MAKERS OF THE AMERICAN MIND

Makers

OF THE

American Mind

ROBERT CLIFTON WHITTEMORE

PROFESSOR OF PHILOSOPHY, TULANE UNIVERSITY

"The men I should be tempted to
commemorate would be the originators
of transforming thought. They often
are half obscure, because what the
world pays for is judgment, not the
original mind."

JUSTICE OLIVER WENDELL HOLMES

WILLIAM MORROW & COMPANY
NEW YORK, 1964

Library of Congress Catalog Card Number 64-12525

To my mother
Zelia Duke Whittemore

Contents

Preface

We have been, intellectually and spiritually, a great and vital people, and it may happen that we shall be such again, but we are neither spiritually nor intellectually great and vital now. The life has gone out of our ideals; morally, as well as ideologically, we are sterile. Let us pray that this is but a temporary condition, for the times will not indefinitely permit our continuing preoccupation with the good *things* of life. If we are to survive and prosper at home, if our ideals are to prevail abroad, we must also be prepared to do battle for our socio-political institutions and philosophical traditions, for if we let these wither and die our material prosperity will not for long suffice to delay the darkness. How tragic then that some amongst us do not even know what these traditions and institutions are that need defending, that a larger number have at best a hazy idea of how they evolved, that even those who comprehend and value our intellectual heritage often falter when it comes to justifying that heritage to outlanders. To cure this sad condition should be our common aim; to this end the chapters that follow are dedicated.

In announcing this purpose, I do not mean to imply any intention of adding yet another to the list of histories and interpretations of American civilization already in print. I have no quarrel with the work of Parrington or Gabriel, Schneider, Werkmeister, Persons, Commager or the rest. What they have done has been, for the most part, well done, and I am not out to do their work over. In brief, their aims are not my aim. I have no thesis to propose, no theory to ride, no undocumented generalizations to offer. My purpose is simpler, and, I think, more precise: to present in compact form, and as much as possible in their own words, the essentials of the philosophy of those thinkers and doers whose influence upon our culture is, or has been, such as justify calling them the makers of the American Mind.

As with every program of this sort, the initial problem is always: whom to include, what to leave out, and why? Since this is a book intended to call attention to those ideas and ideals which have been coercive as regards the shaping of our national consciousness, I have omitted mention of many men and some movements whose philosophical contribution has been of greater technical than cultural importance. Thus you will not find in these pages any account of recent and not so recent developments in epistemological or ontological realism and idealism. Nor will you find much theology as such. What you will find is a discussion of every *major* historical figure whose ideals or ideas are of some contemporary relevance. Obviously, this must include many whose primary reputations have been gained in social science, politics, religion, and literature. It includes also some born abroad. As concerns these latter, I count as American any thinker whose major works were written in, and reflect the spirit of, this country, or whose influence is essentially American.

II

I believe that the reader of any discussion of American points of view is entitled to know something of the relevant convictions and prejudices with which the author approaches his subject matter, and these are mine. I take the position that any philosophy worth writing about and reading deserves a positive treatment. Since philosophies conflict, the only way to be fair to all is to present each as its own advocates would. Since conflict endures, candour requires that we recognize the American Mind for what it is today— an unresolved confusion of incompatible standpoints. That such a view of the matter must infuriate those who demand of an historian that he ride one thesis from Cotton to Whitehead, I am thoroughly aware. But I simply do not believe that the course of American thought is explicable in terms of one particular dialectic or interest. Indeed, I take it as a sign of national health that we as a people are still torn between Jefferson and Calhoun, Ward and Sumner, Dewey and Whitehead. Nor am I dismayed that the American Mind is as yet no mind made up.

Even so, I would not hide the fact that for myself I prefer Jefferson, Ward, and Whitehead; that in opposition to Thoreau I find a strong national government a necessary safeguard against those who would destroy us. Thus I find myself out of sympathy with those who in the name of States Rights and Rugged Individualism would weaken the Federal Union. Conversely, I refuse to accept the popular notion that democracy means the leveling down of all individual distinctions. The unlimited extension of the franchise to those who, because of mental or educational deficiencies, are unfitted to exercise it responsibly is, to my way of thinking, the source of much that is wrong with America today. I am appalled by the results of fifty years of progressive education. The idea that it is more important for the child to be well-adjusted than to be well-trained in the basic intellectual disciplines seems to me to border on educational lunacy. The witness of history is, I am sure, against those who think that a people who put happiness ahead of responsibility can long endure.

In those areas of philosophy which, as a teacher and writer, I have chosen for my own, i.e., history, metaphysics and theology, I count myself more idealist than empiricist. I am very far from being convinced that any philosophical problem can be posed or settled in isolation. Invariably, one problem generates another, and that another—until one is caught up in the attempt to describe the whole of things whether he will or not. It may be that the task of defining this whole of things can never be finished, but this does not, I think, excuse us from the obligation to try. To come to know the Whole, and the part as part of that Whole, this alone suffices; in this, I believe, consists such knowledge as we humans may have of God.

I owe and here tender my thanks to Mr. Walter T. Ryan of WYES-TV (New Orleans), producer of my ETV series, The American Mind, and to the anonymous executive of National Educational Television, whose decision to commission portions of that series for network presentation made possible the research on which this book is based; to the Reference Department of Howard-Tilton Memorial Library, Tulane University, for procuring those many source materials without which it could not have been finished; to my colleague Professor Andrew J. Reck, from whose knowledge of American philosophers I have regularly benefited; to the Tulane University Council on Research for a grant of funds to produce the typescript; to Mrs. James Kemp for a flawless job of typing; and, above all, to my wife, Dorothy Gordon Whittemore, for seeing to it that I had no excuses to put off doing what I have done.

I

The Holy Commonwealth

ENGLISH ANTECEDENTS

JOHN COTTON

ROGER WILLIAMS

THE MATHER DYNASTY

SOLOMON STODDARD

JOHN WISE

"The more Theocratical, or
truly Divine any Government
is, the better it is." [1]

RICHARD BAXTER

1. English Antecedents

Now therefore, if ye will obey my voice indeed, and keep my covenant, then ye shall be a peculiar treasure unto me above all people: for all the earth is mine: And ye shall be unto me a kingdom of priests, and an holy nation. These are the words which thou shalt speak unto the children of Israel.[2]

AND GOD WAS SILENT. Then went Moses before his people and told them of God's offer, and they assenting to it the Holy Commonwealth came into being. Or so the Puritans believed, for to them the Books of Moses were the continuation of a history whose beginnings they traced to the mind of God, a history whose last period they thought themselves to be enacting. In the covenant of God with the people of Israel they found direct precedent for their own covenant with the Lord. "The covenant of grace is the very same now that it was under the Mosaical dispensation. The administration differs, but the covenant is the same."[3]

The theology justifying such a conclusion had been a long time in the making. St. Augustine had laid its foundations with his description of The City of God as the community of the saints visible and invisible. His successors identified this visible community with the Church, and in the Lutheran doctrine of the priesthood of all believers the equation of the Church with the congregation was accomplished. In Elizabethan England, the sometime Puritan, Robert Browne, convinced that the congregation derived its authority from its own solemn covenant with God and not from any Established Church, preached separation from the corrupt Church of England and argued for the independence of each church congregation under Christ. The Congregational theory thus advanced was ably defended by the man many scholars consider to be the spiritual father of New England Congregationalism, William Ames. "The Church," declares Ames in his *First Book of Divinity,* "is not one Catholic Church, but there are so many churches as there are companies, or particular congregations, of those that profess the faith, who are joined together by a special band for the constant exercise of the communion of the Saints. . . . Hence divers fixed congregations of the same country and province are always called Churches in the plural number, not one Church. . . . Neither is there anything in all the New Testament of the institution of any larger Church upon which lesser congregations should depend." [4] On the issue of the appointment of ministers, Ames holds with Luther that ordination follows only after election by the congregation: "The episcopal ordination of a minister without title, that is without a Church to which and in which he should be ordained, is as ridiculous as if any should be fained to be a husband without a wife." [5] As earlier the Anglican Church, through Elizabeth I, had repudiated the authority of Rome, so now Ames, in the name of Congregationalism, impugns the authority of Canterbury. If the Bible is the Word of God, and if it is as Martin Luther has said, that man is justified by faith alone, then bishops, vestments, and cathedrals are alike superfluous. The true Church is the congregational elect, the visible community of the saints in covenant with God and with each other.

In England, where the elect had no chance of permanently converting the nation into a Bible State, Congregationalism remained merely another species of nonconformism. In New England, however, it was quite another matter. Here, from the beginning, the Puritans could and did appeal from Luther to Calvin, the founder and leader of the one successful theocracy in Europe—the city-state of Geneva. The Calvinist assumption of power was based upon the proposition, also derived from St. Augustine, that the chief end of government is the glorification of God and the welfare of souls. Since this welfare requires membership in the elect, it follows, according to Calvin, that the first duty of the magistrate is the protection and furtherance of the interests of the Christian community. "For we are born first of all for God, and not for ourselves. As all things flowed from him and subsist in him, as Paul says (Rom. 11:36), they ought to be related to him." [6] It would, however, be a mistake to think of Calvin as the principal architect of the Puritan theocracy. That honor belongs rather to an English clergyman and reformer named Richard Baxter.

Accepting without question the Augustinian view of the chief end of government, and convinced that there is no true worship outside the Christian Church, Baxter proposes, in his treatise on *The Holy Commonwealth* (1659), 244 theses, among them the following:

> Thes. 192. The more Theocratical, or truly Divine any Government is, the better it is.

To deny this, Baxter thinks, is to deny God. For as no man should dare to compare himself with God, so no government should be compared with His.

> Thes. 198. In a Divine Commonwealth the Honor and Pleasing of God, and the salvation of the people are the Principal Ends, and their corporal welfare but subordinate to these.
>
> Thes. 200. In the Administration of a Divine Commonwealth, the Officers should be such as God will own; that is, men fearing God and working righteousness; men sober, righteous and godly, that by Faith and Love are subjected themselves to God their Creator and Redeemer.

In practice, the men whom God will own are those who meet the approval of the ministers of the elect. In effect, all magistrates are church members and subject to church discipline.

> Thes. 202. In a Divine Commonwealth the Laws of God, in Nature and Scripture, must be taken for the principal Laws, which no Rulers can dispense with; and all their Laws must be as by-laws, subordinate to them for the promoting of their execution.
>
> Thes. 203. In a Divine Commonwealth, the sins against God must

be accounted the most heinous crimes; The denying or blaspheming God, or his Essential Attributes or Sovereignty, is to be judged the highest Treason; and the drawing men to other Gods, and seeking the ruin of the Commonwealth in spirituals, is to be accounted the chiefest enmity to it.

It is, perhaps, unnecessary to add that Baxter was no friend to Democracy or to ideas and groups unsanctioned by the Puritan Church.

Thes. 239. It is necessary both to the purity and peace of the Churches, that the publishing or propagating of the certain intolerable Errors be restrained, both by the Magistrate and the Churches: and also the practice of such Errors that are practicable.

It is, Baxter contends, the plain duty of the government to approve and support orthodoxy. "As liberty in things where liberty may be granted, is necessary to the Churches' peace, so is restraint in things intolerable."

Thes. 240. It is necessary to the Churches' Peace, that no private Congregations be gathered, or Anti-churches erected, by any but such as have an Approbation or Toleration for it from the Magistrate: supposing still that such private Assemblies are Allowed of course as are kept by the Approbation of Approved Ministers, in a due subordination to the Church-Assemblies.

Such, then, are the principles which guided the founders of the Holy Commonwealth of Massachusetts Bay.

Across the empty seas they came with no intention of permitting political or religious freedom. They did not come to pioneer a new democracy. They came to set up a Bible State, a holy commonwealth, and they came because they could not have their way in England. They were not renegades, nor were they outcasts. On the contrary, most were men of property, gentlemen of standing, their ministers were learned. Even so, they saw America not as something fair, to be peacefully cultivated and enjoyed. They were not here for enjoyment. They knew that the devil had entered the heart and mind of the Indian. They knew this was the devil's land. The Indians were not fit subjects for the Kingdom of God, and so they killed and took property, for they were fighting the wars of the Lord and in the name of God and the theocracy much was permitted. In this atmosphere of superstition and intolerance, then, the American Mind was born.

2. John Cotton

What is a Christian's comfort, and where doth it chiefly lie, but in this: that the Lord hath made with him an everlasting Covenant, in all things stablished and sure? [7]

To THE MIND of the newly American Puritan, this idea of Covenant is fundamental. Through Abraham,

It has pleased the great God to enter into a treaty and covenant of agreement with us his poor creatures, the articles of which agreement are here comprised. God, for his part, undertakes to convey all that concerns our happiness, upon our receiving of them, by believing on him. Every one in particular that recites these articles from a spirit of faith makes good this condition.[8]

Because all men are the children of Abraham, all, the Puritans believed, are under Abraham's Covenant of Grace, for this it is that gives meaning to human history and makes intelligible God's will for man.

The Covenant is the midst between both God's purposes and performances, by which and in which we come to see the one before the world began, and by a blessed faith (which makes things absent, present) to enjoy the other, which shall be our glory when this world shall be burned up and all things in it shall have an end. For in God's Covenant we see with open face God's secret purpose for time past—God's purposes toward His people being, as it were, nothing else but promises concealed, and God's promises in the Covenant being nothing else but His purposes revealed. As also, in the same Covenant and promises we see performances for [the] future, as if they were accomplishments at present. Where then is a Christian's comfort but in that Covenant? . . .[9]

Where else indeed? In the words of John Cotton, teacher [10] of the First Church of Boston, "This is such an Argument as the strength and wisdome of men and Angels cannot unfold," which being said, he confidently sets himself to the unfolding of it.

As Cotton and his fellow ministers conceive the matter, involved here is not one covenant but three: the Covenant of Grace, the contract between God and the whole seed of Abraham, the invisible church of the saints eternally elect; the Church Covenant, the voluntary agreement between God and the visible congregation of the saints, sealed by profession of faith, baptism, and the Lord's Supper; and lastly, the Civil (or Social) Covenant, the extension of the agreement between God and his churches to all social and civil institutions. It is this that Cotton has in mind when, in the famous letter to Lords Say and Sele, he writes:

It is better that the commonwealth be fashioned to the setting forth of God's house, which is his church: than to accommodate the church frame to the civill state. Democracy, I do not conceyve that ever God did ordeyne as a fit government eyther for church or commonwealth. If the people be governors, who shall be governed? As for monarchy, and aristocracy, they are both of them clearly approoved, and directed in scripture, yet so as referreth the sover-aigntie to himselfe, and setteth up Theocracy in both, as the best forme of government in the commonwealth, as well as in the church.

In practice, then, the three covenants are really one, for as the Church Covenant gives form to the Covenant of Grace, so does the Civil Covenant give power to the Church. He who covenants, alone is fit to rule: such is the sum of John Cotton's political philosophy. This being so, it follows that his prime interest, whether he recognizes it or not,[11] must always be to guard against any doctrine tending to impugn the Covenant. For if the Covenant be denied, or even if it be interpreted in such wise as to minimize its political function, the Bible State collapses, as a building when its foundation is undermined. It is important that you remember this, since it explains much as regards Cotton's role in the great controversies of his time.

Theologically, the Puritans warred constantly against two major heresies, Arminianism and Antinomianism. Both, to their way of thinking, represented religious extremes: Arminianism over-stressing reason and under-emphasizing piety; Antinomianism over-emphasizing piety and under-stressing reason. To every Puritan, therefore, it was a matter of supreme doctrinal concern to cleave always to the middle path between them, for, as Samuel Willard puts it, "the way lyes very narrow between Antinomian and Arminian errours, and therefore needs the greater exactness in cutting the threed true." Just how great an exactness is evidenced by the case of Mistress Anne Hutchinson.

Back in England, she and her husband had been members of Mr. Cotton's congregation, and upon his departure for America they resolved to follow him, which they did. From all accounts Mistress Hutchinson was a woman of great attractiveness, talents, and zeal for the work of the Church. It has been suggested by some scholars, perhaps unfairly, that she craved power, and sought through attacks on the clergy to get it. At all events, she began to rehearse the Sunday sermons for those whose duties prevented their attendance at service. Apparently, she was very skillful at this, for soon her audiences grew, and eventually she added criticism to her recitations. She thought that all the ministers save her beloved Mr. Cotton were far too much concerned with public morals, far too little aware of the work of grace in private revelations, and she said so publicly. She took to holding private religious meetings at her home. Most important, she interpreted the Covenant of Grace in such a way as to imply that those truly under Grace were possessed of a sanctifying spirit of election, an inner light and revelation, setting them apart from those laymen and clergy not so blessed. Worst of all, she claimed a private revelation and admitted to a personal communion with the Holy Ghost. For a time, her ardour and magnetism carried all before it. John Cotton himself found no fault in her theology. To him, as to her, it was obvious that regeneration must be grounded in an immediate experience of God's saving grace. Grace, he thinks, is not something one prepares for.[12] "Drowsie hearts," do not open upon the knocking of Christ, "unless he be pleased to put the finger of his spirit into our hearts, to open an entrance for himselfe." Unfortunately for both of them, it soon became apparent that the practical outcome of their position, its theological soundness notwithstanding, was to pose a threat to the future of the theocracy. Any spread of private piety could only result in a weakening of church control over public affairs; to make personal experience of regeneration the test of election would, in time, empty the churches of all but a few of the saints. Faced with a choice between theology and theocracy, the clergy chose theocracy. Henceforth, the Covenant of Grace would be interpreted moralistically. Pietism was a luxury the Holy Commonwealth could hardly afford. At all costs, the cancer of Antinomianism must be cut out. And so they asked John Cotton to reconsider his position, which, being a prudent man, he did. "I the next morning did of my self freely declare to them publikely, my consent with them in the point, which they gladly accepted." Anne Hutchinson was not so lucky. Brought to trial in November 1637, she was convicted of misconduct and banished from the colony. Some short time later she died, killed, so the story has it, by an Indian tomahawk. To the theocrats it seemed as if God himself had vindicated their action, and they waxed content in the righteousness of their ways.

3. Roger Williams

IN THESE SAME YEARS, one Roger Williams was also ruffling the theological waters of Massachusetts Bay. He was a scholarly and pious man, and such was his reputation that on his coming to Boston in 1631 he was offered, and refused, that teachership of the First Church which two years later was given to Cotton. The reason for his refusal was straightforward: he was an avowed separatist, and the congregation of the First Church would not yield to his demand that they repent of their ties with the Church of England, nor would they withdraw their recognition of the right of magistrates to deal with breaches of the law in cases of conscience. After some spirited negotiations, and over the disapproval of the General Court, he was called to the church at Salem. Here his radical views on the relations of church and state soon led him further into trouble. He urged his people not to pray with the unregenerate, even though the latter were of their own family. He thought the cross on the Colony Flag idolatrous and popish, and prevailed upon the Governor to remove it. When his own church refused to renounce communion with its neighbors, he renounced it and, like Anne Hutchinson, took to having private meetings in his own home. When he began to preach against the Charter, and to question the right of the magistrates to tender the oath to unregenerate jurors, the authorities took steps to have him transported back to England. Forewarned, he fled to Narragansett Bay, and there founded Providence Plantation, from which safe vantage point he passed the remainder of his days, an intellectual and political thorn in the side of the Holy Commonwealth.

As a pioneer in the fight for religious toleration, Roger Williams is justly renowned; nonetheless, his importance in the history of the Holy Commonwealth, as well as to posterity, is not so much religious as it is political. For his was the first serious challenge to the political theory on which the Bible State was founded. It cannot be, he argues, that God should require a uniformity of religion in any civil state. Better always that church and state be separate, for in any commonwealth, however holy, the truly pious are always a minute minority. Still, should not this minority, small though it be, rule? Cotton had argued that the godly ruled by divine right. Williams flatly denies it. All men, he thinks, are fallible, the saint no less than the sinner, and no man speaks for God. Ultimately, the foundation of all government must be the consent of the governed.

.... from this grant I infer, as before hath been touched, that the sovereign, original, and foundation of civil power, lies in the people— whom they must needs mean by the civil power distinct from the government set up: and if so, that a people may erect and establish what form of government seems to them most meet for their civil condition. It is evident that such governments as are by them erected and established, have no more power, nor for no longer time, than the civil power, or people consenting and agreeing, shall betrust them with. This is clear not only in reason, but in the experience of all commonweals, where the people are not deprived of their natural freedom by the power of tyrants.[13]

That one synonym for "tyrants" was "theocrats," Mr. Cotton, to whom these sentiments were addressed, was well aware. In his *The Bloudy Tenent washed white in the Bloud of the Lambe* (1647) he undertakes anew the task of showing that, "that Form of Government wherein the power of Civil Administration is denied unto unbelievers, and committed to the Saints, is the best Form of Government in a Christian Commonwealth." In the main, he rests his case on the authority of Moses and every Christian prince and scholar from the Apostle Paul to William Ames. If he convinced himself and his fellow theocrats, he did not, however, convince Williams. That doughty warrior again took pen in hand to wash the dirty linen of theocracy in his: *The Bloudy Tenent yet more bloudy by Mr. Cotton's endeavour to wash it white in the Bloud of the Lambe; of whose precious Bloud, spilt in the Bloud of his Servants; and of the bloud of millions spilt in former and later Wars for conscience sake, that most bloudy Tenent of Persecution for cause of conscience upon a second Tryal is found more apparently and more notoriously guilty* (1652). As the title tells the story, it is sufficient to note his conclusion:

> Every lawful Magistrate whether succeeding or elective, is not only the Minister of God, but the Minister or servant of the people also (what people or nation soever they be all the world over), and that Minister or Magistrate goes beyond his commission who intermeddles with that which cannot be given him in commission from the people. . . .[14]

And there, Mr. Cotton having passed to his reward, the matter rested. Rhode Island became a haven for the religious unwashed, while Massachusetts Bay grew more narrowly theocratic. With the adoption of the Cambridge Platform, written by Richard Mather and containing a preface by John Cotton, by the Synod of 1646-48, the Holy Commonwealth entered upon a new stage in its history. The Age of Mather had begun.

4. The Mather Dynasty

THOSE WHOSE MISFORTUNE it is to lead a state in decay cannot expect much sympathy from their posterity. History invariably judges harshly the architects of an age of decline, and the Mather family is no exception. They were the very symbols of the theocracy at its most intolerant, and its flaws and failures are properly their responsibility. In the Cambridge Platform, Richard Mather, minister of the church at Dorchester, had laid it down that "the work & duty of the people is expressed in the phrase of obeying their Elders," and his son (Increase) and grandson (Cotton) saw no reason to modify that dictum one whit. To preserve the rule of the saints, that was the task as they conceived it, and to achieve that end they were willing to compromise when- and wherever necessary.

The first major test of Mather resolve came in the 1650's. The problem was one of baptism—occasioned by an exploding birth rate and the failure of more than a small minority of parents to make formal profession of their faith. These parents, although technically unregenerate, regarded themselves, and were regarded by their congregations, as members of the church in good standing by virtue of regular attendance and financial support. Naturally, they wished to have their children baptized. Just as naturally the Elders demurred. To allow such baptisms would mean that by the third or fourth generation the composition of church membership would be overwhelmingly unregenerate, the requirements of formal profession being such that few would care to undertake them. On the other hand, to refuse baptism to the children of the technically unregenerate would in time mean the emptying of the churches. Either way, it was the beginning of the end of the Holy Commonwealth. But optimistically refusing to face the inevitable, the majority of the clergy chose to sacrifice principle to expediency by compromising on the issue. Led by Richard Mather, they drew up a report recommending that the children of the unregenerate second generation be baptized, but that neither children nor parents be allowed to partake of the Lord's Supper. Members they would be, but not communicants. This report, dubbed the Half-Way Covenant, was formally adopted by the Synod of 1662 over the vehement objections of a minority whose principal light was Richard Mather's son Increase, pastor of the North Church in Boston. Logic as well as theology favored the minority, and ultimately they might have prevailed had not Increase Mather deserted to the compromisers. Thus, by a tarnishing of holiness, the power of the saints was saved—but not for long.

In 1692 the devil reappeared in Massachusetts. Whether he had ever really been absent is a matter of conjecture. The jeremiads preached by three generations of Puritan divines indicate a continuing awareness of the need to wrest the devil's land from Satan, and loosen his grip upon the souls of the unregenerate. Increase Mather's book of old wives' tales, *An Essay for the Recording of Illustrious Providences* (1684), no less than his son Cotton's imitation, *Memorable Providences Relating to Witchcrafts and Possessions* (1689), certainly helped to set the stage for the hysteria that struck Salem Village in March of that fatal year. By the time the madness had run its course, twenty persons had been executed and eight more condemned. The extent of Mather responsibility is a matter of debate; that they saw in the witchcraft issue a tool whereby they might discredit that rationalism (Sadduceeism, as Cotton Mather called it) which in their opinion threatened the theocracy is plain. At all events, their contemporaries did not find them blameless. Both were to live another thirty years, but from that time forward their influence was on the wane. The excesses of the theocrats forecast the finish of the theocracy.

5. Solomon Stoddard

BY THE TURN OF THE CENTURY, the theocrats were everywhere on the defensive. Boston ceased to take its guidance from the Mathers, and out on the frontier at Northampton a new type of congregationalism was in the making. Solomon Stoddard, having succeeded Increase Mather's brother Eleazer and married his widow, was taking the Half-Way Covenant seriously. Everyone who assented to the articles of faith was baptized and admitted to full communion. In justification of his action, Stoddard published in 1687 *The Safety of Appearing at the Day of Judgment,* a work which was to have a decisive influence in shaping the religious revival known as The Great Awakening. Scorning the elaborate rationalizations of the Boston theologians, Stoddard aimed to call men back to the notion of God's arbitrary and irresistible grace. "The only reason why God sets his love on one man and not upon another is, because he pleases." The Covenant of Grace is not reasonable. "The meer pleasure of God does decide it, who shall be the objects of his love and his hatred." Election and damnation are fates known to God alone, and no man can be sure that he is saved, since no objective criteria exist for distinguishing the sinner from the saint. Such assurance as is possible can only come from within. Objectively, regenerate and unregenerate are alike—all in the same boat. All, therefore, who profess themselves Christians are entitled to baptism and the Lord's Supper. So Stoddard reasoned, and thus in 1687 the challenge to the right of the saints to rule was made good. Unlike Anne Hutchinson, Stoddard was too far removed from Boston power to banish. Henceforward, the way of the Congregational Churches would be towards democracy.

6. John Wise

> . . . it seems most agreeable with the Light of Nature, that if there
> be any of the Regular Government settled in the Church of God it
> must needs be
> A Democracy.[15]

SUCH IS THE FINDING of the man whose work marks the end of
the theocracy in Massachusetts. His name is John Wise, and he
deserves a greater fame. In the same year (1687) that Stoddard's
book was raising the hackles of the Mathers and their cohorts,
Wise was leading the people of Ipswich in resisting the taxation
laid upon them by the Royal Governor, Andros. For this he went—
briefly—to jail. Later he served as chaplain in the British expedi-
tion against Quebec. His was one of the very few clerical voices
raised against the Salem witchcraft trials. He sponsored paper
money and smallpox inoculation. Legend has it that he was a
champion wrestler. In fact, he was the first to advocate the philosophy of natural rights in this country, the first to defend in print the
democratic basis of Congregational church polity. His major work
was *A Vindication of the Government of New-England Churches*
(1717), and in it he has this to say about the evils of theocracy:

> This Government (aristocracy, theocracy) might do to support the
> Church in its most valuable Rights, etc., If we could be assured they
> would make the Scripture, and not their private Will, the Rule of
> their Personal and Ministerial Actions: And indeed upon these terms
> any Species of Government might serve the great design of Redemp-

tion; but considering how great an Interest is imbarkt, and how frail a bottom we trust, though we should rely upon the best of Men, especially if we remember what is in the hearts of Good Men, (viz. Much ignorance, abundance of small ends, many times cloked with a high Pretence in Religion; Pride Skulking and often breeding revenge upon a small affront; and blown up by a pretended Zeal; Yet really and truly by nothing more Divine than Interest, or ill Nature) and also considering how very uncertain we are of the real goodness of those we esteem good Men; and also how impossible it is to secure the Intail of it to Successors: And also if we remind how Christianity by the foresaid Principle has been peel'd, rob'd and spoiled already; it cannot consist with the Light of Nature to venture again upon such Perils, especially if we can find a safer way home.[16]

In a world where there are no saints—as far as complete indifference to private interest is concerned, the only safe way home is that form of government which represents the power of all the people. Right reason, no less than the congregational structure of the churches, declares this one best form to be Democracy.

For certainly if Christ has settled any form of power in his Church he has done it for his Churches safety, and for the Benefit of every Member: Then he must needs be presumed to have made choice of that Government as should least Expose his People to Hazard, either from the fraud, or Arbitrary measures of particular Men. And it is as plain as day light, there is no Species of Government like a Democracy to attain this End.[17]

The whole of Wise's *Vindication* is a justification of that conclusion, and he did his work well. The poison of Wise's cursed libel, as Cotton Mather called it, spread throughout the Commonwealth, completing what Stoddard had begun. The rule of the saints in Zion was over. For a generation the sinners enjoyed a democratic peace, all unaware that it was only temporary, a sleep before the Great Awakening.

SUGGESTED READINGS

Of good books on the Puritan era, there are more than enough, and most are readily available. The best of the lot, in my opinion, is Herbert Schneider's *The Puritan Mind* (Ann Arbor: paperback, 1960). Professor Schneider's scholarship is impeccable, but it is his wit and brilliant style that make this study a delight to read. For the more seriously minded, there is Perry Miller's exhaustive and ponderous *The New England Mind: The Seventeenth Century* (New York: Macmillan, 1939) and its sequel *The New England Mind: From Colony to Province* (Cambridge: Harvard University Press, 1953). Professor Miller omits nothing save the footnotes, and his bibliography is thorough. *Orthodoxy in Massachusetts,* an earlier work by the same author, covering much the same ground, is now available in paperback (Boston: Beacon Press, paperback, 1959), as is Miller's anthology *The American Puritans, Their Prose and Poetry* (New York: Doubleday Anchor, paperback, 1956). The selection is representative enough, albeit rather light on Puritan philosophy and theology. Finally, for those primarily interested in the daily life and culture of the Bay Colonists, there is Thomas Jefferson Wertenbaker's *The Puritan Oligarchy* (Scribner, 1947) also in paperback (Grosset Universal Library).

In the area of biography, choice is rather more limited, except as regards Roger Williams. Here one has his pick of: James Ernst, *Roger Williams, New England Firebrand* (New York: Macmillan, 1932); Samuel Brockunier, *The Irrepressible Democrat, Roger Williams* (New York: Ronald, 1940); Perry Miller, *Roger Williams: His Contribution to the American Tradition* (Indianapolis: Bobbs-Merrill, 1953); and Ola Elizabeth Winslow, *Master Roger Williams* (New York: Macmillan, 1957). Of the four, Miller is philosophically the most substantial; Winslow is the best balanced. For the Mather Dynasty see Kenneth Murdock, *Increase Mather: The Foremost American Puritan* (Cambridge: Harvard, 1925), and Barrett Wendell, *Cotton Mather the Puritan Priest* (New York, Dodd, Mead, 1891). John Wise has been well served by his only biographer, George Allan Cook, *John Wise, Early American Democrat* (New York: King's Crown Press, 1952). There are no book-length studies of John Cotton and Solomon Stoddard. For the career and theology of the latter, however, see Perry Miller, "Solomon Stoddard, 1643-1729," *Harvard Theological Review,* Vol. XXXIV (1941), pp. 277-320.

Two source books demand mention. Each, in its way, is invaluable. Williston Walker, *The Creeds and Platforms of Congregationalism* (New York: Scribner, 1893), contains all of the important documents of the Puritan era complete and unabridged, together with explanatory essays on each by the editor. Smith, Handy, and Loetscher, *American Christianty,* 2 Vols. (New York: Scribner, 1960) provides a critical interpretation, complete with relevant documents, of the major men and movements, plus an extensive survey of the literature of each of the periods covered.

REFERENCES

1. *A Holy Commonwealth* (London: Thomas Underhill and Francis Tyton, 1659), Thesis 192.

2. Exodus 19:5-6.

3. William Brattle, MS Sermons, Harvard College Library. Quoted in T. J. Wertenbaker, *The Puritan Oligarchy* (New York: Scribner, 1947), pp. 58-59.

4. Quoted in Wertenbaker, pp. 24-25.

5. Ibid.

6. *On the Christian Faith* (New York: Liberal Arts Press, 1957), p. 194.

7. Thomas Shepard, Preface to Peter Bulkeley, *The Gospel Covenant: or the Covenant of Grace Opened* (London, 1651, 2nd edition).

8. Richard Sibbes, quoted in Perry Miller, *The New England Mind: The Seventeenth Century* (New York: Macmillan, 1939), p. 377.

9. Thomas Shepard, *op. cit.*

10. In the churches of the Holy Commonwealth the office of teacher was co-equal with that of pastor, the former being responsible for the nourishment of the minds of the congregation, the latter being concerned for the welfare of their souls. Thus, in the First Church, Cotton preached as teacher, while John Wilson practiced as pastor. According to the *Platform of Church Discipline*, "The pastor's special work is to attend to exhortation, and therein to administer a word of wisdom; the teacher is to attend to doctrine and therein to administer a word of knowledge." It is easy to see how, in the hands of a forceful personality, this latter office could become, as it did with Cotton, the real source of ecclesiastical power.

11. That he did not always recognize it, was made clear to him by John Winthrop during the Antinomian crisis of 1637. For the story of the Anne Hutchinson case and Cotton's part in it, see Perry Miller, *The New England Mind: From Colony to Province* (Cambridge: Harvard University Press, 1953), pp. 57-63.

12. Technically, the issue here is whether or not sanctification, i.e., acceptance as one of the saints in congregation, is evidence of justification, i.e., election by God. Anne Hutchinson denied it; John Cotton, by implication, at first denied it and then recanted. The theocrats accepted it as necessary to the operation of the Holy Commonwealth. In other words, the theocrats maintained that it was not only possible but necessary to prepare for grace by works, whereas Mistress Hutchinson and Mr. Cotton denied that works made any real difference, since the Covenant of Works had been annulled by the fall of Adam, and the Covenant of Grace implied nothing about preparation.

13. *The Bloudy Tenent of Persecution for cause of conscience discussed and Mr. Cotton's Letter examined and answered* (London: J. Haddon, 1848), pp. 214-15.

14. *The Works of Roger Williams*, edited by members of the Narragansett Club, 6 Vols. (Providence, 1866-1874), IV, p. 187.

15. John Wise, *A Vindication of the Government of the New-England Churches* (Boston, 1717), p. 60. Facsimile reproduction by Scholar's Facsimiles and Reprints (Gainesville, 1958).

16. Vindication, pp. 56-57.

17. Ibid., pp. 62-63.

II

The Great Awakening

THEODORE J. FRELINGHUYSEN

GILBERT TENNENT

GEORGE WHITEFIELD

JONATHAN EDWARDS

"A man's having much affection,
don't prove that he has any
true religion: but if he has
no affection, it proves that
he has no true religion." [1]

JONATHAN EDWARDS

1. Theodore J. Frelinghuysen

TOWARDS THE END OF JANUARY in the year 1720 a young German-born minister of the Dutch Reformed Church, the ancestor of three distinguished Americans bearing the same name, Theodore Jacobus Frelinghuysen arrived in the Raritan Valley of north central New Jersey. He had come to take up the pastorate of four Dutch Reformed congregations lately established around New Brunswick, and before he had been a month about his duties, the stolid complacency of his congregations was shaken to the core. They wanted from religion only the preservation of their Dutch traditions and the comforts of self-righteousness. He demanded humility and the passion of true repentance. They strove for outward conformity; he insisted upon a personal experience of regeneration. Nothing less, in his eyes, qualified a person to partake of the sacrament of holy communion. No unregenerate person need approach; the ungodly must be repelled. To his parishioners, he put it thus:

> Much-loved hearers, who have so often been at the Lord's table, do you know that the unconverted may not approach? Have you then, with the utmost care examined, whether you be born again? Were you aware what is required in order to an acceptable observance, when you so composedly approached? Or did you go blindly forward, not only without a wedding garment, but even without concern respecting it? not examining whether you were of the number of those who are invited? Say you, I was not aware that so much is required? You should have known it. . . .
>
> Remain, I beseech you, my hearers, no longer, ignorant respecting this truth, but at length lay it to heart; for, if there be aught con-

cerning which we should be circumspect, it is this. Let us then here be careful, if we would anywhere be so! He who loves danger, deserves to fall into it: nowhere is danger so great as here! here, by a morsel, and swallow, can the covenant of God be desecrated; his wrath brought upon the whole congregation; and ourselves made liable to temporal and eternal punishment. Reflect, therefore, upon, and bear in mind this truth; and remember, that though moral and outwardly religious, if still you be unregenerate and destitute of spiritual life, you have no warrant for an approach to the table of grace.[2]

Unaccustomed to such plain speaking, Frelinghuysen's flock of respectable Dutch farmers reacted at first with bitter resentment. Many of his fellow ministers were scandalized by the extravagant passion of his preaching, and they organized to resist his crusade for regeneration. His removal was sought, but not granted, and he continued to preach the Christianity of spiritual vitality, not disdaining the strategy of terror to whip his people to conversion. Here, for example, is an excerpt from one of his early sermons.

Come hither, ye careless, at ease in sin, ye carnal and earthly minded, ye unchaste whoremongers, adulterers, ye proud, haughty men and women, ye devotees of pleasure, drunkards, gamblers, ye disobedient, ye wicked rejectors of the Gospel, ye hypocrites and dissemblers, how suppose ye it will go with you? The period of grace is concluded. All earthly satisfaction ceaseth. Your agonies and pains as to soul and body have no end, for ye shall be cast into that lake which burns with fire and brimstone, where is weeping and gnashing of teeth, where the smoke of their torment ascendeth forever, where your worm dieth not and your fire is not quenched. . . . Be filled with terror, ye impure swine, adulterers and whoremongers, and consider that without true repentance, ye shall soon be with the impure devils; for I announce a fire hotter than that of Sodom and Gomorrah to all that burn in their lusts.[3]

Gradually, his words took effect, and many now began to experience the pain and joy of a new birth in Christ. By 1727 the fervour of revival sparked by Frelinghuysen was sweeping through the Middle Colonies. Shortly, it would spread north to New England and south to Virginia and the Carolinas. The Great Awakening was underway.

2. Gilbert Tennent

ITS SPREAD WAS NO LESS denominational than geographic. What Frelinghuysen had begun among the Dutch Reformed, his young friend Gilbert Tennent continued among the Presbyterians. Tennent, eldest son of William Tennent, minister and founder of the famed revivalist "Log College" at Neshaminy, Pennsylvania, came into the Raritan Valley in the fall of 1727. Ironically enough, his call to the Presbyterian Church at New Brunswick had been signed by many of the Dutch, some in the hope that the presence of an English Presbyterian would embarrass Frelinghuysen, others believing that a new minister would help to spread the revival to their Scotch-Irish neighbors. Under Frelinghuysen's influence, Tennent's evangelical inclinations flowered early, and he soon surpassed the older man in the violence of his revivalistic zeal. The great English revivalist George Whitefield, who heard him preach in New York in 1738, described him as a "son of thunder" and declared that "Hypocrites must either soon be converted or enraged at his preaching." What Whitefield meant is easily understood in the light of such sermons as that which Tennent preached at Nottingham, Pennsylvania, on March 8th, 1740. His subject was "The Danger of an Unconverted Ministry," and by "Unconverted" he understood any minister opposed to the revival. Needless to say, he was no respecter of such persons. To him they were "plastered Hypocrites," "Servants of Satan," "moral Negroes." For those who followed their teaching he had only bitter irony and contempt.

. . . such who are contented under a dead Ministry, have not in them the Temper of that Saviour they profess. It's an awful Sign, that they are as blind as Moles, and dead as Stones, without any spiritual Taste and Relish. And alas! isn't this the case of Multitudes? If they can get one, that has the Name of a Minister, with a Band, and a black Coat or Gown to carry on a Sabbath-days among them, although never so coldly, and insuccessfully; if he is free from gross Crimes in Practice, and takes good Care to keep at a due Distance from their Consciences, and is never troubled about his Insuccessfulness; O! think the poor Fools, that is a fine Man indeed; our Minister is a prudent charitable Man, he is not always harping upon Terror, and sounding Damnation in our Ears, like some rash-headed Preachers, who by their uncharitable Methods, are ready to put poor People out of their Wits, or to run them into Despair; O! how terrible a Thing is that Despair! Ay, our Minister, honest Man, gives us good Caution against it. Poor silly Souls! [4]

Better, he thinks, that a pious man should turn away from such Ministers and listen to a godly layman than to persist in hypocrisy.

Such subversion of the organized ministry could not long be allowed to go unchallenged, and in 1741 the Synod of Philadelphia expelled Tennent and his fellow revivalists of the New Brunswick Presbytery. That they were right in so doing, Tennent himself soon seemed to recognize, for two years later in a letter to Jonathan Dickinson [5] we find him condemning "The practice of openly exposing ministers, who are supposed to be unconverted in public discourses." The practice, he thinks, can do no public good. Nor, he now feels, can it do any real good to send out "unlearned men to teach others, upon the supposition of their piety," since this "seems to bring the ministry into contempt; to cherish enthusiasms, and bring all into confusion." He had learned his lesson; for him the years of revivalistic excess were over. In 1743, having accepted a call to the newly-formed Second Presbyterian Church of Philadelphia, he left New Brunswick and ceased itinerating. For all that he now muted his attacks upon the unconverted, however, he did not abandon his revivalist emphasis. To the end of his life he continued to preach the necessity of personal conversion. His constant thought, which he is at pains to impress upon his Philadelphia congregation, is that sinners must awake.

I beseech you, Friends, by all the happiness of heaven, by all the torments of hell, for the sake of God, the Father, Son and Spirit, by all the regard you owe to your deathless souls, your reason, your conscience, as well as the ambassadors of Christ among you, that ye *awake*. I beseech you as a messenger of the great God, as on my bended knees, by the groans, tears, and wounds of Christ that ye would *Awake*. Yea, I charge you all by the curses of the law, and blessings of the gospels, that ye would *Awake*. My friends, you are witnesses against yourselves, that I have set Death and Life before you; O choose Life that ye may live. *Let the wicked man forsake his way, and the unrighteous man his thoughts, and turn to God and he will have mercy upon him, and to our God for he will abundantly pardon!* O Sirs! consider these things, as ye would answer at the Tribunal of Christ on the last day.[6]

3. George Whitefield

It is unlikely that Tennent's congregation really needed this exhortation, for by 1743 the eastern seaboard from Boston to Savannah was already religiously wide awake, and this mainly because of the activity of one man—the English evangelist George Whitefield. Unfettered by denominational ties or theological niceties, he rode through the colonies awakening the sinners and electrifying the saints. He preached his personalized Calvinism to all who would listen, and few indeed were those who would not, for neither in England nor America was there a preacher who could compare with him in the art of public speaking. From all accounts, his voice was magnificent, and he had an actor's command of it. To Benjamin Franklin, who knew him well and often heard him preach, "every accent, every emphasis, every modulation of voice was so perfectly tuned and well placed, that without being interested in the subject, one could not help being pleased with the discourse." [7] It was a shrewd assessment, for as regards content Whitefield's sermons were nothing out of the ordinary. He rang the standard changes on the traditional Calvinist themes, and there is nothing in his writings to suggest that they might arouse an audience to frenzy. His critics have pointed out the shallowness of his mind. "I heard him once," said Jonathan Mayhew, "and it was as low, confused, puerile, conceited, ill-natured, enthusiastic a performance as I ever heard." The Faculty of Harvard rebuked his Enthusiasm and denounced him for "a censorious, uncharitable Person, and a Deluder of the People." What Harvard and Mayhew both failed to see was the complete sincerity and devoutness of the man. His single aim was to save souls, and if in the heat of enthusiastic self-righteousness he alienated some, he converted many more. He made no pretense of being a theologian. He cared nothing for liturgical form, and, unlike every American preacher of note, he never spoke from a prepared text. Everything was extempore; all hung upon the inspiration of the moment. "O earth, earth, earth, hear the word of the Lord," [8] he would cry, and the word poured forth from his mouth in a clear articulate stream. He was a preacher, nothing more, but he was the best there was—and he knew it. Such, then, was the man who on September 18th, 1740, came to Boston and brought the simmerings of revival in New England to a boil.

4. Jonathan Edwards

THE AWAKENING OF MASSACHUSETTS WAS NOT, however, a sudden thing. Out on the frontier at Northampton, Solomon Stoddard had garnered five harvests of souls before his death in 1729. His grandson and successor, Jonathan Edwards, had in the winter and spring of 1734-35 led a notable revival. By 1739 his account of the matter, *A Faithful Narrative of the Surprising Work of God in the Conversion of Many Hundred Souls in Northampton and the Neighboring Towns and Villages,* had gone through three editions and twenty printings and made its author famous. Thus, as Perry Miller has pointed out,[9] when Whitefield came to New England, he came to a land already possessed of an orator greater than himself, and a model for the revival sermon whose literary and philosophical quality he could hardly hope to match. Small wonder that Whitefield, after a single day with Edwards in Northampton, should record in his Journal his

> wonderful Satisfaction in being at the House of Mr. *Edwards*. He is a Son himself, and hath also a Daughter of *Abraham* for his wife. A sweeter Couple I have not yet seen. Their Children were dressed not in Silks and Satins, but plain, as becomes the Children of those who, in all Things, ought to be Examples of Christian Simplicity.[10]

He was no less impressed by the services in Edwards' church.

Our Lord seem'd to keep the good Wine till the last. I have not seen four such gracious Meetings together since my Arrival.[11]

Dear Mr. Edwards is a solid, excellent Christian, but at present weak in Body. I think, I may say I have not seen his Fellow in all New England. When I came into his Pulpit, I found my Heart drawn out to talk of scarce any Thing besides the Consolations and Privileges of Saints, and the plentiful Effusion of the Spirit upon the Hearts of Believers. And, when I came to remind them of their former Experiences, and how zealous and lively they were at that Time, both Minister and People wept much; and the Holy Ghost enabled me to speak with a great deal of Power.[12]

This weeping minister so graced by the Holy Ghost was at the time thirty-seven years of age, and no clergyman in New England could look back upon a more auspicious beginning or anticipate a brighter future. The only son in a family of ten daughters, Jonathan Edwards was born in the parsonage at East Windsor, Connecticut, on October 5th, 1703. His father, the Reverend Timothy Edwards, had come to the church at East Windsor fresh out of Harvard in 1694. His mother, nee Esther Stoddard, was a daughter of the famous Solomon. Their son was a very precocious youth. He had an eye for nature and at eleven wrote a treatise on spiders which, considering the circumstances and the age, was a notable effort. At thirteen he entered Yale; at sixteen, having discovered Locke and hit upon the basic idea of Berkeley, he graduated. Two years of theological studies followed, and then in 1722, aged eighteen, he received his first call—to a Presbyterian church in New York City. Nine months later, his congregation having dissolved, he was back in East Windsor waiting for a call to Bolton, Connecticut. It having failed to materialize, he accepted an appointment as Tutor in Yale College. About this time, the Church at Northampton began looking for a man to succeed the aging Solomon Stoddard. "Pope" Stoddard approved highly of young Edwards, and after three months' trial the congregation invited him to settle. On February 15th, 1727, he signed the Northampton Town Book and was ordained minister. In July he married Sarah Pierrepont. The pattern of his life was now to all intents and purposes permanently fixed.

Four years later he went up to Boston to deliver the traditional

Thursday Lecture. Held at the First Church every Thursday morning, this lecture had been instituted by the earliest settlers as a slake to their thirst for the Word. Since every clergyman who could attended, it was, in effect, a display case for the wares of the Puritan ministry, and Edwards knew it. The title of his sermon indicates his theme, *God Glorified in the Work of Redemption by the Greatness of Man's Dependence upon him, in the Whole of it.* There is, he told them,

> an absolute and universal dependence of the redeemed on God. The nature and contrivance of our redemption is such, that the redeemed are in every thing directly, immediately, and entirely dependent on God: They are dependent on him for all, and are dependent on him every way.[13]

From this, according to Edwards, it follows that

> Those that are called and sanctified are to attribute it alone to the good pleasure of God's goodness by which they are distinguished. He is sovereign, and hath mercy on whom he will have mercy.[14]

Hence,

> when a man is made holy, it is from mere and arbitrary grace: God may for ever deny holiness to the fallen creature if he pleases, without any disparagement to any of his perfections.[15]

To none of this could his hearers take exception. That the redeemed depend directly and in every way upon God was a doctrine to which all of the Puritan clergy must and did pay lip-service. It was not what Edwards said, but what he left unsaid that was disturbing. For nowhere in his sermon was there any mention of assurance of mercy through participation in the Covenant of Grace. The traditional acknowledgement that the arbitrariness of God's decree was modified by God's acceptance of the covenant with man in the moment of man's conversion was conspicuous by its absence. Edwards had dwelt at length upon man's utter unworthiness, and intimated that the true mark of salvation is a personal experience of the Holy Spirit, but of the sacraments as seals of a covenant he had said not a word.

The significance of the omission was not immediately appreciated. It was only later, when reports of the Northampton revival began to circulate and Edwards published his *Faithful Narrative,* that the full meaning of this new Calvinism without covenant became plain. For what Edwards was saying was, that if man is utterly dependent upon God then there can be no covenant because man by his fall has forfeited *all* rights, including that of obligating God. Before God, man really is as nothing. In Adam's fall all have sinned and come short, and the eternal wrath of God rests justly upon the heads of Adam's posterity. Unfortunately for man, in his pride he fails to realize this and thinks to bargain with God rather than, as he should, approaching Him in faithful fear and trembling, begging for that mercy he does not deserve. Thus it is that he (man) needs to be awakened to the terror of that hell into which he is likely to fall if he does not repent.

> If there really be a hell of such dreadful and never-ending torments, . . . Why should they not be told as much of the truth as can be? If I am in danger of going to hell, I should be glad to know as much as I possibly can of the dreadfulness of it. If I am very prone to neglect due care to avoid it, he does me the best kindness, who does most to represent to me the truth in the case, that sets forth my misery and danger in the liveliest manner.[16]

If hell really exists and the Lord is a God of Wrath, then Edwards' defense of the revival and of his own part in it is surely well taken. And that both propositions are true, he never doubts.

> The God that holds you over the pit of hell, much as one holds a spider, or some loathsome insect over the fire, abhors you, and is dreadfully provoked: his wrath towards you burns like fire; he looks upon you as worthy of nothing else, but to be cast into the fire. . . .[17]
>
> O sinner! Consider the fearful danger you are in: it is a great furnace of wrath, a wide and bottomless pit, full of the fire of wrath, that you are held over in the hand of that God, whose wrath is provoked and incensed as much against you, as against many of the damned in hell. You hang by a slender thread, with the flames of

divine wrath flashing about it, and ready every moment to singe it, and burn it asunder; and you have no interest in any Mediator, and nothing to lay hold of to save yourself, nothing to keep off the flames of wrath, nothing of your own, nothing that you have ever done, nothing that you can do, to induce God to spare you one moment.[18]

O that you would consider it, whether you be young or old! There is reason to think, that there are many in this congregation now hearing this discourse, that will actually be the subjects of this very misery to all eternity. We know not who they are, or in what seats they sit, or what thoughts they now have. It may be that they are now at ease, and hear all these things without much disturbance, and are now flattering themselves that they are not the persons, promising themselves that they shall escape. If we knew that there was one person, and but one, in the whole congregation, that was to be the subject of this misery, what an awful thing would it be to think of! If we knew who it was, what an awful sight would it be to see such a person! How might all the rest of the congregation lift up a lamentable and bitter cry over him! But, alas! instead of one, how many is it likely will remember this discourse in hell? And it would be a wonder, if some that are now present should not be in hell in a very short time, even before this year is out. And it would be no wonder if some persons, that now sit here, in some seats of this meeting-house, in health, quiet and secure, should be there before tomorrow morning.[19]

Therefore, let every one that is out of Christ, now awake and fly from the wrath to come. The wrath of Almighty God is now undoubtedly hanging over a great part of this congregation: Let every one fly out of Sodom: "Haste and escape for your lives, look not behind you, escape to the mountain, lest you be consumed." [20]

For us who live in a century whose capacity for holocaust pales that of the devil, such hellfire preaching may seem to serve more to amuse than to terrify. But to those unhappy souls of Enfield who listened as the thin-lipped, cold-eyed, quiet-voiced Edwards pronounced them all Sinners in the Hands of an Angry God it was no laughing matter. To Edwards' way of thinking, it was "a reasonable thing to fright persons away from hell." And frightened they were. All across New England in that fearful summer of 1741 the ministers of the revival were hammering home the terrors of damnation. Inevitably, public peace and morality were seriously impaired, and no man was safe from denunciation as unconverted. In some places the lunatic fringe gained control and in the name of the Holy Spirit performed so extravagantly that the few religious men of reason left in Massachusetts began to wonder in print whether the revival was the work of God or Satan.

A war of pamphlets now ensued as the clergy debated among themselves as to the authenticity of the "Great Work." Edwards, convinced that the revival for all its excesses was still a work of God, contributed two treatises to the controversy. In the first, *The Distinguishing Marks of a Work of the Spirit of God* (1741), he undertook to specify those particular marks or signs whereby one might distinguish the genuine from the spurious work of the spirit. Freely conceding that the physical and psychological manifestations of such works were wholly natural, he insisted that it was reasonable, nonetheless, to expect the spirit to work through the body, for "Such is our nature, that we cannot think of things invisible, without a degree of imagination." [21] Challenged by Charles Chauncy [22] to produce some incontrovertible evidence of the operation of God in these imaginings, he replied with *Some Thoughts Concerning the Present Revival of Religion in New England* (1742). As evidence the book was a failure. Instead of trying to prove the handiwork of God in specific cases of conversion involving emotional and physical disturbances (which is what Chauncy and his supporters expected him to do), Edwards assayed the much more difficult task of showing that any true religion must have its emotional (affectionate) as well as its rational side. Like Pascal, he knew that the heart has its reasons, and in this "sense of the heart" he thought to find the essence of the spiritual life. His only error was to be a century and a half ahead of his time. The Boston religious mind of 1742 was not yet sophisticated enough to grasp the psychological subtlety of religion as change of heart. That one could at the same time retain emotion and repudiate enthusiasm was something neither Boston nor Northampton could quite understand, and as the furore of the Great Awakening gradually died away they lost all interest in trying. When Edwards' final word on the subject, *A Treatise concerning Religious Affections*, appeared in 1746 it attracted few readers and persuaded none. To the end of his days, Chauncy believed that Jonathan Edwards was a "visionary enthusiast, and not to be minded in anything he says."

It is the verdict of history that Chauncy was mistaken. Completely unappreciated by his own generation, Edwards is today generally recognized as the greatest theologian of the spiritual life America has yet produced. Miller has called the *Religious Affections* "the most profound exploration of the religious psychology in all American literature," and if it is not quite that, it is still a landmark in the history of American theology. The question it seeks to answer is fundamental to every faith in any age: "What is the nature of true religion? and wherein do lie the distinguishing notes of that virtue and holiness, that is acceptable in the sight of God?" [23] Edwards' reply is as sweeping as it is simple: "True religion, in great part, consists in holy affections." [24] These affections, or fruits of the Spirit, he defines as "the more vigorous and sensible exercises of the inclination and will of the soul." [25] As instances of these affections, he cites the *peace* of God, the joy of believing, the *light of knowledge* of God's glory in Christ, and last and most important, the *love* of God indwelling in the heart of the converted.[26] Only in these "fervent exercises of the heart" is true religion truly found, for

> If we ben't in good earnest in religion, and our wills and inclinations be not strongly exercised, we are nothing. The things of religion are so great, that there can be no suitableness in the exercises of our hearts, to their nature and importance, unless they be lively and powerful. In nothing, is vigor in the actings of our inclinations so requisite, as in religion; and in nothing is lukewarmness so odious. True religion is evermore a powerful thing; and the power of it appears, in the first place, in the *inward* exercises of it in the heart, where is the principle and original seat of it. Hence true religion is called the power of godliness, in distinction from the external appearances of it, that are the form of it.[27]

Had Chauncy carefully studied this passage, he must have seen how one might retain emotion while yet rejecting enthusiasm. Religion is a force so vital to everything in life that it cannot be something merely intellectual or formal. True religion is engagement as well as observance. On the other hand, the inwardness of true religion renders suspect the emotional excesses of the Great Awakening. The sense of the heart, then, should not be confused with the physical frenzy of the revival. The affections are more than passions.

> The *affections* and *passions* are frequently spoken of as the same; and yet, in the more common use of speech, there is in some respect a difference; and affection is a word, that in its ordinary signification, seems to be something more extensive than passion; being used for all vigorous lively actings of the will or inclination; but passion for those that are more sudden, and whose effects on the animal spirits are more violent, and the mind more overpowered, and less in its own command.[28]

The mind in its own command inclined to love in faith for Christ, in this, Edwards teaches, does true religion consist.

> That religion which God requires, and will accept, does not consist in weak, dull and lifeless wouldings,[29] raising us but a little above a state of indifference: God, in his Word, greatly insists upon it, that we be in good earnest, fervent in spirit, and our hearts vigorously engaged in religion: . . . "And now Israel, what doth the Lord thy God require of thee, but to fear the Lord thy God, to walk in all his ways, and to love him, and to serve the Lord thy God, with all thy heart, and with all thy soul?" (Deut. 10:12) . . . 'Tis such a fervent, vigorous engagedness of the heart in religion, that is the fruit of a real circumcision of the heart, or true regeneration, and that has the promises of life; "And the Lord thy God will circumcise thine heart, and the heart of thy seed, to love the Lord thy God, with all thy heart, and with all thy soul, that thou mayest live" (Deut. 30:6).[30]

Having marshalled the scriptural evidence for his thesis, Edwards turns next to consider the empirical. By what signs or marks shall we know that a man has those affections whose practice constitutes true religion, and whose manifestation indicates one who is saved? That, Edwards contends, is the basic question, and he proposes two approaches to it. First, he feels, we must guard against being drawn into error by judging of affections by false signs, for there are "some things, which are no signs that affections are gracious, or that they are not." Thus,

'Tis no sign one way or the other, that religious affections are very great, or raised very high.[31]

'Tis no sign that affections have the nature of true religion, or that they have not, that they have great effects on the body.[32]

'Tis no sign that affections are truly gracious affections, or that they are not, that they cause those who have them, to be fluent, fervent and abundant, in talking of the things of religion.[33]

'Tis no sign that the religious affections which persons have are such as to have in them the nature of true religion, or that they have not, that they dispose persons to spend much time in religion, and to be zealously engaged in the external duties of worship.[34]

Nothing can be certainly known of the nature of religious affections by this, that they much dispose persons with their mouths to praise and glorify God.[35]

'Tis no sign that affections are right, or that they are wrong, that they make persons that have them, exceeding confident that what they experience is divine, and that they are in a good estate.[36]

Nothing can be certainly concluded concerning the nature of religious affections, that any are the subjects of, from this, that the outward manifestations of them, and the relation persons give of them, are very affecting and pleasing to the truly godly, and such as greatly gain their charity, and win their hearts.[37]

The outward manifestations of revival, the shrieking and speaking in tongues, the ostentatious devoutness and reputation of holiness, are no certain signs of true religious affection. That they are evidences of sham or hypocrisy, Edwards does not go so far as to say; but the implication is there. The man who only ten years earlier had borne witness in his *Faithful Narrative* to the operation of the spirit in the morbid mouthings of Abigail Hutchinson and the neurotic hysteria of the child Phoebe Bartlett, who only five years before had himself deliberately stirred his hearers to frenzy with his hellfire sermonizing, had at last awakened to a nobler vision of the work of the Holy Spirit. Once the negative had been supplemented by the positive, the vision would be complete.

The second, or positive, approach to the problem of distinguishing signs of truly gracious and holy affections is the topic of the third, and by far the longest, section of Edwards' Treatise. There are, according to his analysis, twelve such signs, and he devotes some two hundred and seventy pages to proving from experience, reason and scripture that the really religious affections (1) "arise from those influences and operations on the heart, which are *spiritual, supernatural* and *divine*"; [38] (2) reflect the transcendent excellence of divine things in themselves; (3) are founded on the loveliness of the moral excellency of divine things; (4) enlighten the mind to the apprehension of divine things; (5) are attended with evangelical humiliation and (6) a reasonable conviction of the reality of divine things; (7) involve a change of nature; (8) naturally beget and promote the imitation of Christ; (9) soften the heart; (10) have symmetry and proportion; (11) tend to increase spiritual appetite; and (12) "have their exercise and fruit in Christian practice." [39] He, then, is truly elect whose life exhibits these twelve signs of gracious regeneration. Even so, we must not make the mistake of judging a man sinner or saint to the precise degree to which he manifests or lacks these signs of religious affection, for in these matters, as Edwards clearly sees, there is no precision to be found. "I am," he tells us at the outset, "far from undertaking to give such signs of gracious affections, as shall be sufficient to enable any certainly to distinguish true affection from false in others; or to determine positively which of their neighbors are true professors, and which are hypocrites." [40]

> Though it be plain that Christ has given rules to all Christians, to enable 'em to judge of professors of religion, whom they are concerned with, so far as is necessary for their own safety, and to prevent their being led into a snare by false teachers, and false pretenders to religion; and though it be also beyond doubt, that the Scriptures do abound with rules, which may be very serviceable to ministers, in counseling and conducting souls committed to their care, in things appertaining to their spiritual and eternal state; yet, 'tis also evident, that it was never God's design to give us any rules, by which we may certainly know, who of our fellow professors are his, and to make a full and clear separation between sheep and goats: but that on the contrary, it was God's design to reserve this to himself, as his prerogative.[41]

Nor, he adds, are any such signs to be expected

> that shall be sufficient to enable those saints certainly to discern their own good estate, who are very low in grace, or are such as

have much departed from God, and are fallen into a dead, carnal
and unchristian frame. It is not agreeable to God's design . . . that
such should know their good estate: nor is it desirable that they
should; but on the contrary, every way best that they should not. . . .[42]

For no man, however high or low his estate, however clear the
sign or lack of sign of his salvation, can know for sure God's
verdict on his life.

'Tis not God's design that men should obtain assurance in any other
way, than by mortifying corruption, and increasing in grace, and
obtaining the lively exercises of it. And although self-examination
be a duty of great use and importance, and by no means to be
neglected; yet it is not the principal means, by which the saints do
get satisfaction of their good estate. Assurance is not to be obtained
so much by self-examination, as by action.[43]

The words are at once the fruit and epitaph of the Great Awakening. They mark the peak of Edwards' insight into religious truth.
He had twelve years yet to live,[44] and in this time he would write
three major theological works,[45] but as a philosopher of the revival
his work was done. By mid-century the colonial mind had passed
beyond Enthusiasm to Enlightenment. America was about to attain the age of reason.

SUGGESTED READINGS

Edwin Scott Gaustad, *The Great Awakening in New England* (New
York: Harper, 1957), is a careful and thorough study of the movement
in all its phases. Excellent bibliography of the primary sources. Somewhat narrower in scope, but equally if not more thorough in treatment,
is Leonard J. Trinterud's re-examination of colonial Presbyterianism,
The Forming of an American Tradition (Philadelphia: Westminster,
1949). This too includes a valuable bibliography of original materials.
The whole course of American revivalism is surveyed in very readable
style by William Warren Sweet, *Revivalism in America: Its Origin,
Growth and Decline* (New York: Scribner, 1945). Out of print, but
available in many libraries.

The major philosophical work to come out of the Great Awakening,
Jonathan Edwards' *A Treatise Concerning Religious Affections* comprises Volume Two of the new Yale edition of the complete works. The

best single-volume introduction to the whole of Edwards' writings is still Faust and Johnson, *Jonathan Edwards, Representative Selections* (New York: American Book Co., 1935). It too is out of print, but your local library may have it. Douglas J. Elwood, *The Philosophical Theology of Jonathan Edwards* (New York: Columbia University Press, 1960), argues for a panentheistic interpretation of Edwards' theology. His failure, to my way of thinking, to make out his case does not, however, detract significantly from the value of his study. There are two excellent biographies: the most recent, Perry Miller's *Jonathan Edwards* (New York: Sloane, 1949; Meridian paperback, 1959), emphasizes the theologian more than the man; Ola Elizabeth Winslow, *Jonathan Edwards* (New York: Macmillan, 1940), stresses the man rather than the theologian.

REFERENCES

1. *A Treatise Concerning Religious Affections* (New Haven: Yale, 1959), p. 121. Hereafter cited as Religious Affections.

2. *Sermons by Theodorus Jacobus Frelinghuysen* (New York, 1856), pp. 67-70.

3. Ibid., pp. 311-14.

4. *The Danger of an Unconverted Ministry, Considered in a Sermon* (Boston, 1742), pp. 11-12.

5. Published in the Boston Evening Post, July 26th, 1742.

6. *Twenty-Three Sermons Upon the Chief End of Man* (Philadelphia, 1744), Sermon XXI.

7. William Warren Sweet, *Revivalism in America* (New York: Scribner, 1945), p. 108.

8. Jeremiah 22:29.

9. *Jonathan Edwards* (New York: Meridian Books, 1959), p. 141.

10. *A Continuation of the Reverend Mr. Whitefield's Journal, From a few Days after his Return to Georgia to his Arrival at Falmouth on the 11th of March, 1741* (London, 1741), pp. 46-47.

11. Ibid., p. 47.

12. Ibid., pp. 45-46.

13. *The Works of President Edwards,* 8 Vols. (Worcester: Isaiah Thomas, 1809), VII, p. 469. Hereafter cited as Works.

14. Ibid., p. 472.

15. Ibid., p. 473.

16. "The Distinguishing Marks of a Work of the Spirit of God," in *Works of President Edwards,* 4 Vols. (New York, 1843), I, pp. 535f.

17. "Sinners in the Hands of an Angry God," Works, VII, p. 496.

18. Ibid., pp. 496-97.

19. Ibid., pp. 501-2. The Worcester (or Austin) edition of the sermon ends with this passage.

20. Works, edited by Sereno E. Dwight, 10 Vols. (New York: 1829), VII, p. 177.

21. Quoted by Miller, *Jonathan Edwards*, p. 170.

22. The only clergyman in Boston to keep his religious sense of balance

throughout the revival, Chauncy (1705-1787) was minister of the First Church from 1736 until his death. His *Seasonable Thoughts on the State of Religion* (1743) was a massive attack upon the revival in general and Edwards in particular. It was Chauncy's belief that, "The plain Truth is, an enlightened Mind, not raised Affections, ought always to be the Guide of those who call themselves Men," and to demonstrate this is the one major aim of all of his theological work.

23. Religious Affections, p. 84.
24. Ibid., p. 95.
25. Ibid., p. 96.
26. Ibid., p. 7.
27. Ibid., pp. 99-100. My italics.
28. Ibid., p. 98.
29. In a footnote to the text, the editor, John E. Smith, notes that "JE coined this word to refer to very weak inclinations which do not represent genuine convictions and do not issue in action; it is as if a man were always to say that he 'would' believe or perform but never actually does." Ibid., p. 99n.
30. Ibid., p. 99.
31. Ibid., p. 127.
32. Ibid., p. 131.
33. Ibid., p. 135.
34. Ibid., p. 163.
35. Ibid., p. 165.
36. Ibid., p. 167.
37. Ibid., p. 181.
38. Ibid., p. 197.
39. Ibid., p. 383.
40. Ibid., p. 193.
41. Ibid.
42. Ibid., pp. 193-94.
43. Ibid., p. 195.
44. By and large, they were bitter years. In 1750 a growing series of personal and theological differences between Edwards and his congregation culminated in his dismissal as pastor of the Northampton church. Physically unequal to the task of another large pastorate, he refused several offers of pulpits and accepted an invitation to become a missionary to the Stockbridge Indians. Here, on the frontier, he lived until January of 1758, preaching, converting, and writing theology. The October previous he had been chosen to succeed his son-in-law Aaron Burr as President of Princeton College, and in February, 1758, he was formally inducted into this office. A month later he was dead, killed by smallpox contracted by inoculation. He was buried at Princeton.
45. In his *Enquiry into the modern prevailing Notions of the Freedom of Will* (1754), Edwards undertook to defend Calvinist orthodoxy against its American detractors. As against the objection that the Calvinist doctrine of the absolute sovereignty of God must imply a denial of man's free will, Edwards argued that man is free so far as his choices are concerned, but conditioned as regards the motives determining these choices. By this formula he sought to secure man's moral responsibility without derogating

from the omnipotence of God. To modern scholars, however, the book's chief merit lies not in its rationalization of Calvinist doctrine (most think it of dubious validity), but in its brilliant critique of the Arminian position. Edwards' other major works are *The Nature of True Virtue* (he finds it to consist in the emotion of disinterested benevolence), written in 1755 but not published until 1765, and *The Great Christian Doctrine of Original Sin Defended,* published posthumously in 1758.

III

The Enlightenment in Colonial America

EUROPEAN ANTECEDENTS

SAMUEL JOHNSON

JONATHAN MAYHEW

CHARLES CHAUNCY

CADWALLADER COLDEN

"There is no Doctrine of Faith, but it perfectly accords with the Principles of true
Reason: Nor otherwise might it be received
as an Article of Faith. We should never
therefore oppose Faith and Reason; but rather
consider them as Helps and Supports to each
other; for so they really are: Nor can there
be Faith without Reason." [1]

CHARLES CHAUNCY

1. European Antecedents

IN THE INTELLECTUAL HISTORY of Western Europe, the Seventeenth and Eighteenth centuries constitute a period of high mental adventure. Scientifically, it was the Age of Newton; philosophically, it was a time of liberation from the Schoolmen. The long night of Faith was over; the new day of Reason had arrived; a decent respect for the rights of man and the opinions of mankind now replaced reliance on religious authority. In England the new watchword was "common-sense," and in the writings of Locke, Berkeley and Hume it was polished to a high gloss. Atheistic materialism was the philosophical fashion of France, and it had many practitioners, Condillac, Diderot and De la Mettrie among them. Voltaire preached deism, Holbach and Helvetius denounced the ignorance and superstition of Christianity, and Rousseau proclaimed the sovereignty of the people. Across the Rhine Lessing, Hamann and Herder were championing religious and cultural liberty in Germany, and it was the Germans who gave the spirit of the times its name: they called it Die Auflkärung (The Enlightenment), and like their French and English contemporaries optimistically assumed that they were describing the state of all times to come.

There were, of course, backward cultures where men still honored the older ways of thought, and sought in Theology the answers that the enlightened believed only Science could give. One such was colonial America, and it was only as the works of the European Enlightenment found their way piecemeal into the libraries of Harvard and Yale, and thence into the hands of the curious few, that the new modes of thought gradually took root in the American Mind. Since most serious American readers were either clergymen, or in training to become same, it was natural that the first fruits of the American Enlightenment should be theological.

2. Samuel Johnson

IN THE YEAR 1722, Mr. Samuel Johnson, bred up in Congregationalism, recently graduated from Yale College, and newly established
as the pastor of the Congregational Church at West Haven, Connecticut, concluded after an agonizing reappraisal of his personal
convictions that he must take Holy Orders in the Church of England, and to that end he embarked from Boston early in November
with two friends similarly minded. He had been, as he wrote in his
Autobiography,[2]

> always much embarrassed with the rigid Calvinistical notions in
> which he had been bred. He thought that he must believe them
> because everybody else did and because some sounds in Scripture
> seemed to favor them, but then as some things there seemed quite
> inconsistent with them, he could never be entirely satisfied in them.
> . . . He had also an early dislike to the independent or congregational
> form of church government, in which every brother has a hand;
> which as well as the *extempore* way he plainly saw tended too much
> to conceit and self-sufficiency and to endless feuds, censoriousness
> and uncharitableness while the discipline was often on mere human
> frailties and made a means to revenge little private quarrels and
> issued in great animosities and often in virulent separations. He
> was convinced that a way so entirely popular could but very poorly
> and he thought not long subsist, to answer any ends of government;
> but must from the nature of it crumble to pieces, as every individual
> seemed to think himself infallible. These observations prepared his
> mind, when he came to read and understand the nature of the
> episcopal government of the church readily to see the reasonableness

and great advantage of it and indeed the superior excellency of the Government of England; both in church and state.

It is hard to imagine today the consternation aroused by this simple decision of Johnson and his friends. We tend to forget that the congregational form of church government had only been won after long years of struggle, and that to the Puritan divines of Connecticut and Massachusetts the concession of the right of Anglicans to minister and have colonial bishops was the opening wedge of a plot to return religion and the state to the immediate control of the English crown. But Johnson and his companions were not to be stopped. They were ordained in England, and Johnson returned to America to become the minister to the Anglican community at Stratford, Connecticut. What he had realized, many others soon came to see: New England was not God's headquarters on earth, but merely another province of the British Empire, and like most provinces, intellectually backward and culturally uncouth. If a man would acquire genuine learning he must look not to the ministers of Boston but to the scientists and philosophers of Europe.

During his college years he had been cautioned against reading Descartes, Locke and Newton because, as he tells us, "the new philosophy it was said would soon bring in a new divinity and corrupt the pure religion of the country." [3] By accident, however, he lighted upon a copy of Sir Francis Bacon's *Advancement of Learning,* and a new world opened to his eyes. From Bacon he learned respect for scientific method; later he got from Newton's *Principia Mathematica* the essentials of his world-view; more important, though, than either was his reading of John Locke. Locke's *Essay Concerning Human Understanding* provided Johnson with his basic philosophical outlook and went far towards determining his views on religion. Indeed, so great was the influence of this book, not only on Johnson but on every major American thinker from Jonathan Edwards to Thomas Jefferson, that no one can claim to understand the colonial American Mind who is not familiar with its themes.

The heart of Locke's philosophy is his conviction that whatever can be known must have its origin in the senses. There is nothing in the mind, he teaches, that was not first in the senses. At birth the mind is like a perfectly smooth wax tablet (*tabula rasa*) completely devoid of any impressions. The notion that man is born with certain innate ideas or dispositions is simply false. Not even the laws of thought are innate, since, as Locke points out, infants and savages are ignorant of them. It follows, then, that whatever we know is due to our experience of the external world, and to our combining in thought the impressions of qualities experienced. What we call our ideas are simply *representations* in our minds of the external objects of our experience. Ideas are classified as simple or complex, the latter being combinations of the former. Such ideas as we may think to have of things we have never experienced are neither true nor false, for the true and the experienced are one and the same.

So much did Samuel Johnson in his early enlightenment learn and accept. That such a view must involve a new conception of the sources and nature of our knowledge of God, he was well aware. If what can be known is what can be experienced, then God can be known and understood only as man has some experience of Him. This is why Jonathan Edwards and the other theologians of the Great Awakening were so insistent that religion is an affair of the heart, a personal communion with God. Having accepted Locke's basic premises, they could argue no other way—and remain true to common sense. Unfortunately for the cogency of their arguments, the Lockean account of knowledge suffered from one glaring defect. For Locke had failed to realize that if all ideas are simply *representations* or mental pictures of things existing outside the mind, then the mind can never know for sure that these ideas are true, since it has no way of knowing whether or not its ideas correspond to the objects they represent. In other words, the knower knows only the contents of his own mind; but whether those contents are in fact identical with the *things* they represent, he cannot know—because in order to know that any idea corresponds to (or represents) its object, he would have antecedently to know *both object and idea of object,* whereas if Locke is right he really knows only his own ideas.

It is to the credit of Samuel Johnson that when this fatal flaw in the representational (Lockean) theory of knowledge was pointed out to him by George Berkeley, the distinguished Anglo-Irish philosopher-priest whom Johnson had come to know during the two and one-half years that Berkeley had lived at Newport, Rhode Island, he had sense enough to see (as many thinkers of his own and later times did not) the cogency of Berkeley's objections, and adaptability enough to change his (Johnson's) own point of view. By 1729 Johnson had become Berkeley's foremost American disciple; in 1751 appeared his *Elementa Philosophica* largely derived from Berkeley. It was the first philosophical textbook published in America, and its wide circulation did much to focus the attention of the colonial collegians on the philosophy of the newly made Anglican Bishop of Cloyne.

Bishop Berkeley holds, as against Locke, that there neither is nor can be any such thing as a substance completely external to and absolutely independent of all mind. If what we can know is our own ideas, and only our own ideas, as Locke has shown, then it must be that to exist and to be perceived are one and the same. *Esse est percipi,* to be is to be perceived. This, Berkeley contends, is the truth upon which every philosophy must build. To be is to be perceived, and nothing exists that is not perceived by some mind. Does this mean that the external world ceases to exist when I or anyone else perceived it? Emphatically not, says Berkeley.

> When I deny sensible things an existence out of the mind, I do not mean my mind in particular, but all minds. Now, it is plain, they have an existence exterior to my mind; since I find them, by experience, to be independent of it. There is, therefore, some other mind wherein they exist, during the intervals between the times of my perceiving them: as, likewise, they did before my birth, and wou'd do after my supposed annihilation.[4]

This "other mind" he goes on to describe as that *"omnipresent, external mind,* which knows and comprehends all things, and exhibits them to our view in such a manner, and according to such rules, as He himself has ordained. . . ."[5] Thus the very fact of our having ideas guarantees the existence of God.

> Men commonly believe that all things are known or perceived by God, because they believe the being of a God; whereas I, on the

other side, immediately and necessarily conclude the being of a God, because all sensible things must be perceived by him.[6]

In sum, if nothing can exist unperceived by some mind, then God (the cosmic mind) must exist, for otherwise that vast expanse of the universe unperceived by any finite minds could have no ground for being. The very fact that there is a world around us is, therefore, the ultimate and adequate proof of the existence of God. It is hardly to be wondered that the ministerial mind of Samuel Johnson should see here an argument that

> left no room for endless doubts and uncertainties. His denying matter at first seemed shocking, but it was only for want of giving a thorough attention to his meaning. It was only the unintelligible scholastic notion of matter he disputed, and not anything either sensible, imaginable or intelligible; and it was attended with this vast advantage, that it not only gave new incontestible proofs of a deity, but moreover the most striking apprehensions of his constant presence with us and inspection over us, and of our entire dependence on him and infinite obligations to his most wise and almighty benevolence. On these accounts (as well as to inure one to a close and exact way of thinking) Mr. Johnson wished his works might be thoroughly studied and well considered especially his wonderfully ingenious theories of vision as well as his principles and dialogues, in which he has plainly outdone both Mr. Locke and Sr. Isaac (Newton) in some particulars.[7]

Of course, Mr. Johnson did not accept Berkeley's views *in toto*. In his correspondence with the bishop he announces his difficulties with certain features of Berkeley's system, particularly those wherein the doctrine seems to run counter to that taught by Sir Isaac Newton. The problem of the independent existence of other minds troubles him, as does the Berkeleian emphasis on the passivity of the mind in its acts of perception. Mind, he thinks, is essentially self-activity. The principle of intelligence is at once a principle of action, as much in finite spirits as in God. Writing to Cadwallader Colden, he argues that intelligent beings alone are properly called causes. This advance beyond Berkeley is, he feels, necessary if we are to account for the ordering of events in nature. Beyond the view of Berkeley also is his idea that we are immediately conscious of a kind of intellectual light within us. . . . whereby we not only know that we perceive the object, but directly apply ourselves to the consideration of it. . . . so our minds are as passive to this intellectual light, as they are to sensible light, and can no more withstand the evidence of it, than they can withstand the evidence of sense. Thus I am under the same necessity to assent to this, that I am or have a being, and that I perceive and freely exert myself, as I am of assenting to this, that I see colors or hear sounds. I am as perfectly sure that 2 plus 2 equals 4, or that the whole is equal to all its parts, as that I feel heat or cold. . . . I am intuitively certain of both. . . .

Now if it be asked, whence does this light derive . . . I answer, I have no other way to conceive how I come to be affected with this intuitive intellectual light, whereof I am conscious, than by deriving it from the universal presence and action of the Deity. . . . For I know I am not the author of it. . . . Therefore, tho' I cannot explain the manner how I am impressed with it (as neither can I that of sense) I do humbly conceive that God does as truly and immediately enlighten my mind internally to know these intellectual objects, as he does by the light of the sun (his sensible representative) enable me to perceive sensible objects. . . . And this intuitive knowledge, so far as it goes, must be the first principles, from which the mind takes its rise, and upon which it proceeds in all its subsequent improvements in reasoning, and discovering both truth in speculation, and right in action; so that this intellectual light must be primarily and carefully attended to, if we would avoid and be secure from either error or vice.[8]

In this conviction Johnson recurs to a motif dating clear back to St. Augustine, although it is probable that he derived it from Descartes, and its echoes are to be found in Locke. Whether it is thoroughly consistent with the empiricism of Locke and the immaterialism of Berkeley is another question, and one into which we cannot here take time to go. In any case, what is important about Johnson's advance beyond Berkeley is that in so doing he anticipates Kant and his synthetic a priori, and lays the foundations of that Idealism which, in the works of the Transcendentalists and the St. Louis Hegelians, dominates the mind of mid-nineteenth century America.

In January, 1754 Samuel Johnson was chosen to be the first president of the newly founded King's College in the City of New

York. After much soul-searching (the College was to be non-denominational, and Johnson was fifty-seven years old and in poor health) he accepted and served until illness forced his retirement in 1763. During his tenure of office he worked for the modernization of the traditional collegiate curriculum, and sought to make education something to be enjoyed rather than simply endured. In many of his ideas and practices he anticipated by a century and a half the progressivism of John Dewey and his school. Johnson wrote textbooks on Logic, Ethics, and Metaphysics, as well as a Hebrew and English grammar. He was a teacher of note, and the survival of King's was a tribute to the soundness of his administration. His work done, his reputation secure, he passed quietly away, like his great and good friend Berkeley, seated in his chair, surrounded by his family, on January 6th, 1772.

3. Jonathan Mayhew

JUST WHEN the Enlightenment came to Boston is hard to say. Its great themes, natural rights and religious liberty were at first so mixed with the traditional theology as to render impossible any hard and fast distinction between orthodox and heterodox. Such pillars of orthodoxy as Increase and Cotton Mather had waxed enthusiastic about the natural philosophy of Newton, and John Wise apparently thought it consistent to teach natural rights and preach Calvinism. Nonetheless, as the Eighteenth Century wore on towards its middle decades, the mood of optimism generated by the growing prosperity of New England issued in a general softening of the Calvinist sense of sin. The emotional excesses of the Great Awakening simply accelerated the rise of that religious rationalism whose basic tenets were already known to the few who kept up with the new accessions to the Harvard Library. Such authors as the English dissenter John Taylor persuaded many New Englanders of the falsity of the doctrine of original sin. "We are," according to Taylor, "born neither righteous nor sinful; but capable of being either as we improve or neglect the Goodness of God." [9] That God was truly good and interested only in the welfare and happiness of His creatures was a belief soon to become widespread. Cotton Mather's *The Christian Philosopher* was but the earliest expression of a conviction of universal benevolence eventually shared by the majority of proper Bostonians. Inevitably, as religious optimism grew, so did men's confidence in their own ability to rationalize the ways of God and man. Psychologically, the churchgoers of

Boston were ready by 1745 to hear the case for religious liberalism. They had not long to wait. In 1747 the West Church called Jonathan Mayhew, son of the Reverend Experience Mayhew, to be its second pastor. At the age of twenty-seven, Mayhew had already acquired a reputation for religious individualism. At Harvard he had absorbed the liberalism of Samuel Clarke and John Locke, and a subsequent period of residence with the rationalist Ebenezer Gay of Hingham just about completed his weaning away from the five fundamentals of Calvinism, i.e., predestination, limited atonement, total depravity, irresistible grace, and perseverance of the saints. At his ordination not a single Boston clergyman put in an appearance. Even the liberal Chauncy stayed away. To the local ministers, Mayhew was that Vineyard heretic, well liked for all of that, but never to be invited into the Congregational club.

When we consider his theological views, it is easy to see why. His heresies were manifold and major. His rejection of original sin established him in the eyes of his colleagues as a Pelagian. Worse still, he had no respect for the Trinity. "The Dominion and Sovereignty of the universe is," he insists, "necessarily *one* and in ONE." [10] To the orthodox this was Arianism, and Mayhew's jibes at the "Athanasians" only made it the more overt. He was, in fact, the first New England Unitarian, and like most theological pioneers he had to pay the price of clerical censure and community disapproval. Boston was ripe for the liberalist gospel, but it was not yet quite prepared to go so far as to accept Mayhew's notion of religion as private judgment.

> Did I say, we have a right to judge and act for ourselves? I now add—it is our *indispensable duty* to do it. This is a right which we cannot relinquish, or neglect to exercise, if we would, without being highly culpable. . . . God and nature and the gospel of Christ injoin it upon us as a duty to maintain the right of private judgment.[11]

On one issue, however, Mayhew did command the solid support of the Congregational clergy. In opposing the practice of the Anglican ministry in New England and the establishment of an American episcopate, Mayhew spoke for all colonials who feared that British bishops meant Crown encroachment and an end to religious freedom. The Mayhew Controversy, as the war of pamphlets between the minister of the West Church and his Anglican opponents was known, for all its ostensible concern with bishops, was actually an American challenge to British authority, a challenge, moreover, which Mayhew had raised as early as 1750 in his celebrated sermon, *A Discourse Concerning Unlimited Submission.* Therein he had called in question the hereditary and divine right of kings to command the unlimited obedience of their subjects. Such a notion, he argues, finds no warrant in revelation or reason. On the contrary,

> A people really oppressed to a great degree by their sovereign, cannot well be insensible when they are so oppressed. . . . For a nation thus abused to arise unanimously, and to resist their prince, even to the dethroning him, is not criminal; but a reasonable way of vindicating their liberties and just rights. . . .[12]

For no government, he thinks,

> is to be submitted to, at the expence of that which is the sole end of all government;—the common good and safety of society. . . . The only reason of the institution of civil government; and the only rational ground of submission to it, is the common safety and utility. . . . All besides, is mere lawless force and usurpation; neither God nor nature, having given any man a right of dominion over any society, independently of that society's approbation, and consent to be governed by him.[13]

Presumably, Mayhew was speaking in commemoration of the execution of Charles I, but his hearers would hardly fail to apply the principles he laid down to George II and his son. For the first time in Massachusetts, a man had dared to use his pulpit to proclaim the rights of free men against their Royal Governors. The plain talk that earlier had damned him for a heretic now caused him to be praised for a hero. Unfortunately, he would not live to know that he had fired the morning gun of the American Revolution.[14]

4. Charles Chauncy

OF THAT SMALL BAND whose lives spanned the long decades between the Calvinism of the Mathers and the religious liberalism of the Revolutionary era, none better exemplifies the transition from Puritanism to Enlightenment than Charles Chauncy. He began as a Calvinist, moderate to be sure, but a Calvinist nonetheless. As late as 1741, in his celebrated sermon, *The New Creature Describ'd,* he was warning sinners of the bottomless pit awaiting those out of Christ, and the virulence of his description yielded nothing to the hellfire rhetoric of Jonathan Edwards. However, as noted earlier, the fanaticism engendered by the Great Awakening awoke him to the inherent evils of enthusiasm. By 1744 he could recognize that

> There have always been visionary, enthusiastical Men; pretending to an extraordinary Mission from GOD, and preaching for Doctrines of his, the Suggestions of their own vain Imaginations. So it was in Old Testament Times. . . . And so it has been in all Ages of the Christian Church; yea, there have not been wanting Instances, even in our own Day, of those, who under the vain Notion of being extraordinarily sent of God, have gone about venting their own wild Imaginations for divine Truths, to the great Reproach of CHRIST, and Scandal of Religion.[15]

Against such, he had made a strong case in his *Seasonable Thoughts on the State of Religion* (1743). Henceforward he would lean to liberalism and follow the lead of Mayhew.

As pastor of the venerable First Church, Chauncy was a power to be reckoned with in Boston, and the rise of liberalism to religious respectability was due in no small part to his advocacy of it. On the other hand, the very eminence of his position tended to make him more conservative than his colleague Mayhew. Chauncy never publicly avowed himself a unitarian, nor did he ever declare explicitly for the right of private judgment in religious matters. Even so, his *Compleat View of Episcopacy* was no less anti-Anglican in its opposition to colonial bishops than the Mayhew pamphlets; his denunciation of the Stamp Act was unequivocal, and he was as sure as his friend from the West Church that

> There is no Doctrine of Faith, but it perfectly accords with the Principles of true Reason.[16]

True reason it was that gradually impressed upon his mind the conviction that it cannot be God's purpose to condemn the mass of men to everlasting damnation. No rational God could, to his way of thinking, possibly wish anything less than the ultimate happiness of all his creatures. For many years his fear of offending the orthodox inhibited him from publishing the conclusions he had arrived at some years before 1768. At last, however, in 1784 he screwed his courage to the printing point and brought out his twofold contribution to the liberal theology, *The Benevolence of the Deity* and *The Salvation of All Men*.

The basic theological assumption from which any Christian concerned with the designs of God must start is, Chauncy contends in these works, that all men are originally made for salvation. Not hellfire but happiness is, then, the ultimate destiny of man. That such a presumption ran counter to every Calvinist precept he had ever learned, Chauncy knew full well. No one understood better than he that what was required was a theology at once explanatory of the errors of Calvinism and the truth of Optimism. To this end his two treatises were written, and not in vain—as the subsequent triumph of Optimism in American religion attests.

He begins by calling attention to some passages in Holy Scripture which appear, on their face, to justify the pessimism of the Puritan Calvinists. "It should seem," he notes, from several passages in the New Testament, as though the greater part of mankind would miss of happiness in the state that follows next upon this. To this purpose is that of our Saviour, "Strait is the gate, and narrow the way, which leadeth unto life; and *few* there be that find it." And, when one came to him with that question, "Lord, are there *few* that be saved?" he plainly concedes that it was so, by the reply which he makes in the following verse, "Strive to enter in at the strait gate; for *many*, I say unto you, will seek to enter in, and *shall not be able.*" And it is observable, the conclusion of two of his parables is summed up in these emphatical words, "For many are called, and few are chosen." To these and such like texts it may be owing, that the salvation of comparatively but a few of the human race has been received as an undoubted doctrine of the bible. And I see not, I confess, but that such texts would be a full confirmation of this doctrine, if it were a truth (as has been generally supposed) that the next is the final state of men.[17]

But is this "next state" final? That, insists Chauncy, is precisely the question upon the answer to which everything depends, and, he thinks, it must be answered in the negative.

. . . if this [i.e., the belief that the next state is final] instead of a truth, should turn out a false notion, grounded on mistaken apprehensions of the genuine sense of scripture, the above declarations, importing that many shall not be saved in the next state, are no inconsistencies with the affirmation we have laid down to be proved. And that it is a mistake, and a very gross one too, greatly tending to the discomfort of mankind, as well as giving occasion for unworthy reflections on the Deity; I say, that it is a mistake to suppose the next state a final one, we shall endeavour to evince, in its proper place; where it will be seen, that the scripture is so far from asserting this, that it very plainly and frequently insinuates the contrary, and cannot indeed be understood, as to the main thing it has in view, upon any other supposition.[18]

This is not to say, he is careful to add, that some men will not endure great misery after death. The agonies of Hell are real enough. Still, it does not follow that because Hell is real, it is eternal, nor must it be thought of, as the Calvinists always do, simply as a state of punishment. Punishment yes, but punishment for a purpose, and that regeneration. Not retribution but restoration, not vengeance but discipline, is the purpose for which, according to Chauncy, God established Hell. In sum, while man is a free agent, and as such tempted to sin, it is from all eternity God's intention to persuade him to so act as to be worthy of the fruits of heaven, for a perfectly good God could desire no less and will no less than the complete and ultimate felicity of all his creatures.

> The salvation of the whole human kind is indeed the great thing aimed at, in the scheme, the bible has opened to our view, as now in prosecution, by the benevolent Deity, under the management of that glorious personage, Jesus Christ; who, we are there assured, will go on prosecuting this design, till all the individuals of the human race that ever had, now have, or ever will have, existence, shall be fixed in the possession of compleat and everlasting happiness. . . .[19]

So much, Chauncy believed, does Reason teach us, and his enlightened contemporaries saw no cause to disagree. As men who knew themselves endowed by their Creator with the inalienable right to the pursuit of happiness on earth, they would find nothing surprising in the prospect of such pursuit continuing in heaven or in hell. For to them, the Calvinistic sense of the utter worthlessness of man no longer existed. Just when it had been lost, no one could say for sure, but for the vast majority it was gone never to return. Today, as in 1787, Chaunceyan optimism is the dominant mood of the American religious mind.

5. Cadwallader Colden

THAT THIS GROWTH of emphasis on reason and the pursuit of happiness should affect colonial understanding of God's role in the affairs of men was inevitable. To Chauncy, as indeed to all of those of his contemporaries and predecessors we have examined, Jesus Christ is still the Son of God. For the liberal Christians, no less than for their Calvinist opponents, Jesus remains the divine mediator come to secure the salvation of men. But to others, not educated to a primary allegiance to some faith, it soon became clear that if reason was the ruling force in human and cosmic affairs, then men had no direct need of God at all. The discovery that the world was governed entirely by natural laws open to human understanding fostered the notion that God's role in things had ended with the Creation. According to the Deists, as the men who held such views were called, revelation is superfluous. Of course, men would do well to pay heed to the moral code enjoined upon us by that amiable and virtuous man Jesus Christ, but that Jesus saves is a proposition no man of reason need concern himself about. Better that he should spend his time in contemplation of the prospect that the great Sir Isaac Newton has unfolded to our view. If man would know God, let him study Nature.

In colonial America the foremost exponent of this new naturalism was a transplanted Scotsman named Cadwallader Colden. The son of a Scots minister, educated in medicine at Edinburgh, in 1710 Colden came to Philadelphia in search of a practice. In 1718, on the invitation of the royal governor, he moved to New York and accepted an appointment as surveyor-general. In 1760 he became lieutenant-governor of New York, continuing in that office until his death in 1776. As an amateur of science, Colden enjoyed wide renown. He did experimental work of value in botany, and in medicine pioneered in cancer research and epidemiology. He studied Newton carefully, and came away from the *Principia* convinced that

> We have no knowledge of substances, or of any being, or of any thing, abstracted from the action of that thing or being. All our knowledge of things consists in the perception of the power, or force, or property, or manner of acting of that thing; that is, of the action of that thing on our senses, or of the effects of that thing on some other thing, whose action affects, or is the object of our senses, and in the perception of the relations or ratios of these actions to each other.[20]

In sum,

> The essence of things or of substances, so far as we can discover it, consists in the power, or force, or manner of acting of those things.[21]

Since Newton is preeminently the one man to have offered a truly scientific explanation of this manner of acting, it is with Newton that we must begin if we would understand the workings of our world. Colden was himself enough of a scientist to recognize that the Newtonian physics was not of itself a sufficient account of things. He found Newton's expression of the law of gravitation inadequate, and in the Preface to his principal work, *The Principles of Action in Matter,* etc. (1751) he prides himself on having improved upon Sir Isaac's presentation. In his correspondence with Samuel Johnson, he derides the Berkeleian notion of a passive matter informed by an active intelligence. "I cannot," he writes,

> have any idea of anything merely passive or without any kind of action. I can have no idea of a mere negative, and since, as I observed, all our ideas of everything external to us must arise from the actions of those things on our minds, everything of which we

have any idea must be active. This is my fundamental argument, to which I suspect you have not given sufficient attention; and from whence I conclude that all matter is active.[22]

Moreover, this activity must, as Colden sees it, be perfectly natural. He professes not to understand Johnson's idea that activity implies intelligence.

One thing I am desirous to be more fully informed of from you, how consciousness and intelligence become essential to all agents that act from a power in themselves. As to my own part, I do not perceive the necessary connection between power or force and intelligence or consciousness. We may certainly in a thousand objects of our senses discover power and force without perceiving any intelligence in them. And though this power or force should be only apparent, and the consequence or effect of some other primary cause, yet I am certainly to be excused in my thinking it real till it appear otherwise to me. . . . In the next place I must beg you will give me a definition of matter, or of any other being merely passive, without any power or force or action. Such a being I cannot conceive, and therefore as to me does not exist.[23]

Eventually Johnson brought him to admit an intelligent creator of matter, but that was as far as Colden would go. To the end he resisted the notion of God's interference in the affairs of His creation. "The intelligent agent (God) never acts in opposition or contradiction to the material agents; for if it did, nothing but confusion, contradiction and absurdity could ensue: and there could be no need or use of machinery, or of a certain order and disposition of the parts of matter in the several systems, which compose the universe." [24] The order that reason has discovered requires no divinity as principle of explanation. Let God, then, be banished to the beginning of all things. Henceforth our guide is sovereign reason, and our proper business—science. As a prominent Tory and high public official, Colden neither would nor could put the matter quite so bluntly. Nonetheless, the whole tenor of his work implies it, and in the revolutionary world of 1776 there would be no lack of Deists ready to proclaim this final insight of the colonial enlightenment.

SUGGESTED READINGS

The history of the enlightenment in colonial America has not yet been written. Clinton Rossiter, *Seedtime of the Republic* (New York: Harcourt, Brace, 1953), covers much of the ground, but his emphasis is primarily political. Chapter Nine of this work summarizes the life and opinions of Jonathan Mayhew. Most large libraries will have Herbert and Carol Schneider, *Samuel Johnson, His Career and Writings,* 4 Vols. (New York: Columbia University Press, 1929). Volume 1 contains Johnson's Autobiography; Volume 2 includes Herbert Schneider's essay, "The Mind of Samuel Johnson," and the Colden-Johnson correspondence. Chapter Five of Anderson and Fisch, *Philosophy in America* (New York: Appleton, 1939), offers a summary of Colden's life and thought, and extracts from his principal work, *The Principles of Action in Matter.* For those with access to a microfilm reader, there is Harold B. Wohl's doctoral dissertation, *Charles Chauncy and the Age of Enlightenment in New England* (Ann Arbor: University Microfilms AC-1, No. 18, 565, 1956). Additional material and selections from the works of Chauncy and Mayhew may be found in Smith, Handy, and Loetscher, *American Christianity,* Vol. I (New York: Scribner's, 1960).

Indispensable to a thorough understanding of all the above is a familiarity with the central themes of the antecedent European Enlightenment. Good and readily available in paperback is Sir Isaiah Berlin, *The Age of Enlightenment* (Mentor Books). Introduction, with interpretative commentary and selections from Locke, Berkeley, Voltaire, Hume, Reid, Condillac, and their German critics.

REFERENCES

1. *Ministers exhorted and encouraged to take heed to themselves, and to their Doctrine* (Boston: Rogers and Fowle, 1744), p. 17.

2. "Autobiography," in Herbert and Carol Schneider, *Samuel Johnson, His Career and Writings,* 4 Vols. (New York: Columbia University Press, 1929), I, pp. 11-12. Hereafter cited as Johnson.

3. Johnson, I, p. 6.

4. George Berkeley, *Works,* 3 Vols. Edited by A. C. Frazer (Oxford: Clarendon Press, 1871), I, p. 325.

5. Ibid.

6. Ibid., p. 304.

7. Johnson, I, pp. 25-26.

8. Ibid., II, pp. 379-80.

9. *The Scripture-Doctrine of Original Sin Proposed to Free and Candid Examination,* 3rd Edition (Belfast, 1746), p. 422.

10. Jonathan Mayhew, *Sermons* (Boston, 1755), p. 268.

11. Mayhew, *Seven Sermons* (Boston, 1749), p. 86.

12. *A Discourse Concerning Unlimited Submission and Non-Resistance to the Higher Powers* (Boston: D. Fowle, 1750), pp. 38, 40.

13. Ibid., p. 38n.

14. Mayhew died on July 9th, 1766, of "an obstinate nervous disorder in his Head." "To draw the character of Mayhew," wrote John Adams, "would be to transcribe a dozen volumes. This transcendent genius threw all the weight of his great frame into the scale of his country in 1761, and maintained it there with zeal and ardor till his death." *The Works of John Adams,* 10 Vols. (Boston: Little & Brown, 1851), X, p. 288.

15. Ministers exhorted, etc., pp. 23, 24.

16. Ibid., p. 17.

17. *The Mystery Hid from Ages and Generations, made manifest by the Gospel-Revelation: or, The Salvation of All Men* (London: Charles Dilly, 1784), pp. 7-8.

18. Ibid., pp. 8-9.

19. Ibid., p. 3.

20. Cadwallader Colden, *The Principles of Action in Matter,* etc. (London, 1751), p. 1. Hereafter cited as Principles.

21. Principles, p. 4.

22. Johnson, II, p. 297.

23. Ibid., p. 289.

24. Principles, p. 163.

IV

Poor Richard's Philosophy

BENJAMIN FRANKLIN

"A good Example is the best
sermon." [1]

POOR RICHARD

VI

Poor Richard's Philosophy

BENJAMIN FRANKLIN

"A good Example is the best sermon."   POOR RICHARD

1. Benjamin Franklin

Early to bed and early to rise,
Makes a man healthy, wealthy, and
wise.[2]

OR SO WE ALL HAVE HEARD. However, the fact of the matter in our time seems to be that for the vast majority, industriousness and thrift are virtues in abeyance. The modern standard of ambition is rather—security from the cradle to the grave, and few today are the job-seekers whose first question to their prospective employers has not to do with retirement benefits and hours off. The early American gospel of get-on, work and save has everywhere given way to the ideal of more pay for less labor in circumstances of maximum comfort. Still, this contemporary passion for protection is not yet so firmly established in the American heart as to make impossible a future return to those virtues of self-reliance on which our very survival as a people may well depend. We are not yet so enamoured of security as to be unable to profit from the homely wisdom of Poor Richard. Poor Richard,[3] as everyone knows, is Benjamin Franklin, and of no man in our history has it been said with greater truth that in his person and his life we find exemplified those qualities which, in the eyes of the world, have ever been the source of American greatness. If we would make a beginning at recovering that self-reliance which we as a nation have somehow left behind us, we can do no better than to start with him whom Phillips Russell has called "the first civilized American."

Ben Franklin learned self-reliance early. For all that he was his father's favorite, intended by him for the Church, the ninth son of Josiah Franklin, silk-dyer cum tallow-chandler, did not have an easy youth. Colonial Boston in the first quarter of the Eighteenth Century was no place for the weak in body or in spirit. Such harshness as Nature failed to supply was amply made up by the Lord's anointed, Increase and Cotton Mather, while west and north beyond the horizon the French and Indian enemies waited. Nonetheless, Ben thrived and even gave signs of being a prodigy. At five he was reading the Bible; at seven he had the rudiments of writing. "I was," he tells us in his *Autobiography,*

> put to the grammar-school at eight. . . . My early readiness in learning to read (which must have been very early, as I do not remember when I could not read), and the opinion of all his friends, that I should certainly make a good scholar, encouraged him in this purpose of his.[4]

A scholar, however, he was not to be, for his father,

> in the meantime, from a view of the expense of a college education, which having so large a family he could not well afford, and the mean living many so educated were afterwards able to obtain—reasons that he gave to his friends in my hearing—altered his first intention, took me from the grammar-school, and sent me to a school for writing and arithmetic, kept by a then famous man, Mr. George Brownell, very successful in his profession generally, and that by mild, encouraging methods. Under him I acquired fair writing pretty soon, but I failed in the arithmetic, and made no progress in it.[5]

And so at the age of ten he was taken out of school for good and apprenticed to the family business. He never liked it; he wished to run away to sea, and fearful of his resolve, his father finally signed indentures apprenticing him to his elder brother James, a printer by trade. Henceforth he would style himself, Ben Franklin, printer.

In 1721 James Franklin founded the *New-England Courant,* and Ben soon discovered a new outlet for his talents. It seems that his brother had some ingenious men among his friends, who amus'd themselves by writing little pieces for this paper. . . . Hearing their conversations, and their accounts of the approbation their papers were received with, I was excited to try my hand among them; but, being still a boy, and suspecting that my brother would object to printing any-thing of mine in his paper if he knew it to be mine, I contrived to disguise my hand, and, writing an anonymous paper, I put it in at night under the door of the printing-house. It was found in the morning, and communicated to his writing friends when they call'd in as usual. They read it, commented on it in my hearing, and I had the exquisite pleasure of finding it met with their approbation. . . .

Encouraged . . . by this, I wrote and convey'd in the same way to the press several more papers which were equally approv'd; and I kept my secret till my small fund of sense for such performances was pretty well exhausted, and then I discovered it, when I began to be considered a little more by my brother's acquaintance, and in a manner that did not quite please him, as he thought, probably with reason, that it tended to make me vain.[6]

As time passed, elder brother James became successively more displeased with the precocity and forwardness of his apprentice. His treatment now became "harsh and tyrannical," and then, all of a sudden, the situation changed. James Franklin was arrested for printing material offensive to authority, and during his month in jail Ben took charge of the paper. His brother having been for-bidden on his release to resume publishing, it was decided that the paper should continue under the name of Ben Franklin, even though little brother was still regarded by the family as being under indenture.

At length, a fresh difference arising between my brother and me, I took it upon me to assert my freedom, presuming that he would not venture to produce the new indentures. It was not fair in me to take this advantage, and this I therefore reckon one of the first errata of my life; but the unfairness of it weighed little with me, when under the impressions of resentment for the blows his passion too often urged him to bestow upon me, though he was otherwise not an ill-natur'd man: perhaps I was too saucy and provoking.[7]

Affairs between the brothers now reached the breaking point, and

Ben resolved to run away. Secretly, he took ship for New York, hoping there to find work as a printer. Unfortunately, New York had nothing to offer, but there was, he was told, a vacancy in a printing-shop in Philadelphia. To this city, the runaway now repaired, and after some difficulties, amusingly recounted in the *Autobiography,* he arrived at last in the city which was to be his permanent home. He got his job, and began to make his way in business. By 1729 he had prospered sufficiently to buy in partnership with Hugh Meredith the *Pennsylvania Gazette.* Meredith's father, grateful for Franklin's good influence upon his son, put up most of the money. A year later, however, the partnership was dissolved, Meredith withdrawing voluntarily when it became obvious to all that his alcoholism was of no help to the company. Three years later, in the issue of December 28th, 1732, appeared the following advertisement:

JUST PUBLISHED, FOR 1733: POOR RICHARD: An ALMA-NACK containing the Lunations, Eclipses, Planets Motions and Aspects, Weather, Sun and Moon's rising and setting, Highwater, &c. besides many pleasant and witty Verses, Jests and Sayings, Author's Motive of Writing, Prediction of the Death of his friend Mr. Titan Leeds, Moon no Cuckold, Batchelor's Folly, Parson's Wine and Baker's Pudding, Short Visits, Kings and Bears, New Fashions, Game for Kisses, Katherine's Love, Different Sentiments, Signs of a Tempest, Death a Fisherman, Conjugal Debate, Men and Melons, H. the Prodigal, Breakfast in Bed, Oyster Lawsuit, &c. by RICHARD SAUNDERS, Philomat. Printed and sold by B. Franklin. . . .[8]

Entertainment-wise, it was a good buy, a deft mixture of fact, sex, and sound advice. Commercially, it was a huge success; for most of the twenty-odd years that Franklin published his Almanac, the annual sales exceeded 10,000 copies, and the contents and format were shamelessly pirated here and in England throughout the Eighteenth and well on into the Nineteenth Century. Any work so popular might be expected to have influenced the outlook of its readers, but not even Ben Franklin could have foreseen the permanent imprint of the pragmatic philosophy of Poor Richard on the American Mind.

Generations have gotten his maxims by heart, and accepted without question the philosophy they imply. As Poor Richard says, "God helps them that help themselves." "Sloth, like rust, consumes faster than labor wears; while the used key is always bright," [9] therefore, Poor Richard advises, do not waste time. "The sleeping fox catches no poultry. There will be sleeping enough in the grave." Industry and frugality are, then, the ways to wealth, and wealth is the goal of every prudent man, for as Poor Richard says, " 'Tis hard for an empty bag to stand upright."

> Get what you can, and what you get hold;
> 'Tis the stone that will turn all your lead into gold, . . .

Virtue abides in free enterprise. As Poor Richard says, "Keep thy shop, and thy shop will keep thee."

Corollary to this celebration of the virtue of gainful toil is the belief that immorality and impracticality go hand in hand. "Leisure," says Poor Richard, "is the time for doing something useful." That a man should cultivate leisure for its own sake was something Franklin never could understand, and so successful was he in communicating his puzzlement to his posterity that the life of intellect or art for itself has ever since been frowned upon by all right-thinking Americans as being not quite proper. Our modern glorification of applied science, no less than our suspicion of the wastefulness of pure research, is the fruit of Franklin's practicality. That Ben himself would have been appalled at the anti-intellectualist conclusions that later generations have drawn from Poor Richard's philosophy does not lessen Franklin's responsibility. The preacher of the practical still owes the price of his preaching.

Of course, on the credit side of the ledger it must be noted that he never took Poor Richard too seriously. As long as it was expedient for him to do so, he followed his own advice, but once the way to wealth was won he quietly and quickly retired to enjoy life. This is not to say that he hibernated. On the contrary, the years of his middle age were among the busiest of his life. The important thing was—that he was doing what he wanted to do. If he stayed on for years in England as colonial agent, it was as much his delight in English society as his duty that bade him to remain. To interest, then, and not to any resurgence of piety, should we ascribe the renewal of his interest in religion. As a young man he had been persuaded of the merits of Deism, and had solemnly written out for his personal use a creed and liturgy in which he affirmed his faith in one Supreme and Perfect Being. Now, in his sixties, he joined with the English rake, Lord le Despencer, to produce a revision of the English Prayer Book, the idea being, as Franklin explains in his Preface,

> to prevent the old and faithful from freezing to death through long ceremonies in cold churches; to make the services so short as to attract the young and lively; and to relieve the well-disposed from the affliction of interminable prayers.[10]

All flippancy notwithstanding, Franklin's purpose was serious enough. He aimed to get at the essentials of religion, omitting all that was the product of arid theologizing, and all that portrayed God as bent on vengeance. Like Jefferson with his abridgement of the New Testament, he had in view to clarify the basic truth of Christian revelation—that God is love and intends charity to all. From this conviction he never wavered. A month before his death, answering a letter of Ezra Stiles', he summed up his religious beliefs in these words:

> You desire to know something of my Religion. It is the first time I have ever been questioned upon it. But I cannot take your Curiosity amiss, and shall endeavor in a few Words to gratify it. Here is my Creed. I believe in one God, Creator of the Universe. That he governs it by his Providence. That he ought to be worshipped. That the most acceptable Service we render to him is doing good to his other Children. That the soul of Man is immortal, and will be treated with Justice in another Life respecting its conduct in this. These I take to be the fundamental Principles of all sound Religion, and I regard them as you do in whatever Sect I meet with them.
>
> As to Jesus of Nazareth, my Opinion of whom you particularly desire, I think the System of Morals and his Religion, as he left them to us, the best the World ever saw or is likely to see; but I apprehend it has received various corrupting Changes, and I have, with most of the present dissenters in England, some Doubts as to his Divinity; tho' it is a question I do not dogmatize upon, having

never studied it, and think it needless to busy myself with it now, when I expect soon an Opportunity of knowing the Truth with less Trouble. I see no harm, however, in its being believed, if that Belief has the good Consequence, as probably it has, of making his Doctrines more respected and better observed; especially as I do not perceive that the Supreme takes it amiss, by distinguishing the Unbelievers in his Government of the World with any peculiar Marks of his Displeasure.[11]

This concern with the "good Consequence" is the hallmark of Franklin's thought. As Clinton Rossiter remarks, "Pragmatism as a rule of conscious political action has never had a more eminent exponent than Benjamin Franklin." [12] He was a man for facts, and if these were not plain, then he would make do with convention, but always he had regard to what might work, to what might work well! With the *theory* of pragmatism he was unconcerned. It is doubtful that he would have appreciated the dialectics of Peirce and Dewey. To him the pragmatic was rather a way of life, in religion no less than in politics, business, or society. As Poor Richard says, "What is Serving God? 'Tis doing Good to Man." [13]

Precisely because he was so practical in his outlook, his political views are very hard to pin down. That he was in sympathy with the social and political ideals of the Revolution, his participation in it attests. Like his age, he respected the rights of property, although unlike his Federalist friends he did not hold it especially sacred.

All Property, indeed, except the Savage's temporary Cabin, his Bow, his Matchcoat, and other little Acquisitions, absolutely necessary for his Subsistence, seems to me to be the Creature of public Convention. Hence the Public has the Right of Regulating Descents, and all other Conveyances of Property, and even of limiting the Quantity and the Uses of it. All the Property that is necessary to a Man, for the Conservation of the Individual and the Propagation of the Species, is his natural Right, which none can justly deprive him of: But all Property superfluous to such purposes is the Property of the Publick, who, by their Laws, have created it, and who may therefore by other Laws dispose of it, whenever the Welfare of the Publick shall demand such Disposition. He that does not like civil Society on these Terms, let him retire and live among Savages.

> He can have no right to the benefits of Society, who will not pay his Club towards the Support of it.[14]

As the passage shows, he was a natural democrat, impatient of all pretensions to special privilege by virtue of inheritance. Like many men forced to make their own way in life, he had no tears to shed for those unwilling to make their own fortune.

> It has been an opinion that he who receives an estate from his ancestors is under some kind of obligation to transmit the same to their posterity. This obligation does not lie on me, who never inherited a shilling from any ancestor or relation.[15]

The obligation to support such institutions as are dedicated to the improvement of education, however, was another matter, and one of which Franklin was conscious all his life. He founded not a few, and gave gladly of his time and money to others. In his *Proposals Relating to the Education of Youth in Pennsylvania* he spells out his ideas on the sort of training he would give to American youth. "It would be well," he thinks,

> if they could be taught *every Thing* that is useful, and *every Thing* that is ornamental: But Art is long, and their Time is short. It is therefore propos'd that they learn those Things that are likely to be *most useful* and *most ornamental*. Regard being had to the several Professions for which they are intended.
>
> All should be taught to write a *fair Hand,* and swift, as that is useful to All. And with it may be learnt something of *Drawing,* by Imitation of Prints, and some of the first Principles of Perspective.
>
> *Arithmetick, Accounts,* and some of the first Principles of *Geometry* and *Astronomy.*
>
> The English Language might be taught by *Grammar.* . . . Reading should also be taught, and pronouncing, properly, distinctly, emphatically; not with an even Tone, which *under-does,* nor a theatrical, which *over-does* nature.[16]

History, he feels, should be a constant part of their reading, for by its example may be learnt geography, customs, morality and religion.

With the History of Men, Times and nations, should be read at proper Hours or Days, some of the best *Histories of Nature,* which would not only be delightful to Youth, and furnish them with Matter for their Letters, &c. as well as other History; but afterwards of great Use to them, whether they are Merchants, Handicrafts, or Divines; enabling the first the better to understand many Commodities, Drugs, &c. the second to improve his Trade or Handicraft by new Mixtures, Materials, &c. and the last to adorn his Discourses by beautiful Comparisons and strengthen them by new Proofs of Divine Providence.[17]

Always the emphasis is on the practical. In matters spiritual, material, and profane alike, it is as Poor Richard says, that God helps them that help themselves.

Benjamin Franklin was a very sane and a very wise man, perhaps the wisest and sanest that America has yet produced, and his advice to the new nation his efforts had helped to bring into being was and is deserving of our careful attention. In May of 1784, writing to Charles Thomson, he has this to say:

A few years of Peace will improve, will restore and encrease our strength; but our future safety will depend on our union and our virtue. . . . If we do not convince the world that we are a Nation to be depended on for fidelity in Treaties; if we appear negligent in paying our Debts, and ungrateful to those who have served and befriended us; our reputation, and all the strength it is capable of procuring, will be lost, and fresh attacks upon us will be encouraged and promoted by better prospects of success. Let us therefore beware of being lulled into a dangerous security; and of being both enervated and impoverished by luxury; of being weakened by internal contentions and divisions; of being shamefully extravagant in contracting private debts, while we are backward in discharging honorably those of the public; of neglect in military exercises and discipline, and in providing stores of arms and munitions of war, to be ready on occasion; for all these are circumstances that give confidence to enemies, and diffidence to friends; and the expenses required to prevent a war are much lighter than those that will, if not prevented, be absolutely necessary to maintain it.[18]

Or, as Poor Richard says, "Love your neighbor; yet don't pull down your hedge."

SUGGESTED READINGS

The new Yale edition of *The Papers of Benjamin Franklin* (Volumes I-VI published to date) contains all of the numbers of Poor Richard, as well as everything else that Franklin wrote up to the end of the year 1758. Eventually the edition will encompass all of Franklin's writings, including much material hitherto unpublished. In the meantime, make do with the ten volumes of *The Writings of Benjamin Franklin* edited by Albert Henry Smyth. Most libraries will have sets of this last. An excellent sampler is Nathan Goodman's *A Benjamin Franklin Reader*. This includes some of Franklin's racier letters, as well as his *Autobiography*. Phillips Russell, *Benjamin Franklin, The First Civilized American* (New York: Brentano, 1926), is a very readable and occasionally flippant study of a man obviously regarded by his biographer as a great human being. Bernard Fay, *Franklin, The Apostle of Modern Times* (London: Sampson Low, Marston & Co., 1929), is rather more ponderous. It is Fay's belief that much of Franklin's social and public success, as well as much of his philosophy, is owing to his Masonic affiliation. Fortunately, he does not ride his thesis to the extent of distorting the facts of Franklin's life, all of which are reported in considerable detail.

REFERENCES

1. *The Papers of Benjamin Franklin* (New Haven: Yale University Press, 1959-   ), Vol. III, p. 104. Hereafter cited as Papers.

2. Papers, Vol. II, p. 9.

3. The name derives from a combination of the title and author of two famous English almanacs, *Poor Robin Almanack,* afterwards published at Newport by Ben's brother, James Franklin, and *The English Apollo* by Richard Saunders. Whereas the latter was serious in intent and literary in tone, the former stressed the bawdy and sought to titillate its readers. The junction of the two as Poor Richard was Franklin's way of indicating his intention of preserving in his own publication the best qualities of these its predecessors.

4. "Autobiography," in Albert Henry Smyth (editor), *The Writings of Benjamin Franklin,* 10 Vols. (New York: Macmillan, 1905-1907), I, p. 232. Hereafter cited as Writings.

5. Writings, I, p. 233.

6. Ibid., pp. 246-47. In all, fourteen papers were printed. Untitled by Franklin, they are now known as the Silence Dogood Letters, after the signature of their supposed author. The complete text of the Letters is given in the first volume of *The Papers of Benjamin Franklin.*

7. Writings, I, p. 249.

8. Papers, Vol. I, p. 280.

9. Ibid., Vol. III, p. 398.

10. Phillips Russell, *Benjamin Franklin, The First Civilized American* (New York: Brentano's, 1926), p. 225.

11. Writings, X, p. 84.
12. *Seedtime of the Republic* (New York: Harcourt, Brace, 1953), p. 294.
13. Papers, Vol. III, p. 105.
14. Writings, IX, p. 138.
15. Ibid., X, p. 502.
16. Papers, Vol. III, pp. 404-5, 407.
17. Ibid., pp. 415-16.
18. Writings, IX, p. 213.

V

Free Thoughts in the Young Republic

ETHAN ALLEN

TOM PAINE

ABNER KNEELAND

FRANCES WRIGHT

"My own mind is my own church." [1]

THOMAS PAINE

1. Ethan Allen

FREE THOUGHT, meaning by that phrase the liberty of the mind to frame its own judgments on matters of religion and custom without regard for the opinions of authority, is an ancient American dream. The Plymouth Pilgrims had it, so did Roger Williams, and John Wise too; but it was not until after the American Revolution that the dream became a reality. Before the War no American had dared to challenge publicly the historic foundation of Christian faith and morality. True, the Calvinist interpretation of that faith had, as we have seen, been for a century slowly losing ground to liberal Christianity; but the liberals, no less than their Puritan opponents, still held fast to the divinity of Jesus and the authenticity of His revelation. After the War, much was changed. Independence made non-conformity permissible if not respectable. The old morality was no more, and a new religion of reason named Deism now began to make its voice heard. And appropriately enough its first American exponent [2] was a man whose primary distinction was as a hero of the Revolutionary War.

Ethan Allen was born at Litchfield, Connecticut, on January 10th, 1739.[3] Shortly thereafter his father removed the family to the new townsite of Cornwall where he established a farm. Joseph Allen, from all reports, was a man of strong opinions and forceful personality. A professed Arminian, he is reputed to have converted the Congregational (Calvinist) minister of Cornwall Church to the idea of free will, and certainly he was instrumental in shaping the religious opinions of his eldest son. Ethan was a precocious boy, hungry for knowledge; he read every book he could lay his hand on, and was a willing listener to anyone with information to impart His father, aware of his intellectual bent, encouraged his studie and hoped to send him to college. Unfortunately, Joseph Alle died in 1755 and left Ethan with no choice but to stay on the farn and tend the family interests. Possessed of great energy, a good head for business, and the gift of gab, young Allen prospered. Fron farming he branched out into mining and smelting. In 1763 he married [4]—for money as some believed. In this same year the country between Lake Champlain and the Connecticut River (Ver mont) was opened to settlement, and men with an eye to rising land values began to move into the territory. Among them wa Ethan Allen. Just when, and to what extent, he was involved in land speculation in the Hampshire Grants (as the region was called) remains obscure, but in 1770 the Hampshire settlers chose him to represent their interests in the rapidly developing controversy be tween the Governors of New York and New Hampshire over title to the Grants. The courts favoured the claims of New York, but the Hampshiremen were on the land and determined to defend their rights by force if necessary. They organized an irregular militia (the Green Mountain Boys) and Ethan Allen became its Colone Commandant. It was a proud title for a man who, in fact, was no more than the outlaw leader of a rural gang. Nonetheless, in this capacity he ruled the Grants from 1770 to 1775, and in May of '75 he earned his place in the annals of the Revolution by leading the motley army that overran the virtually undefended Fort Ticon-deroga. Four months later Colonel Allen was a prisoner of the British, captured outside Montreal. He was taken to England repatriated, and in May of 1778 exchanged. His requests for a line commission in the Continental Army were ignored, but the in-dependent State of Vermont elected him Brigadier-General of its Militia, and henceforward Ethan Allen would be dedicated to its service.

In 1779 he published in the Pennsylvania Packet *A Narrative of Colonel Ethan Allen's Captivity*. As literature it wasn't much, but as propaganda for the cause of Liberty it proved to be an instantaneous success. In two years it went through eight editions and brought its author a comfortable amount of cash. Undoubtedly

he reception accorded his *Narrative* encouraged Allen to write
down his thoughts on the more serious subject of natural religion.
His opinions had been a long time in the making. As he notes in his
Preface to *Reason the only Oracle of Man*,

> In my youth I was much disposed to contemplation, and at my
> commencement in manhood, I committed to manuscript such senti-
> ments or arguments, as appeared most consonant to reason, least
> through the debility of memory my improvement should have been
> less gradual. . . .[5]

Man of action though he was, he managed throughout his life to
find time for theology, and in 1784 appeared the fruit of his reflections, the book on which his reputation as a free-thinker rests.
From the outset, he wishes to leave no doubt as to where he
stands.

> In the circle of my acquaintance (which has not been small) I have
> generally been denominated a Deist, the reality of which I never
> disputed, being conscious I am no Christian, except mere infant
> baptism makes me one; and as to being a Deist, I know not strictly
> speaking, whether I am one or not, for I have never read their
> writings. . . .[6]

Actually, this was not quite the truth of the matter; although in
all fairness to Allen, he may not himself have realized the extent
of his theological indebtedness to Thomas Young and Charles
Blount. Allen was still in his teens, anticipating college, and living
at Salisbury with his tutor Reverend Jonathan Lee, when he first
made friends with Young, an itinerant doctor who lived and practiced in the vicinity. By the standards of the times, Young was a
learned man. He had attended Yale, gained an M.D., and was
well versed in the writings of Locke and the English Deists. His
saddle-bags probably contained a copy of Locke's *Essay,* and he
had for his own benefit copied out long extracts from those authors
who had interested him. For Calvinism in general and the prophets
of the Great Awakening in particular he had only scorn, and many
a night the young doctor and the farm boy sat before the tavern
fire, the one raptly attentive as the other poked orthodoxy full of

holes. Young's favorite author was an English free-thinker named Charles Blount, and Blount's were the ideas that Allen absorbed. That he himself ever read Blount's *Oracles of Reason* is doubtful, but he was certainly familiar enough with the work to borrow its title and expound its central theme: "As far as we understand nature, we are become acquainted with the character of God; for the knowledge of nature is the revelation of God." [7]

However, with revelation in the traditional sense Allen will have nothing to do. The circumstances of the composition of the Bible declare its fallibility. The many pious frauds perpetuated by the Popes over a long succession of ages equally forbid any inscription of infallibility to their pronouncements. And as for miracles,

> To suppose that God should subvert his laws (which is the same as changing them) would be to suppose him to be mutable; for that it would necessarily imply, either that their eternal establishment was imperfect; or that a premised alteration thereof is so. To alter or change that which is absolutely perfect, would necessarily make it cease to be perfect, inasmuch as perfection could not be altered for the better, but for the worse; and consequently an alteration could not meet with the divine approbation; which terminates the issue of the matter in question against miracles. [8]

Reason, then, and the evidence of the senses, must ever be our guide, since

> There is not any thing, which has contributed so much to delude mankind in religious matters, as mistaken apprehensions concerning supernatural inspiration or revelation; not considering, that all true religion originates from reason, and can no otherwise be understood but by the exercise and improvement of it. . . . [9]

> Was a revelation to be made known to us, it must be accommodated to our external senses, and also to our reason, so that we could come at the perception and understanding of it, the same as we do to that of things in general. *We must perceive by our senses, before we can reflect with the mind.* Our sensorium is that essential medium between the divine and human mind, through which God reveals to man the knowledge of nature, and is our only door of correspondence with God or with man. [10]

So speaks Allen, but his words no less than his thoughts are those of John Locke.

For the man who believes with Locke that there is nothing in the mind that was not first in the senses, the sacraments and such doctrines as original sin, predestination, and omnipotence are senseless, and Allen argues their meaninglessness at length. Nor does the orthodox doctrine of the Trinity seem to him any more reasonable.

> To say that there are three eternals in the trinity, and yet that there are not three eternals therein, is a contradiction in terms, as much as to say, that there are three persons in the trinity and yet there are not three persons in the trinity.
>
> The plain English is, that the three persons in the trinity are three eternals, individually considered, and yet they are not three eternals but one eternal.[11]

One eternal, and this God—infinite and transcendent, for

> ONE God can have but one essence, which must have been eternal and infinite, and for that reason precludes all others from a participation of his nature, glory, and universal and absolute perfection.[12]

It follows from this, according to Allen, that Jesus Christ is no more God than you or me. "That God should become a man, is impossible, and that man should become a God, is equally impossible and absurd.[13]

> For God and man are not and cannot be one and the same, for that there is an infinite disproportion between them; for which reason they cannot be hypostatically united in one nature or essence.[14]
>
> But we are told, that the hypostatical union is a mysterious one. Nevertheless it is a union or not a union, if it is a union of the divine and human natures, they must be comprized in one and the self-same essence, or otherwise it is such a mysterious union, that it is not a union, which is no mystery at all, but a barefaced absurdity.[15]

Sentiments such as these could hardly fail to arouse the clergy and their hearers, and in consequence Allen was denounced for an atheist from pulpits up and down the land. His denial of the divinity of Jesus was taken for a repudiation of religion, which of course it was not. His attack on original sin was interpreted as a blow at morality, whereas in truth Allen throughout his book emphasizes the moral function of true religion. Lamentably few people bothered to give his work the careful reading it deserved. The public that so avidly bought up the *Narrative* would have nothing to do with the *Oracle*. Financially, the book was a failure. To pay the publication costs Ethan was forced to borrow on his land and sell his interest in the family home. In his last years he was often hard pressed for ready cash, and he died on January 17th, 1789, a relatively poor man.

2. Tom Paine

THAT RADICAL VIEWS ON RELIGION, or, for that matter, on politics also, could be economically as well as socially disastrous no man of the Eighteenth Century could better testify than Thomas Paine.

The apostle of the American and French Revolutions was born at Thetford, England, on 29 January, 1737. His father, Joseph Paine, was a Quaker by religion and by trade a staymaker, and he taught young Tom the rudiments of both. After grammar school, he followed for some years the staymaker's trade, the while studying science on his own. In 1762 he wangled an appointment to the Customs Service: three years later he was discharged for failure to perform his duties properly. In 1768 he successfully petitioned for reappointment, but in 1774 was discharged again and quitted the Service for good. Through friends, he met Benjamin Franklin, then colonial agent in London, and Franklin gave him a letter of introduction to his son-in-law. Armed with this, he sailed for America and arrived at Philadelphia in November of 1774. For a while he worked as a tutor and acquired the literary reputation which led to his being offered employment as a journalist. He wrote essays and poems for various Philadelphia periodicals, and for a brief period worked as an editor. In January of 1776 he published *Common Sense,* a pamphlet defending the American Revolution. It was an immediate success and made Paine famous. At the outbreak of hostilities, he joined the Army, but soon decided that he could serve his adopted country better with his pen. For the remainder of the war he worked as a propagandist for the American cause, his best known contribution being the thirteen essays published under the title *The American Crisis*. In 1787 he embarked for France, hoping to sell the French government on the idea of building one or more single-arched iron bridges on a model he had designed. The hope proving abortive, he decided to try his luck next in England. Here too the venture failed, and he now turned his energies from business back to politics.

In 1790, aroused by Edmund Burke's pamphlet *Reflections on the Revolution in France,* he undertook to state the case for the revolutionaries, and in 1791 appeared *The Rights of Man*. As earlier with *Common Sense,* so here too Paine's book was widely read, and in France his reputation was made. In England, however, it was a different story. Worried by the growing popularity of Paine's writings, the authorities brought Paine to trial for seditious libel. Tried in absentia (he in the meantime having gone to France), he was convicted and was henceforth an outlaw in his native land. In France though he was a hero. Three constituencies vied for the honor of having Paine represent them in the French National Convention, and he accepted election from the Pas de Calais. Now he journeyed to Paris, where immediately he began to take an active part in the affairs of the Convention. Unfortunately for his future, he sided too often with the moderate (Girondist) faction, and shortly after this group fell from power, Paine was arrested, imprisoned in the Luxembourg, and only by accident escaped the guillotine. Released in November of 1794, he remained awhile in Paris finishing up Part II of *The Age of Reason* (Part I had been completed just prior to his arrest). Predictably, the book provoked new storms of criticism. To the charge of anarchist was now added the epithet—atheist, and during the next decade refuting Paine became the prime concern of orthodox theologians everywhere. In 1802, broke and hoping to recoup his fortunes, Paine returned to America in search of the rewards he felt his services to the Revolution had merited. Here again he suffered disappointment, and his last years were spent in profitless pamphleteering. At his death there was hardly a friend left to mourn his passing, and his burial went unnoticed by the world his writings had done so much to change.

The earliest of these writings is the pamphlet *Common Sense*.

Of the circumstances of its composition, little is known. The title was suggested by Dr. Benjamin Rush, and the author was identified only as "an Englishman." Paine himself tells us that it was the events of April 19th, 1775, at Lexington and Concord which convinced him that a declaration of independence was the only reasonable course for America to take, and the tenor of his argument makes plain his concern over the possibility that his fellow-Americans might yet choose the easier course of compromise within the framework of colonialism. That it was a justifiable concern is evidenced by the fact that his was the first voice in America to speak out publicly for independence. For all that the idea was in the wind, it was no native-born American but the "Englishman" who first dared cry defiance.

Paine begins by drawing a distinction between society and government. "The former," says he, "promotes our happiness *positively* by uniting our affections, the latter *negatively* by restraining our vices. The one encourages intercourse, the other creates distinctions. The first is a patron, the last a punisher." [16]

> Society in every state is a blessing, but government, even in its best state, is but a necessary evil; in its worst state an intolerable one: for when we suffer, or are exposed to the same miseries *by a government,* which we might expect in a country *without government,* our calamity is heightened by reflecting that we furnish the means by which we suffer. Government, like dress, is the badge of lost innocence; the palaces of kings are built upon the ruins of the bowers of paradise.[17]

For monarchy in general and the British Crown in particular he has only scorn. It is, he argues, an institution without warrant in Scripture or justification in history:

> could we take off the dark covering of antiquity and trace them (the race of kings) to their first rise, we should find the first of them nothing better than the principal ruffian of some restless gang; whose savage manners of pre-eminence in subtilty obtained him the title of chief among plunderers: and who by increasing in power and extending his depredations, overawed the quiet and defenceless to purchase their safety by frequent contributions. . . . Of more worth

is one honest man to society, and in the sight of God, than all the crowned ruffians that ever lived.[18]

Hereditary succession is, he insists, "an insult and imposition on posterity."

For all men being originally equals, no one by birth could have a right to set up his own family in perpetual preference to all others for ever, and though himself might deserve some decent degree of honors of his contemporaries, yet his descendants might be far too unworthy to inherit them. One of the strongest natural proofs of the folly of hereditary right in kinds, is that nature disapproves it, otherwise she would not so frequently turn it into ridicule, by giving mankind an *ass* for *a lion*.[19]

Having thus disposed of kingship and the character of George III, Paine turns next to consider "The Present State of American Affairs." In his opinion, it is a time of unparalleled opportunity:

The sun never shone on a cause of greater worth. 'Tis not the affair of a city, a country, a province, or a kingdom; but of a continent— of at least one eighth part of the habitable globe. 'Tis not the concern of a day, a year, or an age; posterity are virtually involved in the contest, and will be more or less affected even to the end of time, by the proceedings now. Now is the seed-time of continental union, faith and honor. The least fracture now will be like a name engraved with the point of a pin on the tender rind of a young oak; the wound would enlarge with the tree, and posterity read it in full grown characters.

By referring the matter from argument to arms, a new era for politics is struck—a new method of thinkings has arisen. All plans, proposals, &c. prior to the nineteenth of April, i.e., to the commencement of hostilities, are like the almanacks of the last year; which though proper then, are superceded and useless now.[20]

Nonetheless, since there are some who still believe a reconciliation with Great Britain not only possible but desirable, he would and does set forth at length the folly of such a course. He reprobates the argument that Britain is the parent, the mother country, from whom the child has no moral right to break away:

the phrase *parent* or *mother country* hath been jesuitically adopted by the king and his parasites, with a low papistical design of gaining an unfair bias on the credulous weakness of our minds. Europe, and not England, is the parent country of America. This new world hath been the asylum for the persecuted lovers of civil and religious liberty from *every part* of Europe. Hither have they fled not from the tender embraces of the mother, but from the cruelty of the monster; and it is so far true of England, that the same tyranny which drove the first emigrants from home, pursues their descendants still.[21]

There is, he holds, no single advantage that this continent can reap by being connected with Great Britain. On the contrary, "It is the true interest of America to steer clear of European contentions, which she never can do, while, by her dependence on Britain, she is made the makeweight in the scale of British politics." [22] Independence, and independence alone, is, then, the one best course for America, " 'Tis repugnant to reason, to the universal order of things, to all examples from former ages, to suppose that this continent can long remain subject to any external power." [23]

Small islands not capable of protecting themselves are the proper objects for government to take under their care; but there is something absurd, in supposing a Continent to be perpetually governed by an island. In no instance hath nature made the satellite larger than its primary planet; and as England and America, with respect to each other, reverse the common order of nature, it is evident that they belong to different systems. England to Europe: America to itself.[24]

Of the present ability of America to control its own destinies, he had no doubts. Here was a country rich in natural resources, free of debt, and ideally situated for the military purposes at hand. "Our present numbers," he thinks, "are sufficient to repel the force of all the world."

The continent has at this time the largest body of armed and disciplined men of any power under heaven: and is just arrived at that pitch of strength, in which no single colony is able to support itself, and the whole, when united, is able to do anything. Our land force is more than sufficient, and as to naval affairs, we cannot be insensible that Britain would never suffer an American man of war to be built, while the continent remained in her hands. Wherefore, we should be no forwarder a hundred years hence in that branch than we are now.[25]

The time is now; this is his constantly restated theme. We must, Paine pleads, grasp the opportunity the moment affords. We may never again be so well situated.

Should we neglect the present favorable and inviting period, and independence be hereafter effected by any other means, we must charge the consequence to ourselves, or to those rather whose narrow and prejudiced souls are habitually opposing the measure, without either inquiring or reflecting. There are reasons to be given in support of independence which men should rather privately think of, than be publicly told of. We ought not now to be debating whether we shall be independent or not, but anxious to accomplish it on a firm, secure, and honorable basis, and uneasy rather that it is not yet began upon. Every day convinces us of its necessity.[26]

We have it in our power to begin the world over again. A situation, similar to the present, hath not happened since the days of Noah until now. The birthday of a new world is at hand, and a race of men, perhaps as numerous as all Europe contains, are to receive their portion of freedom from the events of a few months. The reflection is awful, and in this point of view, how trifling, how ridiculous, do the little paltry cavilings of a few weak or interested men appear, when weighed against the business of a world.[27]

These passages were designed to stir men's souls, and in that they succeeded. No matter that their logic was not faultless, nor their political theorizing beyond reproach; Paine was not writing for philosophers, but for the people, and the people got the message. The troops before Boston heard his words and took courage. They were read to the legislature of South Carolina, and short days later it reversed its opposition to independence and voted to send its delegates to Philadelphia instructed to vote for the Republic. Washington himself reported their powerful impact on the minds of the men of Virginia. When the author of *Common Sense* became known, Paine was a national hero. Throughout the war, he was to remain the United States' foremost propagandist. The argument begun with

Common Sense was continued in his famous series of papers on The American Crisis, and at revolution's end his reputation was at its highest. Unfortunately, so was his ego, and the rewards proffered him by his countrymen striking him as inadequate, in 1787 he sailed for France and a new fortune.

The Rights of Man, probably the best, and certainly the most influential celebration of the philosophy of democracy ever written, was published at London in March of 1791. It made Paine famous in England, a hero in France, and everywhere it infuriated conservatives. Against Edmund Burke and the lesser proponents of tradition and hereditary right, Paine argued the thesis of the equal right of all men to self-government. The French, no less than the Americans, have, he insists, the right to decide for themselves just what sort of government they will abide.

> Every age and generation must be as free to act for itself, *in all cases,* as the ages and generation which preceded it. . . .
>
> Man has no property in man; neither has any generation a property in the generations which are to follow. . . .
>
> Every generation is, and must be, competent to all the purposes which its occasions require. It is the living, and not the dead, that are to be accommodated. . . .
>
> That which a whole nation chooses to do, it has a right to do.[28]

Burke to the contrary, there are no hereditary rights. The privileges of aristocracy are not inheritable, and the mere fact that they may have been exercised for centuries past is, Paine holds, no justification for their continuation. To no one, king or noble, is the right reserved to rule the present on the basis of the past; to no man is it given to bind and loose the future.

Disturbing as such views were to the English ruling class, they still suffered them for a while. After all, Paine had stopped short of advocating revolution, and many others higher placed than he had no appetite for monarchy. To vilify the King, however, was one thing; to attack the British Constitution and invite Englishmen to revolt, as Paine did in Part II of *The Rights of Man* (published in 1792), was entirely another, and soon after publication the authorities took steps to suppress the book and silence the author. Unfortunately for their purpose, the latter was out of the question (Paine having slipped away to France), while the former was rendered extraordinarily difficult by the curiosity of everyone to read a work likely to be prohibited. In consequence, sales soared, and by the year's end some 200,000 copies of the two parts combined were in circulation. Even so, it would be a mistake to conclude that sensationalism alone made Paine's work popular. The thousands who read him did so as much for the freshness of his vision of social reform as for his arguments against the Crown. Living as we do in an age and a society which can seriously entertain, even if it cannot yet entirely accept, such Painean notions as medical care and maintenance for the aged and indigent, government guarantee of employment and compensation, and free education for all, we tend to forget just how revolutionary all of this sounded to late Eighteenth Century Englishmen. To the landed and titled classes, Paine's proposals for social and fiscal reform were synonymous with the destruction of society as they knew and cherished it, and the example of the Revolution in progress across the English Channel seemed ample confirmation of their fears. That the leaders of this Revolution should honor Paine with a seat in their Convention was to conservative Englishmen evidence enough of his sedition. Henceforward, in Tory eyes, the name of Paine would stand for renegade and anarchist.

In 1794 appeared *The Age of Reason,* and conservatives in England and America were reinforced in their convictions that they had made no mistake in their estimate of the character of Paine. Few books before and not many since have been so roundly abused and denounced. Christians everywhere reacted as if the antichrist had suddenly appeared in their midst. Indeed, so virulent was the hatred engendered by this work that a century and a half have hardly sufficed to rehabilitate its author's name. To many Americans, including some who should know better, Paine is still what he was to Theodore Roosevelt, "a filthy little atheist."

Obviously, Roosevelt had not read the profession of faith with which the book begins, or, if he had, he did not take it seriously. And yet, what Paine here declares is consistent with everything he ever wrote in any book or pamphlet touching on the subject of religion.

I believe in one God, and no more; and I hope for happiness beyond this life. I believe in the equality of man; and I believe that religious duties consist in doing justice, loving mercy, and endeavoring to make our fellow-creatures happy.

But lest it should be supposed that I believe many other things in addition to these, I shall, in the progress of this work, declare the things I do not believe, and my reasons for not believing them.

I do not believe in the creed professed by the Jewish Church, by the Roman Church, by the Greek Church, by the Turkish Church, by the Protestant Church, nor by any church that I know of. My own mind is my own church.[29]

Like Allen, he sees reason as the only oracle of man, and his reason tells him that "it is a contradiction in terms and ideas, to call anything a revelation that comes to us at second-hand, either verbally or in writing."

When Moses told the children of Israel that he received the two tables of the commandments from the hands of God, they were not obliged to believe him, because they had no other authority for it than his telling them so; and I have no other authority for it than some historian telling me so. The commandments carry no internal evidence of divinity with them; they contain some good moral precepts, such as any man qualified to be a lawgiver, or a legislator, could produce himself, without having recourse to supernatural intervention.[30]

When also I am told that a woman called the Virgin Mary said, or gave out, that she was with child without any cohabitation with a man, and that her betrothed husband, Joseph, said that an angel told him so, I have a right to believe them or not; such a circumstance required a much stronger evidence than their bare word for it; but we have not even this—for neither Joseph nor Mary wrote any such matter themselves; it is only reported by others that *they said so*—it is heresay upon hearsay, and I do not choose to rest my belief upon such evidence.[31]

Jesus Christ "was a virtuous and an amiable man. The morality that he preached and practised was of the most benevolent kind," [32] but that he was or is God is something that no man of reason should be expected to credit. The story of his resurrection shows "every mark of fraud and imposition stamped upon the face of it." [33] It is the product of a Christian mythology which, Paine feels, "for absurdity and extravagance, is not exceeded by anything that is to be found in the mythology of the ancients." [34]

In fact, most of what Christians profess about Jesus Christ is, Paine holds, obviously based upon fables freely taken from antiquity. To show that this is so is one main purpose of his work, and both Parts I and II [35] contain extensive analyses and criticisms of Holy Scripture. There is, he contends, little or nothing in either the Old or New Testament to justify our honoring these books by calling them the word of God. That Church authorities have decided by majority vote to designate them as such is no valid reason for believing them to be so, and of revelation, in the strict sense of the word, Paine finds none. The Old Testament is mostly bad history and brutal anecdote, liberally salted with obscenity disguised as poetry. The Gospels are altogether anecdotal, the epistles are likely forgeries, and the Revelation to John is an enigma inaccessible to reasonable men.

> What is that we have learned from this pretended thing called re-vealed religion? Nothing that is useful to man, and everything that is dishonorable to his Maker. What is it the Bible teaches us? rapine, cruelty, and murder. What is it the Testament teaches us?—to believe that the Almighty committed debauchery with a woman engaged to be married, and the belief of this debauchery is called faith.[36]

> Of all the systems of religion that ever were invented, there is none more derogatory to the Almighty, more unedifying to man, more repugnant to reason, and more contradictory in itself, than this thing called Christianity. Too absurd for belief, too impossible to convince, and too inconsistent to practise, it renders the heart torpid, or pro-duces only atheists and fanatics. As an engine of power, it serves the purpose of despotism; and as a means of wealth, the avarice of priests; but so far as respects the good of man in general, it leads to nothing here or hereafter.[37]

Predictably, the storm broke early. The orthodox had been hurt where they lived, and their answer was—defamation. *Common Sense* was forgotten as the pious Americans vied with their English Tory counterparts to blacken Paine's name.[38] It made no difference that his views on religion were virtually identical with those of Allen,

Franklin, and the spiritual heirs of Mayhew. What mattered was that he had put them publicly in such a way that even the commonest man could understand, and this the orthodox could not tolerate. It was all very well for intellectuals to talk up Deism in the comparative privacy of salon or study; it was something else again to broadcast it in terms that all the world could grasp. What would become of organized religion if John Bull or Yankee Doodle were to be persuaded of the truth of this pernicious religion of reason? Obviously, in the best interests of society it must be repressed, and if innuendo, smear, and downright misrepresentation would do it— why, let it be done. And done it was, as Paine and his freethinking successors could wryly testify.

3. Abner Kneeland

CONSIDER, FOR INSTANCE, as did all New England from 1834 to 1838, the case of Abner Kneeland. Born at Gardner, Massachusetts, in 1774, Kneeland was the fourth son of a Scots farmer who proudly traced his ancestry back to Robert Bruce. His formal education was limited to the common school at Gardner plus one term at Chesterfield (N.H.) Academy; his proficiency in Hebrew, Greek, and Latin he acquired on his own. In his early twenties he joined the Baptist Church, and later served it briefly as a preacher. His liberalism soon alienated his congregation, and facing charges of heresy if he remained, he withdrew. In 1803 he was licensed as a Universalist preacher, and for the next twenty-five years he served various pastorates of that denomination. As he grew older, however, his views grew steadily more radical, and in 1829 he suspended himself from the Universalist Church and began a new career as editor and writer. In 1831 he founded at Boston a weekly newspaper, *The Investigator,* dedicated to the dissemination of freethought, and it was his articles in this journal that led in 1834 to his indictment for blasphemy. In December of 1833 he had published in *The Investigator* an article, the substance of which was the following set of propositions:

1. Universalists believe in a God which I do not; but believe that their God, with all his moral attributes (aside from nature itself) is nothing more than a chimera of their own imagination.
2. Universalists believe in Christ, which I do not; but believe that

the whole story concerning him is as much a fable and fiction as that of the god Prometheus. . . .

3. Universalists believe in miracles, which I do not; but believe that every pretension to them can be accounted for on natural principles, or else is to be attributed to mere trick and imposture.

4. Universalists believe in the resurrection of the dead, in immortality and external life, which I do not; but believe that all life is mortal, that death is an extinction of life to the individual who possesses it, and that no individual life is, ever was, or ever will be eternal.

On the face of it, this would seem to indicate a matter concerning only Kneeland and the members of the Universalist Church which he had for twenty-five years served as pastor and apologist. Actually, it was to provide the pretext for bringing this free-thinker to trial, and thereby stopping his mouth and pen. Conservative Boston was appalled at Abner Kneeland. In the same issue in which the offending propositions appeared, he had printed an article questioning the Virgin Birth, and given space to a piece ridiculing prayer and comparing God to General Jackson. More important, he had published in the columns of his paper *The Fruits of Philosophy,* a pioneering discussion of the desirability and technique of birth control. This last, rather than the propositions concerning religion, was, according to Stewart Holbrook, the real reason why Kneeland was indicted. Unwilling to debate publicly the virginity of Mary or give further circulation to the facts of contraception, the Boston brahmins charged him with uttering a "certain profane, impious, and scandalous libel on and concerning God," and in January of 1834 he was brought to trial for blasphemy.

From the standpoint of free-thought, the point at issue in the Kneeland case was simply whether or not society (i.e., The Commonwealth of Massachusetts) had the right and duty to suppress an unpopular opinion in the name of the public interest. The State, represented by Mr. S. D. Parker, contended that it had: "There have been," he argued,

other infidels, Hume, Gibbon, Voltaire, Volney, etc. but the works of these persons were read only by men of literary habits—necessarily a few. But here is a journal, a newspaper, cheap, and sent into a thousand families. Where one man would be injured by Hume,

Gibbon, or Volney, a thousand may be injured by this newspaper, so widely circulated, so easily read, so coarsely expressed, so industriously spread abroad.[39]

It was the same objection as had been raised against the work of Paine, and it was to be brought forward many times during the four trials of Abner Kneeland.[40] The relevance to the present case of the argument urged against Paine was remarked by Judge Thacher in his charge to the jury at the first trial. "I cannot," he told them, "omit to repeat the observation of the illustrious Erskine in the trial of Thomas Williams for publishing Paine's Age of Reason. . . .

> Of all the human beings, he says, the poor stand most in need of the consolations of religion, and the country has the deepest stake in their enjoying it, not only from the protection which it owes them, but because no man can be expected to be faithful to the authority of man, who revolts against the government of God.[41]

That the poor might be the better for being exposed to reason, neither Erskine nor Thacher nor, as a matter of fact, the majority of the judges who heard Kneeland's final appeal seriously considered. Best that the poor be not disturbed in their religious ignorance, lest they rise to challenge the rule of the righteous. As for the liberty of the press guaranteed by the constitution of the Commonwealth, it did not, in the opinion of the Court, apply here. Chief Justice Shaw spoke for the majority of his colleagues when he declared, in his opinion affirming Kneeland's conviction, that

> every act, however injurious or criminal, which may be committed by the use of language, may be committed with impunity if such language is printed. . . . Not only would the article in question become a general license for scandal, calumny, and falsehood against individuals, institutions and governments . . . but all incitation to treason, assassination, and all other crimes however atrocious, if conveyed in printed language, would be dispunishable.[42]

It mattered not to Justice Shaw that there was in the instance under judgment no question of slander or of specific injury to any individual; the fact remained that the ordinance of 1782 prohibiting blasphemy had been violated, the public peace had been disturbed, the common man must be protected against himself. A majority of his fellow justices concurring, appeal was denied, and, as Theodore Parker put it in a letter to his friend Ellis, "Abner was jugged for sixty days; but he will come out as beer from a bottle, all foaming, and will make others foam."

As things turned out, Parker's prediction was not quite accurate. The intellectuals foamed, and petitions were gathered; newspapers throughout the State united to denounce the resurgence of religious intolerance; but it was all to no avail. As for Kneeland himself, it was a disappointed and somewhat bitter man who emerged from prison in the fall of 1838. With puritan Boston he wished to have no more to do, and so in 1839 he and some of his friends in the Society of Free Enquirers acquired a large tract of land in Iowa with the intention of founding thereon a community of free men. Shortly thereafter he moved west and out of history. Five years later he was dead, and the utopia he had sought to found died with him.

4. Frances Wright

UTOPIANISM PER SE, however, remained very much alive. Throughout the first half of the Nineteenth Century, Kneeland's experiment in communal living was to be tried many times. Brook Farm, Fruitlands, New Harmony, Nashoba—all were settled by men and women of like mind with the free enquirer of Boston, all owed their origin to the dream of a society of free men, freely sharing their goods, their work, and, to the eternal scandal of respectable society, their women one with another. All, naturally, drew upon themselves the ire of the custodians of convention, but none more so than those who sanctioned free love, and of these none was more viciously attacked and violently denounced than Fanny Wright's Nashoba community.

Frances Wright, eldest daughter of James Wright, a prosperous Scottish linen-merchant, and his wife, Camilla Campbell (of the Campbells of Inverary), was born on September 6th, 1795, in the family mansion at Dundee. Both her parents died when she was but three years old, and she, together with her younger sister Camilla, was sent to England to be raised by their Campbell grandfather, a well-to-do British general with excellent social connections. Tall, handsome, and an heiress, Frances might have anticipated an advantageous marriage and the leisurely life of the English upper class; but for these she had no taste. Her world was one of books and scholars, and she cultivated both with zeal. Soon she had outgrown the shallow religiosity of her upbringing. At twenty-one she had so far formed her views as to write *A Few Days in Athens,* a literary exposition of the Epicurean philosophy. Soon after she conceived the notion of visiting America, and in 1818, having come of age and into her money, she, in company with Camilla, sailed for New York. The fruit of this first American visit was *Views of Society and Manners in America,* etc. Published in 1821 it had an excellent sale, was translated into several European languages, and made its author famous. She was introduced to Bentham and became an intimate of Lafayette. She took a dashing Spanish lover, and when he left her she decided to accompany Lafayette on his tour of America. It was during this tour that she saw at first hand the misery of the Negro slaves and resolved to devote herself to the eradication of this cancer from the body politic of her beloved America. Jefferson, whom she had visited at Monticello, had acquainted her with the economics of the Negro problem, and her travels to the utopian communities of Pennsylvania and Ohio opened her mind to the means whereby the problem might be solved. She would found an experimental community of her own, and on it white and Negro would live in harmony while the latter was educated to freedom and the standards of the former. To this end she acquired in 1825 six hundred and forty acres near Memphis, and set about recruiting. With the arrival of her sister Camilla, a white friend, George Flower, his wife and three children, five male and three female Negro slaves, the community got under way in February of 1826.

In theory, the place was to be a free-thinker's paradise. The Negroes would do the hard work, and in return would be trained for freedom by the whites, who in their leisure would enjoy the delights of spiritual and physical intercourse with congenial companions. As Miss Wright firmly believed in the equality of the sexes, the women of the community were to be emancipated from the slavery of marriage. Everyone was to be free to live with whom they chose and to exchange partners as they wished—without any regard to color. "By such means," she was convinced,

the amalgamation of the races shall take place in good taste and good feeling and be made, at once, the means of sealing the tranquility and perpetuating the liberty of the country, and of peopling it with a race more suited to its southern climate, than the pure European.[43]

Fanny Wright's Free Love Colony her horrified detractors called it, and they rejoiced that it didn't seem to be working out. The easy treatment made the slaves lazy, and the work of the farm went undone. Educating the Negroes up to white standards turned out to be much harder than anyone had anticipated. The climate proved abominable, and the health of the whites suffered. For three years Frances Wright poured all of her energy and most of her money into her Tennessee utopia, and then in 1829, yielding to the pleas of her lover Robert Dale Owen, she abandoned Nashoba for the more civilized pleasures of New Harmony.

Shortly thereafter she took to the lecture platform. From all accounts she was extremely effective as a speaker, and this conjoined with an impressive public personality attracted crowds wherever she went. The Priestess of Beelzebub, as the strait-laced called her, was for a decade a goddess to the workingmen whose cause she championed. To spread the gospel of Free-Thought ever wider, she founded and wrote for *The New York Free Enquirer*. In its pages she argued vigorously for the abolition of capital punishment and imprisonment for debt, demanded the vote for women, civil rights for all minorities, and sought a system of public education completely free from religious bias. To the churchgoers she was a holy terror, and the respectable upper class came to shun her as they would a social disease. Meeting halls gradually became harder to rent, and the audiences, for all their enthusiasm, grew steadily smaller. Finally, in the late 30's she gave up lecturing altogether. Now she devoted herself to her family,[44] to writing, and to her business interests. In the main, she was unsuccessful. Her marriage foundered, her writing grew incoherent, and her last years were spoiled by constant quarrels over money.

No more than she deserved, you say? Perhaps. What Frances Wright stood for, few men even today care or dare to preach. Yet, if she offended, she offended gloriously. The role of women, the life of the Negro, the rights of the workingman, the freedom of the press—all were bettered for her efforts. To these goals she sacrificed her youth, health, fortune, and good name. She had a vision of a freer, more tolerant America, and she did her level best to bring it to reality. There are hardly any of her critics of whom it can in truth be said they did a tithe as much.

SUGGESTED READINGS

Herbert M. Morais, *Deism in Eighteenth Century America* (New York: Columbia University Press, 1934), emphasizes the speculative side of American Deism. Less scholarly, and narrower in compass, is G. Adolf Koch, *Republican Religion* (New York: Holt, 1933). Both books provide bibliographies. Albert Post, *Popular Freethought in America, 1825-1850* (New York: Columbia University Press, 1943), is a Ph.D. dissertation rewritten.

A photographic copy of the 1784 edition of Ethan Allen's *Reason the Only Oracle of Man* with Appendix (Essay on the Universal Plentitude of Being), published by Scholar's Facsimiles (New York, 1940), is available in some libraries. It includes an Introduction and biographical note by John Pell. All libraries should possess one or more editions of the works of Thomas Paine. The most compact and convenient is that of Philip S. Foner, *The Complete Writings of Thomas Paine,* 2 Vols. (New York: Citadel Press, 1945). Introduction by the editor, with explanatory notes on each of Paine's works. Of the works of Abner Kneeland and Frances Wright, there is nothing readily available apart from the items cited in the text.

Few men in American history have aroused more biographical passion than Thomas Paine. There are a score of lives, some describing a devil incarnate, others canonizing a saint. Among those that try to strike a balance are Hesketh Pearson, *Tom Paine, Friend of Mankind* (New York: Harper, 1937), W. E. Woodward, *Tom Paine, America's Godfather* (New York: Dutton, 1945), and, most recent, Alfred Owen Aldridge, *Man of Reason, the Life of Thomas Paine* (New York: Lippincott, 1959). There are two biographies of Ethan Allen: John Pell, *Ethan Allen* (Boston: Houghton Mifflin, 1929), and Stewart Holbrook, *Ethan Allen* (Portland, Oregon: Binfords and Mort, 1958). Only the latter is currently in print, but the former will be in most libraries. A. J. G. Perkins and Theresa Wolfson, *Frances Wright, Free Enquirer* (New York: Harper, 1939), state all the facts but somehow fail to communicate the personality of one of the Nineteenth Century's most fascinating women. About Abner Kneeland there is nothing, and that is a shame.

REFERENCES

1. *The Life and Works of Thomas Paine*, 10 Vols. (New Rochelle: Thomas Paine National Historical Association, 1925), VIII, p. 5. Hereafter cited as Works.

2. In the view of some religious historians, Benjamin Franklin ranks as the earliest professed American deist. However, since Franklin neither engaged in religious controversy nor published his opinions on the subject at any length, he hardly deserves to be called an *exponent* of Deism.

3. The date is in doubt. John Pell, Allen's biographer, gives the year as 1738; Allen himself, writing in his wife's copy of *Reason the Only Oracle of Man,* makes the day January 21st.

4. Mary Brownson (Allen) was the daughter of a well-to-do Connecticut Valley farmer. Delicate, devout, devoid of humour and illiterate, she was thirty when she married the twenty-four-year-old Allen. At forty-nine she died of consumption, having borne her husband four daughters and a son. A year later (1784) Ethan married the "dashing" young heiress and widow, Fanny Montresor. For the details of Allen's personal life see John Pell, *Ethan Allen* (Boston: Houghton Mifflin, 1929).

5. *Reason the Only Oracle of Man* (Bennington: Haswell & Russell, 1784). Photographic facsimile of this edition, with an Introduction by John Pell, Scholar's Facsimiles & Reprints, New York, 1940. Hereafter cited as Oracle.

6. Oracle, Preface.

7. Ibid., p. 30.

8. Ibid., p. 235.

9. Ibid., p. 200.

10. Ibid., p. 226. My italics.

11. Ibid., p. 346. I have reversed the order of quotation.

12. Ibid., p. 348.

13. Ibid., p. 417.

14. Ibid., p. 418.

15. Ibid., p. 419.

16. Works, II, p. 97.

17. Ibid., pp. 97-98.

18. Ibid., pp. 115, 122.

19. Ibid., p. 114.

20. Ibid., pp. 123-24.

21. Ibid., p. 127.

22. Ibid., p. 130.

23. Ibid., p. 135.

24. Ibid., pp. 136-37.

25. Ibid., p. 151.

26. Ibid., p. 180.

27. Ibid., pp. 179-80.

28. Ibid., VI, pp. 20-21.

29. Ibid., VIII, pp. 4-5.

30. Ibid., p. 8.

31. Ibid., p. 9.

32. Ibid., p. 11.

33. Ibid., p. 13.

34. Ibid., p. 14.

35. Part I deals with revelation in general. When Paine composed it, he had no Bible to hand, and his critics attacked his conclusions on the basis of the authority of Holy Writ. Part II, which analyzes the biblical account in detail, was written with the motive of confounding his critics by showing forth the inadequacy of the Scriptural authority on which their alleged refutations rested.

36. Works, VIII, pp. 271-72.

37. Ibid., p. 278.

38. Their task was made easier by Paine's already deserved reputation as a heavy drinker, by his personal slovenliness and his overbearing egotism. Building on these foundations, successive generations of conservatives have argued the falsity of Paine's political and religious principles on the (formally fallacious) grounds that nothing true is to be expected from the pen of a smelly, loudmouthed, deadbeat drunk. Probably he was none of these; possibly he was a bit of each.

39. Henry Steele Commager, "The Blasphemy of Abner Kneeland," *The New England Quarterly,* Vol. VII (1935), pp. 32-33.

40. The first trial ended in a conviction, with the judge (Thacher) sentencing Kneeland to three months in the common jail. He promptly appealed to the Supreme Court of Massachusetts. The second and third trials ended in hung juries. In the fourth trial the jury returned a verdict of guilty, and the judge (Wilde) sentenced the prisoner to sixty days. From this conviction, Kneeland appealed to the full Court (Chief Justice Shaw presiding). His appeal was denied, and in August of 1838 he finally went to jail.

41. Commager, op. cit., p. 35.

42. Leonard W. Levy, "Satan's Last Apostle in Massachusetts," *American Quarterly,* Vol. V (1953), p. 26.

43. A. J. G. Perkins and Theresa Wolfson, *Frances Wright, Free Enquirer* (New York: Harper, 1939), p. 193.

44. In 1831, her sister having died, and she in consequence having put an end to her affair with Owen and returned to France, she married Phiquebal D'Arusmont, an itinerant French physician and educator some sixteen years her senior. Of the life of the one child of this union, Frances Sylvia D'Arusmont, very little is known.

VI

The Federalists and Their Foes

ISSUES AND ADVOCATES

ALEXANDER HAMILTON

JOHN JAY

JAMES MADISON

RICHARD HENRY LEE

JOHN ADAMS

"A Nation, without a national government, is, in my view, an awful spectacle." [1]

ALEXANDER HAMILTON

1. Issues and Advocates

Whereas there is provision in the Articles of Confederation & perpetual Union for making alterations therein by the Assent of a Congress of the United States and of the legislatures of the several States; And whereas experience hath evinced that there are defects in the present Confederation. . . .

Resolved that in the opinion of Congress it is expedient that on the second Monday in May next a Convention of delegates who shall have been appointed by the several states be held at Philadelphia for the sole and express purpose of revising the Articles of Confederation and reporting to Congress and the several legislatures such alterations and provisions therein as shall when agreed to in Congress and confirmed by the states render the federal constitution adequate to the exigencies of Government & the preservation of the Union.[2]

ON MAY 14th, 1787, the Convention assembled: four months later it had completed its work, and sent to the several States for confirmation a new constitution. In so doing, it clearly exceeded the instructions laid down in the call to Convention.[3] Nonetheless, a constitution was what the nation needed, and a new constitution was what it got. By July of the following year the required nine of thirteen States having ratified,[4] the Federal Constitution took effect and the United States of America took its place among the nations of the earth.

The events of those momentous summer months of 1787 have been recorded time and again, and I shall not here add another description to the list. In any case, it is not so much the events themselves as it is the conflict of philosophies underlying them that compels the attention of every responsible American. For the issues of that conflict are still very much with us. Where yesterday men spoke of the Federalists and their foes, they speak today of the Republicans and their Democratic opposition. But only the names have changed: the issues remain as before.

Like much else in our intellectual life, these issues arise out of the various philosophies imported into colonial America from the English homeland; in this instance, those of James Harrington and John Locke. According to the former, economic power is the true source of political power, thus Harrington's dictum: "Empire follows the balance of property." The protection of property, therefore, is the cardinal interest of any government, and as in all societies the predominant propertied interest is that of the owners of the land, it follows, as Harrington sees it, that political control should be vested in the natural aristocracy of landowners. That the power should belong to those who owned the property, Locke agreed. But whereas Harrington had thought of property primarily in terms of land, Locke saw that the real property lay with those who held the money. Those who have a monetary stake in society should, then, Locke believes, run the government. On this stake-in-society theory, those who have no stake, either in money or in land or in other real property, deserve no voice, since "The Reason why Men enter in Society is the preservation of their Property; and the end why they chuse and authorize a Legislative, is, that there may be Laws made, and Rules set, as Guards and Fences to the Properties of all the Members of the Society, to limit the Power, and moderate the Dominion of every Part and Member of the Society." [5] That a legislature composed, either in whole or in part, of unpropertied men could or would serve the property interest is not to be expected. In consequence, this propertied interest being paramount, reason demands the restriction of the franchise to those possessing the property qualification. All men, Locke had declared, are entitled to life, liberty, and *property,* and in approving the changing of this last to read "pursuit of happiness," the sponsors of the American Declaration of Independence intended no slight to the inalienable right of property. All were men of means, and of those among them who a decade later assembled at Philadelphia to write a constitution for the American States, there was hardly a man whose political philosophy was out of tune with those of Harrington and Locke.

Given such a similarity of philosophical belief, and considering the political and economic unrest in the country,[6] it is not surprising that the delegates, for all their debate and wrangling, were able to complete in four months a draft which has so well stood the test of time. Indeed, the basic problem was not to get the Constitution written but to get it ratified. Many of its provisions were new, some were open to variant interpretation, and no one could say for sure how any would work out in practice. Doubts multiplied and hardened into opposition as various factions took up the fight to preserve what they took to be a federal threat to regional and local interests. Even those with no particular axe to grind could say Amen to DeWitt Clinton's anti-federalist prayer:

> From the insolence of great men—from the tyranny of the rich—from the unfeeling rapacity of the excise-men and Tax-gatherers—from the misery of despotism—from the expence of supporting standing Armies, Navies, Placemen, sinecures, federal cities, Senators, Presidents, and a long train of etceteras, Good Lord deliver us.[7]

A bare ten days after the final draft of the proposed Constitution was finished and signed at Philadelphia, Governor George Clinton of New York published in the City press the first of a series of letters denouncing the proposed Constitution. Alexander Hamilton was moved to reply, and in the months that followed, while ratification hung in the balance, the federalists [8] and their foes filled the columns of the newspapers with letters and articles, and kept the presses busy turning out broadsides and pamphlets pro and con the Constitution. Both sides mustered able advocates. Against ratification stood Richard Henry Lee and the agrarian democrats of Virginia and Carolina. Standing for it were most of the great names of the Revolution. Of these, however, none was more eloquent or astute in argument than Publius, the pseudonymous author of a series of eighty-five articles appearing in the New York press between October 1787 and May 1788. Publius was, in fact, three men, Alexander Hamilton, James Madison, and John Jay, and their articles in collected form constitute the work we know as *The Federalist*. No better defense of the federal system of government has ever been written. Anyone who would know the case for the Constitution, and understand the Federalist philosophy, must of necessity begin here.

As we do so, however, it is essential that we keep in mind the fact that *The Federalist* is, after all, campaign literature, specifically designed by its authors to sell the federal system of government to the voters of the State of New York, and hence it is not entirely free from the taint of bias and special pleading. It is worthy of note that Publius never defines exactly what he means by "federal system." As the phrase is used throughout *The Federalist,* it signifies just as much and no more Union than is required to promote the general welfare and secure the common defense. That these are essential purposes for any government, both sides agree. But as to the amount or nature of the Union needed to accomplish them, there is no agreement at all. Just how much Union of what sort does America need? That is the fundamental question at issue between those in favor of and those opposed to the Constitution.

2. Alexander Hamilton

HAMILTON FINDS THE ANSWER to lie in the basic reason underlying the failure of the Articles of Confederation. "The great and radical vice in the construction of the existing Confederation is," he writes in No. 15 of *The Federalist,*

> in the principle of LEGISLATION for STATES or GOVERNMENTS, in their CORPORATE or COLLECTIVE CAPACITIES, and as contradistinguished from the INDIVIDUALS of which they consist. Though this principle does not run through all the powers delegated to the Union, yet it pervades and governs those on which the efficacy of the rest depends. Except as to the rule of apportionment, the United States has an indefinite discretion to make requisitions for men and money; but they have no authority to raise either, by regulations extending to the individual citizens of America. The consequence of this is, that though in theory their resolutions concerning those objects are laws, constitutionally binding on the members of the Union, yet in practice they are mere recommendations which the States observe or disregard at their option.[9]

In other words, the Union the general welfare requires is a Union of *individuals* rather than of States. For unless the Union has not only the privilege but the power to levy taxes against the *individual,* unless it has the right and means to recruit the *individual* for its defense, there is no real Union at all, but merely a loose confederation of sovereign States free to ignore the Union as they wish. This, of course, is exactly what the anti-federalists thought the Union should be. Thus Patrick Henry, speaking in the Virginia Convention against ratification asks:

> Have they said, We, the States? Have they made a proposal of a compact between States? If they had, this would be a confederation. It is otherwise most clearly a consolidated government. The question turns, sir, on that poor little thing—the expression, We, the *people,* instead of the *states,* of America.[10]

And so it does. But the point remains, as Hamilton sees and Henry does not, that unless the Union is one of "We, the *people,*" it is no true *Union* at all.

For his own part, Hamilton preferred a strong centralized *national* government, with all power administered by and for those with the strongest stake in society. There was in his mind no doubt whatever about who should run the government: "That power which holds the purse-strings absolutely, must rule." But since federalism was the best he could persuade his more democratically inclined colleagues to accept, he would use his pen in its defense—but his heart was hardly in his work. Inalienably aristocratic in his personal bearing and outlook, he had only contempt for the common herd: "The people!—the people, is a great beast." Such were his sentiments, and if he defended the Union of "We, the people," it was only because he saw in direct government control over individual affairs the safest course for the new nation to pursue.

3. John Jay

JAY TOO WAS CONCERNED WITH SAFETY, but in a more obvious sense. In each of the five articles that he contributes to *The Federalist,* the emphasis throughout is on the need of a strong Union as the best insurance against attack from without and subversion from within.

> Leave America divided into thirteen or, if you please, into three or four independent governments—what armies could they raise and pay—what fleets could they ever hope to have? If one was attacked, would the others fly to its succor, and spend their blood and money in its defence? Would there be no danger of their being flattered into neutrality by its specious promises, or seduced by a too great fondness for peace to decline hazarding their tranquillity and present safety for the sake of neighbors, of whom perhaps they have been jealous, and whose importance they are content to see diminished. . . .
>
> But admit that they might be willing to help the invaded State or confederacy. How, and when, and in what proportion shall aids of men and money be afforded? Who shall command the allied armies, and from which of them shall he receive his orders? Who shall settle the terms of peace, and in case of disputes what umpire shall decide between them and compel acquiescence? [11]

The difficulties are endless, and the end, Jay is sure, must ever be the same; a house divided cannot stand indefinitely, a nation incapable of unity must finally say, "FAREWELL! A LONG FAREWELL TO ALL MY GREATNESS."

4. James Madison

ON THIS, Madison thinks,[12] all practical men will agree. But unlike Hamilton and Jay, he does not feel it is enough to have secured a strong Union. If this Union be not republican in character, if its power be not of, by, and for the people, if it be not established to promote the common good, then Madison would have it die.

> If the plan of the convention, therefore, be found to depart from the republican character, its advocates must abandon it as no longer defensible.[13]

It would be a mistake to infer from the statement that Madison is, what Hamilton very probably thought him to be, an idealist out of touch with reality. No one of the founding fathers is more clearly aware than Madison of the impracticability of *pure* democracy. "Such democracies," he notes in No. 10, "have ever been spectacles of turbulence and contention; have ever been found incompatible with personal security or the rights of property; and have in general been as short in their lives as they have been violent in their deaths." [14] On the other hand, the great advantage of a republican form of government, i.e., "a government which derives all its powers directly or indirectly from the great body of the people, and is administered by persons holding their offices during pleasure, for a limited period, or during good behavior," [15] is simply that it is the one truly representative form of Union strong enough to cope with the evils of faction.[16]

If a faction consists of less than a majority, relief is supplied by the republican principle, which enables the majority to defeat its sinister views by regular vote. It may clog the administration, it may convulse the society; but it will be unable to execute and mask its violence under the forms of the Constitution. When a majority is included in a faction, the form of popular government, on the other hand, enables it to sacrifice to its ruling passion or interest both the public good and the rights of other citizens.[17]

Even so,

It is *essential* to such a [republican] government that it be derived from the great body of the society, not from an inconsiderable proportion, or a favored class of it; otherwise a handful of tyrannical nobles, exercising their oppressions by a delegation of their powers, might aspire to the rank of republicans, and claim for their government the honorable title of republic. It is *sufficient* for such a government that the persons administering it be appointed, either directly or indirectly, by the people; and that they hold their appointments by either of the tenures just specified; otherwise every government in the United States, as well as every other popular government that has been or can be well organized or well executed, would be degraded from the republican character.[18]

On neither count, he thinks, need we have any fear. The Constitution as drawn plainly provides for a government essentially and sufficiently republican.

Yet even as he reaches this conclusion, Madison knows that for the adversaries of the Constitution a proven republicanism is not enough. For they are not so much concerned with rights and proper representation of individuals as they are with preserving power to the several States. They care not whether there is justice for all, but only that there is sovereignty for themselves.

The adversaries to the plan of the convention, instead of considering in the first place what degree of power was absolutely necessary for the purposes of the federal government, have exhausted themselves in a secondary inquiry into the possible consequences of the proposed degree of power to the governments of the particular States. But if the Union, as has been shown, be essential to the security of the people of America against foreign danger; if it be essential to their security against contentions and wars among the different States; if it be essential to guard them against those violent and oppressive factions which embitter the blessings of liberty, and against those military establishments which must gradually poison its very fountain; if, in a word, the Union be essential to the happiness of the people of America, is it not preposterous, to urge as an objection to a government, without which the objects of the Union cannot be attained, that such a government may derogate from the importance of the governments of the individual States? Was, then, the American Revolution effected, was the American Confederacy formed, was the precious blood of thousands spilt, and the hard-earned substance of millions lavished, not that the people of America should enjoy peace, liberty, and safety, but that the government of the individual States, that particular municipal establishments, might enjoy a certain extent of power, and be arrayed with certain dignities and attributes of sovereignty? [19]

5. Richard Henry Lee

When the advocates of states-rights press their claims to the point of imperiling the safety of the Union, they deserve the contempt of every patriotic American, for in the name of freedom they would destroy the very conditions which make any genuine freedom possible.

It is a harsh judgment, and to the adversaries of the Constitution, one most unjust. In their eyes it was they who were preserving freedom. Then as now, the underdogs had good reason to doubt that their governors would always act from that ideal spirit of scrupulousness assumed in every constitution but very rarely found in the practice of any state. They too believed that "The happiness of the people at large must be the great object with every honest statesman," [20] and they too knew that only the free are truly happy. But that true freedom was the fruit of Union—of that they were by no means convinced. For they saw in the proposed Constitution primarily a device whereby all power might be centralized in the hands of the few, and that few the aristocrats and their hangers-on. Thus Richard Henry Lee in his *Letters of a Federal Farmer* remarks his doubts as to the true intentions of those aristocrats who "support and hasten the adoption of the proposed constitution, merely because they think it is a stepping stone to their favorite object." [21] Granted that the proposed plan of Union has many good things in it, still, Lee feels, no government is any better than those who are entrusted with the administration of it. The very haste and eagerness of the aristocratic federalist faction for immediate Union should warn us to proceed with all caution in this matter. There is, Lee insists, no need for hasty action: "If we remain cool and temperate, we are in no immediate danger of any commotions; we are in a state of perfect peace, and in no danger of invasions; the state governments are in the full exercise of their powers; and our governments answer all present exigencies . . . and whether we adopt a change three or nine months hence, can make but little odds with the private circumstances of individuals; their happiness and prosperity, after all, depend principally upon their own exertions." [22] There are, he thinks, many features of this proposed Constitution that call for lengthy and careful study. There is, for example, the question of the right of the federal government to levy taxes. Considering the variety of ordinances necessary to enforce collection, the geographical distances involved, the imperfect organization of the new government—not to mention the possible veniality of its administrators—is it, Lee asks,

wise, prudent, or safe, to vest the powers of laying and collecting internal taxes in the general government, while imperfectly organized and inadequate; and to trust to amending it hereafter, and making it adequate to this purpose? It is not only unsafe but absurd to lodge power in a government before it is fitted to receive it. It is confessed that this power and representation ought to go together. Why give the power first? Why give the power to the few, who, when possessed of it, may have address enough to prevent the increase of representation? Why not keep the power, and, when necessary, amend the constitution, and add to its other parts this power, and a proper increase of representation at the same time? . . .

When I recollect how lately congress, conventions, legislatures, and people contended in the cause of liberty, and carefully weighed the importance of taxation, I can scarcely believe we are serious in proposing to vest the powers of laying and collecting internal taxes in a government so imperfectly organized for such purposes.[23]

I know that powers to raise taxes, to regulate the military strength of the community on some uniform plan, to provide for its defence and internal order, and for duly executing the laws, must be lodged somewhere; but still we ought not so to lodge them, as evidently to give one order of men in the community, undue advantages over others; or commit the many to the mercy, prudence, and moderation of the few.[24]

In short, can we trust the few? Can we trust them not to recruit large standing armies with the monies we give them? Can we trust them not to use our taxes to destroy our hard-won liberties? Perhaps we can, but to Lee it seems only common sense that we should trust them no more than is absolutely necessary.

Of even greater concern to Lee, as indeed to all those who henceforward serve the cause of states-rights, is the power and trust to be vested in the federal judiciary. In No. 78 of *The Federalist*, Hamilton had argued that

> There is no position which depends on clearer principles, than that every act of a delegated authority, contrary to the tenor of the commission under which it is exercised, is void. *No legislative act, therefore, contrary to the Constitution, can be valid.* To deny this, would be to affirm, that the deputy is greater than his principal; that the servant is above his master; that the representatives of the people are superior to the people themselves; that men acting by virtue of powers, may do not only what their powers do not authorize, but what they forbid.[25]

It is, then, to Hamilton's way of thinking, essential to the successful operation of the federal system of government that any act against the Constitution be recognized as void. Lee himself appears to concede as much when he remarks apropos of the authority of federal law that

> It is proper [that] the national laws should be supreme, and superior to state or district laws;

but then, he adds,

> the national laws ought to yield to unalienable or fundamental rights —and national laws, made by a few men, should extend only to a few national objects.[26]

Just what these unalienable and fundamental rights are, he does not spell out; nor has he anything to say on such rights as might happen, in the opinion of the federal courts, to conflict with the Constitution as these courts interpret it. He does, however, have serious reservations about the Supreme Court functioning as a determiner of equity. It is, he thinks,

> a very dangerous thing to vest in the same judge power to decide on the law, and also general powers in equity; for if the law restrain him, he is only to step into his shoes of equity, and give what judgment his reason or opinion may dictate; we have no precedents in this country as yet, to regulate the divisions in equity as in Great Britain; equity, therefore, in the supreme court for many years will be mere discretion. I confess in the constitution of this supreme court, as left by the constitution, I do not see a spark of freedom or a shadow of our own or the British common law.[27]

The "many years" have now stretched to one hundred and seventy-three, and in the minds of not a few Americans today the belief persists that these general powers of equity still rest upon no better foundation than the discretion of the Court. Unfortunately, what Lee and those of his political posterity fail to see is that discretion to interpret what the Constitution means must ultimately rest with someone, and if not with the Supreme Court, then with whom? Certainly not the people or the States!

6. John Adams

CERTAINLY NOT, according to John Adams. "The proposition that the people are the best keepers of their own liberties is not true. They are the worst conceivable, they are no keepers at all; they can neither judge, act, think, or will, as a political body." [28] Shaken by passion and driven by greed, the people must inevitably destroy any society of which they gain control. "Remember, democracy never lasts long. It soon wastes, exhausts, and murders itself. There never was a democracy that did not commit suicide." [29] If, as Adams believes, the great aim of any government is to secure the rights of every man to the enjoyment of his life, liberty, and property, then the greatest error any society can commit is to vest all power in the people. "If you give more than a share in the sovereignty to the democrats, that is, if you give them the command or preponderance in the sovereignty, that is, the legislature, they will vote all property out of the hands of you aristocrats, and if they let you escape with your lives, it will be more humanity, consideration, and generosity than any triumphant democracy ever displayed since the creation." [30] That power should rest with the owners of property, was to Adams a self-evident truth. "The moment the idea is admitted into society, that property is not as sacred as the laws of God, and that there is not a force of law and public justice to protect it, anarchy and tyranny commence." [31]

It is agreed that "the end of all government is the good and ease of the people, in a secure enjoyment of their rights, without oppression"; but it must be remembered, that the rich are *people* as well as the poor; that they have rights as well as others; that they have as clear and as sacred a right to their large property as others have to theirs which is smaller; that oppression to them is as possible and as wicked as to others.[32]

For all his defense of the property rights of the rich, however, Adams was no simple economic royalist. He lacked Hamilton's confidence in the moral superiority of the economic aristocracy, and if he was careful to protect the interests of the wealthy, he was no less concerned for the right of the middle and lower classes to representation.

The poor should have a bulwark against the same dangers and oppressions; and this can never be without a house of representatives of the people. But neither the rich nor the poor can be defended by their respective guardians in the constitution [the Senate, in his opinion, being the guardian of the interests of the rich], without an executive power, vested with a negative, equal to either, to hold the balance even between them, and decide when they cannot agree.[33]

With this formula of the balance of powers, Adams believed himself to have solved the problem of representative government. In fact, however, his solution presupposed a false premise, for it has never been the case that Senate, House, and Executive have represented respectively the interests of rich, poor, and public. In truth, such balance of powers as has existed has always been *within* the branches rather than between them. Had Adams realized this, and framed the policies of his Presidency accordingly, the campaign of 1800 might have had a different ending. As it was, the Adams policies satisfied no one, and he failed to win a second term. The Federalists had finally fallen to their foes.

They never really rose again. Hamilton's death at the hands of Burr in 1804 deprived them of their one remaining leader of stature sufficient to challenge the agrarian democrat Jefferson and the federalist-cum-democrat Madison. Yet the Federalists had done their job well. The loose Confederacy had been tightened into a Union strong enough to survive. The institutions envisaged in the

Constitution had been successfully established. As the Nineteenth Century dawned, the United States was a going concern.

SUGGESTED READINGS

Edward M. Earle (editor), *The Federalist, A Commentary on the Constitution of the United States* (New York: Modern Library, 1937), offers the complete text plus The Declaration of Independence, The Constitution, and other relevant documents. Introduction and biographical notes by the editor. Charles A. Beard (editor), *The Enduring Federalist* (New York: Doubleday, 1948), rearranges the text by topic, and provides an analysis of each. For Richard Henry Lee's *Letters from the Federal Farmer to the Republican* and other writings pro and con the proposed Constitution for the United States, see Paul Leicester Ford, *Pamphlets on the Constitution of the United States* (Brooklyn, 1888). Unfortunately, this last is long out of print, but is available in many libraries.

The person wanting background will find in A. H. Kelly and W. Harbison, *The American Constitution, Its Origins and Development* (New York: Norton, 1948), a readable survey couched in relatively untechnical terms. See especially Chapters Three through Seven. A somewhat more scholarly analysis is provided by Gottfried Dietze, *The Federalist* (Baltimore: Johns Hopkins, 1960); a good bibliography. Carl L. Becker, *The Declaration of Independence* (New York: Vintage Books, paperback, 1958), is a classic study of the making of the Declaration, and of the philosophy for which its stands.

REFERENCES

1. *The Federalist, A Commentary on the Constitution of the United States,* edited by Henry Cabot Lodge (New York: Putnam's Sons, 1888), p. 552. All subsequent references are to this edition.

2. The Call for the Federal Constitutional Convention. Resolution of Congress, February 21st, 1787.

3. The justification for having exceeded the instructions of the call to Convention is argued by Madison in No. 40 of *The Federalist.* "Will it," he asks there, "be said that the *fundamental principles* of the Confederation were not within the purview of the convention, and ought not to have been varied? I ask, What are these principles? . . . . The truth is, that the great principles of the Constitution proposed by the convention may be considered less as absolutely new, than as the expansion of principles which are found in the articles of Confederation. The misfortune under the latter system has been, that these principles are so feeble and confined as to justify all the charges of inefficiency which have been argued against it, and to require a degree of enlargement which gives to the new system the aspect of an entire transformation of the old. . . .

"The sum of what has been here advanced and proved is, that the charge against the convention of exceeding their powers, except in one instance little urged by the objectors, has no foundation to support it; that if they had exceeded their powers, they were not only warranted but required, as the confidential servants of their country, by the circumstances in which they were placed, to exercise the liberty which they assumed; and that finally, if they had violated both their powers and their obligations, in proposing a Constitution, this ought nevertheless to be embraced, if it be calculated to accomplish the views and happiness of the people of America." *The Federalist,* pp. 243, 244, 248.

4. North Carolina and Rhode Island refused to ratify but agreed later to abide by the will of the majority.

5. John Locke, *Two Treatises of Government,* edited by Peter Laslett (Cambridge: University Press, 1960), The Second Treatise (An Essay etc.), Section 222, p. 430.

6. The Convention met during a period of widespread depression. The financial system was shaky; inflation threatened; in Massachusetts the discontent of the farmers had flared into Shays' Rebellion. Forced to operate under the utterly inadequate Articles of Confederation, the national government found itself impotent at home and held in contempt abroad. The nation faced dissolution from within while its weakness invited aggression from without. The situation as it then was is vividly described by Madison and Hamilton in Numbers 15-22 of *The Federalist.*

7. Quoted in Charles A. Beard, *The Enduring Federalist* (New York: Doubleday, 1948), p. 360.

8. The term "federalist" as here employed refers to those who favored the adoption of the federal system of government embodied in the Constitution. In somewhat broader context it refers to those who made up the Federalist Party, in power during the administrations of Washington and John Adams. In its years of office, i.e., 1789 to 1801, this Party, whose membership was drawn for the most part from the ranks of the moneyed and propertied, championed the cause of strong centralized government and served the interests of the well-to-do. Defeated by the Jeffersonians in 1800, the Federalists became the chief opposition party in Congress and remained such until its demise from lack of voter support in 1820. Subsequently, its traditions were carried on by the Whigs and, since 1860, by the Republicans.

9. *The Federalist,* No. 15, p. 86.

10. Richard Hofstadter, *Great Issues in American History,* 2 Vols. (New York: Vintage Books, 1960), I, p. 119.

11. *The Federalist,* No. 4, pp. 20-21.

12. In view of Madison's subsequent break with Hamilton, and his turn to Jefferson, a shift of allegiance which later greatly facilitated his successful bid for the Presidency, it seems open to question that he was ever truly Federalist in his politics. In the limited sense of the term, as referent to anyone favoring a strong Union, he must, I think, be counted as of the same party with his fellow aristocrats Hamilton and Jay. But certainly he was far more liberal in his views and refreshingly free from the class bias which marred most Federalist statesmanship.

13. *The Federalist,* No. 39, p. 232.

14. Ibid., No. 10, p. 56.

15. Ibid., No. 39, p. 233.

16. "By a faction, I understand," writes Madison, "a number of citizens, whether amounting to a majority or minority of the whole, who are united and actuated by some common impulse of passion, or of interest, adverse to the rights of other citizens, or to the permanent and aggregate interests of the community." *The Federalist*, No. 10, p. 53.

17. *The Federalist*, No. 10, p. 55.

18. Ibid., No. 39, p. 233.

19. Ibid., No. 45, p. 286.

20. Richard Henry Lee, *Letters from the Federal Farmer to the Republican*, in Paul Leicester Ford, *Pamphlets on the Constitution of the United States* (Brooklyn, 1888), p. 286. Hereafter cited as Federal Farmer.

21. Federal Farmer, p. 321.

22. Ibid., pp. 280-81.

23. Ibid., pp. 302-3.

24. Ibid., p. 306.

25. *The Federalist*, No. 78, p. 485. My italics.

26. Federal Farmer, p. 308.

27. Ibid., p. 312.

28. *The Works of John Adams*, 10 Vols. (Boston: Little & Brown, 1851), VI. Hereafter cited as Works. Quoted in V. L. Parrington, *Main Currents in American Thought*, 3 Vols. (New York: Harcourt, Brace, 1927), I, p. 316.

29. Ibid.

30. Letter to John Taylor, Works, VI, p. 516.

31. "Defence of the Constitution," Works, VI, p. 9.

32. Ibid., p. 65.

33. Ibid.

VII

Philosopher-President

THOMAS JEFFERSON

"A patient pursuit of facts, and cautious combination and comparison of them, is the drudgery to which man is subjected by his Maker, if he wishes to attain sure knowledge." [1]

THOMAS JEFFERSON

Thomas Jefferson

THE PUBLIC LIFE of the third President of the United States is, or should be, known to every educated American, and I do not propose to add another to the many excellent accounts already in print. The philosophy of Thomas Jefferson is, however, not well known at all, and yet it is in this, the most important of his many roles as far as his posterity is concerned, that he commands the attention of all who would know the American Mind.

That Jefferson's philosophy should not be well known is not surprising, since he wrote nothing that could be described with any accuracy as a philosophical treatise. What he did write was letters, thousands of them, and it is in these, and in his public papers, that his philosophy is to be found. Thus, in a letter to John Adams written in 1820, he remarks the fundamental assumptions from which his thought proceeds and reveals the sources whence his philosophical creed derives:

I feel, therefore I exist, I feel bodies which are not myself: there are other existences then. I call them *matter*. I feel them changing place. This gives me *motion*. Where there is an absence of matter, I call it *void*, or *nothing*, or *immaterial space*. On the basis of sensation, of matter and motion, we may erect the fabric of all the certainties we can have or need. . . . When once we quit the basis of sensation, all is in the wind. To talk of *immaterial* existences, is to talk of *nothings*. To say that the human soul, angels, God, are immaterial, is to say, they are *nothings*, or that there is no God, no angels, no soul. I cannot reason otherwise: but I believe I am supported in my creed of materialism by the Lockes, the Tracys and the Stewarts.[2]

An Englishman, a Frenchman, and a Scot; these are Jefferson's philosophical antecedents: in their thought his ideas find their ground. From Locke, the Englishman, comes the basic principle of sensationalism: there is nothing in the mind that was not first in the senses. The Frenchman, Tracy, or rather, de Tracy, provides the schematism; while Stewart, the Scot, contributes that philosophy of common sense from which the sage of Monticello never far departs.

It must be remarked that all three are materialists only insofar as they all subscribe to the proposition that matter, in some shape or form, is the ordinary terminus or object of thought. None are materialists in the radical sense in which that term describes the views of Helvetius, d'Holbach, Cabanis, and Flourens. None insist, as do these latter, that the universe consists wholly of material particles moving in empty space; none hold that man is a being purely physical. It is important to note this, the more so since Jefferson's writings reveal his thorough knowledge and unbounded admiration of the works of these radical French materialists. Yet even as he admires their complete devotion to the physical fact, Jefferson hesitates. Beyond experiment and observation, he himself does not wish to go; on the other hand, he cannot quite bring himself to accept in full the denial of all purpose that seems to follow from the reduction of everything psychological to physiology. Like Stewart, he would steer "a steady course of inquiry, between implicit credulity and unlimited scepticism." [3]

In Jefferson's eyes, Dugald Stewart was a great man. He honoured his Scots honesty and common sense, carefully studied the volumes of his writings that Stewart sent him, and ranked him (with de Tracy) as the ablest of investigators of the human faculty of thought. In this last, he surely overestimated his man, and by so doing, he pointed up a weakness in both their philosophies. It was Stewart's belief, elaborated in his *Elements of the Philosophy of the Human Mind,* that philosophy had properly to do only with the discovery and analysis of the principles of mental activity. In other words, true philosophy is simply the science of the psychology of the human mind; all else is metaphysical moonshine.

With these sentiments, Jefferson was in virtually complete accord. No more than Stewart had he any toleration to spare for those spiritualists and immaterialists who would indulge in speculation beyond the range of fact. "I am," he wrote to Adams, "satisfied, and sufficiently occupied with the things which are, without tormenting or troubling myself about those which may indeed be, but of which I have no evidence." [4] These are, he feels, enough "for all the purposes of life, without plunging into the fathomless abyss of dreams and phantasms." But are they enough for the purposes of philosophy, particularly a philosophy aspirant to the status of a science? It would scarcely seem so. A philosophy which consistently refused to press beyond the dictates of common sense must leave science untouched. For science, properly conceived, only begins where Jefferson and Stewart would have it end—with the collation of observations. To maintain that philosophy should so limit itself for fear of falling into scepticism is, in effect, to refuse the philosophic enterprise as such. Of this, Jefferson seems to have been at least partly aware, since his own scientific investigations testify to a philosophy of science of far greater subtlety than Stewart's theory would allow. That Stewart's view is incomplete, he admits by implication in another of his letters to Adams. "Stewart," he writes, "seems to have given its natural history from facts and observations; Tracy its modes of action and deduction, which he calls Logic and Ideology; and Cabanis has investigated anatomically, and most ingeniously, the particular organs in the human structure which may most probably exercise that faculty." [5] In short, observation requires to be supplemented by theory and confirmed by experiment.

It might seem that this last was far and away the most important, and that Jefferson was fascinated by the physiological experiments of Cabanis and Flourens, his letters make clear. Even so, his greatest enthusiasm was reserved not for the work of these, but for the ideological theory of Destutt de Tracy. It was not merely, as in the case of Stewart, that Jefferson recommended his writings to all and sundry of his correspondents; he did much more: he translated and edited many of the ideological writings of de Tracy, arranged for their American publication, advertised the work of the author, and protected his legal rights. Indeed, that Ideology became known in America at all was almost entirely due to Jefferson's efforts on its behalf.

What is Ideology? To Adams, Jefferson defined it thus:

Tracy comprehends, under the word "Ideology," all the subjects which the French term *Morale,* as the correlative to *Physique.* His works on Logic, Government, Politics, Economics and Morality, he considers as making up the circle of ideological subjects, or of those which are within the scope of the understanding, and not of the senses.[6]

De Tracy's own definition is somewhat simpler, yet no less sweeping. Ideology, as he conceives it, is a branch or subclass of the science of zoology; specifically, that subclass having to do with the natural history of the human function of thought in all its aspects, and to analyze its products—ideas.

In the history of European thought, the first to perform that task, *le premier ideologiste,* according to de Tracy, was Locke's French follower, Condillac. For himself, de Tracy claimed only the honors due a systematizer. Actually, however, his role was far greater, for not only did he give the movement its name; he gave it its method, and freed it once and for all from the tyranny of metaphysics by defining its zoological context. It was not Condillac but de Tracy who saw that Descartes' "I think, therefore I am," was inadequate to its aim of being the one irrefutably true proposition; it was de Tracy who was first to see that this honor belonged rather to the proposition, "I feel, or, more simply, I am cold or hot, I thirst, therefore I am."

I touch something, and it resists my touch; on this sensation of resistance, de Tracy holds, my certainty of my own existence and that of the external world is founded. I am aware that I have willed the touching; I remember what it is that I have touched, and I make a judgment concerning the quality of the object I have felt. In this complex act I discover the irreducible modes of sensation—sensibility, judgment, memory, and will, and I come to see how these in combination constitute my mind. The life of this mind, in all its physical and social manifestations, is de Tracy's constant subject throughout the five volumes of his *Elements of Ideology;* it is the key to his *Political Economy,* the basis of *The Commentary and Review of Montesquieu.* All of these Jefferson read with enthusiasm; the last two he translated, firm in his conviction that "These two works will render more service to our country than all the writings of all the saints and holy fathers of the church have rendered." [7]

This is strong praise, considering that these are works which to-day have been all but forgotten; and with every due allowance for Jefferson's fondness for the superlative, it is not easy for the modern reader to see what could have so enthused him. These books, indeed all of de Tracy's works, are, by contemporary standards, deadly dull going, even for one antecedently interested in their subject matter. Perhaps it was their illustration of the ideological method, possibly the scheme of classification they put forth, that appealed to Jefferson's orderly mind. Most probably, however, he was inspired to exaggeration by de Tracy's dream of a unified science wherein each fact would have its proper place, and that which was not fact would have no place at all. For Jefferson also, the organization of fact was the only key to truth in science or philosophy. "A patient pursuit of facts, and cautious combination and comparison of them, is the drudgery to which man is subjected by his Maker, if he wishes to attain sure knowledge." [8]

It is, moreover, a drudgery as necessary in ethics and religion as it is in science. In matters of faith and morals, as elsewhere, Jefferson would have all men follow the advice he dispenses to his nephew Peter Carr:

Fix reason firmly in her seat, and call to her tribunal every fact, every opinion. Question with boldness even the existence of a God; because, if there is one, he must more approve of the homage of reason, than that of blindfolded fear. You will naturally examine first, the religion of your own country. Read the Bible, then, as you would read Livy or Tacitus. The facts which are within the ordinary course of nature, you will believe on the authority of the writer. . . . But those facts in the Bible which contradict the laws of nature, must be examined with more care, and under a variety of faces. Here you must recur to the pretensions of the writer to inspiration from God. Examine upon what evidence his pretensions are founded, and whether that evidence is so strong, as that its falsehood would be more improbable than a change in the laws of nature, in the case he relates. . . . You will next read the New Testament. It is the history of a personage called Jesus. Keep in your eye the opposite pretensions: 1, of those who say he was begotten by God, born of a virgin, suspended and reversed the laws of nature at will, and ascended bodily into heaven; and 2, of those who say he was a man of illegitimate birth, of a benevolent heart, enthusiastic mind, who set out without pretensions to divinity, ended in believing them, and was punished capitally for sedition, by being gibbeted. . . . Do not be frightened from this inquiry by any fear of its consequences. If it ends in a belief that there is no God, you will find incitements to virtue in the comfort and pleasantness you feel in its exercise, and the love of others which it will procure you. If you find reason to believe there is a God, a consciousness that you are acting under his eye, and that he approves you, will be a vast additional incitement. . . . In fine, I repeat, you must lay aside all prejudice on both sides, and neither believe nor reject anything, because any other persons, or description of persons, have rejected or believed it. Your own reason is the only oracle given you by heaven, and you are answerable, not for the rightness, but uprightness of the decision.[9]

Such sentiments, for all that they bespoke an enlightened mind, earned Jefferson no credit in American religious circles. As in France the Churchmen regarded the ideologists as open enemies, and succeeded at last in having their movement banned; so in America the orthodox saw in the fact-minded Jefferson a foe of all organized religion, most likely an atheist, a Deist by his own admission, and how that man could ever get to be President of the United States they just could not understand.

That Jefferson was, in fact, a foe to the dogmatic pretensions of organized religion was true enough. "To the corruptions of Christianity I am," he writes to Benjamin Rush, "indeed, opposed;

but not to the genuine precepts of Jesus himself. I am a Christian, in the only sense in which he wished any one to be; sincerely attached to his doctrines, in preference to all others; ascribing to himself every human excellence; and believing he never claimed any other.[10]

We must, he thinks,

strip off the artificial vestments in which they [the moral teachings of Jesus] have been muffled by priests, who have travestied them into various forms, as instruments of riches and power to themselves. We must dismiss the Platonists and Plotinists, the Stagyrites and Gamalielites, the Eclectics, the Gnostics and Scholastics, their essences and emanations, their Logos and Demiurgos, Aeons and Daemons, male and female, with a long train of etc., etc., etc., or, shall I say at once, of nonsense. We must reduce our volume to the simple evangelists, select, even from them, the very words only of Jesus, paring off the amphibolisms into which they have been led, by forgetting often, or not understanding, what had fallen from him, by giving their own misconceptions as his dicta, and expressing unintelligibly for others what they had not understood themselves. There will be found remaining the most sublime and benevolent code of morals which has ever been offered to man.[11]

Having himself performed this editorial task to his own satisfaction, Jefferson issued the result—forty-six pages of the sayings of Jesus culled from the Gospels—under the title *The Life and Morals of Jesus of Nazareth,* hoping thereby that Christianity might be understood for what he, Jefferson, always maintained it actually was—the ethical teachings of the man Jesus.

In light of such a view of Christianity, the issue of Jefferson's church affiliation, about which so much fuss has been raised, seems rather academic. His denial of the divinity of Christ, coupled with his often-stated contempt for the minutiae of creeds and doctrine, would naturally preclude his belonging to any denomination which held these matters important. They would not, of course, prevent his being a Unitarian; and largely on the basis of remarks made in letters to Benjamin Waterhouse and the Rev. Thomas Whittemore, the Unitarians have claimed him as one of their own. However, as the whole tenor of his writings on the subject of religion makes apparent, his Unitarianism [12] was hardly more than that to which any Deist might assent: that God is one, intelligent, and benevolent, and that He has made us as free moral agents, is the sum of Jefferson's faith, the substance of his hope. In truth, he belonged to no sect, nor did he care to. He counted himself a follower of the man Jesus, and Jesus, as Jefferson read his teachings, "has told us only that God is good and perfect, but has not defined him.

I am, therefore of his theology, believing that we have neither words nor ideas adequate to that definition. And if we could all, after this example, leave the subject as undefinable, we should all be of one sect, doers of good, and eschewers of evil.[13]

And, he might well have added, eschewers of sectarianism, for in this, and in its fossil, institutionalism, lies everything pernicious in religion. So strongly does he feel this, that he can write in reply to Adams "If by *religion* we are to understand *sectarian dogmas,* in which no two of them agree, then your exclamation on them is just, 'that this would be the best of all possible worlds, if there were no religion in it.' " [14]

We would be less than just to Jefferson if we failed to recognize that "religion" here means "institutional religion." For religion in the broader, moral sense he had only praise, as the conclusion of the passage just quoted shows; but for Christian institutionalism he had nothing good to say. His own experience had shown him, as indeed it had shown most Americans of the revolutionary era, the raw evil to which a Christian institutionalism could give rise. Of an institutionalism which could condone a Christian ruler's carrying into slavery "a distant people who never offended him," he wanted no part. In the catalogue of offences imputed to that *"Christian* king" George III in his rough draft of a Declaration of Independence he makes clear his contempt for that institution which would, in the name of Christianity, tolerate such acts, and his implication is plain: perhaps in declaring our independence of the British Empire, we ought also to declare our independence of that Christian church with which it stands. It tells us quite a bit, I think, about the religious climate of opinion prevailing in the Continental Congress, that the other members of the drafting committee saw to it that the Jefferson polemic against slavery and its Christian practitioners was stricken from the final draft of the Declaration of Independence offered for congressional approval. America was not then, and perhaps is not still, quite ready to take the teachings of Jesus as seriously as did that "prince of infidels" Thomas Jefferson.

One doctrine preached by Jefferson that they did take seriously, however, was his advocacy of natural rights. This doctrine was not, of course, private to, or original with, Jefferson. The ideas to which he gave such magnificent expression in his rough draft of the Declaration of Independence were, as he himself freely admitted, common to the age:

Not to find out new principles, or new arguments, never before thought of, not merely to say things which had never been said before; but to place before mankind the common sense of the subject, in terms so plain and firm as to command their assent. . . .[15]

Such was his intention. "I did not," he writes, "consider it as any part of my charge to invent new ideas altogether and to offer no sentiment which had ever been expressed before."[16]

Neither aiming at originality of principle or sentiment, not yet copied from any particular and previous writing, it [the Declaration] was intended to be an expression of the American mind, and to give to that expression the proper tone and spirit called for by the occasion. All its authority rests then on the harmonizing sentiments of the day, whether expressed in conversation, in letters, printed essays, or in the elementary books of public right, as Aristotle, Cicero, Locke, Sidney. . . .[17]

and, he might have added, Montesquieu, since the basic principles on which every modern defense of natural rights rests, have their origin in his famous work *On the Spirit of the Laws*.

The first, and most important, of these principles laid down by Montesquieu is that all laws are as such local to the society and the time of their propounding. From this it follows, he contends, that as societies change and their environments evolve, so must their laws evolve and change. Thus, as against the Church, he denies the existence of external law, and as for natural law; that, he thinks, is simply the reflection of the social climate of the particular epoch in question. Such, then, is the view that Jefferson has in mind when he declares to Madison

that no society can make a perpetual constitution, or even a perpetual law. The earth belongs always to the living generation: they may manage it, then, and what proceeds from it, as they please, during their usufruct. They are masters, too, of their own persons, and consequently may govern them as they please. But persons and property make the sum of the objects of government. The constitution and the laws of their predecessors are extinguished then, in their natural course, with those whose will gave them being. This could preserve that being, till it ceased to be itself, and no longer. Every constitution, then, and every law, naturally expires at the end of thirty-four years. If it be enforced longer, it is an act of force, and not of right.[18]

The earth belongs to the living; the dead have no rights. "They are nothing; and nothing cannot own something. Where there is no substance, there can be no accident. This corporeal globe, and everything upon it, belong to its present corporeal inhabitants, during their generation. They alone have a right to direct what is the concern of themselves alone, and to declare the law of that direction; and this declaration can only be made by their majority." [19] The truth of this principle justifies the right of revolution. Because it is so, we are, Jefferson maintains in his Rough Draft, warranted in proclaiming

that all men are created equal & independent; that from that equal creation they derive rights inherent & inalienable, among which are the preservation of life, & liberty, & the pursuit of happiness; that to secure these ends, governments are instituted among men, deriving their just powers from the consent of the governed; that whenever any form of government shall became destructive of these ends, it is the right of the people to alter or to abolish it, & to institute new government, laying it's foundation on such principles & organizing it's powers in such form, as to them shall seem most likely to effect their safety & happiness.[20]

Government, then, rests on compact, and compact is made precisely that men's inherent rights might be secured. This is Montesquieu's second basic principle, and from it he infers man's duty to dissolve any compact in violation of those rights. In Jefferson's thought, this duty is no less moral for being political.

There are circumstances, which sometimes excuse the non-performance of contracts between man and man; so are there also between nation and nation. When performance, for instance, becomes *impossible*, non-performance is not immoral: so if performance becomes self-destructive to the party, the law of self-preservation overrules the laws of obligation in others.[21]

In such circumstances, the law of self-preservation is the moral law. The natural right of revolution vindicated, it remains to develop a positive philosophy of government, and this Jefferson thinks to have provided by his theory of republicanism. In Jeffersonian usage, republicanism means

> a government by its citizens in mass, acting directly and personally, according to rules established by the majority; and that every other government is more or less republican, in proportion as it has in its composition more or less of this ingredient of the direct action of the citizens.[22]

A pure republic, therefore, would be one in which the people have the maximum of control over the organs of their government. Obviously, in a nation as large and populous as the United States, such pure republicanism is, he recognizes, quite impractical. The nearest practical approach to a pure republic on such a large scale would be

> where the powers of government, being divided, should be exercised each by representatives chosen either *pro hac vice* (for the occasion), or for such short terms as should render secure the duty of expressing the will of their constituents.[23]

Our House of Representatives, he thinks, conforms in part to this ideal; but on the other hand, the Senate, Executive, and Judiciary, as chosen in Jefferson's time, are, to his view, hardly republican at all.

To remedy these defects, and to provide for the adequate representation of all the people, Jefferson proposes that the nation shall be subdivided into units called wards, each of which shall compose an area of about six miles square, or less depending on the local density of population. Each ward, consisting of no more than that number of citizens able to govern themselves by direct action, in accordance with the republican ideal described above, would manage its own schools, muster its own militia, provide its own police and judges, care for its own poor, and in general secure to its inhabitants all essential public services. The value of such a radical decentralization of the functions of government, as Jefferson sees it, is that it preserves the liberties of the people at the same time as it educates them to their duty as citizens. Hereby it illustrates the republican ideal of good government, since the way to have good and safe government, is not to trust it all to one; but to divide it among the many, distributing to every one exactly the functions he is competent to: *let the National government be entrusted with the defence of the nation, and its foreign and federal relations; the state governments with the civil rights, laws, police and administration of what concerns the state generally;* the counties with the local concerns of the counties; and each Ward direct the interests within itself. It is by dividing and subdividing these republics from the great National one down thro' all its subordinations, until it ends in the administration of every man's farm and affairs by himself; by placing under every one what his own eye may superintend, that all will be done for the best.[24]

For Jefferson, no less than for Lincoln, the ideal of all good government is that it shall be—literally—of the people, by the people, and for the people. "I am not," he declares in a letter to Samuel Kercheval, "among those who fear the people. They, and not the rich, are our dependence for continued freedom." [25] In the wisdom of the people, and in their majorities, we can and must place our trust. "Absolute acquiescence in the decisions of the majority," this is "the vital principle of republics, from which there is no appeal but to force, the vital principle and immediate parent of despotism. . . ." [26] Republicanism, properly defined, is, therefore, that philosophy of government which, rejecting every appeal to force or despotism, accepts the "rightful" will of the "fair" majority as the natural law of every society of reasonable men. However, he would have everyone

bear in mind this sacred principle, that though the will of the majority is in all cases to prevail, that will, to be rightful, must be reasonable; that the minority possess their equal rights, which equal laws must protect, and to violate which would be oppression.[27]

Unfortunately, he nowhere clearly explains how he proposes to reconcile such instances of conflict as must invariably arise between those exercising the natural right of the minority to dissent and those insistent on the equally natural right of the majority to rule. Optimistic to the core, he simply assumes that in all such instances reason and good-will will find a way. That reason's dictates might be ambiguous, or good-will lacking, are eventualities he never seriously considers.

A similar failure to think through the implications of his position is evident in his doctrine of states rights. It is, he feels, entirely consistent with the republican principles of majority rule and equal rights to hold, as he does in his Kentucky Resolutions, that the Federal Government has no right to exercise powers not expressly granted to it by the Constitution. To hold otherwise would, he is sure, conduce to the gradual erosion of liberty and facilitate the rise of despotism. Anything, therefore, that tends to diminish the power of the Federal Government must be in the best interests of the individual. That State which interposes its authority between the citizen and the national power is, therefore, deserving of its people's full support, since its sovereignty is their best guarantee of continued freedom. That the State might ever function to repress the natural rights of its inhabitants is, again, a contingency that Jefferson does not take into account. Nor is he at all concerned about the possibility of conflict between states rights and individual right. Since both are natural rights, he assumes that the interests of the one must ever be the same as those of the other. Convinced that the Federal Union rests upon a compact of the various states, he assumes that this compact is identical in kind with that from which, according to Montesquieu, the state itself originates. Nowhere in his writings does he undertake to examine either assumption in detail. They are, he seems to think, self-evident, and on them he confidently rests his case for states rights.

On this case all subsequent discussion of the matter has built, and there are today many who would rate his doctrine of states rights as his most important contribution to the American Mind. Apparently, however, he himself thought otherwise. In an appendix to his Autobiography, written near the end of his life, he posed to himself this striking question: Is my country the better for my having lived at all? Only Jefferson would have thought to ask it, and he alone would have been so modest in his answer. Through his efforts, he tells us, the Rivanna has been opened to navigation, and he feels that he has made some small contribution to the agricultural arts. He notes his work for religious freedom and against slavery. He mentions his part in securing the abolition of entail in Virginia, and marks his role in securing the inheritance rights of Virginia children. Pridefully, he writes the words—The Declaration of Independence. That is all. Of his contributions to the cause of states rights, he has not a word to say.

SUGGESTED READINGS

The literature on Jefferson is extensive, and hardly a month passes but that some item of significance is added to it. What follows, then, is only a beginning. The best buy for the person who knows nothing of the man or his works is still Koch and Peden, *The Life and Selected Writings of Thomas Jefferson* (New York: Modern Library, 1944). Here, in one inexpensive volume, are the Autobiography, Anas, Notes on Virginia, and all the other major literary and public papers, plus some two hundred and twenty letters to various personages, the whole complete with an Introduction by the editors. The Jeffersonian world of ideas is lucidly portrayed in Daniel J. Boorstin's *The Lost World of Thomas Jefferson* (New York: Holt, 1948). More recent and concrete is Adrienne Koch, *The Philosophy of Thomas Jefferson* (Gloucester, Mass.: Peter Smith, 1957). This is the only book specifically devoted to Jefferson's philosophy, and fortunately it has been well done. Unfortunately, it has not been written with the beginner in philosophy in mind. The author assumes throughout an acquaintance with the thinkers and 'isms she discusses. Good bibliography. Jefferson's religious views are carefully examined by Henry Wilder Foote, *The Religion of Thomas Jefferson* (Boston: Beacon Press, 1947; paperback edition, 1960). Jefferson's posthumous reputation and its influence on American political thought from the 1820's to the 1930's are ably explored in Merrill D. Peterson, *The Jefferson Image in the American Mind* (New York: Oxford University Press, 1960).

There are several biographies. Each of the following has its virtues, and all are readable. Available in paperback are Saul Padover, *Jefferson* (Mentor, paperback, 1952) and Gilbert Chinard, *Thomas Jefferson, The Apostle of Americanism* (Ann Arbor, paperback, 1960). Nathan Schachner, *Thomas Jefferson* (New York: Appleton, 1951), is, as of this writing, in print; Phillips Russell, *Jefferson, champion of the free mind* (New York: Dodd, Mead, 1956), is not, but most libraries will have a copy.

REFERENCES

1. *Notes on Virginia,* viii, p. 314. In Paul Leicester Ford, *The Writings of Thomas Jefferson,* Vol. III (New York: Putnam, 1894), p. 170n.

2. *The Writings of Thomas Jefferson* edited by Albert Ellery Bergh, 20 Vols. (Washington: Jefferson Memorial Association, 1903), XV, pp. 273-74. Hereafter cited as Writings.

3. Adrienne Koch, *The Philosophy of Thomas Jefferson* (Gloucester: Peter Smith, 1957), p. 53. Hereafter cited as Koch.

4. Writings, XV, p. 276.

5. Ibid., p. 240.

6. Ibid., p. 97.

7. Gilbert Chinard (editor), *The Letters of Lafayette and Jefferson* (Baltimore: Johns Hopkins University Press, 1929), p. 397.

8. Writings, II, p. 97.

9. Ibid., VI, pp. 258-61.

10. Ibid., X, p. 380.

11. Ibid., XIII, pp. 389-90.

12. "I am anxious," he writes, "to see the doctrine of one god commenced in our state. But the population of my neighborhood is too slender, and is too much divided into other sects to maintain any one preacher well. I must therefore be contented to be an Unitarian by myself, although I know there are many around me who would become so, if once they could hear the questions fairly stated." Letter to Benjamin Waterhouse, January 8th, 1825; manuscript in the Jefferson Collection, Library of Congress. Reproduced in Koch, p. 27. See also, Henry Wilder Foote, *The Religion of Thomas Jefferson* (Boston: Beacon Press, 1960), pp. 69-76.

13. Writings, XV, p. 203.

14. Ibid., p. 109.

15. Ibid., XVI, p. 118.

16. Carl Becker, *The Declaration of Independence* (New York: Alfred A. Knopf, 1958), p. 25.

17. Writings, XVI, pp. 118-19.

18. Ibid., VII, p. 459.

19. Ibid., XV, p. 43.

20. Ibid., p. 142.

21. Ibid., III, p. 228.

22. Ibid., XV, p. 19.

23. Ibid.

24. Ibid., XIV, p. 420.

25. Ibid., XV, p. 39.

26. Ibid., III, pp. 321-22.

27. Ibid., p. 318.

VIII

The Cast-Iron Southerner

JOHN C. CALHOUN

"Our federal Union—next to our
liberties the most dear! May we all
remember that it can only be preserved
by respecting the rights of the States
and distributing equally the benefit
and burthen of the Union." [1]

JOHN C. CALHOUN

John C. Calhoun

STATES RIGHTS! Of all the slogans that have stirred the American Mind none has had further reaching consequences than this. It has divided North from South. We fought a civil war to settle the issue, and we settled nothing. From Jefferson to Kennedy, States Rights has been debated up and down the land, and it is the perennial tragedy of American politics that on no issue have so many spoken with so much passion about a problem they so little understood. For make no mistake about it, States Rights is not a simple problem. Its ramifications are manifold; it goes straight to the heart of any American's political philosophy. In the intellectual history of our country no one has realized this more clearly than the man who did so much to pose the problem and to call his fellow-Americans to account concerning it—South Carolina's John Caldwell Calhoun.

The English critic, Harriet Martineau, dubbed him the cast-iron man, and cast-iron he was. Born of pioneer stock on the western frontier of Carolina in 1782, he grew up on a farm and tasted democracy as a field hand working with Negro slaves. The Calhoun family prospered, and it was decided that John should study for the law. Off he went to Yale, graduating with high honors in 1804. After three more years of study, eighteen months of it at the Litchfield, Connecticut, Law School, he returned to South Carolina and the practice of law. He really didn't like the law very much, that is, he didn't like the tedium of legal routine although he seems to have enjoyed riding the circuit. In 1808 he was elected to the State Legislature; in 1810, when he was but twenty-eight years old, the voters sent him to Washington and to the U.S. Congress. Henceforth, for forty tumultuous years, first as Congressman, later as Cabinet member and Vice-President, finally as Senator from South Carolina, Calhoun would be a power to reckon with on the national scene.

For the most part, that power would be exerted throughout his career in the interest of the minority, specifically the minority composing the Southern white middle class into which Calhoun was born, and the aristocracy into which he married.[2] It was an interest easily misunderstood, and Calhoun's conception of democracy has often been called in question. Popular democracy, the rule of a mere numerical majority, he opposes, for, he thinks, it must ever end by tyrannizing the minority. On the other hand, the course of history, as he scans it, is replete with instances of coercion of majorities by organized minorities acting in combination. It follows, therefore, that the only true democracy is that which, avoiding dictation by majority or minority, secures the rights of the former and the toleration of the latter. The formula for this true democracy Calhoun thinks to have found in his theory of the concurrent majority. "There are," he contends, "two different modes in which the sense of the community may be taken;

one, simply by the right of suffrage, unaided; the other, by the right through a proper organism. Each collects the sense of the majority. But one regards numbers only, and considers the whole community as a unit, having but one common interest throughout; and collects the sense of the greater number of the whole, as that of the community. The other, on the contrary, regards interests as well as numbers; —considering the community as made up of different and conflicting interests, as far as the action of the government is concerned; and takes the sense of each, through its majority or appropriate organ, and the united sense of all, as the sense of the entire community. The former of these I shall call the numerical, or absolute majority; and the latter, the concurrent, or constitutional majority.[3]

"Constitutional" because, Calhoun believes, the concurrent rather than the numerical majority is what the Founding Fathers had in mind in setting up our Constitution as a system of checks and balances. And properly so, since only thus is the interest of the minority protected while the right of the majority is secured. Take, for example, the issue of school integration. In a community governed according to the dictates of popular (numerical) democracy, if an absolute majority of all the citizens favor integration, integration must become the rule of the community. However, in a community governed by the will of the concurrent majority, integration would become the rule only if a majority in each of the several interests involved [4] (such as Negroes, whites, teachers, parents, property-owners, business men, other racial groups, etc.), plus a majority of all these interests combined, were to be obtained. Not a mere majority, but a majority of majorities would be required in order to impose integration on the community. And what is true with regard to any particular issue in any specific community is, Calhoun argues, true also as regards general issues concerning the community of these United States. Thus the imposition of any law directed against a single region such as the South, or against a single interest such as that of the whites, would on Calhoun's theory require such a large majority as to render it extremely unlikely that any such law could ever be democratically imposed.

Nonetheless, it is not impossible, and because it is not, the theory of the concurrent majority must be buttressed by the doctrine of States Rights, i.e., the notion that each of the States has sovereign power over its own internal affairs. Doctrine and theory alike, in Calhoun's view, find their ultimate justification in the Declaration of Independence and in the Constitution. The former teaches us that all men have the right to life, liberty, and the pursuit of happiness, and this right is prior to any duty enjoined by government, it takes precedence over any tyranny of the majority, it is alienable. The latter declares that any rights not expressly delegated to the federal government are reserved to the several states. The problem lies in determining the precise extent of these rights reserved. Just what rights does a state have?

Historically, the answer to the question has tended to take the form of an interpretation of the relation between the several states and the federal government. Thus Jefferson in the Kentucky Resolutions of 1798 argues that the Constitution is only a compact between the states, and this being so the right of decision in all issues of constitutionality is reserved to the states. This compact theory is spelled out in detail by Jefferson's disciple, John Taylor of Caroline.

As he sees it, each state in entering into the compact reserves to itself various rights which the federal government cannot and must not abrogate. The rights of property, the rights of the individual, the right to live in accord with the traditions of one's local society, all are rights of the states and they cannot be, nor have they been, surrendered in the act of compact. Yet, what if the relation of the state to the federal power is not of the nature of a compact? The compact theory has been widely challenged. It rests on a somewhat arbitrary interpretation of a not unambiguous passage in the Constitution. Most important, it seems more to describe the relation envisaged by the repudiated Articles of Confederation than that proclaimed in the Tenth Amendment. In light of these difficulties, it is necessary, Calhoun feels, to examine somewhat more closely the ideas of government occupying the minds of the authors of the Constitution.

There are, he contends, three such ideas that must be distinguished. The first of these is what Calhoun calls "confederation," that is to say, a compact made by ambassadors of sovereign states and dissolvable at will. This was the sort of government we had originally under the Articles of Confederation. Each of the states being sovereign, each having the right to withdraw at its pleasure, the Confederation was at will—dissolvable. And that is the important thing. At the opposite pole from this very loose idea of confederation, which was very early in our history found totally inadequate as a means of safeguarding the interests of the united states, is national government. This, as Calhoun defines it, is government in which each single state is subject to the central national agency. Properly speaking, the state in this form of national government is, Calhoun insists, a state in name only. For the very word "state" implies sovereignty. Therefore, if you deny the sovereignty of the state, as under a national government you do, you must end by denying the state itself. This conception and this result Calhoun associates with the Federalists. They aimed at a compound of national and federal, but they ended with a government solely national because to their way of thinking a national government alone can survive. As Franklin punningly put it, "either we hang together or we hang separately." Because they thought that, the makers of the Constitution oscillated from a concern for the rights of individuals to a care for the safety of the nation, but they never really came to rest with either. And there the trouble lies. The third idea of government is federal union. It is, basically, the combination of the first two, and according to Calhoun it is that form which is really represented in our Constitution. Federal Union, to Calhoun, means separate sovereign states united through a central agency: "federal" in that the states are sovereign; "union" in that they are gathered into a central agency with certain specific powers. The key point is that the states are sovereign.

> Ours is a union, not of individuals, united by what is called a social compact—for that would make it a nation; nor of governments—for that would have formed a confederacy, like the one superseded by the present constitution; but a union of States, founded on a written, positive compact, forming a Federal Republic, with the same equality of rights among the States composing the Union, as among the citizens composing the States themselves. Instead of a nation, we are in reality an assemblage of nations, or peoples . . . united in their sovereign character immediately and directly by their own act, but without losing their separate and independent existence.[5]

From this conclusion the right of each state to safeguard its particular sovereignty necessarily follows. In effect, this means the right of Nullification, the right, that is, of the states to repudiate any federal statute they deem inimical to their own best interests. In Calhoun's South Carolina the great issue in 1832 was the tariff. The North wanted it. Its industries needed protection. The South didn't want it. It was bad for the cotton market. Faced with economic disaster as a result of the passage of the tariff act, South Carolina called a constitutional convention and passed an ordinance of nullification designed to prevent the collection of customs duties within the State. President Jackson promptly issued a proclamation threatening the use of Federal troops to enforce collection. Adroit political maneuvering by Senator Calhoun effected a temporary compromise, but the price was the passage by Congress of Jackson's Force Bill authorizing the President to use military force, if necessary, to forestall any nullification of Federal law. South Carolina immediately passed a second ordinance of nullification, this one nullifying the Force Bill. The legal stage was set for civil war.

In such a situation, if neither party backs down, Nullification must lead to Secession, i.e., the withdrawal by the State from the Federal partnership. Now Calhoun himself doesn't think that it ever need come to that, although he does insist that in any system of federal union each sovereign state always retains the prerogative of secession. Rather is he convinced that Nullification is a sufficient legal means of securing equity, for Nullification, as he interprets it, is but the necessary first step in the process of bringing about constitutional amendment, and this process, operative in a democracy ruled by concurrent majority, must, he believes, suffice to resolve any issue arising between the States and the Federal Union. And in his time it did suffice.

In the meantime, the basic issue—slavery—continued unresolved. The South could not abandon an institution whose property value Calhoun himself computed to be nine hundred and fifty million dollars. The North, even as it recognized the economic necessity of slavery, found it morally intolerable. As in all such impasse situations, so too in this one, economic necessity bred moral justification. Thus the necessary evil becomes in Calhoun's public pronouncements after 1836—the positive good. The basic premise by which this conclusion is attained is the natural inferiority of the Negro race. "In the whole history of man," Calhoun argues, "there is no instance whatever of any civilized colored race, of any shade, being found equal to the establishment and maintenance of free government." [6] Like Aristotle, he believes that some men are slaves by nature, just as other men are naturally free. For the shibboleth that all men are born equal he has only scorn.

Taking the proposition literally (it is in that sense it is understood), there is not a word of truth in it. It begins with "all men are born," whch is utterly untrue. Men are not born. Infants are born. They grow to be men. And concludes with asserting that they are born "free and equal," which is not less false. They are not born free. While infants they are incapable of freedom, being destitute alike of the capacity of thinking and acting, without which there can be no freedom. Besides, they are necessarily born subject to their parents, and remain so among all people, savage and civilized, until the development of their intellect and physical capacity enables them to take care of themselves. They grow to all the freedom, of which the condition in which they were born permits, by growing to be men. Nor is it less false that they are born "equal." They are not so in any sense in which it can be regarded; and thus, as I have asserted, there is not a word of truth in the whole proposition, as expressed and generally understood.

If we trace it back, we shall find the proposition differently expressed in the Declaration of Independence. That asserts that "all men are created equal." The form of expression, though less dangerous, is not less erroneous. All men are not created. According to the Bible, only two—a man and a woman—ever were—and of these one was pronounced subordinate to the other. All others have come into the world by being born, and in no sense, as I have shown, either free or equal.[7]

It is, therefore,

a great and dangerous error to suppose that all people are equally entitled to liberty. It is a reward to be earned, not a blessing to be gratuitously lavished on all alike;—a reward reserved for the intelligent, the patriotic, the virtuous and deserving;—and not a boon to be bestowed on a people too ignorant, degraded and vicious, to be capable either of appreciating or of enjoying it.[8]

You may not agree. Still, in the light of current events in Africa and the American South, you must, I think, concede the contemporary relevance of Calhoun's views. States Rights has become civil rights, the slave has been replaced by the second-class citizen, but otherwise the issue is unchanged. Calhoun's ideas, now as much as when he wrote them down one hundred and eleven years ago, are dynamite.

SUGGESTED READINGS

The least expensive and most readily available edition of Calhoun is C. Gordon Post, *John C. Calhoun, A Disquisition on Government and Selections from the Discourse* (New York: Liberal Arts Press, paperback, 1953). Professor Post's Introduction makes clear Calhoun's relation to the issues of his time and ours. Complete with chronology and selected bibliography. John M. Anderson (editor), *Calhoun: Basic Documents* (State College, Pa.: Bald Eagle Press, 1952), contains *A Disquisition on Government*, plus eleven representative speeches from all stages of Calhoun's career. Pedestrian is the word for August O. Spain's *The Political Theory of John C. Calhoun* (New York: Bookman Associates, 1951), although all the basic ideas are adequately covered, and there is a bibliography. The most recent and balanced of the twentieth century biographies is Gerald Capers, *John C. Calhoun —Opportunist, A Reappraisal* (Gainesville: University of Florida Press, 1960). Good bibliography. Charles M. Wiltse, *John C. Calhoun,* 3 Vols. (Indianapolis: Bobbs-Merrill, 1944-51), is a major scholarly achievement marred by special pleading and right-wing bias. Arthur Styron, *The Cast Iron Man: John C. Calhoun and American Democracy* (New York: Longmans, 1935), is as much a portrait of the age as of the man. Regrettably, the most widely read study of Calhoun's life, Margaret L. Coit's *John C. Calhoun, American Portrait* (Boston: Houghton Mifflin, 1950), is, from the standpoint of scholarship, inadequate. Mrs. Coit over-dramatizes her subject's life and underestimates her reader's intelligence. Worse still, she manages in some mysterious way to make the issues and events of Calhoun's life rather less colorful than they actually were.

REFERENCES

1. Quoted in Gerald M. Capers, *John C. Calhoun—Opportunist, A Reappraisal* (Gainesville: University of Florida Press, 1960), p. 127.

2. In 1811 Calhoun married his second cousin, Floride Bonneau, the wealthy heiress of Bonneau Plantation near Charleston. His pride prohibited him from accepting any marriage settlement, but it did not hinder his circulation in the aristocratic Charleston circles to which his marriage gave him entrée.

3. *The Works of John C. Calhoun* in 6 volumes, edited by Richard K. Cralle (Charleston, 1851-1857), I, p. 28. Hereafter cited as Works.

4. In those cases where one individual might represent several interests (for instance, a white teacher who was also a parent and a property-holder), presumably he would cast a vote for each of the interests he represented.

5. Works, IV, pp. 80-81.

6. Ibid., p. 411.

7. Ibid., pp. 507-8.

8. Ibid., I, p. 55.

IX

Prophet Out of Concord

RALPH WALDO EMERSON

"Do not craze yourself with thinking,
but go about your business anywhere.
Life is not intellectual or critical,
but sturdy. Its chief good is for
well-mixed people who can enjoy what
they find, without question. . . .
If we will take the good we find,
asking no questions, we shall have
heaping measures. The great gifts
are not got by analysis. Everything good is on the highway." [1]

RALPH WALDO EMERSON

Ralph Waldo Emerson

FOR ALL THAT WE ARE not noted among the peoples of the earth for our contributions to the spread of culture, there is one intellectual institution which we have pioneered and developed into something distinctively American, and that institution is—the lyceum. Nowadays, what with television and radio making possible instant communication with millions, the lyceum takes somewhat of a back seat. But all through the Nineteenth Century it was the cultural and social center of every community, large or small. To it, the great men of the day, politicians, poets, philosophers, reformers, and literati of all sorts, came to speak their piece, preach, or entertain. It made some of them famous, and a few rich; for others it was just a living, and not a very easy one at that. In its heyday it was the chief instrument for shaping the American Mind, and it was so used by many of its most illustrious ornaments.

Among these, none stood higher than, and few equalled, Ralph Waldo Emerson. For nearly forty years he traveled about America, from Boston to St. Louis, "emptying his decanters and demijohns of popular wisdom" into the minds of all who would pay to listen. His books grew out of his lectures, and the lectures made a market for the books, which in turn made him famous and led to still more lyceum engagements. Unfortunately, for all his popularity and skill as a lecturer, he was much too poor a businessman to grow wealthy at it. In any case, money wasn't his prime motive. He enjoyed traveling; he felt that he was doing good by educating the masses; and there was always enough coming in to enable him to live comfortably in Concord. He wanted nothing more; there was, he thought, nothing more worth wanting.

Emerson was just thirty when he gave his first lyceum lecture. Its title was "The Uses of Natural History"; the theme was Nature as "a metaphor or image of the human mind," and the audience was reported as being highly gratified by the lecturer's remarks. Whether they understood them is another matter; for even this earliest of his essays abounds in phrases of oracular obscurity, i.e.,

> The world is emblematic. Parts of speech are metaphors, because the whole of nature is a metaphor of the human mind. The laws of moral nature answer to those of matter as face to face in a glass. "The visible world and the relation of its parts, is the dial plate of the invisible." The axioms of physics translate the laws of ethics.[2]

Is he saying that mind alone is real, and that what we call nature is merely its appearance? Is he, then, an absolute idealist?—understanding by this phrase one who believes that the rational alone is real, and that this real is of the nature of a cosmic mind or consciousness whose adventures are the evolution of this universe. The passage seems to lend itself to such interpretation, and Emerson does suggest in a subsequent chapter of *Nature* that he who has never doubted the existence of matter has yet to reach the age of reason. On the other hand, in his essay on Plato, he reluctantly concedes that philosophy, and Plato for him is philosophy, can never really explain nature away. The universe resists dismissal as image or illusion; nature will not be disposed of. "No power of genius has ever yet had the smallest success in explaining existence. The perfect enigma remains."[3] Nature is real, for all that it is a metaphor of mind.

In nature, moral law and physics meet face to face. Does Emerson mean by this that all things are ensouled? Is matter panpsychic? There are in *Nature* several statements which appear to imply as much. "Every natural process," he tells us, "is a version of a moral sentence. The moral law lies at the centre of nature and radiates to the circumference. It is the pith and marrow of every substance, every relation, and every process."[4] "Nature," he insists, "is not fixed but fluid. Spirit alters, moulds, makes it."[5] "All things

are moral; and in their boundless changes have an unceasing reference to spiritual nature."

> Therefore is nature glorious with form, color, and motion; that every
> globe in the remotest heaven, every chemical change from the rudest
> crystal up to the laws of life, every change of vegetation from the
> first principle of growth in the eye of a leaf, to the tropical forest and
> antediluvian coal-mine, every animal function from the sponge up
> to Hercules, shall hint or thunder to man the laws of right and wrong,
> and echo the Ten Commandments.[6]

Yet here, as before, Emerson shies away from any concrete commitment. That all things are ensouled, he will not come right out
and say. There is, he thinks, a "bruteness," an "immobility," about
nature that no spirit can dissolve.

Emerson's philosophy is not, then, absolute idealism, nor yet
panpsychism, even though it bears a strong resemblance to both.
Is it, perhaps, pantheism? There is a famous passage in the first
chapter of *Nature,* to which those who would make him out to be
a pantheist always refer. He has been talking about the "wild
delight" of walking under the open sky, and of the feeling of
"sanctity" that comes upon him when he is alone in the woods.
Then he has this to say:

> Standing on the bare ground—my head bathed by the blithe air and
> uplifted into infinite space—all mean egotism vanishes. I become a
> transparent eyeball; I am nothing; I see all; the currents of the
> Universal Being circulate through me; I am part or parcel of God.[7]

Does he intend that we shall take him at his word—literally? I
believe that he does not. Nowhere in his writings is there any plain
equation of the universe with God. That the universe testifies to
God, he clearly believes; that it is "a remoter and inferior in-
carnation of God, a projection in the unconscious," [8] he specifically
states; but that it *is* God, he will not admit. How, then, is it that
he has been so often damned for a pantheist?

The answer is, I suggest, twofold. First of all, Emerson is a
mystic. To be sure, his mysticism is always of this world; the
practical Yankee is always there behind the dreamer; but a mystic

he is, and about that hardly any critic has been disposed to argue. Moreover, he is a poet, with a poet's manner of expressing his thoughts, and this despite the fact that he writes in prose. From such people, linguistic precision is not to be expected. Poetry plus mysticism adds up to hyperbole and fosters misinterpretation. Second, and most important, Emerson was an apostate, and all his life he had to bear the disapproval of the Unitarian orthodox for having given up his pulpit. To them it mattered not that he remained a profoundly religious man, one whose every published thought reflected this lifelong awareness of, and reverence for, the divine. He had renounced his ministry, and that, in their eyes, was enough to damn him. If his life and works gave the lie to the charge of atheism, then he must be a pantheist. So the Boston brahmins reasoned, and their difficulty in following his poetic flights of fancy served only to confirm their fears.

The trouble was that there were in the 1830's no words in the philosophical lexicon to describe the sort of thing that Emerson was proposing in *Nature*. Today we should call him an existentialist; for himself he preferred the name "transcendentalist," and when we understand what he meant by that, we shall, perhaps, be better equipped to interpret the philosophy of *Nature*.

In his essay, The Transcendentalist, he defines the term briefly thus: "What is popularly called Transcendentalism among us, is Idealism; Idealism as it appears in 1842." [9] And what is Idealism in 1842? To Emerson it is faith in the spiritual character of events:

> The Transcendentalist adopts the whole connection of spiritual doctrine. He believes in miracle, in the perpetual openness of the human mind to new influx of light and power; he believes in inspiration, and in ecstasy. He wishes that the spiritual principle should be suffered to demonstrate itself to the end, in all possible applications to the state of man, without the admission of anything unspiritual; that is, anything positive, dogmatic, personal. Thus the spiritual measure of inspiration is the depth of the thought, and never, who said it? And so he resists all attempts to palm other rules and measures on the spirit than its own. [10]

Why, he had asked in his Introduction to *Nature*, "Why should not we also enjoy an original relation to the universe? Why should not we have a poetry and philosophy of insight and not of tradition, and a religion by revelation to us, and not the history of theirs?" [11] What had they that we have not? Only this: the sense of being permeated by spirit; the joy of being alive to nature; and these we to can have.

> Know then that the world exists for you. For you is the phenomenon perfect. What we are, that only can we see. All that Adam had, all that Caesar could, you have and can do. Adam called his house, heaven and earth; Caesar called his house, Rome; you perhaps call yours, a cobbler's trade; a hundred acres of ploughed land; or a scholar's garret. Yet line for line and point for point your dominion is as great as theirs, though without fine names. Build therefore your own world. As fast as you conform your life to the pure idea in your mind, that will unfold its great proportions.[12]

That this "pure idea" was there in mind waiting to be unfolded, Emerson believed Kant to have shown. But whereas Kant had equated the pure idea with the structure of the knowing mind itself, Emerson identified it with instinct (intuition), and thought of it as a mysterious spiritual something in man answering to spirit in nature. In brief, mind in man answers to matter in nature because spirit permeates both. The axioms of physics translate the laws of ethics because in both mind is married to matter. That this is so, your own experience must prove; it cannot be demonstrated otherwise. "Shall we say then that Transcendentalism is the Saturnalia of faith; the presentiment of a faith proper to man in his integrity, excessive only when his imperfect obedience hinders the satisfaction of his wish?" Emerson answers—yes.

II

The American Scholar is Emerson's most famous lecture. Oliver Wendell Holmes Senior called it "our intellectual Declaration of Independence," and subsequent generations have echoed his estimate. With this oration, the American Mind comes of age. Emerson's theme was nothing new; others before him had urged the development of an American literature conceived in independence of "the courtly muses of Europe." The newness lay rather in his realization that any such development must presuppose the coming of a new breed of scholars. As Emerson sees him, the man of this breed will be, first of all, creative, *Man Thinking* rather than man absorbing and regurgitating other men's thoughts. He will not forget that his great European predecessors were only young men in libraries when they wrote their books; he will not be subdued by his instruments or pinned down by the past. Nor will he shut himself away from men, refusing the lessons of life.

> There goes in the world a notion that the scholar should be a recluse, a valetudinarian—as unfit for any handiwork or public labor as a penknife for an axe. The so-called "practical men" sneer at speculative men, as if, because they speculate or *see,* they could do nothing. . . . As far as this is true of the studious classes, it is not just and wise. Action is with the scholar subordinate, but it is essential. Without it he is not yet man. Without it thought can never ripen into truth. Whilst the world hangs before the eye as a cloud of beauty, we cannot even see its beauty. Inaction is cowardice, but there can be no scholar without the heroic mind. The preamble of thought, the transition through which it passes from the unconscious to the conscious, is action. Only so much do I know, as I have lived. . . . A great soul will be strong to live, as well as strong to think.[13]

In the final analysis, for Emerson character counts more than intellect. "Thinking is the function. Living is the functionary." [14] Perhaps so, but in his zeal for living, Emerson here comes dangerously close to saying that the objectives of scholarship are no more and none other than those of the more abundant life; and this is a viewpoint which, in practice, must end with the death of scholarship—understood as the pursuit of truth for its own sake. To verify this, we need only to reflect upon the American scholar in our own day. All that Emerson asks, he is: he lends his skills to the production of marvels of engineering ingenuity; through his efforts we live, as he lives, well. Of course, as a pure scientist he leaves much to be desired. Most often, when it is a question of basic research, we have found it necessary to rely on European scholars of less character than intellect. God grant they may remain in good supply for so long as it takes us to learn that intellect counts more than character when the stake is the survival of society.

In justice to Emerson, it should be noted that he does not seek to force his pragmatic vision of the role of the American scholar on the academic community. Unlike his great admirer, John Dewey, he has no program of reform to press upon our educational system. Indeed, it is most probable that he would be shocked by the present state of American scholarship, and, I suspect, he would wish no part of a system which, far from encouraging his beloved self-reliance, subordinates it to the interests of material prosperity. Here, as in *Nature,* Emerson is riding two divergent horses, and is blinded to the realization of it by the brilliance of his own prose. As before with mind and matter, so now with living and scholarship, he assumes a unity and compatibility that may not, in truth, exist.

III

For a year Emerson enjoyed the reputation The American Scholar had earned him. His lectures on Human Culture, given at Boston during the winter of 1837-38, were a fiscal as well as a literary success; at home in Concord he worked in his garden and basked in the admiration of his neighbors. It was a happy time, and yet, at the back of his mind, he was troubled. His journal for the period reveals his growing disenchantment with religious orthodoxy. He thought the moment near when he must "sit and think and then write a discourse to the American clergy, showing them the ugliness and unprofitableness of theology and churches at this day, and the glory and sweetness of the moral nature out of whose pale they are almost wholly shut." [15] Three days later he was to note that the moment had come in the form of an invitation from the half-dozen seniors of the Harvard Divinity School to deliver "the customary discourse, on occasion of their entering upon the active Christian ministry." And so, one Sunday evening in July of 1838 he went up to Cambridge prepared to challenge the preachers on their home ground.

His beginning was not calculated to offend the sensibilities of the orthodox. He remarked the beauties of the summer season, paid tribute to the inquiring nature of the human spirit, and recommended to them the sentiment of virtue. His definition of this sentiment as "a reverence and delight in the presence of certain divine laws" would have struck them as nothing strange. Perhaps it was stretching the moral aspect a trifle far to claim, as Emerson now did, that this sentiment was the essence of all religion; but even this was well within the Unitarian tradition. The implications that Emerson drew from his "sentiment of virtue" were, however, quite another matter. For as he continued his remarks, it gradually became plain to all that he regarded the intuition of this sentiment as the only true revelation of God to man. By means of it, man comes to know himself as grounded in spirit; in spirit he is united to God. The point was, that all of this must be at first hand.

> Truly speaking, it is not instruction, but provocation, that I can receive from another soul. What he announces, I must find true in me, or reject; and on his word, or as his second, be he who he may, I can accept nothing. On the contrary, the absence of this primary faith is the presence of degradation. As is the flood, so is the ebb. Let this faith depart, and the very words it spake and the things it made become false and hurtful. Then falls the church, the state, art, letters, life. The doctrine of the divine nature being forgotten, a sickness infects and dwarfs the constitution. Once man was all; now he is an appendage, a nuisance. And because the indwelling Supreme Spirit cannot wholly be got rid of, the doctrine of it suffers this perversion, that the divine nature is attributed to one or two persons, and denied to all the rest, and denied with fury. The doctrine of inspiration is lost; the base doctrine of the majority of voices usurps the place of the doctrine of the soul. Miracles, prophecy, poetry, the ideal life, the holy life, exist as ancient history merely; they are not in the belief, nor in the aspiration of society; but, when suggested, seem ridiculous. Life is comic or pitiful as soon as the high ends of being fade out of sight, and man becomes near-sighted, and can only attend to what addresses the senses.[16]

By now the clergy in his audience were definitely uncomfortable; even so, had he stopped here, all might have been well. But relentlessly the thesis is pressed to its, by now obvious, conclusion. The true Christian finds his provocation to virtue in the life of the *man* Jesus; but from the *god* Christ he can gain nothing, for none such exists.

Historical Christianity has fallen into the error that corrupts all attempts to communicate religion. As it appears to us, and as it has appeared for ages, it is not the doctrine of the soul, but an exaggeration of the personal, the positive, the ritual. It has dwelt, it dwells, with noxious exaggeration about the *person* of Jesus. The soul knows no persons. It invites every man to expand to the full circle of the universe, and will have no preferences but those of spontaneous love. But by this eastern monarchy of a Christianity which indolence and fear have built, the friend of man is made the injurer of man. The manner in which his name is surrounded with expressions which were once sallies of admiration and love, but are now petrified into official titles, kills all generous sympathy and liking. All who hear me, feel that the language that describes Christ to Europe and America is not the style of friendship and enthusiasm to a good and noble heart, but is appropriated and formal—paints a demi-god, as the Orientals or the Greeks would describe Osiris or Apollo. Accept the injurious impositions of our early catechetical instruction, and even honesty and self-denial were but splendid sins, if they did not wear the Christian name. One would rather be

"A pagan, suckled in a creed outworn,"

than to be defrauded of his manly right in coming into nature and finding not names and places, not land and professions, but even virtue and truth foreclosed and monopolized. You shall not be a man even. You shall not own the world; you shall not dare and live after the infinite Law that is in you, and in company with the infinite Beauty which heaven and earth reflect to you in all lovely forms; but you must subordinate your nature to Christ's nature; you must accept our interpretations, and take his portrait as the vulgar draw it.[17]

To his clerical hearers, this was heresy! It was not so much that he denied the divinity of Christ; after all, that was something every good Unitarian denied. It was rather that what he asserted, if taken seriously, must lead to a denial of the Church itself! Here was a man, himself an ordained minister and preacher in good standing, admonishing candidates for ordination

to go alone; to refuse the good models, even those which are sacred in the imagination of men, and dare to love God without mediator or veil.[18]

Here was a man, himself a son of Unitarian Harvard, telling Harvard seminarians in chapel that

> the prayers and even the dogmas of our church are like the zodiac of Denderah and the astronomical monuments of the Hindoos, wholly insulated from anything now extant in the life and business of the people.[19]

They would, he firmly believed, be better advised to cast conformity behind them, and acquaint men at first hand with Deity.

> Look to it first and only, that fashion, custom, authority, pleasure, and money, are nothing to you—are not bandages over your eyes, that you cannot see—but live with the privilege of the immeasurable mind.[20]

He would have them aware always that

> The spirit only can teach. Not any profane man, not any sensual, not any liar, not any slave can teach, but only he can give, who has; he only can create, who is. The man on whom the soul descends, through whom the soul speaks, alone can teach. Courage, piety, love, wisdom, can teach; and every man can open his door to these angels, and they shall bring him the gift of tongues. But the man who aims to speak as books enable, as synods use, as the fashion guides, and as interest commands, babbles. Let him hush.[21]

This was advice most of those present could not take, and would not tolerate. The clergy united in condemning Emerson. The leading Unitarian periodical, *The Christian Examiner,* took care to reassure its readers that the lecturer's views, "so far as they are intelligible, are utterly distasteful to the instructors of the School, and to Unitarian ministers generally, by whom they are esteemed to be neither good divinity nor good sense." [22] Orthodoxy, under the leadership of the "hard-headed Unitarian Pope," Andrews Norton, castigated this "latest form of infidelity." Emerson's name was linked anew with that of the blasphemer, Abner Kneeland, and conservative Bostonians were now taught "to abhor and abominate R. W. Emerson as a sort of mad dog."

Not all, however, were against him. Elizabeth Peabody declared herself "enraptured." Theodore Parker found in the lecture a mandate for theological reform, and was inspired to carry his own speculations beyond Unitarianism. In general, the transcendentally inclined rejoiced that they had found a new prophet.

The prophet himself, however, was not so sanguine. Disillusioned by the reception accorded his lecture, he retired to Concord and refused any further role in the debate his views had aroused. His career as a preacher was almost at its end.[23] Henceforward, his profession would be that of author and lyceum lecturer; but for the present, he would be silent.

IV

In 1841 appeared *Essays, First Series; Essays, Second Series* followed in 1844. On these two collections of revised lectures, Emerson's reputation as a philosopher largely rests. In them, the ideas previously thrown out at random in *Nature* and the two Addresses are organized into some semblance of unity, and the whole developed with considerable care. He was striving, so he wrote, "to spin some single cord out of my thousand and one strands of every color and texture." This "single cord," twisting through every essay, is the freedom of each of us to believe his own thoughts and make his own life. "Every mind must know the whole lesson for itself—must go over the whole ground. What it does not see, what it does not live, it will not know." [24] "Civil and natural history, the history of art and of literature, must," he tells us in the first of his essays, "be explained from individual history, or must remain words. There is nothing but is related to us, nothing that does not interest us—kingdom, college, tree, horse, or iron shoe—the roots of all things are in man. . . . The true poem is the poet's mind; the true ship is the shipbuilder." [25]

In all American literature there is no clearer, or better known, expression of this individualism than *Self-Reliance*. Into this essay Emerson pours his soul; it is, without doubt, the most existential of all his works. Like his great contemporary, Kierkegaard, his root assumption is that truth is subjectivity.

To believe your own thought, to believe that what is true for you in your private heart is true for all men—that is genius. Speak your latent conviction, and it shall be the universal sense; for the inmost in due time becomes the outmost. . . . Trust thyself: every heart vibrates to that iron string.[26]

So he believes, and is not afraid to face down the scorn of coldly logical men.

A foolish consistency is the hobgoblin of little minds, adored by little statesmen and philosophers and divines. With consistency a great soul has simply nothing to do. He may as well concern himself with his shadow on the wall. Speak what you think now in hard words and to-morrow speak what to-morrow thinks in hard words again, though it contradict every thing you said to-day.—'Ah, so you shall be sure to be misunderstood.'—Is it so bad then to be misunderstood? Pythagoras was misunderstood, and Socrates, and Jesus, and Luther, and Copernicus, and Galileo, and Newton, and every pure and wise spirit that ever took flesh. To be great is to be misunderstood.[27]

Be, then, confident of your greatness. "Absolve you to yourself, and you shall have the suffrage of the world." [28] It would be easy to misinterpret such advice. Taken in isolation, such statements have the ring of egomania. Even so, Emerson is no egomaniac nor megalomaniac either, but rather a man who finds it absolutely necessary to overstate his case: how otherwise shall the complacent American be awakened to his maverick heritage? Are you not a non-conformist? Then, he thinks, are you hardly a man. For what is a man if not sweat and spirit hacking out new paths into the jungle of the future. "Whoso would be a man, must be a non-conformist. He who would gather immortal palms must not be hindered by the name of goodness, but must explore if it be goodness." [29] Too often in our country has goodness justified conformity. "I am," confesses Emerson,

ashamed to think how easily we capitulate to badges and names, to large societies and dead institutions. Every decent and well-spoken individual affects and sways me more than is right. I ought to go upright and vital, and speak the rude truth in all ways. If malice and vanity wear the coat of philanthropy, shall that pass? If an angry bigot assumes this bountiful cause of Abolition, and comes to me with his last news from Barbadoes, why should I not say to him, "go love thy infant; love thy wood-chopper; be good-natured and modest; have that grace; and never varnish your hard, uncharitable ambition with this incredible tenderness for black folk a thousand miles off. Thy love afar is spite at home." Rough and graceless would be such greeting, but truth is handsomer than the affectation of love. Your goodness must have some edge to it—else it is none.[30]

That Emerson's own goodness had an edge to it, Daniel Webster could well testify. Few great men have had their moral shortcomings so ruthlessly exposed as were Webster's in Emerson's address on the Fugitive Slave Law. In vain might Webster protest that his course alone could save the Union; to Emerson he was only a man who for all his large understanding "had not what is better than intellect, and the source of its health." [31] For his own part, Emerson would put his trust in his moral intuition:

If slavery is good, then is lying, theft, arson, homicide, each and all good, and to be maintained by Union societies.

These things show that no forms, neither constitutions, nor laws, nor covenants, nor churches, nor bibles, are of any use in themselves. The Devil nestles comfortably into them all. There is no help but in the head and heart and hamstrings of a man. Covenants are of no use without honest men to keep them; laws of none but with loyal citizens to obey them. To interpret Christ it needs Christ in the heart. The teachings of the Spirit can be apprehended only by the same spirit that gave them forth.[32]

Withal, some there are who more than others have the gift of spiritual interpretation. These, for Emerson, are the poets, the readers of the handwriting on the walls of that temple which is the world. Among partial men they stand for the complete man; for it is they who are the Sayers, the Namers, and the Language-Makers.

The world being thus put under the mind for verb and noun, the poet is he who can articulate it. For though life is great, and fascinates and absorbs; and though all men are intelligent of the symbols through which it is named; yet they cannot originally use them. We are symbols and inhabit symbols; workmen, work, and tools, words and things, birth and death, all are emblems; but we sympathize with the symbols, and being infatuated with the economical uses of things, we do not know that they are thoughts. The poet, by an ulterior intellectual perception, gives them a power which makes their old use forgotten, and puts eyes and a tongue into every dumb and inanimate object. He perceives the independence of the thought on the symbol, the stability of the thought, the accidency and fugacity of the symbol. As the eyes of Lyncaeus were said to see through the earth, so the poet turns the world to glass, and shows us all things in their right series and procession.[33]

That men of such capacity are very rare, Emerson well knows. Not every man who claims the title "Poet" is worthy of the name. Indeed, if Emerson is to be believed, none so deserving has yet appeared on the shores of America.

I look in vain for the poet whom I describe. We do not with sufficient plainness or sufficient profoundness address ourselves to life, nor dare we chaunt our own times and social circumstance. . . . We have yet had no genius in America, with tyrannous eye, which knew the value of our incomparable materials, and saw, in the barbarism and materialism of the times, another carnival of the same gods whose picture he so much admires in Homer; then in the Middle Age; then in Calvinism. . . . Our log-rolling, our stumps and their politics, our fisheries, our Negroes and Indians, our boats and our repudiations, the wrath of rogues and the pusillanimity of honest men, the northern trade, the southern planting, the western clearing, Oregon and Texas, are yet unsung. Yet America is a poem in our eyes; its ample geography dazzles the imagination, and it will not wait long for metres.[34]

It was his truest prophecy. Twelve years later he would hail Walt Whitman's *Leaves of Grass* as *the* American poem; all unaware that it was his own thought that had brought the simmering poet to the boil. Nor was the solitary singer alone his spiritual debtor. Whittier, Lowell, Holmes Senior and Junior, Emily Dickinson, and Robert Frost, all publicized their owing. Parker, Peirce, James, and Dewey, all later found in Emerson's work their philosophic inspiration. His greatest disciple, however, was none of these, but rather his friend and neighbor, Henry David Thoreau, the one man in Concord, or in America, who really tried to live the life the prophet merely preached.

SUGGESTED READINGS

The best, and least expensive, one-volume introduction to Emerson is Brooks Atkinson, *The Complete Essays and Other Writings of Ralph Waldo Emerson* (New York: Modern Library, 1950). Introduction and short reading list by the editor. Frederic Carpenter, *Emerson Handbook* (New York: Hendricks House, 1953), offers a valuable synopsis of Emerson's life, works, ideas, and place in world literature. Detailed bibliography. The most recent biography is Ralph Rusk's, *The Life of Ralph Waldo Emerson* (New York: Scribner, 1949). Comprehensive and scholarly in tone, although the organization of the material leaves something to be desired. Stephen E. Whicher, *Freedom and Fate, An Inner Life of Ralph Waldo Emerson* (Philadelphia: University of Pennsylvania Press, 1953), limits himself to the exploration of the development of Emerson's mind, but does a good job of interpreting its many facets. Includes a chronology of the outer life. Sherman Paul, *Emerson's Angle of Vision* (Cambridge: Harvard University Press, 1952), is portentous and pretentious, but behind the verbiage lie ideas worth pondering.

REFERENCES

1. "Experience," in *The Complete Works of Ralph Waldo Emerson* with a biographical Introduction and Notes by Edward Waldo Emerson (Centenary Edition), 12 Vols. (Boston: Houghton Mifflin, 1903), III, pp. 59, 62. Hereafter cited as Works.

2. "Nature," Works, I, pp. 32-33.

3. "Plato; or, The Philosopher," Works, IV, p. 78.

4. Works, I, pp. 41-2.

5. Ibid., p. 76.

6. Ibid., pp. 40-41.

7. Ibid., p. 10.

8. Ibid., pp. 64-65. This may be what Emerson means by his notion of the "Over-Soul." "May," because his descriptions of this mysterious entity are of such a vagueness and ambiguity as to allow the interpretation of the Over-Soul as God. If such an interpretation be allowed, then Emerson is surely a pantheist. On the other hand, if, as I believe, Emerson understands the Over-Soul to be the incarnate Word of God rather than God *in se,* then his view is not pantheism; it is—panentheism.

9. Works, I, p. 329.

10. Ibid., pp. 335-36.

11. Ibid., p. 3.

12. Ibid., p. 76.

13. Ibid., pp. 94-95, 99.

14. Ibid., p. 99.

15. *The Heart of Emerson's Journals* edited by Bliss Perry (Boston: Houghton Mifflin, 1926), p. 125.

16. Works, I, pp. 127-28.

17. Ibid., pp. 130-31.

18. Ibid., p. 145.

19. Ibid., p. 139.

20. Ibid., p. 146.

21. Ibid., p. 135.

22. Ralph L. Rusk, *The Life of Ralph Waldo Emerson* (New York: Scribner, 1949), p. 271.

23. Following the Divinity School Address, Emerson preached four sermons; twice at Watertown and twice at Concord. His diary records his final sermon as being that given at Concord on January 20th, 1839. After that, the prophet went no more to the pulpit.

24. Works, II, p. 10.

25. Ibid., p. 17.

26. Ibid., pp. 45, 47.

27. Ibid., pp. 57-58.

28. Ibid., p. 50.

29. Ibid.

30. Ibid., p. 51.

31. Ibid., XI, p. 223.

32. Ibid., p. 234.

33. Ibid., III, p. 20.

34. Ibid., pp. 37-38.

X

The Sage of Walden Pond

HENRY DAVID THOREAU

"If a man lose his fowls or his
dogs, he knows how to seek them.
There are those who lose their
hearts and know not how to seek
them. The duty of the student
is no other than to seek his
lost heart." [1]

HENRY DAVID THOREAU

Henry David Thoreau

As ANYONE WHO HAS ever taken seriously any particular philosophy knows, it is one thing to preach a point of view; it is entirely another to practice what you preach. A life of lip-service to an ideal comes easy, but a life lived honestly in accordance with the truth one's mind acknowledges—that is hard, no less hard for a New England Transcendentalist than for anybody else. The Transcendentalist idea that man is a god in ruins needing only to recapture his kinship with Nature to realize his divinity is a magnificent vision. Too bad that Emerson, who had the vision, couldn't really live by it. But could anyone? In Concord or any place? The answer is—yes. And it is to Ralph Waldo Emerson's everlasting credit that he championed the one Transcendentalist in Concord who actually did practice what he preached—Henry David Thoreau.

By Boston standards, the Thoreaus were foreigners. Henry David's grandfather had emigrated from the island of Jersey just before the American Revolution, and had prospered as a merchant. John Thoreau Junior, Henry's father, unfortunately did not inherit his parent's business sense. His merchandising experiments soon cost him his share in the store. Seeking a living, he moved his family from Boston to Concord. There, on July 12th, 1817, Henry David Thoreau was born. Little is known of his childhood years. He attended Concord Academy and at the age of sixteen entered Harvard. He made only average grades, and some have seen in this fact evidence of a late maturing. The truth of the matter is that he missed most of his junior year: for months he was out with an illness that may have been an early warning of the tuberculosis that eventually killed him, although at the time its only visible effect was to lower his academic standing. In 1837 he graduated and returned to Concord and a job teaching in the town school. It lasted three weeks. He didn't believe that sparing the rod spoiled the child, and ordered to lay on, he protested and soon found himself laid off. It was a bad time to be out of work. The depression of 1837 was in full swing, and for many months Thoreau was idle. Whether from necessity or inclination is hard to judge, since if Perry Miller [2] is correct, any Harvard man, depression or not, could be fairly certain of commercial success—if he was willing to work for it. Thoreau, however, had other ideas, and in 1838, in collaboration with his brother John, he opened a private school in the family home. His progressive teaching methods must have produced results, for the school soon had all the pupils it could accommodate. Unfortunately, this successful venture was cut short in March of 1841 by the failing health of John Thoreau. His brother's tragic death the following January was a profound shock to Henry, and undoubtedly influenced the subsequent direction of his life. He required his freedom, and the townsman's idea of spending his days in working just so as to have money enough to conform to town standards of living seemed to him a terrible waste. It was, he thought, a fool's life to pass the years "laying up treasures which moth and rust will corrupt and thieves break through and steal." [3] He had long cherished the notion of memorializing a river journey he had taken with his brother on the Concord and the Merrimack for a week in 1839, and for that project he needed solitude and leisure for reflection. His opportunity for both materialized in 1845, and gratefully he took it.

In October of the previous year, Ralph Waldo Emerson had purchased a tract of woods on the north shore of Walden Pond, a mile and a half south of Concord. Thoreau now made an agreement with his friend Emerson [4] whereby he (Thoreau) would clear part of the woods for a garden in return for being allowed to build and live in a cabin on the property. He started felling trees in March of 1845 and on July 4th he moved into his finished hut. In the two years and two months he was to spend in the woods, he would write *A Week on the Concord and Merrimack Rivers* and finish the greater part of his masterpiece *Walden*. However, his own account of what he hoped to accomplish by living on the shores of the pond reveals a motivation rather more basic than the mere writing of books.

> I went to the woods because I wished to live deliberately, to front only the essential facts of life, and see if I could not learn what it had to teach, and not, when I came to die, discover that I had not lived. I did not wish to live what was not life, living is so dear; nor did I wish to practise resignation, unless it was quite necessary. I wanted to live deep and suck out all the marrow of life, to live so sturdily and Spartan-like as to put to rout all that was not life, to cut a broad swathe and shave close, to drive life into a corner, and reduce it to its lowest terms, and, if it proved to be mean, why then to get the whole and genuine meanness of it, and publish its meanness to the world; or if it were sublime, to know it by experience, and be able to give a true account of it in my next excursion.[5]

Such was his expressed reason. At the back of his mind, however, unconscious and inexpressible, there may have been another. In April, 1844, not quite a year before the felling of the trees at Walden, Thoreau had carelessly set fire to the Concord woods and put the town itself in mortal danger. His biographers have tended to play down the incident as something of small significance, yet in his lifetime the people of Concord never forgave him. For all his later fame, to the villagers of Concord and to their descendants, Henry Thoreau had always been the man who burned the woods and ran away to watch the spectacle in safety from Fair Haven Cliff.[6] *Six years later,* Thoreau himself still felt sense of guilt enough to write down in his Journal these incredible sentences of exculpation.

> Hitherto I had felt like a guilty person,—nothing but shame and regret. But now I settled the matter with myself shortly. I said to myself: "Who are these men who are said to be the owners of these woods, and how am I related to them? I have set fire to the forest, but I have done no wrong therein, and it is as if the lightning had done it. These flames are but consuming their natural food." (It has never troubled me from that day to this more than if the lightning

had done it. The trivial fishing was all that disturbed me and disturbs me still.) [7]

Perhaps so. Yet nowhere in his writings does Thoreau teach such a complete identification of man with nature as the analogy of the lightning implies, and the very fact of his having the incident in mind long years later belies his dismissal of it as trivial. Did he, then, go to the woods because he could no longer bear the censure of the town? Was it some semi-conscious desire for atonement that drove him to Walden Pond? We shall never know. Thoreau's Journals tell us nothing; no one of the Concord Group took written notice of the matter, and the people of the town lie silent in their graves.

II

The making of *Walden,* as Lyndon Shanley [8] has pointed out, was a matter of several years and seven revisions. The book had its origin in the curiosity of Thoreau's townsmen about the nature of his life in the woods.

Some have asked what I got to eat; if I did not feel lonesome; if I was not afraid; and the like. Others have been curious to learn what portion of my income I devoted to charitable purposes; and some, who have large families, how many poor children I maintained.[9]

Thoreau's answer was "Economy," first delivered as a lyceum lecture in the winter of 1846-47, and subsequently incorporated as the first chapter of *Walden.* Why "Economy"? Because, Thoreau contends, Economy is the first chapter of life. Until we have determined the true necessaries of daily existence and distinguished what we need from what we should be better off without, we have hardly begun the business of *living.* "The mass of men," he thinks, "lead lives of quiet desperation," [10] wasting their precious substance on the non-essentials. Self-condemned slaves to land, husbandry, and possessions, they never realize that

Most of the luxuries, and many of the so-called comforts of life, are not only not indispensable, but positive hindrances to the elevation of mankind.[11]

For what commodities does man really require? Food, Shelter, Clothing, and Fuel, and of these the last three are wholly or half unnecessary.

At the present day, and in this country, as I find by my own experience, a few implements, a knife, an axe, a spade, a wheelbarrow, etc., and for the studious, lamplight, stationery, and access to a few books, rank next to necessaries, and can all be obtained at a trifling cost. Yet some, not wise, go to the other side of the globe, to barbarous and unhealthy regions, and devote themselves to trade for ten or twenty years, in order that they may live,—that is, keep comfortably warm,—and die in New England at last.[12]

Better that they were employed the whole while in learning the economy of nature, in trying the experiment of getting a spiritual living rather than piling up the material treasure no man can take with him. Better that they should go into the proper business of mankind, the business that is of finding themselves and appreciating the God-given gift of life.

I would say to my fellows, once for all, As long as possible live free and uncommitted. It makes but little difference whether you are committed to a farm or the county jail.[13]

Freedom, then, is the antidote for desperation, and true freedom is life uncluttered by the paraphernalia of conventional existence. Like the Stoics, Thoreau finds happiness to lie not in increase of possessions but in decrease of wants.

In short, I am convinced, both by faith and experience, that to maintain one's self on this earth is not a hardship but a pastime, if we will live simply and wisely. . . . It is not necessary that a man should earn his living by the sweat of his brow, unless he sweats easier than I do.[14]

Like Whitman, he would loaf and invite his soul, and to those townspeople who wondered that he should not spend his idleness doing good for others, he has this to say:

> I confess that I have hitherto indulged very little in philanthropic enterprises. I have made some sacrifices to a sense of duty, and among others have sacrificed this pleasure also. There are those who have used all their arts to persuade me to undertake the support of some poor family in the town; and if I had nothing to do—for the devil finds employment for the idle—I might try my hand at some pastime as that. However, when I have thought to indulge myself in this respect, and lay their Heaven under an obligation by maintaining certain poor persons in all respects as comfortably as I maintain myself, and have even ventured so far as to make them the offer, they have one and all unhesitatingly preferred to remain poor.[15]

Why, therefore, pity them? The poverty one should really pity is not that arising from the lack of those things necessary to maintain oneself in town society, but rather that which instances a condition of slavery to those things. It is, Thoreau believes, no genuine charity to provide men with the means to their continued enslavement. Rather provide them with an example of self-reliance, and teach them that true idleness consists not in contemplation of nature but in poverty of soul.

> Let a man then know his worth, and keep things under his feet. Let him not peep or steal, or skulk up and down with the air of a charity-boy, a bastard, or an interloper in the world which exists for him.[16]

So much had Thoreau learned from Emerson. It was, however, his own experience that told him that the simple life according to nature was man's best means to such an end. "In proportion as he simplifies his life, the laws of the universe will appear less complex, and solitude will not be solitude, nor poverty poverty, nor weakness weakness." [17] Every man, therefore, may profit spiritually from a season in the woods.

The temporal limitation is deliberate, for Thoreau does not preach nature as a permanent mode of life. The woods are not a hermitage but a place of renewal, a place of retreat where one may practice the economy of regeneration. Every man is the better for a vacation from society, but when the vacation is over, the retreat finished, the renewal accomplished, it is time to return to the haunts of men. Thus Thoreau, having found himself, left the woods and returned to Concord. He had, as he said, "several more lives to live, and could not spare any more time for that one." [18]

III

Back among the townsmen, he took up surveying. It was, he figured, the best of jobs for a man who so enjoyed the woods and fields of Concord. He renewed his lecturing, and in February, 1848 delivered to the Concord Lyceum the first version of his famous essay on Civil Disobedience. His theme was the right of the individual to stand against the State according to the dictates of his conscience, and it is, in his opinion, a right inalienable.

> Must the citizen ever for a moment, or in the least degree, resign his conscience to the legislator? Why has every man a conscience, then? I think that we should be men first, and subjects afterward. It is not desirable to cultivate a respect for the law, so much as for the right. The only obligation which I have a right to assume is to do at any time what I think right.[19]

Not the will of the majority, then, but the rule of conscience should prevail. It is enough, he thinks, that the righteous have God on their side; it is enough because "any man more right than his neighbors constitutes a majority of one already." [20]

In giving voice to such radical views, Thoreau was not simply indulging himself in the expression of an abstract political ideal. He was vitally concerned, as were many of his fellow-citizens in the decades just before the Civil War, about the right of government to enforce slavery. To him it was a question of immense practical importance as to whether any American citizen was under any obligation to obey the dictates of a government which condoned an institution so repugnant to individual conscience. As for himself, he had no doubts.

> How does it become a man to behave toward this American government to-day? I answer, that he cannot without disgrace be associated

with it. I cannot for an instant recognize that political organization as *my* government which is the *slave's* government also.[21]

And so he refused to pay his poll-tax, and went to jail for a night. Some one, he tells us, paid it for him (much to his disgust), and the next morning he was away to the woods captaining a huckleberry party. But he had made his point: "Under a government which imprisons any unjustly, the true place for a just man is also a prison." [22]

It was a principle destined to exert an enormous influence on the evolution of Twentieth Century society. Mohandas K. Gandhi, long years before he received the accolade "Mahatma," read Thoreau, and found in the following the inspiration for his revolution by non-violence.

A minority is powerless while it conforms to the majority; it is not even a minority then; but it is irresistible when it clogs by its whole weight. If the alternative is to keep all just men in prison, or give up war and slavery, the State will not hesitate which to choose. If a thousand men were not to pay their tax-bills this year, that would not be a violent and bloody measure, as it would be to pay them, and enable the State to commit violence and shed innocent blood. This is, in fact, the definition of a peaceable revolution, if any such is possible. If the tax-gatherer, or any other public officer, asks me, as one has done, "But what shall I do?" my answer is, "If you really wish to do anything, resign your office." When the subject has refused allegiance, and the officer has resigned his office, then the revolution is accomplished.[23]

Thoreau could not foresee that a century after his death these words would provide a program for American Negroes seeking civil rights; he could not anticipate that he would be honored in Asia even as his works gathered dust on the shelves of American libraries; but it goes without saying that he would have been tremendously pleased.

There are in America today many who disapprove of Henry Thoreau and all that he stands for. To these, his rejection of the authority of every government save that of the wise and the conscientious smells of communism. Of course, he was no communist, or socialist either, except perhaps in the same spiritual sense that Christ and Confucius were such. In many ways he represents the arch-conservative point of view. He would, I think, if alive today, be extremely disgusted with the notion that the government should support us and sustain us from the cradle to the grave. He would, I am sure, have hooted at Social Security. For better than any man of his time, he exemplified the typically American virtue of maverick independence. Emerson spoke no more and no less than the truth when he remarked that "No truer American existed than Thoreau."

IV

By mid-century the freest years of Thoreau's life lay behind him. He had acquired responsibilities; he was taking a larger share in the operation of the family pencil business. In 1850 the Thoreaus bought a large house on Main Street and Henry moved in to stay. As if chafing at the new bonds, he began to wander farther afield. There were excursions to Cape Cod and to Canada in 1850, and to the Maine Woods in 1853; it was back to Cape Cod in 1855 and 1857, and up to Vermont in 1856. *Walden* had finally come out in 1854, and sold well enough to make Thoreau's name known outside of Concord. He began to attract disciples. One of these, F. B. Sanborn, introduced him to John Brown, the abolitionist, and before and after Brown's notorious raid on Harper's Ferry, Thoreau spoke out in Brown's defense. Bronson Alcott took him to Brooklyn to meet Walt Whitman, and each recognized in the other a kindred soul.

Thoreau's original work on the succession of forest trees (his only notable contribution to science) took up much of his time in the late Fifties. It was while examining tree stumps in December of 1860 that he caught the severe cold which was to flower into bronchitis, and eventually into acute tuberculosis. In a last desperate bid for health, he set out in May of 1861 for Minnesota; unfortunately, his strength was not up to the hard journey, and by July he was back in Concord in bed. Knowing that he had not long to live, he now undertook to put his manuscripts in order. Ironically, the demand for his works had picked up, and publishers were anxious for such contributions as he had to offer. He had none, and would have none, for he was dying. The end came quietly on May 6th, 1862. Emerson delivered the eulogy, and in it described his subject thus:

> He interrogated every custom, and wished to settle all his practice on an ideal foundation. He was a protestant *a outrance*, and few lives contain so many renunciations. He was bred to no profession; he never married; he lived alone; he never went to church; he never voted; he refused to pay a tax to the State; he ate no flesh, he drank no wine, he never knew the use of tobacco; and, though a naturalist, he used neither trap nor gun. He chose, wisely no doubt for himself, to be the bachelor of thought and Nature. He had no talent for wealth, and knew how to be poor without the least hint of squalor or inelegance.[24]

Thoreau would have thought it as fine an epitaph as any man could wish.

SUGGESTED READINGS

The Modern Library edition of Thoreau's writings, edited by Brooks Atkinson, *Walden and Other Writings* (New York, 1950), includes the complete text of *Walden*, major portions of *A Week on the Concord and Merrimack Rivers*, *Cape Cod*, and *The Allegash* and *East Branch*; together with the essays on *Walking*, *Civil Disobedience*, *Slavery in Massachusetts*, *A Plea for Captain John Brown*, and *Life without Principle*. Introduction by the editor. Perry Miller, *Consciousness in Concord* (Boston: Houghton Mifflin, 1958), contains the text of Thoreau's hitherto "Lost Journal," with notes and a commentary. J. Lyndon Shanley, *The Making of Walden* (Chicago: University of Chicago Press, 1957), provides an exhaustive and exhausting analysis of the various stages in the composition of *Walden*.

For those who enjoy reading other people's mail, Walter Harding and Carl Bode have edited *The Correspondence of Henry David Thoreau* (New York: New York University Press, 1958). This is the first complete collection of all, and I mean *all*, the letters, notes, and other trivia sent to or by Thoreau. Also by Walter Harding is *A Thoreau Handbook* (New York: New York University Press, 1959). A book mostly about books about Thoreau, this offers valuable analyses of all the standard biographies and critical works, including various unpublished dissertations. Exhaustive bibliography. Detailed chronology of Thoreau's life and summary of his main ideas. The most recent, and probably the best, critical study of these ideas is Sherman Paul, *The Shores of America: Thoreau's Inward Exploration* (Urbana: University of Illinois Press, 1958).

REFERENCES

1. *The Dial,* Vol. IV (1843), p. 206.
2. *Consciousness in Concord* (Boston: Houghton Mifflin, 1958), p. 9. That Thoreau was interested at all in making money is very doubtful. At Harvard, in a colloquy on "The Commercial Spirit," he had advocated a one-day work-week and freedom to spend the other six absorbing "the soft influences and sublime revelations of Nature."
3. *The Writings of Henry David Thoreau,* 20 Vols. (Boston: Houghton Mifflin, 1906), II, p. 6. Hereafter cited as Writings.
4. Emerson settled in Concord in 1835, and it is probable that he met Thoreau soon thereafter. At all events, in 1841 he offered him room and board in return for his services as a man of all work. Thoreau accepted and lived with the Emersons for two years. It is likely that the double tragedy of the deaths of Thoreau's brother John and Emerson's son Waldo occurring only fifteen days apart in 1842 brought the two men closer together. In later years they drew apart. Each noted in his Journal the other's failure to understand him. Thoreau was undoubtedly sensitive of Emerson's greater fame, and Emerson would not have been human had he not resented Henry's ability to practice what he Emerson could only preach. Even so, they remained friends to the last, and it was Emerson who delivered Thoreau's funeral oration and saw to the publication of a number of his works.
5. Writings, II, pp. 100-101.
6. For a detailed account of the incident, see Miller, *Consciousness in Concord,* pp. 119-21.
7. *The Journal of Henry D. Thoreau,* edited by Bradford Torrey and Francis H. Allen, 14 Vols. (Boston: Houghton Mifflin, 1949), II, p. 23.
8. J. Lyndon Shanley, *The Making of Walden* (Chicago: University of Chicago Press, 1957).
9. Writings, II, p. 3.
10. Ibid., p. 8.
11. Ibid., p. 15.
12. Ibid.
13. Ibid., p. 93.
14. Ibid., p. 78.
15. Ibid., p. 80.
16. *The Works of Ralph Waldo Emerson,* 14 Vols. (Boston: Houghton Mifflin, 1883), II, p. 62.
17. Writings, II, p. 356.
18. Ibid., p. 355. The day of his return (September 6th, 1847) was undoubtedly dictated by the fact that Emerson was about to leave for England on a lecture tour. Since the Emerson family would be left behind, Lydia Emerson had invited Thoreau to spend the winter, keeping them company and taking care of the necessary chores. It was an invitation Henry would hardly refuse, considering his literary debt to "Waldo" and his affection for Lydia and the children.

19. Writings, IV, p. 358.
20. Ibid., p. 369.
21. Ibid., p. 360.
22. Ibid., p. 370.
23. Ibid., p. 371.
24. Emerson, *Complete Essays* (ed. Atkinson), pp. 896-97.

XI

Missionary to the Popular Education

HORACE MANN

"The interests of a client are small
compared to the interests of the next
generation. Let the next generation
be my client." [1]

HORACE MANN

Horace Mann

. . . any man more right than his neighbors, constitutes a majority of one already.

There is no evidence to suggest that Horace Mann had ever read these words of Thoreau's, but if he did he surely must have gained a bitter satisfaction from them; for of all the reformers in ante-bellum Massachusetts, none had a more righteous cause or vigorous opposition, none employed his majority of one to greater lasting effect. "He took up the common schools of Massachusetts in his arms and blessed them . . . He was the father of Normal Schools. His good work here will live; one hundred years hence three generations will have tasted its blessed influence, the last the deepest of all." [2] A century has passed since Theodore Parker, a friend of Mann's as much aware of his deficiencies as of his virtues, wrote these words to Samuel Howe; the time has served to vindicate his judgment: the children of today, no less than those three genera-tions past, are debtors to the work of Horace Mann.

That he could feel so deeply the needs of children was due in no small part to his own experience of growing up. His childhood was not a happy one. His parents, fifth generation Massachusetts farmers, were dirt poor. The father, Thomas Mann, died when Horace was thirteen, and on the shoulders of his children the whole burden of support descended. His early schooling was thoroughly inadequate; in his time "there was no such thing as oral instruction. Books designed for children were few, and their contents meagre and miserable." [3] His "teachers were very good people; but they were very poor teachers." "Until the age of fifteen," he "had never been to school more than eight or ten weeks in a year." [4] One facet of his training, however, was not neglected. The glory of Franklin Township was its Calvinist pastor, Nathanael Emmons, "a man of pure intellect, whose logic," according to Mann, "was never softened in its severity by the infusion of any kindliness of sentiment. He expounded all the doctrines of total depravity, election, and reprobation, and not only the eternity, but the extremity, of hell-torments, unflinchingly and in their most terrible significance; while he rarely if ever descanted upon the joys of heaven, and never," to Mann's recollection, "upon the essential and necessary happiness of a virtuous life." The end result on so sensitive a boy as young Horace Mann, as might be expected, was disastrous. Throughout his life he would be in revolt against that Calvinism whose teachings he could never quite bring himself to disbelieve.

At nineteen, chance, in the form of a small inheritance, changed the direction of his life. Leaving the farm, he traveled down to Providence and enrolled at Brown. Following his graduation in 1819, he stayed on for two years as college tutor, and afterwards entered Judge Tapping Reeve's Law School at Litchfield, Connecticut. In 1823, upon his admission to the Massachusetts Bar, he opened a law office in Dedham, entered politics, and (in 1830) married Charlotte Messer, daughter of the President of Brown. Earlier, in 1827, he had been elected to the Massachusetts House of Representatives; two years later, in 1832, his wife died, and now he moved to Boston and resumed the practice of law. In 1833 he won election to the State Senate, rising to its Presidency in 1836.

Trust thyself, advised Emerson, and Horace Mann did. That the causes he espoused were just, his Calvinist conscience never doubted. To Parker, he was the sort of lawyer who "never took a case that he did not conscientiously think he ought to win." [5] As a legislator, he never backed a bill of whose righteousness he was not personally sure. He demanded better quarters and better treatment for the insane, and he got it. He insisted that drunkenness be made a felony, and the legislature agreed. He was, as Hinsdale has noted, "ethical in everything. His heart went only where his head recognized benevolence." [6] To the mind of Edmund Dwight, influential member of the newly-constituted State Board of Education, it was obvious that Senate President Mann, for all his lack of practical experience in the field of education, was peculiarly fitted to fill the vacant post of Secretary to the Board, and Dwight resolved that he should have it despite the fact that the first choice of the Governor, the Board, and the educators of the state was James G. Carter, an extremely able and well-liked teacher and writer on educational subjects. Dwight prevailed; Mann was offered the position, and on July 1st, 1837, having resigned his seat in the senate and quitted the profession of the law, he entered upon what was to be his greatest work.

Most of his friends did not at the time see it so. They thought him foolish to sacrifice his political and professional prospects for a post which Mann himself described as one "whose returns for effort and privation must be postponed to another generation." [7] As usual, however, he was sure that what he was doing was the right thing. "Is it not better," he writes to his sister,

> to do good than to be commended for having done it? If no seed were ever to be sown save that which would promise the requital of a full harvest before we die, how soon would mankind revert to barbarism! If I can be the means of ascertaining what is the best construction of [school] houses, what are the best [school] books, what is the best arrangement of studies, what are the best modes of instruction; if I can discover by what appliance of means a non-thinking, non-reflecting, non-speaking child can most surely be trained into a noble citizen ready to contend for the right and to die for the right,—if I can only obtain and diffuse throughout this State a few good ideas on these and similar subjects, may I not flatter myself that my ministry has not been wholly in vain? [8]

"The interests of a client are small compared to the interests of the next generation . . . Let the next generation be my client." And for the next twelve years it was.

There is a prevalent misconception, fostered by some of Mann's more uncritical admirers, that he entered upon his duties as Secretary with a completely open mind and a pure reforming zeal. In truth he did neither. The practical Yankee in him saw clearly that the price of educational progress was constant compromise. To

Samuel May, Mann-appointed principal of the Lexington Normal School, who had injudiciously taken a group of his female students to a local anti-slavery meeting, and by so doing had aroused the ire of community conservatives, Mann wrote:

> A public interest and sympathy are now excited throughout the Commonwealth in behalf of the cause of education. With the exception of Mr. Dwight's donation, more has been given by rich men during the last year for its general promotion, probably, than ever before. . . . If I had not succeeded in producing a conviction, that, while I am engaged in administering the cause, it will be kept clear of all collateral subjects, of all which the world chooses to call fanaticisms or hobbies, I should never have obtained the co-operation of thousands who are now its friends. I have further plans for obtaining more aid; but the moment it is known or supposed that the cause is to be perverted to, or connected with, any of the exciting party questions of the day, I shall never get another cent. . . . You must not mistake my motives; and, if you think I am speaking too plainly, you must pardon it for the zeal I have in the cause. . . .[9]

Withal, his puritanism is presupposed throughout his educational philosophy. That God exists and enjoins man's absolute obedience to his laws, he took for granted. On these assumptions his moral argument for common schools is founded. "In obedience to the laws of God and to the laws of all civilized communities, society is," he argues,

> bound to protect the natural life; and the natural life cannot be protected without the appropriation and use of a portion of the property which society possesses . . . But why preserve unborn embryos of life, if we do not intend to watch over and to protect them, and to expand their subsequent existence into usefulness and happiness? As individuals or as an organized community, we have no natural right; we can derive no authority or countenance from reason; we can cite no attribute or purpose of the divine nature, for giving birth to any human being, and then inflicting upon that being the curse of ignorance, of poverty and of vice, with all their attendant calamities. We are brought, then, to this startling but inevitable alternative. The natural life of an infant should be extinguished as soon as it is born, or the means should be provided to save that life from being a curse to its possessor; and therefore every State is bound

to enact a code of laws legalizing and enforcing Infanticide, or a code of laws establishing Free Schools! [10]

Logically, the argument hardly bears inspection, but then Mann was a reformer, not a logician. What mattered was the conclusion; to reach this he would use whatever arguments came to hand.

A month before his election as Secretary, he had finished "that most valuable book, 'Combe on the Constitution of Man.'" [11] Vastly impressed by the social and educational theories of its author, the Scottish reformer and phrenologist, George Combe, he soon adopted Combe's views as his own. In 1839 Combe visited Boston on his American lecture tour, and Mann grasped the opportunity to make his acquaintance. Their common interest in reform, conjoined with Mann's conversion to phrenology, cemented a friendship that was to last until Combe's death two decades later. Intellectually, the initiative was all Combe's. The relation between the two men, as their correspondence shows, was essentially always that of master and disciple. For the most part, Mann's acceptance of Combe's system of phrenology, and the educational and social outlook it implied, was entirely uncritical. As above, it was a case of conclusions justifying reasons. That phrenology was thought by many to be a fraud, bothered Mann not at all. He found its methods and its teachings useful and vigorously advocated their adoption by the public schools. Through Mann, the principles of phrenology passed into the American educational system, and there some of them remain today.

To those for whom phrenology means simply the study of head bumps, such an assertion must seem fantastic, but phrenology as preached by Combe and understood by Mann was much more than that. Its fundamental postulate, that brain is the organ of mind, was then, as it is now, presupposed by every variety of philosophical materialism and behavioristic psychology. Where phrenology differed from these was in its belief that mind, so conceived, was organized into a specific number of faculties, each having its seat in a definite region of the brain, correspondent to a specific area on the surface of the skull. The measurement of a person's skull formations, then, must, so the phrenologists thought, provide a reliable index to his mental capacities. When subsequent physiological research discovered no such correlation between the bumps and the faculties alleged to lie directly beneath them, phrenology was permanently discredited as a science. Even so, there was much in the detail of it that, to Mann and those of like mind, seemed of sound educational worth. By its emphasis on observation and experiment, it fostered the study of human nature and took the children's noses out of books; its assumption that everything is governed by physical laws encouraged investigation of the environment; its identification of mind as body promoted emphasis on physical education and training. Indeed, wherever in Mann's writings we find him stressing the physical and natural environment of the child, we can be sure that here is an echo of George Combe. As we contemplate the major role of physical education in our schools and colleges today, we would do well to remember that it mostly began with phrenology.

II

Horace Mann wrote no books.[12] What he had to say is contained, for the most part, in his twelve annual reports as Secretary of the Board of Education to the people of Massachusetts, and in the ten volumes of the *Common School Journal* that he edited. On these his reputation largely rests. Therein is to be found his social and educational philosophy—such as it is. The qualification is very much in order, since these essays and reports offer very little worthy of the name of philosophy. The fact is, as Hinsdale and the other commentators have pointed out, "that Mr. Mann was not a theorist, philosopher, or scientific pedagogist. His writings show no trace of speculative talents. In all his work, he was devoted to the practical or useful." [13] If the truth be known, Mann was essentially a propagandist, albeit one with absolute faith in his cause. Rightly regarded, those sections of his reports not directly concerned with the actual state of the Massachusetts schools, are propaganda and nothing more. This is not to derogate from their importance. Rather is it to say that the full appreciation of that importance comes only as we realize just how successful a propagandist Mann really was.

In 1837 the attitude of the great majority of the citizens of Massachusetts towards their public schools was one of indifference bordering on hostility. Hardly anybody really cared. The politicians were concerned only to effect economies in operations: "for a series of years previous to 1837, the school system of Massachusetts had been running down. Schoolhouses had been growing old, while new ones were rarely erected. School districts were divided, so that each part was obliged to support its schools on the moiety of a fund, the whole of which was," in Horace Mann's opinion, "a scanty allowance." [14] Nor did those who stood to lose the most appreciate their loss. To the illiterate and poverty-stricken masses, education seemed not so much an opportunity as a diabolical scheme to deprive them of the fruits of their children's labor. "It was found that children could be profitably employed in many kinds of labor,—in factories, in the shoe-making business, and in other mechanical employments; and this," Mann pointed out, "swelled the already enormous amount of non-attendance and irregularity." [15] Inevitably, "the business of school-keeping fell more and more into the hands of youth and inexperience; so that, in rare instances only, did the maturity of years preside over the indiscretions of the young . . . To crown the whole, and to aggravate the deterioration which it proved to exist, the private school system was rapidly absorbing the funds, patronizing the talent, and withdrawing the sympathy, which belonged to the Public Schools." [16] The educated and the well-to-do were generally content to emulate the British system of private schools. After all, these had served to provide the leadership that had built Britain into a world power! The class system, so they argued, was natural to society. Why, then, encourage an institution that could serve only to disrupt it?

As one who took seriously the democratic ideal enshrined in the *Declaration of Independence* and the *Constitution,* Mann was appalled by such reasoning. What was needed was "an energetic and comprehensive system of Popular Education, good enough for the richest, open to the poorest. . . ." [17] In his Twelfth Report, Mann recalls how this end was to be achieved:

The intelligence of the State was to be invoked to justify such a system, and its liberality to support it. Improvements were to be sought for, whether to be found at home or abroad; and to be adopted with equal alacrity, whether coming from proud Jerusalem or from despised Nazareth. The incompetency of teachers was to be exposed in a spirit of justice, tempered with kindness;—for, that union of justice and kindness which leads a man to abandon his error, or supply his shortcomings, is the loveliest form of mercy. Committees were to be informed and stimulated, that they might both know and discharge their duty. Money, for the more liberal payment of teachers, was to be won from the pockets of the wealthy by persuasion, or exacted by law. By appeals to duty, to decency, and to parental love; by rebuke or by ridicule; by any means not absolutely criminal; all that class of wretched, pain-inflicting, disease-creating structures called schoolhouses, was to be swept from the face of the State;—a work, which, could it have been consummated at once, would not have left [in Mann's estimation], a hundred schoolhouses standing in the Commonwealth.[18]

The first year things went fairly well. Some coldness and indifference there was, but it was more than offset by the financial windfall which made possible the foundation of the first American Normal School at Lexington. However, in 1839, Marcus Morton, an economy-minded Jacksonian democrat and no friend of public schools, won election as Governor of Massachusetts by exactly one vote over the incumbent, Governor Edward Everett. Convinced that he had a mandate to sweep clean, Morton moved at once to effect economies, and his first target was Secretary Mann, "a reckless extravagance at a salary of fifteen hundred dollars a year." For months it seemed likely that the Board would be abolished and its functions returned into "the hands of town and district meetings," but fortunately it was not to be. The friends of public education rallied their legislative forces and in March 1840 "signally defeated" the motion to abolish. Henceforward, Massachusetts would stand firmly committed to public education.

Now things began to go really well. By 1842 Mann counted three Normal Schools permanently established. "Language," he wrote in his diary, "cannot express the joy that pervades my soul at this vast accession of power to that machinery which is to carry the cause of education forward." [19] With this triumph came public recognition. He was much in demand for speeches, and his cup ran over when Boston tendered him an invitation to deliver the traditional Fourth of July Oration. It was a golden opportunity to strike a public blow for common schools, and Mann took full advantage of it. "It is," he warned them, "not enough that a bare majority should be intelligent and upright. We need general intelligence and integrity as we need our daily bread. By the vote of a few wicked men, or even of one wicked man, honorable men may be hurled from office and miscreants elevated to their places . . . If votes come from ignorance and crime, the fire and brimstone that were rained on Sodom and Gomorrah would be more tolerable." [20] Having thus disposed of Morton's supporters, he turned his face on the anglophiles. "Select schools for select children should be discarded. Instead of the old order of nobility, a new order should be created— an order of Teachers, wise, benevolent, filled with Christian enthusiasm and rewarded and honored by all." Let our motto be, he cried in closing, *"Teach this People."* And apparently the people were eager to be taught, for in August, Mann would report seventeen thousand copies of his oration in print and another ten thousand in the press.

On May Day, 1843, Horace Mann married Mary Peabody and sailed for Europe. It was not exactly a honeymoon. Mann had obtained leave from the Board to study, at his own expense, European systems of education, and for five months Mary Mann trailed her husband around England, Germany, and France while he did just that. The substance of his findings, constituting the core of his Seventh Annual Report, was presented to the legislature in January of 1844. He had found, he told them, "many things abroad which we, at home, should do well to imitate; things, some of which are here, as yet, mere matters of speculation and theory, but which, there, have long been in operation, are now producing a harvest of rich and abundant blessings." [21] Particularly, he had been impressed by the organization and pedagogy of the Prussian schools.

On reviewing a period of six weeks, the greater part of which I spent in visiting schools in the North and middle of Prussia and in Saxony . . . I call to mind three things about which I cannot be mistaken. In some of my opinions and inferences, I may have erred, but of the following facts, there can be no doubts:—1. During all this time, I never saw a teacher hearing a lesson of any kind (excepting a reading or spelling lesson), *with a book in his hand.* 2. I never saw a teacher *sitting,* while hearing a recitation. 3. Though I saw hundreds of schools, and thousands,—I think I may say, within bounds, tens of thousands of pupils,—*I never saw one child undergoing punishment, or arraigned for misconduct. I never saw one child in tears from having been punished, or from fear of being punished.*[22]

That Mann should have been so impressed by conduct we today would take for granted indicates clearly just how sorry the quality of teaching must have been in many Massachusetts classrooms. Nor was he unaware that his praise of Prussian pedagogy would be taken as disparagement of Massachusetts methods. Anticipating just such a reaction, he is at pains to reassure the legislators that he intends no personal criticism.

I mean no disparagement of our own teachers by the remark I am about to make. As a general fact, these teachers are as good as public opinion has demanded; as good as the public sentiment has been disposed to appreciate; as good as public liberality has been ready to reward; as good as the preliminary measures taken to qualify them would authorize us to expect. But it was impossible to put down the questionings of my own mind,—whether a visiter [sic] could spend six weeks in our own schools without ever hearing an angry world spoken, or seeing a blow struck, or witnessing the flow of tears.[23]

This was putting it as gently as possible, but even so the schoolmasters of Massachusetts realized that they had been damned with the very faintest of praise, and they reacted vigorously. Shortly appeared a lengthy pamphlet entitled *Remarks on the Seventh Annual Report,* etc.; the collective effort of thirty-one Boston schoolmasters, it denounced Mann as an academic and moral amateur unqualified to criticize experienced teachers. So offensive was its tone that Mann was stung into writing a *Reply.* This led to a *Rejoinder* by the schoolmasters, which drew from Mann a second pamphlet, *Answer to the Rejoinder.* Into the details of this acrimonious squabble it is unnecessary to go. Suffice it to say that the Boston public felt Mann to have won. The end result was a wave of reform adopting nearly all of the positions for which Mann had fought. Corporal punishment was curtailed, and the standards for qualifying teachers were raised. Most important, public interest in the schools was reawakened. From this time forward, Mann enjoyed a steadily increasing measure of popular support.

He needed every bit of it, for soon he had to face a serious challenge from another quarter. The common school revival had not escaped the attention of the religious community. As early as 1838, the denominational press had begun to question the effect of the Board's policies on religious instruction in the schools. The controversy with the Boston schoolmasters had not yet run its course, when an article appeared in the Episcopalian *Christian Witness and Church Advocate* charging Mann with having sought to inflict upon the people a system of education designed to rob them of their faith. A return to Puritan practice and principles was called for, but the call went unheeded by the public, and soon died away. In 1846 the issue flared up anew in consequence of a sensational sermon preached by the Reverend Matthew Hale Smith attacking Mann and all his works. Smith, a die-hard Calvinist not far removed from the lunatic fringe, was convinced that the abundance of sin in Boston was traceable to the malevolent design of the Board of Education in excluding the Bible from the curriculum and sectarian books from the school libraries. Mann himself was portrayed as a modern Uzzah, neglectful of the divine commandments, and deserving, like the Uzzah of the Bible, to be struck dead for his wickednesses. The fact of the matter, as Mann pointed out in a letter replying to Smith's charges, was that the Board had no jurisdiction whatever over the teaching of religion and the use of the Bible in the common schools. These matters, he noted, were strictly within the province of the local school committees to decide. As for his (Mann's) attitude towards the use of the Bible in schools, his Eighth Annual Report had argued at length in favor of Bible readings. Moreover, he added, "The Bible was never so extensively used in our schools as at the present time; and its use has been constantly increasing ever since the influence of the Board was brought to bear on the subject." [24] True, the Board had refused to introduce into the schools the American Sunday School Library; but this was necessary, since any introduction of sectarianism must be fatal to the future of the public schools. In his *Sequel to the so-*

called Correspondence between Rev. M. H. Smith and Horace Mann, Mann explains why:

> One sect may have the ascendency to-day, another to-morrow. This year there will be three Persons in the Godhead; next year but one; and the third year the Trinity will be restored to hold its precarious sovereignty until it shall be again dethroned by the worms of the dust it has made. This year, the everlasting fires of hell will burn to terrify the impenitent; next year, and without any repentance, its eternal flames will be extinguished, to be rekindled forever, or to be quenched forever as it may be decided at annual town meetings . . . This year the ordinance of baptism is inefficacious without immersion; next year one drop of water will be as good as forty fathoms. Children attending the district school will be taught one way; going from the district school to the town high school they will be taught another way. In controversies involving such momentous interests, the fiercest party spirit will rage, and all the contemplations of heaven be poisoned by the passions of earth . . . Can aught be conceived more deplorable, more fatal to the interests of the young than this? [25]

Mann thought not, and the majority agreed. In time the controversy died away, but not before it had been settled for once and for all, that in Massachusetts "no one sect shall obtain any advantage over other sects by means of the school system, which, for purposes of self-preservation, it has established." [26]

His last years as Secretary were, on the whole, the happiest years of Mann's life. His work was everywhere bearing fruit. He had recently built the home of his dreams, and his family was growing. The Twelfth Annual Report would justly claim "very remarkable results." Appropriations for common schools—nearly doubled; use of female teachers—increased by almost two thousand; the Normal Schools—prospering; school construction and attendance at all time highs; curricula and textbooks improved and standardized. The *Boston Transcript,* in an editorial reviewing Mann's years in office, thought it a "great work . . . well done." "There is," the *Transcript* continued,

> sensation in every nerve, power in every muscle, and activity in every limb of the Commonwealth . . . but the impulse given to

education has not been confined to Massachusetts. At this moment there is not, probably, a state in the Union which has not been moved, and which is not looking up to Massachusetts for direction and encouragement. The states from Maine to Texas are blessed, or to be blessed, by the example and recorded labors of Massachusetts; and while we allow something to the cooperation of many worthy minds, and many noble hearts, who does not know, who is not willing to confess, that all this is mainly the work of Horace Mann? [27]

In view of his growing fame, it is not surprising that the Whigs should have tapped him as their candidate to fill the Congressional seat vacated by the death of John Quincy Adams in January of 1848. The offer was one which neither his financial straits [28] nor his educational ambitions (he cherished hopes of becoming National Secretary of Education) permitted him to refuse. He made the race; won election by a majority of 904, and on April 13th, 1848, having submitted his resignation to the Board, he took his oath and seat as Representative from Massachusetts.

III

As a politician, Mann was a limited success. During his years in Washington the one great issue was slavery, and all of Mann's speeches and most of his energies were devoted to this issue. Surprisingly enough, considering his strong moral streak, he was no abolitionist. Perhaps his term as Secretary had taught him that the art of reform was the pursuit of the possible. At all events, he eschewed the extreme for the moderate. He would oppose slavery with all his heart, but he would not destroy the nation for a principle. And yet, when Daniel Webster came out for compromise in his famous Seventh of March speech, it was Mann who, as Theodore Parker put it, "smote the champion of slavery a blow which sent him reeling home: it was the heaviest Webster ever had." [29] It evidently was heavy enough, for Webster and his backers succeeded in preventing Mann's renomination by the Whigs in 1850. They could not prevent, however, his re-election. Mann ran as an independent and won handsomely.

Two years later he was out of politics, badly beaten in a try for the Governorship of Massachusetts. Mann attributed his loss to the unholy combination of the liquor interests and the Websterites, but it is more likely that he had simply overestimated his political appeal. With politics closed to him, he turned again to education. The Christian Connection was at this time in the process of organizing a co-educational and non-sectarian college at Yellow Springs, Ohio. They offered Mann the presidency, and stirred by the challenge it posed, he accepted; on October 5th, 1853, he was inaugurated as first president of Antioch College.

For this great occasion he composed and delivered the longest and most polished speech he ever made. His theme was a subject dear to his heart; education as the development of moral character. He passed civilization in review to show forth the destiny of man, and throughout, his emphasis was on the moral capabilities of the human race. To know and do the will of God as God has revealed that will in nature's laws was, he told them, the one grand end for which man, and woman too, was made. If both could be educated to observance of the uniform rules decreed by divine providence, then all, he assured them, must end well. This optimistic faith in the efficacy of God's law he never lost. One finds it in his last Antioch address as in his first: "We must," he counsels the Class of 1859, "learn to obey God's laws; for a perfect knowledge and a perfect obedience of God's laws would introduce all possible happiness into the world, and eliminate all possible misery from it." [30]

And so it might—if only we knew precisely what God's laws were, and what obeying them meant. Unfortunately, Mann's blueprint for beatitude does not extend to filling in the detail. God acts uniformly, and uniformity of act is what we mean by law. This much Mann had learned from George Combe, and for him it was enough. What mattered was a moral mind in a healthy body, and the theological experience of his youth had convinced him that too much theology was a positive hindrance to this end. He was prepared to pay lip-service to the reigning God, and he did so throughout his life—much to the disgust of Theodore Parker.[31] Beyond this, however, he would not and did not go. "He took phrenology for his metaphysics, and knew no psychology but physiology." [32] He needed, so he thought, no more.

Withal, it would be a mistake to conclude from this that Mann's contribution to higher education was nothing significant. Despite his metaphysical shallowness, he had a genius for getting to the heart of the matter, and, what is more important, doing something about it. More clearly than any man of his time, excepting only Theodore Parker, Mann saw that the reform of society must begin with the education of its young men *and* women to an appreciation of, and service to, society's moral needs. As in the common schools, so too at Antioch, all of his energies were bent to this purpose. He made co-education possible by making it respectable; he forced his age to consider that the proper aims of education encompassed more than rote training in classics or technics. A half-century before the advent of progressive education, Horace Mann was preaching and teaching life-adjustment. What Dewey reaped, Mann long since had sowed. The social conscience of American education is largely his memorial; the last sentence of his final baccalaureate address is still its finest expression: *"Be ashamed to die until you have won some victory for humanity."* [33]

SUGGESTED READINGS

Horace Mann wrote no books, and perhaps it is just as well, since the sum total of his reports, lectures, and addresses comprises several volumes. Most important are the Twelve Reports summarizing his secretaryship of the Massachusetts Board of Education. All are available in planographic reproduction, paperback publication by the Hugh Birch-Horace Mann Fund of the National Education Association, 1201 Sixteenth Street, Northwest, Washington 6, D.C. *The Common School Journal*, Vols. I-X (1839-1848), edited by Horace Mann, contains much of his best work. Copies of this Journal are available in most large University and Public Libraries. The important Antioch Addresses and Sermons are reprinted in Joy Elmer Morgan, *Horace Mann at Antioch* (Horace Mann Centennial Fund, National Education Association, Washington, D.C., 1938).

There are three biographies; all tend to idolize their subject. The earliest of these, Mary Peabody Mann's *Life of Horace Mann* (Boston, 1865), was a labor of love and should be judged as such. E. I. F. Williams, *Horace Mann, Educational Statesman* (New York: Macmillan, 1937), is more didactic but no less hero-worshipping. Louise Hall Tharp, *Until Victory, Horace Mann and Mary Peabody* (Boston: Little, Brown and Co., 1953), is primarily a love-story. Those seeking a more objective appraisal will find it in Merle Curti, "Education and Social Reform: Horace Mann," Chapter III in *The Social Ideas of*

American Educators (New York: Scribner, 1935), and in Neil G. McCluskey, *Public Schools and Moral Education,* Part Two (New York: Columbia University Press, 1958). B. A. Hinsdale, *Horace Mann and the Common School Revival in the United States* (New York: Scribner, 1900), is a dated, but nonetheless valuable, assessment of Mann's contribution to American public education. For further references, see *Selective and Critical Bibliography of Horace Mann* compiled by workers of the Federal Writers' Project of the Works Progress Administration in the State of Massachusetts (Boston, 1937).

REFERENCES

1. Louise Hall Tharp, *Until Victory, Horace Mann and Mary Peabody* (Boston: Little, Brown, 1953), p. 136.

2. Theodore Parker to Samuel Gridley Howe, August 26th, 1859, in *Life and Correspondence of Theodore Parker,* 2 Vols. (New York: Appleton, 1864), II, p. 343. Hereafter cited as Parker.

3. Horace Mann to an unidentified friend, in Mary Peabody Mann, *Life of Horace Mann,* 2nd edition (Boston: Lee & Shepard, 1865), p. 11. Hereafter cited as Life.

4. Life, p. 12.

5. Parker, II, p. 344.

6. B. A. Hinsdale, *Horace Mann and the Common School Revival in the United States* (New York: Scribner, 1900), p. 90. Hereafter cited as Hinsdale.

7. Letter to his sister, Life, p. 86.

8. Ibid., pp. 86-87.

9. Ibid., p. 172.

10. *Common School Journal,* Vol. IX (1847), p. 142.

11. Life, p. 71. Correct title, *The Constitution of Man Considered in Relation to External Objects.* First published in England in 1828, and shortly thereafter exported to America, this introduction to Combe's system of phrenology soon became a best seller on both sides of the Atlantic. Horace Mann was not the only distinguished Bostonian converted to Combe's philosophy. His friends, Dr. Samuel Gridley Howe, George Emerson, and Cyrus Pierce, all avowed phrenology.

12. That is to say, he wrote no books as such. He did write two pamphlets of almost book-length (*Reply* and *Answer* to the Boston Schoolmasters), and his annual Reports, if printed together, would make a volume of considerably more than a thousand pages.

13. Hinsdale, p. 266.

14. Twelfth Annual Report, pp. 17-18.

15. Ibid., p. 18.

16. Ibid.

17. Ibid.

18. Ibid., pp. 18-19.

19. *Until Victory,* p. 174.

20. Ibid., pp. 177-78.

21. Seventh Annual Report, p. 21.

22. Ibid., pp. 132-33. Mann's italics.

23. Ibid., p. 138.

24. Hinsdale, p. 223.

25. Ibid., pp. 226-27.

26. Ibid., p. 228.

27. *Boston Transcript,* December 18th, 1848.

28. Considering his meagre personal resources, Mann had, over the years, assumed financial responsibility for far too many educational projects. He had lent money for school construction, supplies, and publications; paid all of his own office and travel expenses, and supported himself and his family—all this on two thousand dollars a year! The effort had cost him such fortune as he had, and had come close to costing him his health as well. Eventually, the Commonwealth of Massachusetts would vote him three thousand dollars in partial reimbursement for his expenditures, but this was hardly adequate to his needs, nor was it anywhere near the total amount he had expended on behalf of the children of Massachusetts. For a detailed account of Mann's financial difficulties, see Hinsdale, pp. 141-44.

29. Parker, p. 344.

30. Joy Elmer Morgan, *Horace Mann at Antioch* (Washington: Horace Mann Centennial Fund, National Education Association, 1938), p. 367. Hereafter cited as Morgan.

31. "I know," wrote Parker to his friend S. G. Howe, "no politician who so hated Calvinism, none who used its language so much, or who, to the public, appeared so much the friend of the ecclesiastic theology of which it is the poison-flower. There was a certain duplicity in the man, at strange variance with the austere purity of his personal life, and the lofty elevation of his purpose. This appears in his work as Secretary of the Board of Education, as Member of Congress, and as President of Antioch College—perhaps more conspicious in the last office. Had the little, bigoted sect of Christians known his profound convictions, and the moral contempt he felt for their absurd and debasing theology, they would never have made him even a teacher in their school, much less its head. If he had lived he must have felt great embarrassment from this cause, to be met by yet farther duplicity. I like not his taking of bread and wine in the meetinghouses of his sect, nor his having prayers three times a-day at his table. It was an official, not a personal act, and savors of hypocrisy. It was done for example —but it was an instance of falseness to his own convictions." Parker, II, p. 342.

32. Ibid.

33. Morgan, p. 389.

XII

Beyond Unitarianism

WILLIAM ELLERY CHANNING
THEODORE PARKER

"We want a revival of religion in the
American church which shall be to the
church what the religion of Jesus was
to heathenism and Judaism . . . We
do not want a religion hierarchically
organized . . . We want a religion
democratically organized, generating
great political, social, domestic
institutions, and ending in a world
full of noble men and women. . . ." [1]

THEODORE PARKER

1. William Ellery Channing

The progress of religion is defined by the denunciation of gods.
The keynote of idolatry is contentment with the prevalent gods.

So SAYS ALFRED NORTH WHITEHEAD, and the progress of religion
in New England from the Seventeenth to the Nineteenth centuries
seems to bear out the truth of his contention. The Puritans landed
on these shores denouncing the scholastic deities of Canterbury
and Rome. Three generations later the Congregationalist Arminians
were denouncing the angry God of the Puritan Elect. By the second
decade of the Nineteenth Century the Unitarians had emerged to
denounce the Trinitarians; by the fourth, they too were being denounced—this time from within.

To us a century and more removed from that struggle for religious reform, the polemic of the Reverend Theodore Parker against
the Unitarian orthodoxy of his day appears mild enough, an affair
primarily, and perhaps exclusively, of interest to the Boston Association of Ministers. In truth it was something more than that,
and as far as Parker himself was concerned, it was by no means
mild. His zeal for social reform was no less than that of his good
friend Horace Mann. What Mann had done for education, Parker
would, and did, do for religion.

It all began back in 1819. Parker was still a boy roaming the
green at Lexington and dreaming of his revolutionary ancestors;
Mann was just about to graduate from Brown. In May of that
year a Boston clergyman named William Ellery Channing journeyed

to Baltimore for the purpose of delivering the sermon at the ordination of his protégé, the Reverend Jared Sparks. Channing was at that time a well-known figure. Since 1803 he had been minister at Boston's Federal Street Church. In 1813 he had helped to found the *Christian Disciple,* a magazine dedicated to the furtherance of Christian liberalism. His tract of 1815, distinguishing the position of the American liberals from that of the English unitarians, had established him as a leading spokesman for American unitarianism. Now, at Baltimore, he was ready to put his creed on record.

He begins with a plain statement of the place of Scripture in religion: "Whatever doctrines seem to us to be clearly taught in the Scriptures, we receive without reserve or exception. We do not, however, attach equal importance to all the books in this collection." [2] The Bible is a library and, like any library, some books in it command a higher regard than others. To Channing, these are the volumes of the New Testament.

> The dispensation of Moses, compared with that of Jesus, we consider as adapted to the childhood of the human race, a preparation for a nobler system, and chiefly useful now as serving to confirm and illustrate the Christian Scriptures. Jesus Christ is the only master of Christians, and whatever he taught, either during his personal ministry or by his inspired Apostles, we regard as of divine authority and profess to make the rule of our lives.[3]

Notice that Channing's emphasis is on the *teachings* of Jesus, rather than on his person. The distinction is of cardinal importance, and in the development of the Unitarian theology it comes to mark a major difference between the liberals and their traditionalist foes. There is, however, something else in the statement worthy of note, and that is the repudiation of the Puritan theocratic tradition implied by the relegation of the Old Testament to minor status. That law and covenant of Moses which was the very model of the Holy Commonwealth is now avowed to be a thing no longer really useful, and this because in the interpretation of Scripture the faith of our childhood must give way before the reason of our maturity.

> We profess not to know a book which demands a more frequent exercise of reason than the Bible. In addition to the remarks now

made on its infinite connections, we may observe that its style no-where affects the precision of science or the accuracy of definition. Its language is singularly glowing, bold, and figurative, demanding more frequent departures from the literal sense than that of our own age and country, and consequently demanding more continual ex-ercise of judgment. . . . With these views of the Bible, we feel it our bounden duty to exercise our reason upon it perpetually, to compare, to infer, to look beyond the letter to the spirit, to seek in the nature of the subject and the aim of the writer his true meaning; and, in general, to make use of what is known for explaining what is difficult and for discovering new truths.[4]

We reason about the Bible precisely as civilians do about the constitution under which we live . . . Without these principles of interpretation, we frankly acknowledge that we cannot defend the divine authority of the Scriptures. Deny us this latitude, and we must abandon this book to its enemies.[5]

Reason, then, is the rule to be adopted in interpreting the Scriptures, and this being settled, Channing now passes to the consideration of some of the doctrines which Scripture, so interpreted, seems to him clearly to express.

The first of these, and preeminently the most important, is the doctrine of the UNITY of God. On this the Unitarian theology rests.

To this truth we give infinite importance, and we feel ourselves bound to take heed lest any man spoil us of it by vain philosophy. The proposition that there is one God seems to us exceedingly plain. We understand by it that there is one being, one mind, *one person,* one intelligent agent, *and one only,* to whom underived and infinite perfection and dominion belong. We conceive that these words could have conveyed no other meaning to the simple and uncultivated people who were set apart to be the depositaries of this great truth and who were utterly incapable of understanding those hairbreadth distinctions between being and person which the sagacity of later ages has discovered. We find no intimation that this language was to be taken in an unusual sense, or that God's unity was a quite different thing from the oneness of other intelligent beings.[6]

We do, then, with all earnestness, though without reproaching our brethren, protest against the irrational and unscriptural doctrine of the Trinity. "To us," as to the Apostle and the primitive Chris-tians, "there is one God, even the Father." With Jesus, we worship the Father as the only living and true God.[7]

What, then, of the Christ? Channing's answer is to proclaim his belief in the unity of Jesus, that is to say, he rejects the orthodox catholic doctrine of the two natures. Jesus Christ is not the God-man, but man sent of God to bring the truth to all the ages. As man he was crucified, as man he suffered, and by his suffering mankind is delivered.

> With regard to the great object which Jesus came to accomplish, there seems to be no possibility of mistake. We believe that he was sent by the Father to effect a moral or spiritual deliverance of mankind; that is, to rescue men from sin and its consequences, and to bring them to a state of everlasting purity and happiness.[8]

At this point the theological waters become a little muddied, for having denied that Jesus is God, Channing now proceeds to invest him with powers and functions that, according to orthodoxy, God alone can possess.

> We believe, too, that he accomplishes this sublime purpose by a variety of methods—by his instructions respecting God's unity, parental character, and moral government . . . by his promises of pardon to the penitent, and of divine assistance to those who labor for progress in moral excellence . . . by his glorious discoveries of immortality; by his sufferings and death; by that signal event the resurrection, which powerfully bore witness to his divine mission, and brought down to men's senses a future life; by his continual intercession, which obtains for us spiritual aid and blessings; and by the power with which he is invested of raising the dead, judging the the world, and conferring the everlasting rewards promised to the faithful.[9]

Withal, Jesus is not empowered to do everything. It is, Channing insists, no part of his function to call forth the mercy of God on our behalf. With the ransom theory of the atonement he will have nothing to do. The idea that man is born totally depraved strikes him as monstrous, and he finds the Calvinist doctrines of election and irresistible grace equally repugnant. As the highest object of Christ's mission "is the recovery of men to virtue or holiness," so man's prime religious responsibility is the cultivation of his moral sense.

We believe that all virtue has its foundation in the moral nature of man, that is, in conscience or his sense of duty, and in the power of forming his temper and life according to conscience. We believe that these moral faculties are the grounds of responsibility and the highest distinctions of human nature, and that no act is praiseworthy any further than it springs from their exertion. . . . Among the virtues we give the first place to the love of God. We believe that this principle is the true end and happiness of our being. . . . We believe, too, that the love of God is not only essential to happiness, but to the strength and perfection of all the virtues. . . .[10]

Nonetheless, Channing thinks, even the love of God should be tempered by reason. Without self-possession, virtue and devotion lose all dignity. Excess of piety only breeds contempt for the pious.

Most certainly, if the love of God be that which often bears its name, the less we have of it the better. If religion be the shipwreck of understanding, we cannot keep too far from it. On this subject we always speak plainly. We cannot sacrifice our reason to the reputation of zeal. We owe it to truth and religion to maintain that fanaticism, partial insanity, sudden impressions, and ungovernable transports are anything rather than piety.[11]

Such is Channing's religion within the limits of reason alone. Its logic is not above reproach, and certainly there is much in it offering excellent grounds for extensive debate. But to a society searching for a creed worthy of the New American Enlightenment it seemed just the thing; remote enough from the angry God of Jonathan Edwards, yet distinguishably Christian all the same. That a religion founded on reason and moral sense was theological dynamite bothered no one at the time. After all, who, in this glorious morning of the new Republic and the Nineteenth Century, had time for theology. And so the Unitarian credo went unchallenged for a season.

2. Theodore Parker

ON MAY 19TH, 1841, at the Hawes Place Church in South Boston, Theodore Parker arose to preach the sermon at the ordination of his friend Charles Shackford. His topic was The Transient and Permanent in Christianity; his theme was the transitoriness of all Christian doctrine and authority as compared with the permanence of "the Christ that is born within us." His fellow Unitarians heard him out with an increasing sense of dismay, for in the name of reason and moral intuition he seemed to them to be dismissing as of little or no account, not only the forms and doctrines of every sect and church (as members of a creedless Church, they expected him to do that), not only the authority of the Old Testament (Channing had accustomed them to doubt of that), but the authority of the New Testament and of Jesus Christ himself! "The ancient belief in the infallible inspiration of each sentence of the New Testament is," they hear him say, "fast changing, very fast."

One writer, not a sceptic, but a Christian of unquestioned piety, sweeps off the beginning of Matthew; another, of a different church and equally religious, the end of John. Numerous critics strike off several epistles. . . . Who shall tell us the work of retrenchment is to stop here; that others will not demonstrate, what some pious hearts have long felt, that errors of doctrine and errors of fact may be found in many parts of the record, here and there, from the beginning of Matthew to the end of Acts? [12]

"Christianity," he concludes, "does not rest on the infallible authority of the New Testament. It depends on this collection of books for the historical statement of its facts." And the facts, he insists, are subject to the judgment of reason. The authority of Jesus fares no better.

> The authority of Jesus, as of all teachers . . . must rest on the truth of his words, and not their truth on his authority. . . . So if it could be proved . . . that the Gospels were the fabrication of designing and artful men, that Jesus of Nazareth had never lived, still Christianity would stand firm, and fear no evil. None of the doctrines of that religion would fall to the ground; for, if true, they stand by themselves.[13]

No wonder that his audience filed out of the church depressed in heart and puzzled in mind, for if Doctrine, Church, Scripture and Teacher are all dispensable, what is left? The theological dynamite fashioned by the Reverend Channing had finally exploded, and many there were who like John Weiss found themselves asking: "What has Mr. Parker done for us? He has with justice annihilated the Transient, but where is the Permanent?" [14]

The man who had in this sermon and other lectures upset the theological sensibilities of Unitarian Boston was no stranger in town. The first Parker had come to Massachusetts Bay in 1635. Theodore's grandfather, Captain John Parker, had commanded the Minute Men on that famous day in '75 when the redcoats marched to Lexington village. For a hundred years Parkers had farmed the Lexington land and lived in the old house where on August 24th, 1810, Theodore was born. There he grew to manhood, from there in 1830 he set off for Boston to teach school and study at Harvard College. He worked hard, made a good impression, and in 1834 entered Harvard Divinity School. His classmates later remembered him as "a prodigious athlete in his studies." He mastered Hebrew, Greek, and German, and got the rudiments of a dozen other languages. The Fathers of the Church and the great German philosophers and theologians were his daily companions. At last, graduation, and the call to a church of his own. West Roxbury parish was small and so was the salary, but no matter, it was enough to get married on. Two months later he was ordained a Unitarian minister and his career began.

His passage to fame was rapid. The clergy took note of his critical reviews of current theology. The Transcendentalists were impressed by his contributions to the *Dial*. Perhaps it was because he was beginning to talk like a Transcendentalist. Like Emerson, he attacked miracles.

> The Gospels are not without their myths—the miraculous conception, the temptation, etc. Do not all the miracles belong to the mythical part? The resurrection—is that not also a myth? I see not where to put up the bar between the true and the false. Christianity itself . . . will stand forever, but I have sometimes thought it would stand better without the New Testament than with it.[15]

But where Emerson, having stated his disagreement with orthodoxy, withdrew from the Unitarian ministry, Parker chose to stay and fight for liberalism from within. Soon he was embroiled in a controversy over miracles that had all the clergy of Boston taking sides. Emerson had started it with his Address to the Students of the Harvard Divinity School. Religion, he had proclaimed,

> is an intuition. It cannot be received at second hand. . . . To aim to convert a man by miracles is a profanation of the soul. . . . The spirit only can teach . . . The man on whom the soul descends, through whom the soul speaks, alone can teach. . . . In the soul then let the redemption be sought.

When Emerson went on from this to disparage the authority of the Church by advising his hearers not to let it interfere with their sense of ministry, the storm broke. Andrews Norton, the leader of the Unitarian brahmins, undertook to reply, and his answer was to read Emerson and transcendentalism out of the Church. A year later, in an address to the alumni of the Divinity School, he characterized the liberal point of view as The Latest Form of Infidelity. It is, he contended,

> distinguished by assuming the Christian name while it strikes directly at the root of faith in Christianity, and indirectly at all religion, by

denying the miracles, the divine mission of Christ. . . . If there are no miracles, there is no religion. No proof of [Christ's] divine commission could be afforded but through miraculous displays of God's power. Nothing is left that can be called Christianity, if its miraculous character be denied. Its essence is gone; its evidence is annihilated. . . . There can be no intuition, no direct perception, of the truth of Christianity, no metaphysical certainty. . . . We must use the same faculties, and adopt the same rules in judging concerning the facts of the world which we have not seen as concerning those of the world of which we have seen a very little.[16]

Then began the war of pamphlets as liberals and brahmins debated miracles and transcendentalism. Parker could not keep silent. The discussion, he thought, was getting out of hand, drifting away from the basic issue Emerson had raised. And so one Levi Blodgett wrote a public letter, and in it undertook to recall Mr. Norton and his supporters to what he (Levi) considered was the real question, the Previous Question heretofore unconsidered.

I will put forth a few thoughts on the PREVIOUS QUESTION, which I think must be decided before we touch the evidence of Christianity. This previous question is as follows: HOW DO MEN COME TO HAVE ANY RELIGION, or, in other words, *on what evidence do they receive the plainest religious truths?* Gentlemen, we must settle the *genus*, before we decide upon the *species*. The evidence for religious truths in *general*, I take it, cannot be different in *kind*, from the evidence for the *special* religious truths of Christianity.[17]

Now the primary and essential truths of all religions are, according to Levi Blodgett,

A BELIEF IN THE EXISTENCE OF GOD, and A SENSE OF DEPENDENCE ON HIM. I call these *primary* and *essential* truths, because without them I cannot conceive any religion possible. I reckon that man is by nature a religious being; i.e., that he was made to be religious, as much as an ox was made to eat grass. The germs of religion, then, both the germs of religious principle and religious sentiment, must be born in man, or innate, as our preacher says. *The existence of God* is a fact given in our nature: it is not something discovered by a process of reasoning; by a long series of deductions from facts; nor yet is it the last generalization from phenomena observed in the universe of mind or matter. But it is a truth fundamental in our nature; given outright by God; a truth which comes to light as soon as self-consciousness begins. Still further, I take *a sense of dependence on God* to be a natural and essential sentiment of the soul, as much as feeling, seeing, and hearing are natural sensations of the body. Here, then, are the religious instincts which lead man to God and religion, just as naturally, as the intellectual instincts lead him to truth, and animal instincts to his food.[18]

This idea that the permanent substance of religion is our intuition of dependence on God, Parker had derived from his reading of the German theologian, Schleiermacher, and throughout his ministry it was to be his mainstay. It is this sense of dependence that is the permanent in Christianity. This is the Christ that is born in us. In sum,

this inborn religious faculty is the basis and cause of all religion. Without this internal religious element, either man could not have any religious notions, nor become religious at all, or else religion would be something foreign to his nature. . . . Without a moral faculty, we could have no duties in respect to men; without a religious faculty, no duties in respect of God. The foundation of each is in man, not out of him. If man have not a religious element in his nature, miraculous or other "revelations" can no more render him religious than fragments of sermons and leaves of the Bible can make a lamb religious when mixed and eaten with its daily food. . . . The religious element existing within us, and this alone, renders religion the duty, the privilege, and the welfare of mankind.[19]

But while this religious element, like human nature itself, remains ever the same in all men, men's thought about religion does not. Modes of worship, forms of religion, and doctrines of theology vary from land to land and age to age. In brief, theology is as transient as religion is permanent. It is essential to keep this in mind, since it is on this distinction of theology from religion that Parker's attack on christendom rests.

The attack begins as a denunciation of the popular theology taught in the Boston churches. As Parker sees it,

There are five doctrines common to [this] theology, namely—the
false idea of God, as imperfect in power, wisdom, justice, benevolence, and holiness; the false idea of man, as fallen, depraved, and by
nature lost; the false idea of the relation between God and man, a
relation of perpetual antagonism, man naturally hating God, and
God hating "fallen" and "depraved" man; the false idea of inspiration, that it comes only by a miracle on God's part, not by normal
action on man's; and the false idea of salvation, that it is from the
"wrath of God," who is "a consuming fire" breaking out against
"poor human nature," by the "atoning blood of Christ," that is by
the death of Jesus of Nazareth, which appeased the "wrath of God,"
and on condition of belief in this popular theology, especially of
the five false ideas.[20]

How, asks Parker,

can you ask men of large reason . . . to believe any one of the
numerous schemes of the Trinity, the miracles of the New or Old
Testament; to believe in the existence of a devil whom God has
made, seeking to devour mankind? How can you ask such men to
believe in the existence of an angry God, jealous, capricious, selfish,
and revengeful, who has made an immeasurable hell under his feet.
. . . Will you ask Humboldt, the greatest of living philosophers, to
believe that a wafer is "the body of God," as the Catholics say? or
M. Comte, to believe that the Bible is "the word of God," as the
Protestants say? Will you ask a man of great genius, of great culture,
to lay his whole nature in the dust, and submit to some little man,
with no genius, who only reads to him a catechism which was
dreamed by some celibate monks in the dark ages of human history?
You cannot expect such men to assent to that. . . .[21]

Nor, he thinks, can you even expect them to assent to the inconsistencies of Unitarianism.

With a philosophy too rational to go the full length of the supernatural theory, too sensual to embrace the spiritual method, and ask
no person to mediate between man and God, it oscillates between the
two; humanizes the Bible, yet calls it miraculous; believes in man's
greatness, freedom and spiritual nature, yet asks for a Mediator
and Redeemer. It censures the traditionary sects, yet sits among the
tombs and mourns over things past and gone; believes in the human-

ity of Jesus, yet his miraculous birth likewise and miraculous powers, and makes him an anomalous and impossible being. It blinds men's eyes with the letter, yet bids them look out for the spirit; stops their ears with the texts of the Old Testament, and then asks them to listen to the voice of God in their heart; it reverences Jesus manfully, yet denounces all such as preach Absolute Religion and Morality, as he did, on its own authority. Well might Jeremiah say of it, "Alas for thee, now thou hast forsaken the promise of thy youth." [22]

The predictable result of such expressions of conviction was a summons to judgment by the Boston Association of Ministers. Parker was invited to tea, accused of deism, pantheism, and subversion, and asked to recant. He defended himself by attempting to provoke a discussion of the theological issues involved. The long and rambling talk which followed ended on a somewhat ludicrous note with members of the Association lauding Parker's goodness and sincerity. And so, as Commager remarks, "the great heresy trial came to an end on a note of bathos."

A year later Parker was in hot water again, this time as a result of his "Great and Thursday Lecture" on The Relation of Jesus to His Age and to the Ages. To Octavius Frothingham, minister of the host First Church, Parker's sentiments were a rejection of Christianity itself, and he took steps to make sure that the heretic could not be invited again to the lectureship. A series of recriminations by both sides culminated with the publication of another open letter by Parker to the Boston ministers. In it he again asked for a specification and discussion of his heresies. None was forthcoming, and soon the breach was widened beyond repair, for in January of 1845 a committee of Parker's Boston friends convened to resolve: "That the Reverend Theodore Parker shall have a chance to be heard in Boston." With a sense of mission, Parker accepted. His friends now organized the Twenty-Eighth Congregational Society, hired the old Melodeon for a church, and in the winter of 1846 Parker preached his inaugural sermon on The True Idea of the Christian Church.

What this "True Idea" was, his opening words made clear:

A Christian church should be a means of reforming the world, of forming it after the pattern of Christian ideas. It should therefore bring up the sentiments of the times, the ideas of the times, and the action of the times, to judge them by the universal standard. In this way it will learn much and be a living church, that grows with the advance of men's sentiments, ideas, and actions, and while it keeps the good of the past will lose no brave spirit of the present day . . . If it would lead, it must go before men; if it would be looked up to, it must stand high.[23]

Good faith, he thinks, means good works.

Does not Christianity say the strong should help the weak? Does not that mean something? It once did. Has the Christian fire faded out from those words, once so marvellously bright? Look round you, in the streets of your own Boston . . . Look at the poor, men of small ability, weak by nature, born into a weak position, therefore doubly weak; men whom the strong use for their purpose, and then cast them off . . . Behold the wicked . . . ask why they became wicked; how we have aimed to reform them; what we have done to make them respect themselves, to believe in goodness, in man and God? and then say if there is not something for Christian men to do, something for a Christian church to do! Every almshouse in Massachusetts shows that the churches have not done their duty, that the Christians lie lies when they call Jesus "master" and men "brothers!" [24]

Surely the true idea of the Christian church has not been well served in Boston.

Consider slavery.

Did not Christ say, whatsoever you would that men should do unto you, do you even so unto them; and are there not three million brothers of yours and mine in bondage here, the hopeless sufferers of a savage doom; debarred from the civilization of our age, the barbarians of the nineteenth century; shut out from the pretended religion of Christendom, the heathens of a Christian land; chained down from the liberty unalienable in man, the slaves of a Christian republic . . . Great God! and has it come to this, that men are silent over such a sin? 'Tis even so. Then it must be that every church which dares assume the name of Christ, that dearest name to men, thunders and lightens on this hideous wrong! That is not so. The church is dumb, while the state is only silent; while the servants of the people are only asleep, "God's ministers" are dead! [25]

The Unitarians of Boston sit silent, saying nothing, doing nothing, playing it safe. For such as these, Parker can scarcely contain his contempt. This "church termagant," peevishly scolding at sin, "mewling and whining, its face turned down, its eyes turned back"; [26] this Unitarian orthodoxy has no future. Let us, then, discard this antiquarian faith, for whatever it may be, it certainly is not—Christian. "Had Christ looked back for counsel, he might have founded a church fit for Abraham or Isaac to worship in, not for ages to come, or the age then"; but Christ looked forward, and so, Parker believes, must we.

> The church that is to lead this century will not be a church creeping on all fours . . . the church which did for the fifth century, or the fifteenth, will not do for this. What is well enough at Rome, Oxford, or Berlin, is not well enough for Boston. It must have our ideas, the smell of our ground, and have grown out of the religion in our soul. The freedom of America must be there before this energy will come. . . . A church that believes in inspiration now will appeal to God; try things by reason and conscience; aim to surpass the old heroes; baptize its children with a new spirit, and using the present age will lead public opinion, and not follow it.[27]

Such was the program Parker laid down for himself and for his congregation, and in the years that followed he did his level best to fulfill it. His fame as a preacher grew with every fiery sermon; the infidel barred from all of the pulpits of Boston save one, ranged far and wide as a Lyceum lecturer. He took up the cause of reform, and worked unceasingly for improvement in the living conditions of those in prison and the working conditions of those forced to labor in factories. When no other preacher in Boston was willing to stand up and be counted against the institution of slavery, he was leading the fight against the Fugitive Slave Law and exposing himself to arrest for harbouring runaways. Inevitably, his scholarly intentions failed of fulfillment. So busy was he practicing Christianity in these years that he never did get around to writing out the theory of the Absolute Theology of the Infinite Perfection of God.

His health suffered; too much work, too little care of his bodily needs, now took their toll. The words that he wrote to describe the American people fitted none better than himself.

All that we do we overdo. It appears in our hopefulness; we are the most aspiring of nations. Not content with half the continent we wish the other half. We have this characteristic of genius, we are dissatisfied with all that we have done. The American soul passes from its work as soon as it is finished. We are more spontaneous than logical; we have ideas rather than facts or precedents. We are not so reflective as forecasting. . . . We are the most restless of people. How we crowd into cars and steamboats; a locomotive would well typify our fuming fizzing spirit. In our large towns life seems to be only a scamper. Not satisfied with bustling about all day, when night comes we cannot sit still but alone of all nations have added rockers to our chairs.[28]

In 1856 Parker contracted pleurisy. It was the first symptom of a tuberculosis already far advanced. Two years later his health broke down again, and in 1859 illness forced him to abandon his pulpit. A final quest for health led him to the West Indies, and from there to Switzerland. Even as Horace Mann was exhorting his students to win victories for humanity, the man who had served humanity as well as or better than any reformer in New England was writing from Montreux to reassure his brother that his quest was prospering. In fact it was not. Parker was slowly dying and he knew it. Seeking the Italian sun, he traveled south to Florence, and there in May of 1860 he died. In November Lincoln won the Presidency. Six months later the Civil War began.

SUGGESTED READINGS

Channing's Baltimore sermon and other essays, edited with an Introduction, Chronology, and Bibliography by Irving H. Bartlett, are available in paperback under the title *Unitarian Christianity and Other Essays* (New York: Liberal Arts Press, 1957). The best introduction to Parker is *Theodore Parker: An Anthology* (Boston: Beacon Press, 1960) edited with Introduction and Notes by Henry Steele Commager. The Centenary Edition of *The Writings of Theodore Parker* in fifteen volumes, published by The American Unitarian Association, is available in most large libraries, as is *Views of Religion* (Boston: American

Unitarian Association, 1885), a selection by James Freeman Clarke of Parker's more important sermons, discourses, speeches, and essays, including "The Transient and Permanent in Christianity."

Of the three biographies of Parker, Commager's *Theodore Parker, Yankee Crusader* (Boston: Little, Brown, 1936), is the most recent, readable, and superficial. Those desiring a somewhat more substantial account should consult Octavius Brooks Frothingham, *Theodore Parker, A Biography* (New York: Putnam's, 1880). Of interest by the same author is *Theodore Parker, A Sermon* (Boston: Walker, Wise, 1860). Preached at a service commemorating Parker's recent passing, it is candid alike in its appraisal of Parker's greatness and shortcomings. Still of value also is John Weiss, *Life and Correspondence of Theodore Parker,* 2 Vols. (New York: Appleton, 1864). The Levi Blodgett letter is reprinted in John E. Dirks, *The Critical Theology of Theodore Parker* (New York: Columbia University Press, 1948).

REFERENCES

1. Theodore Parker, "The Religion which is Needed," in H. S. Commager, *Theodore Parker: An Anthology* (Boston: Beacon Press, 1960), pp. 114-15. Hereafter cited as Parker Anthology.

2. William Ellery Channing, *Unitarian Christianity and Other Essays* (New York: Liberal Arts Press, 1957), p. 4. Hereafter cited as Channing.

3. Ibid.

4. Ibid., pp. 5-6.

5. Ibid., p. 7.

6. Ibid., p. 11. My italics.

7. Ibid., p. 12.

8. Ibid., p. 25.

9. Ibid., pp. 25-26.

10. Ibid., p. 30.

11. Ibid., p. 31.

12. Theodore Parker, "A Discourse of the Transient and Permanent in Christianity," in *Views of Religion* (Boston: American Unitarian Association, 1855), p. 307.

13. Ibid., p. 308.

14. Henry Steele Commager, *Theodore Parker* (Boston: Little, Brown, 1936), p. 76. Years later Weiss would write the first biography of Parker.

15. Parker Anthology, p. 71.

16. Andrews Norton, *A Discourse on the Latest Form of Infidelity* (Cambridge: John Owen, 1839), pp. 22-23.

17. John Edward Dirks, *The Critical Theology of Theodore Parker* (New York: Columbia University Press, 1948), p. 140.

18. Ibid., pp. 140-41.

19. Theodore Parker, "The Religious Element in Man," from "A Discourse of Matters Pertaining to Religion" in *Views of Religion,* p. 13.

20. Dirks, p. 112.

21. Ibid., p. 113.

22. Commager, *Theodore Parker,* p. 85.

23. Parker Anthology, pp. 82, 84.
24. Ibid., p. 85.
25. Ibid., pp. 85-86.
26. Ibid., p. 87.
27. Ibid.
28. Commager, *Theodore Parker,* p. 138.

XIII

Of the People
... For the People

ABRAHAM LINCOLN

"My paramount object in this struggle *is* to save the Union, and is *not* either to save or to destroy slavery." [1]

ABRAHAM LINCOLN

Abraham Lincoln

IT IS ODD, but often true, that the greatness of a man can be a barrier to the understanding of his philosophy. For greatness fosters hero-worship and encourages the making of myths, and truly there are no greater enemies to philosophical understanding than the myth-makers and the hero-worshippers. The former would bury the inconvenient reality in the pleasant fantasy; the latter would have us believe that all the utterances of the great man are beyond reproach. We must, then, take special care to guard ourselves against these enemies, if only because no people on earth is as prone as we Americans to fall prey to them. It is our abiding weakness always to see men and ideas in blacks and whites. We habitually divide all into the good guys and the bad guys, and in the process most often lose the real man in between. Of no figure in our history is this more true than Abraham Lincoln. The literature about him is enormous, and much of it is sentimental trash. If we would know the mind of Lincoln we must put it all behind us and concentrate upon the man's own words. We must forget the mythical character so beloved by partisan politicians and think only of what he actually stood for. The verdict of history has made him the prince of good guys, and perhaps he was. But we must remember that he was only a man, not a saint, and like all men he was fallible and opinionated and not always wise.

He was, as we all know, a self-made man, and those qualities which enabled him to survive and prosper in a frontier society are the keys to the understanding of his thought. The Kentucky wilderness, where in 1809 he was born, like the raw young settlement of New Salem, Illinois, wherein he reached his manhood, prized hard work, respected strength, and admired initiative. The historians are agreed that in each the young Lincoln came up to the mark. Springfield, the new capital to which Lincoln removed in 1837, valued legal acumen and rated speaking ability high, and here too he excelled. He joined the Whigs and stood foursquare for Free Soil, Free Enterprise, and a Strong Union. To these political ideals he was faithful throughout his public life. His political career was strange, to say the least. Prior to his nomination for the Presidency, he had held no important elective office save that of Congressman, and this for but a single term (1847-48). In 1855, and again in 1858, he ran for the Senate against Stephen Douglas and lost both times. His election as President in 1860 was the fortunate consequence of a split between the northern and southern wings of the Democratic Party. Thus, almost by accident, did Lincoln come to that eminence which was to assure his place among the framers of the American Mind.

As he was a maverick in politics, so also in his ethical and religious attitudes he was ever the individualist. Ethically, he was what the professors would call a "moral-sense" man, that is, he believed that every man should in all matters of personal conduct be guided by the dictates of his conscience, and very often in his own career he himself was guided in this way. He has been much criticized for his religion, or rather for what his critics have taken to be his lack of it. Lincoln himself was always aware of the problem. When he was still a young man, and was considering running for Congress, the question as to his religious beliefs having been raised, he wrote an open letter to the voters of his district, and in it he had this to say:

FELLOW CITIZENS: A charge having got into circulation in some of the neighborhoods of this District, in substance that I am an open scoffer at Christianity, I have by the advice of some friends concluded to notice the subject in this form. That I am not a member of any Christian Church, is true; but I have never denied the truth of the Scriptures; and I have never spoken with intentional disrespect of religion in general, or of any denomination of Christians in particular. It is true that in early life I was inclined to believe in what

I understand is called the "Doctrine of Necessity"—that is, that the human mind is impelled to action, or held in rest by some power, over which the mind itself has no control; and I have sometimes (with one, two or three, but never publicly) tried to maintain this opinion in argument. The habit of arguing thus, however, I have entirely left off for more than five years. And I add here, I have always understood this same opinion to be held by several of the Christian denominations. The foregoing, is the whole truth, briefly stated, in relation to myself, upon this subject.[2]

The passage is interesting more for what it does not say than for what it does. Notice that Lincoln takes no position pro or con on any of the basic tenets of the Christian faith. Nor, to be precise, does he actually answer the implications of the charge brought against him. In brief, his personal view of the matter is entirely agnostic. Like most self-made men, he seems to have believed in his heart that God helps those who help themselves. On the other hand, it is only fair to note that throughout his life in his public utterances Lincoln frequently mentioned the name of God. In times of crisis he always invoked His Name, and by his words implied belief in His existence. Withal, Professor William Wolf, in his recent study of Lincoln's religion, *The Almost Chosen People,* concludes that "by the creedal standards of the churches of his day he was not 'an orthodox Christian.' "[3] He was, however, Wolf believes, "a biblical Christian," or, "to use a still more precise definition, Lincoln was a biblical prophet who saw himself as an instrument of God and his country as God's 'almost chosen people' called to world responsibility."[4] Wolf may be right, but, on the other hand, there is the evidence of Lincoln's last view of the subject to be considered.

In September of 1862, that same month in which Jackson's army crossed the Potomac and invaded Maryland, the sorely beset Commander-in-Chief delivered himself of the following:

The will of God prevails. In great contests each party claims to act in accordance with the will of God. Both *may* be, and one *must* be, wrong. God cannot be *for* and *against* the same thing at the same time. In the present civil war it is quite possible that God's purpose is something different from the purpose of either party—and yet the human instrumentalities, working just as they do, are of the best adaptation to effect His purpose. I am almost ready to say that this is probably true—that God wills this contest, and wills that it shall not end yet. By his mere quiet power, on the minds of the now contestants, He could have either saved or destroyed the Union without a human contest. Yet the contest began. And, having begun, He could give the final victory to either side any day. Yet the contest proceeds.[5]

Since Lincoln never intended that this meditation should be published,[6] it must be allowed that it expresses his private thought on the subject. Does it lend itself to Wolf's conclusions? I think not. One gets the impression that for all his acceptance of the *being* of God, the President hasn't much faith in His personal interest in the affairs of men. At all events, he (Lincoln) is going to rely primarily on his generals and on what his conscience tells him is the righteous course. This may come short of satisfying his Christian critics, but then they don't have the responsibility for the preservation of the Union.

The Union must and shall be preserved. This to Lincoln is the one matter of overriding importance. As it colours his attitude towards religion, so also does it shape his philosophical opinions on the subject of slavery. There is a popular misconception, fostered by the hero-worshippers and based upon his signature of the Emancipation Proclamation, that Lincoln is, on the slavery issue, militantly anti-southern. He is invariably represented as absolutely opposed to the *institution* of slavery, as hating and despising it with all the fervour of a Boston abolitionist. The facts of the matter are rather different. Personally, Lincoln disliked slavery. True enough. No more than any other person of humane sensibilities could he condone the human degradation that slavery frequently involved. Philosophically, however, he is of another mind. One question is foremost in his thoughts: What does the Declaration of Independence mean when it says that all men are created equal? "I have said," he answers,

that I do not understand the Declaration to mean that all men were created equal in all respects. *They are not our equal in color;* but I suppose that it does mean to declare that all men are equal in some respects; they are equal in their right to "life, liberty, and the pursuit of happiness." *Certainly the negro is not our equal in color—perhaps not in many other respects;* still, in the right to put into his mouth the bread that his own hands have earned, he is the equal of every other man, white or black.[7]

Philosophically, then, he is ready to concede that there is some difference in equality, and he is ready to deny the pure equality that many have interpreted the Declaration to teach. In the first of his great speeches, at Peoria, Illinois, October 16th, 1854, replying to Douglas, he has this to say:

> When southern people tell us they are no more responsible for the origin of slavery, than we; I acknowledge the fact. When it is said that the institution exists; and that it is very difficult to get rid of it, in any satisfactory way, I can understand and appreciate the saying. I surely will not blame them for not doing what I should not know how to do myself. If all earthly power were given me, I should not know what to do, as to the existing institution. My first impulse would be to free all the slaves, and send them to Liberia,—to their own native land. But a moment's reflection would convince me, that whatever of high hope (as I think there is) there may be in this, in the long run, its sudden execution is impossible. . . . What then? Free them all, and keep them among us as underlings? Is it quite certain that this betters their condition? I think I would not hold one in slavery, at any rate; yet the point is not clear enough for me to denounce people upon. What next? Free them, and make them politically and socially, our equals? *My own feelings will not admit of this;* and if mine would, we well know that those of the great mass of white people will not. . . . *We can not, then, make them equals.* It does seem to me that systems of gradual emancipation might be adopted; but for their tardiness in this, I will not undertake to judge our brethren of the south.[8]

Notice how different this all sounds from the Lincoln of the myth-makers. The speaker of these words is no rabid egalitarian, perhaps not even an integrationist, certainly no abolitionist. "I have," he remarks in his First Inaugural Address, "no purpose, directly or indirectly, to interfere with the institution of slavery in the States where it exists. I believe I have no lawful right to do so, and I have no inclination to do so." [9] Much as he personally dislikes the institu-

tion of slavery, much as he would wish for its eventual extinction
even in its southern homeland, Lincoln concedes its legitimacy
"where it exists." To his way of thinking, the slavery issue is not
whether the institution as it exists should be everywhere abolished
by law; rather is it a question of whether or not slavery shall be
allowed to spread to the territories seeking statehood. This is the
great question at issue in the Lincoln-Douglas debates. In Lincoln's
position on this issue, the heart of his philosophy stands revealed.

A house divided against itself cannot stand.

I believe this government cannot endure, permanently half-*slave*
and half-*free*.

I do not expect the Union to be *dissolved*—I do not expect the
house to *fall*—but I *do* expect it will cease to be divided.

It will become *all* one thing, or *all* the other.

Either the *opponents* of slavery, will arrest the further spread of
it, and place it where the public mind shall rest in the belief that
it is in the course of ultimate extinction; or its *advocates* will push it
forward, till it shall become alike lawful in *all* the States, *old* as well
as *new*—*North* as well as *South*.[10]

These are, next to the Gettysburg Address, Lincoln's best known
lines. As he spoke them, he was fully aware that the die had been
cast, the issue joined whose result must be the dissolution or preservation of the Union. That it was more likely to be the former,
Stephen Douglas was shortly to remind him. For, Douglas would
argue, if you say that it has got to be all one way or the other, you
are in effect already dissolving the Union: "Uniformity is the parent
of despotism the world over." [11] Once deny the right of the people
of any State, present or future, to choose for themselves whether
they will or will not have slavery, and the clear intent of the Founding Fathers—that each of these States shall be sovereign as regards
its own internal affairs—has been done away with. When you shall
have attained uniformity in all things local and domestic, "you will
have converted," Douglas believes, "these thirty-two sovereign, independent states into one consolidated empire, with the uniformity
of despotism reigning triumphant throughout the length and breadth
of the land." [12] It would be a mistake to infer from this ringing
rhetoric that Douglas was any less devoted to the Union than

Lincoln. States Rights man that he was, he was no less determined that the Union must and shall be preserved. But how to do it? By compromise or unilateral choice? Lincoln himself refused to dogmatize about the matter. For him it was not a question of morals but of expediency.

I would save the Union. I would save it the shortest way under the Constitution. The sooner the national authority can be restored; the nearer the Union will be "the Union as it was." If there be those who would not save the Union, unless they could at the same time *save* slavery, I do not agree with them. If there be those who would not save the Union unless they could at the same time *destroy* slavery, I do not agree with them. My paramount object in this struggle is to save the Union, and is not either to save or to destroy slavery. If I could save the Union without freeing *any* slave I would do it, and if I could save it by freeing *all* the slaves I would do it; and if I could save it by freeing some and leaving others alone I would also do that.[13]

According to Vernon Parrington, Lincoln's "practical sense, which is only another name for political realism, restrained his idealism and made him of necessity an opportunist, willing to yield much if he might save the Union." [14] And surely Parrington is right. First and last Lincoln is a nationalist. Always and forever the Union, this is his single aim. No more than Jackson could he drink to Calhoun's toast: "The Union, next to our liberties most dear." Where popular sovereignty conflicts with the national interest, he is ready and firm to sacrifice popular sovereignty—as he did in Kansas-Nebraska. On the other hand, there is the passage from a speech on the Mexican War in which, oddly enough, he champions the right of revolution:

Any people anywhere, being inclined and having the power, have the *right* to rise up and shake off the existing government, and form a new one that suits them better. This is a most valuable,—a most sacred right—a right which we hope and believe is to liberate the world. Nor is this right confined to cases in which the whole people of an existing government may choose to exercise it. Any portion of such people that *can, may* revolutionize, and make their *own,* of so much of the territory as they inhabit. More than this, a *majority* of any portion of such people may revolutionize, putting down a *minority,* intermingled with, or near about them, who may oppose this movement. . . . It is a quality of revolutions not to go by *old* lines or *old* laws; but to break up both, and make new ones.[15]

Perhaps Lincoln should not be held accountable in 1861 for a statement made under different conditions in 1848. Nonetheless, it is often quoted against him by those concerned to legitimize the case for the South. For, they say, no man can be at once against a house divided and for revolution and/or the slave state status quo. Plainly, there is some inconsistency here, and the partisans of the South may derive such comfort from it as they will. At all events, we must not expect to find a thoroughgoing logical consistency in Lincoln's thought. Basically, he was a man possessed of great common sense, actuated by a deep and sincere compassion for his fellow-man, and guided by a profound conviction that the Union must be saved. He was, however, no metaphysician, nor do I think it fair to judge him as such. Had he been minded to couch his beliefs in the language of professional philosophy, he must, I suggest, have come close to taking the position later held by James and Dewey. Indeed, Wolf to the contrary, I doubt not that his perennial appeal owes much to the pragmatic quality of his convictions. Whether or not he was right in those convictions, I leave to you to judge, reminding you only that Lincoln was always completely aware that judgement would some day be passed upon himself and all his works. In his annual message to Congress on December 1st, 1862, in the Union's most trying hour, he put it this way:

Fellow-citizens, *we* cannot escape history. We of this Congress and this administration, will be remembered in spite of ourselves. No personal significance, or insignificance, can spare one or another of us. The fiery trial through which we pass, will light us down, in honor or dishonor, to the latest generation. We *say* we are for the Union. The world will not forget that we say this. We know how to save the Union. The world knows we do know how to save it. We—even *we here*—hold the power, and bear the responsibility. In *giving* freedom to the *slave,* we *assure* freedom to the *free*—honorable alike in what we give, and what we preserve. We shall nobly save, or meanly lose, the last best, hope of earth. Other means may succeed; this could not fail. The way is plain, peaceful, generous, just—a way which, if followed, the world will forever applaud, and God must forever bless.[16]

SUGGESTED READINGS

The Collected Works of Abraham Lincoln (8 Vols.), edited by Roy P. Basler, Marion Dolores Bonzi Pratt, and Lloyd A. Dunlap, and published by the Abraham Lincoln Association and Rutgers University Press in 1953, is the new standard edition replacing the venerable but appallingly inaccurate twelve-volume *Complete Works of Abraham Lincoln* edited by Nicolay and Hay. From this new edition, William E. Baringer has selected those passages which, loosely speaking, constitute Lincoln's philosophy. The result is *The Philosophy of Abraham Lincoln in His Own Words* (Indian Hills, Colorado: Falcon's Wing Press, 1959). Still a best buy for those seeking the most material at a modest price is Philip Van Doren Stern's edition of *The Life and Writings of Abraham Lincoln* (New York: Modern Library, 1940). Herein are all of the major speeches and a good selection of the letters, plus several miscellaneous pieces. The Life (by Stern) is objective and cleanly written. Allan Nevins has contributed a Preface, and there is a thorough chronology. The best of the biographical studies is Carl Sandburg's monumental six-volume *Abraham Lincoln: The Prairie Years and the War Years*. The same, abridged but not mutilated, is available in a one-volume edition published by Harcourt, Brace (New York, 1954). For Lincoln's religious views, see William J. Wolf, *The Almost Chosen People* (Garden City: Doubleday, 1959). This last inculdes as appendices Lincoln's creed, as formulated by William Barton from the President's own words, and a critical bibliography of works on Lincoln's religion.

REFERENCES

1. Lincoln to Horace Greeley, August 22nd, 1862, in *The Collected Works of Abraham Lincoln,* edited by Roy P. Basler; Marion Dolores Pratt and Lloyd A. Dunlap, assistant editors, 9 Vols. (New Brunswick: Rutgers University Press, 1953), V, p. 388. Hereafter cited as Collected Works.

2. Handbill Replying to Charges of Infidelity, July 31st, 1846, in Collected Works, I, p. 382.

3. William J. Wolf, *The Almost Chosen People* (Garden City: Doubleday, 1959), p. 193.

4. Ibid., p. 194.

5. Meditation on the Divine Will, September 2nd, 1862, Collected Works, V, pp. 403-4.

6. John Milton Hay, Lincoln's secretary, made a copy of it, and thus it was preserved for posterity.

7. Speech at Springfield, Illinois, July 17th, 1858, Collected Works, II, p. 520. My italics.

8. Speech at Peoria, Illinois, October 16th, 1854, Collected Works, II, pp. 255-56.

9. Collected Works, IV, p. 263.

10. Speech to the Republican State Convention, Springfield, Illinois, June 16th, 1858, Collected Works, II, pp. 461-62.

11. Paul M. Angle (editor), *Created Equal, The Complete Lincoln-Douglas Debates of 1858* (Chicago: University of Chicago Press, 1958), p. 19.

12. Ibid., p. 20.

13. Collected Works, V, p. 388.

14. *Main Currents in American Thought* (New York: Harcourt, Brace, 1930), II, p. 156.

15. Speech in the U.S. House of Representatives, January 12th, 1848, Collected Works, I, pp. 438-39.

16. Annual Message to Congress, December 1st, 1862, Collected Works, V, p. 537.

XIV

Singer of the Body Electric

WALT WHITMAN

"The average man of a land at last
only is important." [1]

WALT WHITMAN

Walt Whitman

ONE'S-SELF I sing, a simple separate person,
Yet utter the word Democratic, the word En-Masse.

Of physiology from top to toe I sing,
Not physiognomy alone nor brain alone is worthy for the Muse,
   I say the Form complete is worthier far,
The Female equally with the Male I sing.

Of Life immense in passion, pulse, and power,
Cheerful, for freest action form'd under the laws divine,
The Modern Man I sing.[2]

THE SINGER IS WALT WHITMAN; the lines are from one of the most remarkable books in American literature, Whitman's *Leaves of Grass*. It is remarkable for many reasons: it is vigorous and earthy, so earthy that the prudish have often sought to suppress it; it is crude, its cadences bang harshly on the ear. And this is as it should be, for *Leaves of Grass* is the poetic celebration of the common man, the apotheosis of the mind and flesh of the average American, the farmer, laborer, wife and mother, toiler in factory and office, yes, even the bum—as seen and felt by the man who more than anyone else is entitled to be called the poet-philosopher of the American Democracy.

Like Lincoln, whom he revered, he was of the people, for the people. Like Thoreau, for whom he had great admiration, his philosophy was a compound of his life and dreams. Like Parker, his origins were democratic:

My tongue, every atom of my blood, form'd from this soil,
  this air,
Born here of parents born here from parents the same, and
  their parents the same. . . .[3]

Born here at West Hills, Long Island, in the year 1819. The Whit-
mans were poor. Walt's father was a sometime carpenter who tried
his hand at farming and at laboring, and succeeded at neither. His
mother was an over-worked housewife scraping to keep the family
fed. When he was twelve, Walt went out to work as an office boy in
a Brooklyn law firm. Later he was apprenticed in the printing trade.
From seventeen to twenty he taught at various country schools on
the Island. Back in Manhattan, he worked on divers papers as editor
and writer. For a while in the 50's he followed his father's trade and
made his living as a carpenter. It was in these years that he began
to compose the poems that went into the first edition of *Leaves of
Grass.* The book came out in 1855 and caught the attention of
Emerson, the first and, for many years, the only American to
recognize the genius of its author. In December 1862 Walt read
his brother's name in a list of war wounded, and went immediately
to the front to find him. He became an unofficial army nurse, and
for two years served the sick and dying in the hospitals around
Washington. Finally, in 1864 his own health broke. Friends secured
him a place in the office of Indian Affairs as a clerk, and he returned to his poetry. In 1867 the fourth edition of *Leaves of Grass,*
containing much new and revised material, was offered to the
public.

People were beginning to take notice. *Democratic Vistas,* his one
important work in prose, was published in 1870. Rossetti's English
edition of Selections from the *Leaves* made his reputation abroad.
Swinburne and Tennyson saluted his work, while his most ardent
English admirer, Anne Gilchrist, proposed by mail and was diplo-
matically refused. *Democratic Vistas* was translated into Danish.
At home, however, all was still grim and earnest. In 1873 he fell ill,
suffered a paralysis, and lost his job. For a time he lived on the
bounty of friends. The first and only real money he ever made from
his poems came to him in 1882 as proceeds from the eighth
(Philadelphia) edition of the *Leaves of Grass.* With the money he

bought a small house in Camden, New Jersey, and here he settled in to live out the remainder of his years. They were marred by illness and poverty. He suffered a series of paralytic strokes, his royalties dwindled, and it was only the generosity of friends plus the fees from an occasional lecture that kept him going. The end came in 1892 even as the ninth edition of the *Leaves* was coming off the press.

For most authors a book is done when the last proof sheet has been corrected and the final page of type has been set. Into its making they may have poured for a season the whole of their energies and their experience, but once made, once in print, the thing is finished and they go on to other matters. Not so Walt Whitman. The *Leaves of Grass* was his biography, and every edition up to 1882 added new material and altered old. It was his intention that the poems mirror the poet, and everything he did was calculated to this end.

> Camerado, this is no book,
> Who touches this touches a man.[4]

And no ordinary man at that, for Whitman saw himself as the poet of the greatness of the American people, incarnating in his person and poetry their spirit and natural life.

> I CELEBRATE MYSELF, and sing myself,
> And what I assume you shall assume,
> For every atom belonging to me as good belongs to you.[5]

Or rather to all Creation, since all things, Whitman believes, are aspects of one vast universal life and growth. The cosmos is organic; man is its microcosm and the poet is its voice, the successor to that tribe of priests whose day is over. In the Preface to the 1855 edition of the *Leaves,* he puts it thus:

> There will soon be no more priests. Their work is done. They may wait awhile . . . perhaps a generation or two . . . dropping off by degrees. A superior breed shall take their place . . . the gangs of kosmos and prophets en masse shall take their place. A new order shall arise and they shall be the priests of man, and every man shall be

his own priest. The churches built under their umbrage shall be the churches of men and women. Through the divinity of themselves shall the kosmos and the new breed of poets be interpreters of men and women and of all events and things. They shall find their inspiration in real objects today, symptoms of the past and future. . . . They shall not deign to defend immortality or God or the perfection of things or liberty or the exquisite beauty and reality of the soul. They shall arise in America and be responded to from the remainder of the earth.[6]

Such is Whitman's vision of the task of the poet of Modern American Man. If you find it foggy, Nineteenth Century America found it no less so. Emerson hailed *Leaves of Grass* as "the most extraordinary piece of wit and wisdom that America has yet contributed," but Emerson saw something few others did, and even Emerson was distressed by the candor of Whitman's treatment of sex. Indeed, Walt Whitman distressed many people. His frank celebration of the flesh struck most Americans as not quite respectable. He was banned in Boston and read elsewhere for all the wrong reasons. Only the English understood his message, and even they understood it only in part.

Perhaps it was because his poetic ambitions outran his philosophical capacities. Consider, for instance, this catalogue of aims from his long poem *Starting from Paumanok*.[7]

> I will make the poems of materials, for I think they are to be the most spiritual poems,
> And I will make the poems of my body and of mortality,
> For I think I shall then supply myself with the poems of my soul and of immortality.
>
> .   .   .
>
> I will acknowledge contemporary lands,
> I will trail the whole geography of the globe and salute courteously every city large and small,
> And employments! I will put in my poems that with you is heroism upon land and sea,
> And I will report all heroism from an American point of view.

Hitherto, he believes, it has not been done. Emerson, Longfellow, Oliver Wendell Holmes, these most American poets are yet fettered in their expression by their reliance on classical poetic forms and imagery. Who would report the American view must find new forms and images, speak the new American idiom, and make articulate yearnings still unvoiced, emotions not yet captured in a poem.

> I will sing the song of companionship,
> I will show what alone must finally compact these,
> I believe these are to found their own ideal of manly love, indicating it in me,
> I will therefore let flame from me the burning fires that were threatening to consume me,
> I will lift what has too long kept down those smouldering fires
> I will give them complete abandonment,
> I will write the evangel-poem of comrades and of love,
> For who but I should understand love with all its sorrow and joy?
> And who but I should be the poet of comrades? [8]

Egotistic? Yes. Whitman is very egotistic. But then it takes a large ego to challenge convention, to lift the damper from the smouldering existential fires.

> To earn for the body and the mind whatever adheres and goes forward and is not dropt by death;
> I will effuse egotism and show it underlying all, and I will be the bard of personality,
> And I will show of male and female that either is but the equal of the other,
> And sexual organs and acts! do you concentrate in me, for I am determin'd to tell you with courageous clear voice to prove you illustrious,
> And I will show that there is no imperfection in the present, and can be none in the future,
> And I will show that whatever happens to anybody it may be turn'd to beautiful results,
> And I will show that nothing can happen more beautiful than death,
> And I will thread a thread through my poems that time and events are compact,

And that all the things of the universe are perfect miracles,
    each as profound as any.
I will not make poems with reference to parts,
But I will make poems, songs, thoughts, with reference to
    ensemble,
And I will not sing with reference to a day, but with reference
    to all days,
And I will not make a poem nor the least part of a poem
    but has reference to the soul,
Because having look'd at the objects of the universe, I find
    there is no one nor any particle of one but has reference
    to the soul.[9]

Whitman never did get around to writing out the philosophy whose
elements he catalogues in this and other poems. What that philosophy would have been, however, the *Leaves of Grass* makes plain
enough. First of all, it would have been a *panpsychism,* for like
Giordano Bruno, Gustav W. Fechner, and Josiah Royce, Whitman
believes that the universe is animated in every part, that there is no
dead matter anywhere, and that rocks and stars and running water
are ensouled even as man. Second, it should have been a *pantheism,*
since like Benedict Spinoza, Whitman finds God and Nature to be
synonymous terms. Finally, it must have been a *personalism,* because Whitman, like Bronson Alcott and Borden Parker Bowne,
is convinced that the Person is the pre-supposition of all things and
beings. A word of caution, however, is necessary at this point.
We must not take these terms as specifying any precise metaphysic.
Each must be conceived in its loosest and most general sense. For
the truth of the matter is that Whitman was, philosophically, very
much the amateur and frequently the dilettante, absorbing an influence from one, enthused by the ideas of another, impressed by
the system of a third. He read widely and felt deeply, but only once
did he think long and thoroughly enough about any idea to put
it in proper philosophical perspective. The exception is his vision
of the future of democracy as expounded in his long essay *Democratic Vistas.*

Actually, *Democratic Vistas* is two essays awkwardly fused into
one. Both appeared originally as magazine articles.[10] Both argue the

same thesis, i.e., the need for a native literature as the essential condition for the survival of the American Democracy.[11]

> I say that democracy can never prove itself beyond cavil, until it founds and luxuriantly grows its own forms of art, poems, schools, theology, displacing all that exists, or that has been produced anywhere in the past, under opposite influences. . . . Our fundamental want today in the United States, with closest, amplest reference to present conditions, and to the future, is of a class, and the clear idea of a class, of native authors, literatures, far different, far higher in grade, than any yet known, sacerdotal, modern, fit to cope with our occasions, lands, permeating the whole mass of American mentality, taste, belief, breathing into it a new breath of life, giving it decision . . . and, as its grandest result, accomplishing (what neither the schools nor the churches and their clergy have hitherto accomplished, and without which this nation will no more stand, permanently, soundly, than a house will stand without a substratum), a religious and moral character beneath the political and productive and intellectual bases of the States.[12]

That his America was tragically lacking in these spiritual values, Whitman did not doubt.

> I say we had best look our times and lands searchingly in the face, like a physician diagnosing some deep disease. Never was there, perhaps, more hollowness at heart than at present, and here in the United States. Genuine belief seems to have left us. The underlying principles of the States are not honestly believed in (for all this hectic glow, and these melodramatic screamings), nor is humanity itself believed in. . . . I say that our New World democracy, however great a success in uplifting the masses out of their sloughs, in materialistic development, products, and in a certain highly deceptive superficial popular intellectuality, is, so far, an almost complete failure in its social aspects, and in really grand religious, moral, literary, and aesthetic results. . . . It is as if we were somehow being endowed with a vast and more and more thoroughly appointed body, and then left with little or no soul.[13]

When we consider that these words were written in 1867, and think how accurately they describe our present situation, we can take little pride in the accomplishments of the past hundred years. Technologically, we have made enormous advances, spiritually and morally we are no better off than were our great-grandfathers. Having done so poorly by ignoring his advice, it is perhaps time that we gave some serious attention to Whitman's cure for our condition.

> Viewed, today, from a point of view sufficiently over-arching, the problem of humanity all over the civilized world is social and religious, and is to be finally met and treated by literature. The priest departs, the divine literatus comes. Never was anything more wanted than, today, and here in the States, the poet of the modern is wanted, or the great literatus of the modern. At all times, perhaps, the central point in any nation, and that whence it is itself really swayed the most, and whence it sways others, is its national literature, especially its archetypal poems. Above all previous lands, a great original literature is surely to become the justification and reliance (in some respects the sole reliance) of American democracy.[14]

To those accustomed to thinking of the nation's greatness as its military power, scientific know-how, or economic health such a conclusion must seem strange. They have forgotten that the pen is mightier than the sword. They have forgotten that "a new single thought, imagination, abstract principle, even literary style, fit for the time, put in shape by some great literatus, and projected among mankind, may duly cause changes, growths, removals, greater than the longest and bloodiest war, or the most stupendous merely political, dynastic, or commercial overturn." [15]

> In short, as, though it may not be realized, it is strictly true, that a few first-class poets, philosophs, and authors have substantially settled and given status to the entire religion, education, law, sociology, etc., of the hitherto civilized world, by tingeing and often creating the atmospheres out of which they have arisen, such also must stamp, and more than ever stamp, the interior and real democratic construction of this American continent, today, and days to come.[16]

We need, therefore, most of all, "a new-founded literature, not merely to copy and reflect existing surfaces, or pander to what is called taste—but a literature underlying life, religious, consistent with science, handling the elements and forces with competent power, teaching and training men—and, as perhaps the most precious of its results, achieving the entire redemption of woman out of these incredible holds and webs of silliness, millinery, and every kind of dyspeptic depletion. . . ." [17] We require, in short, a literature to inspire, for of books designed to amuse us and pass away the time we have more than enough.

As to the precise nature of this "New World literature" which we need and have not, Whitman offers only general suggestions. It must, he thinks, be a people's literature, giving voice in their language to their culture and aspirations. It should reflect the peculiar genius of the nation and celebrate its manifold heroes. It ought to inspire in all a love of country and foster comradeship between Americans. It has to be a monument to American achievements. But most of all it should glorify the democratic way, and in so doing break clean from all ideas and idioms derived from European sources, for the literature of Europe is dedicated throughout to that feudal ideal which it is the destiny of democracy to destroy. Destroy, that is, by purely peaceful means, for Whitman is no advocate of the military. His own experience of war bred in him a profound distaste for coercive violence and force. For all his celebration of the vigorous and healthy, he holds no brief for armed aggression. Freedom for every individual is his goal; freedom for everyone to realize their own identity.

The purpose of democracy—supplanting old belief in the necessary absoluteness of established dynastic rulership, temporal, ecclesiastical, and scholastic, as furnishing the only security against chaos, crime, and ignorance—is, through many transmigrations and amid endless ridicules, arguments, and ostensible failures, to illustrate, at all hazards, this doctrine or theory that man, properly trained in sanest, highest freedom, may and must become a law, and series of laws, unto himself, surrounding and providing for, not only his own personal control, but all his relations to other individuals, and to the State; and that, while other theories, as in the past histories of nations, have proved wise enough, and indispensable perhaps for their conditions, *this,* as matters now stand in our civilized world, is the only scheme worth working from, as warranting results like those of Nature's laws, reliable, when once established, to carry on themselves.[18]

Some there are who will say that this is not democracy but anarchy, and certainly Whitman's idea of democracy as the autonomy of the average man is not the sort of thing that we Twentieth Century Americans understand by the term. Where we conceive of democracy as meaning equality of opportunity, Whitman takes it to mean everybody absolutely equal and absolutely nobody better than anyone else—in rank, rights, or education. Theoretically, his notion has much to commend it; practically, it is an invitation to chaos, the more so since he never really faces up to the effects of such a democracy on the social, economic, and political institutions of these American States. He is inclined to credit mankind with a capacity for comradeship which few men, in fact, possess. Perhaps Jesus Christ and his disciples had it, but the average American does not and never will. Whitman himself was aware, of course, that his Democratic Vistas were only a dream, but mystic that he was, he saw his dream as a reality in the making and himself as the prophet of its actualization. His mistake was to identify the democratic ideal with the ideal of all religions. He forgot that in no religion is heaven a democracy; he failed to see, what the religious have always seen, that any heaven so conceived and so ordered would, in truth, be hell!

SUGGESTED READINGS

For the person who is a stranger to Whitman, the book to begin with is *The Poetry and Prose of Walt Whitman* (New York: Simon and Schuster, 1949), edited, with biographical introduction by Louis Untermeyer. In addition to the complete and unabridged text of the "deathbed" edition of *Leaves of Grass,* the volume includes, in their entirety, *Specimen Days* and *Democratic Vistas,* plus a selection of letters and shorter prose pieces. Book Two of this work consists of a comprehensive sampling of critical opinion on all phases of Whitman's writings. The serious student of the *Leaves of Grass* will wish also to consult the Inclusive Edition published by Doubleday, Doran (1929). This latter contains the "authorized" text of the Ninth Edition of 1892, complete with Prefaces and Variorum Readings compiled by Trigg. *Democratic Vistas* is available in a paperback edition (New York: Liberal Arts Press, 1949).

The best book to find out the most in the shortest time is Gay Wilson Allen, *Walt Whitman Handbook* (Chicago: Packard & Co., 1946). It offers a detailed chronology of the poet's life; gives the publishing history of all his works; analyzes his fundamental ideas, and assesses his contribution to world literature. The bibliography takes note of practically everything written about Whitman up to 1946. The best of the biographies, also by Allen, is *The Solitary Singer* (New York: Macmillan, 1955). H. C. Gardiner, *American Classics Reconsidered* (New York: Scribner, 1957), contains (pp. 300-4) an excellent critical bibliography on Whitman by Geoffrey Stone.

REFERENCES

1. *Democratic Vistas* in *Complete Prose Works* (Philadelphia: David McKay, 1897), p. 224. Hereafter cited as Prose Works.

2. "One's-Self I Sing," from *Leaves of Grass*. The "Authorized" edition, edited by Emory Holloway (Garden City: Doubleday, Page & Company, 1925), p. 1. Hereafter cited as Leaves.

3. "Song of Myself," Leaves, p. 24.

4. "So Long," Leaves, p. 418.

5. "Song of Myself," Leaves, p. 24.

6. Leaves, pp. 505-6.

7. Ibid., pp. 14-15.

8. Ibid., p. 15.

9. Ibid., pp. 18-19.

10. "Democracy," *Galaxy* (December, 1867), pp. 919-33; "Personalism," *Galaxy* (May, 1868), pp. 540-47.

11. In Whitman's lexicon, the words "America" and "Democracy" are convertible terms.

12. Prose Works, pp. 205-6.

13. Ibid., pp. 210-11.

14. Ibid., p. 206.

15. Ibid., p. 207.

16. Ibid.

17. Ibid., p. 212.

18. Ibid., p. 214.

XV

Hegel in St. Louis

HENRY C. BROCKMEYER

HEGELIAN HERITAGE

WILLIAM TORREY HARRIS

DENTON J. SNIDER

"For after all it is not American *'thought'* so much as American *thinkers* that we want. To *think,* in the highest sense, is to transcend all *natural limits*—such, for example, as national peculiarities, defects in culture, distinctions in Race, habits, and modes of living—to be *universal,* so that one can dissolve away the external hull and seize the substance itself . . . Our province as *Americans* is to rise to purer forms than have hitherto been attained, and thus speak a 'solvent word' of more potency than those already uttered." [1]

WILLIAM TORREY HARRIS

1. Henry Brockmeyer

IN THESE SAME YEARS of Whitman's dreaming there came together at St. Louis, Missouri, a group of men who believed themselves to have found in the System of the German philosopher, Georg Wilhelm Friedrich Hegel, the means to the realization of the democratic millennium envisioned by the poet. Whitman himself shared their enthusiasm: "In my opinion," he wrote in *Specimen Days,* "the . . . formulas of Hegel are an essential and crowning justification of New World democracy in the creative realms of time and space. There is that about them which only the vastness, the multiplicity and the vitality of America would seem to be able to comprehend, to give scope and illustration to, or to be fit for, or even originate." [2] "Only Hegel is fit for America," so Whitman in his innocence believed,[3] and in St. Louis there were knowledgeable students of Hegel's works who knew that he spoke true.

Chief among them was the fabulous Henry Conrad Brockmeyer. Born in 1826 at Minden in Westphalia, Brockmeyer emigrated to America in 1844. By his own account, he landed at New York with twenty-five cents in pocket and a vocabulary of three English words. Energy and native genius, however, he had in abundance. For a decade he roamed the East, Midwest, and South working at a variety of jobs. In northern Mississippi he paused awhile to operate a tannery and shoe factory, made a small fortune, and later lost it all through bad investments. Always, he had a thirst for knowledge. He attended Georgetown University (Kentucky); back East he took courses at Brown. There he had met and studied with

Frederic Henry Hedge, the Unitarian minister whose *Prose Writers of Germany* (1847) was the first important body of translations generally available in America. The selections from Hegel were brief: the Introduction to the *Philosophy of History* plus a short fragment on abstract reasoning; but for Brockmeyer they sufficed. In Hegel's exposition of the dialectic of history he found intimations of what the American State, alive to its Hegelian destiny, might become, and he determined to master the System. Somewhere, somehow, he managed to procure a German edition of Hegel's *Logic,* and in 1854, emulating Thoreau, he retired into the Missouri forest to study and be close to nature. Two years later, ready to rejoin society, and eager to remake it, he walked out of the woods and took a room in St. Louis.

That he should have fixed upon St. Louis was probably no accident. As a German he would naturally be drawn to a city predominantly Germanic in culture and outlook. Perhaps he felt, as did another new arrival, Denton Snider, "the uplift of a strange new spirit . . . the revelation of the peculiar racial consciousness of old Teutonia welling forth just now on the banks of the Mississippi." Certainly, the spirit of St. Louis, manifest as the confidence of its people that theirs was destined to be The Future Great City of the World, must have had its attraction for one dedicated to the propagation of a philosophy of social evolution. Whatever his reasons, they were strong enough; henceforward he would call St. Louis home.

He went to work as an iron-molder, and on such evenings and weekends as he could bear to spend apart from his cherished books, he began to take part in the intellectual life of the city. Probably he joined the St. Louis Literary and Philosophical Society, since it was, presumably, at a Society meeting one Sunday afternoon in 1858 that he met William Torrey Harris.

Like Brockmeyer, Harris was a recent arrival. However, in the latter's case it was business prospects rather than culture which had led him to quit Yale in the middle of his junior year, and seek his fortune in the West. St. Louis, he figured, "was a great place for business as it was the center of business and migration to the West and surrounded by a rich country." So it was, but he found no profit there. Disaster piled on commercial disaster, and to support himself he took a job teaching in the St. Louis public schools. By the standards of the day he was well qualified. Yale had trained him in the classics, and awakened his mind to philosophy. At the time of his meeting with Brockmeyer, he had studied Locke and almost mastered Kant. He was familiar with the works of Cousin, Fichte, Goethe, and Schelling. Most important, Hegel's *History of Philosophy* and his *Logic* were in Harris's library, and by dint of hard study he had acquired enough German to read them. It wanted only the spark to light the Hegelian fire, and that Brockmeyer supplied. The two men hit it off immediately. Brockmeyer would tutor Harris in Hegel; Harris would finance Brockmeyer's translations, and organize their dissemination. Together they would Hegelize America.

Unfortunately, America at that time had Civil War on its mind, and philosophy must wait until the issue was settled. Brockmeyer accepted a colonelcy in the Missouri militia and left on active duty. Harris, who had married in 1858, remained at his post in the St. Louis schools. Throughout the war his would be the task of keeping interest in philosophy alive and the members of the study group in touch with one another; at its end he would take the lead in forming them into the St. Louis Philosophical Society.

This organization, whose founding marks the formal beginning of the St. Louis Movement, came into being in January of 1866. On or about the 19th of that month, seven men, Brockmeyer, Harris, Denton J. Snider, G. H. Howison, J. Z. Hall, J. H. Watters, and Britton Hill, met in Hill's St. Louis office for the purpose of forming a Society to "encourage the study and development of Speculative Philosophy, to foster an application of its results to Art, Religion, and Science, and to establish a philosophical basis for the professions of Medicine, Divinity, Law, Politics, Education, Fine Arts and Literature." Of these seven, Hall, Hill, Howison, and Watters require no further mention, while Brockmeyer and Harris we have already met. Snider, however, is of more immediate importance.

Born in 1841 at Mt. Gilead, Ohio, Denton Jacques Snider was graduated from Oberlin in 1861, served in the Union Army, and in March of 1864, in answer to a Cincinnati newspaper advertisement, came to St. Louis and a job as teacher of languages in the Christian Brothers College. In 1867 he married and gave up his college post for a position in the St. Louis High School. His interest in German culture brought him into contact with Brockmeyer and Harris, and led to his lifelong association with the St. Louis Movement. In 1874 his wife died and for some years thereafter he shunned society [4] and devoted himself to his writing. He produced over a period of fifty years some sixty books,[5] the majority of them on literary subjects. His Hegelian interpretations of Shakespeare, Dante, Homer, and Goethe are important landmarks in the history of literary criticism; his book on *The State, especially the American State Psychologically Treated* constitutes the major contribution of the St. Louis group to American political thought. Far less known, and certainly less influential than either Brockmeyer or Harris, in novelty of thought he easily surpassed them both. He had a creative fire neither could match. He was the one truly original thinker the movement produced, and at his death in 1925 he had long outlived it and all its members.

2. Hegelian Heritage

To THOSE OUTSIDE the immediate vicinity of St. Louis, the earliest and continuing evidence of the existence and vitality of the movement was provided by the *Journal of Speculative Philosophy.*[6] From the beginning, opinion concerning it was sharply divided. The Transcendentalists were delighted, and several contributed essays and poetry to subsequent issues. Many Americans, however, were profoundly disturbed by what they took to be the un-American character of its contents, i.e., the heavy emphasis on the works of Kant, Hegel, and other German thinkers. To the patriotic this emphasis on foreign-born ideas seemed to border on the subversive, and in the fourth issue Harris, the editor, was forced to take account of their objections. Since the issues involved are of such great importance even today, his reply deserves to be quoted in full.

"In what books," he asks them,

is one to find the true "American" type of Speculative Philosophy? Certain very honorable exceptions occur to everyone, but they are not American in a popular sense. We, as a people, buy immense editions of John Stuart Mill, Herbert Spencer, Comte, Hamilton, Cousin, and others; one can trace the appropriation and digestion of their thoughts in all the leading articles of our Reviews, Magazines, and books of a thoughtful character. If this is American philosophy, the editor [Harris] thinks that it may be very much elevated by absorbing and digesting more refined aliment. It is said that of Herbert Spencer's works nearly twenty thousand have been sold in this country, while in England, scarcely the first edition has been bought. This is encouraging for the American thinker: what lofty spiritual culture may not become broadly and firmly rooted here where thoughtful minds are so numerous? Let this spirit of inquiry once extend to thinkers like Plato and Aristotle, Schelling and Hegel—let these be digested and originally reproduced—and what a phalanx of American thinkers we may have to boast of! For after all it is not "American *thought*" so much as American *thinkers* that we want. To *think,* in the highest sense, is to transcend all *natural limits*—such, for example, as national peculiarities, defects in culture, distinctions in Race, habits, and modes of living—to be *universal,* so that one can dissolve away the external hull and seize the substance itself. The peculiarities stand in the way:—were it not for these, we should find in Greek or German Philosophy just the forms we ourselves need. Our province as *Americans* is to rise to purer forms than have hitherto been attained, and thus speak a "solvent word" of more potency than those already uttered. If this be the goal we aim at, it is evident that we can find no other means so well adapted to rid us of our own idiosyncrasies as the study of the greatest thinkers of all ages and all times. May this journal aid such a consummation! [7]

That it was entirely possible for any serious American to accomplish this purpose, Harris and his associates were convinced, for were not "purer forms," in the guise of the philosophies of Kant and Hegel, already available to those possessed of the intellect and will to rise to their attainment? Actually, the matter was not, nor is, that simple, since of all of the philosophies of modern Europe, those of Kant and Hegel are, by common consent, the most difficult to comprehend. This being so, some brief account of the origins and development of these philosophies must now be given. For until we know them in their original outline, we cannot hope to understand how, and to what end, the St. Louis movement appropriated their thought to American uses.

He who would know Hegel must first have understood Kant. Even then to have done so is not enough, since Kant's philosophy originates as a response to a challenge posed by David Hume, who in turn inherits his problems from Berkeley, and before him from Locke. Whom Locke is indebted to we need not here inquire. Suffice it to say that our understanding of Hegel begins with Locke's assertion that there is nothing in the mind that was not first in the senses.

Assuming that this is true, it follows, as Hume points out, that there can be no such thing as a necessary connection of cause and effect, since our perceptions, which are all we have to go on, discover no power in any single event in nature to justify our assuming any such connection. Moreover, if it is true, as Hume contends it is, that "I can never catch *myself* at any time without a perception, and never can observe any thing but the perception," then there is—literally speaking—no *thing* called mind at all! Rather is it that what we call mind is only "a bundle or collection of different perceptions, which succeed each other with an inconceivable rapidity, and are in a perpetual flux and movement . . . They are the successive perceptions only, that constitute the mind; nor have we the most distant notion of the place, where these scenes are represented, or of the materials, of which it is compos'd." [8] Small wonder that Kant should be aroused from his dogmatic slumber by the reading of these passages. If Hume is right, the pursuit of knowledge is an utter waste of time, for in reality there is no knowledge to pursue, nor any mind to know it.

But what of Science? Surely Science is knowledge, and if so Hume must be wrong. So Kant believes; but how to prove it? How is Science possible? To this last question Kant has a twofold answer, and on its cogency the position of Harris largely depends. To begin with, says Kant, Hume was looking in the wrong place for his evidences of causal connection. Instead of seeking them in the world disclosed to experience, he should have searched for them in the mind itself. That there must be a mind is, Kant insists, self-evident, for even if it is true that I can never catch myself without a perception, it remains that my perceptions are *my* perceptions. In other words, there must be something which organizes and synthesizes the raw data of perception, and since it cannot be anything external (as Hume has proved), it must be mind. This being granted, the second, and positive, part of the answer to Hume may now be stated: Science is possible because the laws and principles we erroneously think to have discovered in nature, are in truth the laws of mind imposed by it on nature. Thus space and time are not something of themselves objective and absolute, but rather are those forms of intellectual intuition presupposed in every possible experience. The principle of cause and effect is not, as Hume supposed, something found in things, but is rather one of twelve categories of the mind to which the manifold of sense must conform. Notice that experience is essential. According to Kant, Hume is right to conclude that all knowledge *begins* with sense-perception; his mistake lay in assuming that it *ends* here. True, concepts without percepts are empty; but equally true, percepts without concepts are blind. Like love and marriage they belong together; if Kant is right, in real knowledge you never can find one without the other.

Knowledge of phenomena, then, we can and do have, but this is all. Beyond the phenomenal, i.e., the realm of sense-experience, we cannot go. Of the noumenal world of things-in-themselves, that is, of the external causes of the data sensed, we can know nothing. Of that transcendental unity of apperception, that noumenal self-in-itself, which is our mind as pure structure abstracted from all percepta, we can, Kant says, know nothing. We may, as he does, insist on the existence of this noumenal (transcendent) realm, but our insistence is always and ever an act of faith alone. Beyond the evidence of the senses, reason has no constitutive authority whatever.

To Hegel this conclusion is intolerable. That anything should be beyond the range of reason, he will not admit, and as Kant had found a flaw in the reasoning of Hume, so he thinks to have discerned the flaw that invalidates Kant's limitation of the known to the sensed. For if "cause and effect" is what Kant throughout his *Critique of Pure Reason* maintains it to be, i.e., a category of relation within the structure of the mind itself, then Kant, argues Hegel, has contradicted himself, because the external unknowable thing—or self-in-itself—cannot be a cause, cannot in fact exist, since to say that anything exists which is unknowable is to imply that something exists independent of mind or consciousness, and this Kant has expressly denied! The assertion of the thing—or self-in-itself—having been shown to be a contradiction in terms, no justification remains for assuming its existence as the cause or ground of phenomena. There being nothing behind appearances, nothing is intrinsically unknowable. It is possible, Hegel thinks, that mind may penetrate to comprehension of the Infinite itself, and it may do this because the Real is the rational and the rational is the Real.

This conviction that what can be known and what can *be* are one and the same thing is the continuing theme of all of Hegel's work. "The task of philosophy is," he tells us, "to comprehend what is, and this is possible because what is, is reason." The structure of mind and the structure of reality are one. To see how this is so, we have, he thinks, only to look at language, for language is the essential medium of any knowledge whatever. Certainly all language is conceptual. A moment's reflection suffices to reveal that every word in any language refers beyond the particular to the universal. For instance, I make the statement, "This paper before you is white." Notice that "paper" is a word that refers not only to this paper, but to any paper; just as "this" refers to all "thises," "is" to being in general, "before" to all things prior, and "white" to a quality possessed by an infinity of beings. Even "you" refers to anyone who might by accident or purpose be reading this account. All words are, therefore, concepts, and every concept being a universal term, it follows, according to Hegel, that the truth of sense-certainty is likewise universal. The individual self, led in thought to this consciousness of its object as the universal, gradually discovers its process of realization of the content of the universal as Spirit to be at once the process wherein it comes to consciousness of itself as the universal self of reason, and in its attainment of absolute knowledge, to recognition of the unity of itself and its object as Notion or Absolute Spirit. This voyage of discovery is the Phenomenology of Mind, and with its conclusion that the ultimate truth of the universal is self, conscious of itself as Absolute Spirit, the outline of Hegel's System is complete.

The System itself is that cosmology (*Weltanschauung*), according to which the meaning of the universe is its character as the environment of spiritual being. The rational evolution of the universe is Absolute Spirit (God) coming to consciousness of itself in History. Because this is Panlogism, i.e., the real is the rational. Cosmology is also Logic, for the science of concepts and their relations (Logic) is identical with the science of the structure of reality (Cosmology). Hence Logic, so far from being merely a science of formalized abstractions, has as its content the essence of the universe itself. To understand the universe is, therefore, to grasp the logical process whereby mind passes from the most abstract cosmological conception, the universe as Being, to the most concrete, the universe as Absolute Spirit (Notion, God). The means wherein mind accomplishes this task is Dialectic, the triadic process (thesis antithesis-synthesis) of logical deduction by which the contradictories (thesis-antithesis) are seen to merge themselves in a synthesis that comprehends them as a higher unity. For example, we begin by saying, "The universe is Being." But Being is, as such, absolutely indeterminate. Nothing can be intuited in it; it is pure vacuity, which is to say—Nothing. Thus Being passes over into Nothing, each has been seen to imply the other. Analysis of Being has disclosed a distinction in Being that is no real distinction, since Being and Nothing are not two but one. But what is it that is at once both Being and Nothing? It is Becoming, "the unseparateness of Being and Nothing . . . this determinate unity in which there *is* Being as well as nothing." This synthesis now serves as the thesis of the next higher triad. Out of it is generated an antithesis, and so on until the attainment of the ultimate synthesis, which is to say—God (Notion, Absolute Spirit).

The *Logic* concludes with this realization of the Idea of God as He is in His eternal essence before the creation of Nature and of finite mind. So manifested, God does not yet *exist*. In creation God passes out of Himself into Nature. Essence assumes existence. Logic (thesis) is externalized as Nature (antithesis). The triadic structure of Nature emerges as mechanics, physics, and organics. Dialectic discovers the highest synthesis of organics to be Free Ego, and Nature passes back into Spirit (synthesis) as mind awakens to the realization of the unity of Logic and Nature in the Self (free ego) conscious of itself as Spirit. The Philosophy of Spirit is the unfolding of mind as reason in history (the State is the march of God on earth), in philosophy (a philosophy does not refute but absorbs its predecessors), and in religion (wherein the triad Logic-Nature-Spirit is seen as the kingdom of Father, Son, and Holy Ghost). Viewed thus in its totality, the Hegelian System is this vast dialectic structure of triads within series of triads, encompassing all science, philosophy, history, religion, and art; the infinitude of God as realized by the mind of man.

Small wonder that Harris and his friends, confronting the tremendous sweep and scope of this Hegelian world-view, should echo

Whitman's thought. Here was a philosophy fit for an evolving empire. What did it matter that it was not easily grasped: "He . . . who would ascend into the thought of the best thinkers the world has seen, must spare no pains to elevate his thinking to the plane of pure thought." [9] It had taken Harris himself, by his own admission, twenty-seven years to master the System, and what he had done he would have others do. "Let no one despair, though he seems to be baffled seventy and seven times; his earnest and vigorous assault is repaid by surprisingly increased strength of mental acumen which he will be assured of, if he tries his powers on lower planes after his attack has failed on the highest thought." [10] It was an argument shrewdly calculated to appeal to profit-minded Americans, and it did. Against the rise of evolutionism, against the new fashion of pragmatism, the philosophy of Hegel, as modified and Americanized by Harris and his followers, would hold its own place in the American Mind for the balance of the Nineteenth Century and beyond.

3. William Torrey Harris

THE AMERICANIZATION OF HEGEL was and is essentially a matter of simplification. No other answer explains how so complex and esoteric a philosophy should find favor with an American public largely indifferent to all things Germanic. This is not to say that Harris and those others who contributed to the English translation and exegesis of Hegel in *The Journal of Speculative Philosophy* and various books deliberately simplified the teaching of the master. On the contrary, in most instances their work was more cumbersome and complex than the original they strove to popularize. So cumbersome, indeed, that very few bothered to read, let alone study, these scholarly productions. What great numbers did read and study was the Hegelianized philosophy of Harris, Howison, Snider, Mulford and that host of interpreters who in the last third of the Nineteenth Century sought to adapt "the formulas of Hegel" to the American situation. Inevitably, such adaptation must and did mean the reduction of the System to a few home truths to which any idealist might subscribe.

Thus on the first page of the second volume of *The Journal of Speculative Philosophy* we find Harris setting forth *his* "fundamental position" in these general terms: "Truth can be known by the thinking reason. It has been known by speculative thinkers scattered through the ages. Their systems exist and may be mastered. Their differences are not radical, but lie rather in the mode of exposition —the point of departure, the various obstacles overcome, and the character of the *technique* used. Their agreement is central and pervading . . ." [11] Apart from the implicit assumption that the real is the rational and vice versa, there is nothing in this credo specifically Hegelian, and in fact the central presuppositions of Harris, as subsequently discovered in the pages of *The Journal of Speculative Philosophy,* turn out to be from Kant rather than from Hegel!

Three Kantian ideas, Space, Time, and Cause, are, he thinks, the ground of any Philosophic Knowing: "Space and Time—as the conditions of nature or the world, as the necessary presuppositions of extension and multitude—will furnish us occasion to consider the infinite and the possibility of knowing it. The idea of Cause will lead us to the fundamental insight on which true philosophy rests." [12] Just how these ideas are to do this, Harris undertakes to explain in his Philosophy in Outline. Assuming (with Kant) Space and Time as the preconditions of any possible experience, and with Hegel "that these *a priori* conditions of experience are both subjective and objective, both conditions of experience, and likewise conditions of the existence of phenomena," Harris concludes that, "whatever be the things and processes of the world, we know that mind as revealed in its *a priori* nature is related to the world as the condition of its existence." [13] "All conscious beings in the possession of the conditions of experience—in being rational, in short—participate in the principle that gives existence to the world, and that principle is reason." [14] Grant this, and the way to "the fundamental insight" lies open.

For analysis of this "condition" discloses it to be the principle of causality; examination of causality yields the knowledge that it implies both Space and Time included in it in a certain sense; a closer look reveals a ground deeper than causality itself, which ground is self-activity. "Self-activity is called *Causa sui* to express the fact of its relation to causality . . . *Causa sui,* or self-cause, is, properly speaking, the principle, *par excellence,* of philosophy. It is the principle of life, of thought, of mind—the idea of a creative activity, and hence also the basis of theology as well as of philosophy." [15] This is the fundamental insight: on self-activity all true philosophy rests. "Self-cause, or eternal energy, is the ultimate presupposition of all things and events. Here is the necessary ground of the idea of God. It is the presupposition of all experience and of all possible existence. By the study of the presuppositions of experience one becomes certain of the existence of One eternal Energy which creates and governs the world." [16]

It is to be regretted that nowhere in his Outline, or in any other of his metaphysical writings, does Harris offer extended arguments to support these generalizations. All is assumed; nothing is proved. His conception of causality, no less than his idea of God as eternal energy, goes far beyond anything attributable to the authority of Hegel or of Kant. His idea of self-activity, particularly as it applies to God, he thinks to have drawn directly from Hegel; but here his concern to show this notion compatible with the Christian notion of the Trinity leads him to expound a view which Anselm or Aquinas might recognize as their own, but that Hegel surely would not. Having borrowed something from both camps, he ends with a system consistent with neither, a metaphysical monument to a speculative unanimity that never was.

Oddly enough, the inconsistency that marred his metaphysics helped make Harris' reputation as an educator. His Christian orthodoxy established him as a defender of the faith, at the same time as his Hegelianism marked him a prophet of the future. More important, his social views and educational philosophy, elaborated in scores of lectures and addresses during his twenty-two years as superintendent of St. Louis Public Schools, had the political merit of appealing to nearly all and offending hardly any. It was unlikely that this combination would long go unnoticed in Washington, and in fact it did not. In August 1889, the newly-elected President, Benjamin Harrison, acting on the recommendations of General Thomas J. Morgan, Nicholas Murray Butler, and other leaders of American education, offered Harris the post of United States Commissioner of Education. Harris accepted, and on September 12th, 1889, took office.

Then, as now, it was a position of high dignity and little positive power. Much depended upon what the man who held the job made of it. A strong commissioner with a sense of mission and great academic prestige could exert, as Harris did, a major influence on the nation's schools. For seventeen years his would be a strong Washington voice for moral and spiritual values in education. "Education," he remarked in the Preface to his *Psychological Foundations of Education,* "can not be wisely administered except from the high ground of the spirit of civilization," and throughout his tenure of office he conceived his mission as the education of the teachers and the taught to the nature of that "spirit."

Punctuality, silence, and industry were, he thought, habits that every school-child must acquire at the outset of his training. Without these moral education could hardly begin; with them the child was properly equipped to undertake the course of studies Harris prescribed: at the elementary level, reading, writing, arithmetic, grammar, geography, and American history; in the high school, algebra, geometry, trigonometry, physical geography (comprising ethnology, zoology, botany, geology, meteorology and astronomy), physics and chemistry, Latin, Greek, one modern language, English literature, "and perhaps some general or special study of the history of the fine arts . . . for the aesthetic side of man." It is noteworthy that he finds no room or time for the cultural trivia that clutter up the curricula of today's schools. For Harris the supreme task of the school is to train the student in the fundamentals, to the end that he or she might be properly prepared for entry into that study of the realms of spirit which is the first and final object of higher education.

Considering his emphasis on the moral and spiritual aims of education, it would be natural to suppose that Harris would favor religious instruction in the public schools. In fact he opposed it— not, let it be quickly added, because of any bias against organized religion, but rather because the sublime truth of religion requires that "religious instruction should be surrounded with solemnity. It should be approached with ceremonial preparation, so as to lift up the mind to the dignity of the lesson received . . . In religious lessons wherein the divine is taught as revealed to the human race, it is right that the raw, immature intellect of youth shall not be called upon to exercise a critical judgment, for the youth at his best cannot grasp the rationality of the dogmas which contain the deepest insights of the religious consciousness of the race." [17] Such instruction, he thought, is properly the province of family and church. "If there is irreligion, practical atheism in the community, the Church is evidently not as efficient as it ought to be, and the family is also derelict. If the school secures good behavior and a knowledge of letters and science, it has contributed its share." [18] To each institution, then, its own. "The principle of religious instruction is authority; that of secular instruction is demonstration and verification. It is obvious that these two principles should not be brought into the same school, but separated as widely as possible." [19] Nor should exception be made for non-sectarian instruction in the Bible or the bare being of God. "It is," Harris thinks, "impossible to make a generalization of Christianity without depriving it of something that is necessary to the form of religion, namely, an appeal to the senses and the imagination." [20] Precisely because religion is so much more than an intellectual exercise, it must be preserved from those who would have to treat it, in all fairness, as such. The founding fathers in their almost infinite wisdom have decreed the separation of Church and State. So be it.

As to which of these possesses the ultimate authority, Harris, unlike Hegel, refuses to say. He does remark in his address To the Reader in the first number of *The Journal of Speculative Philosophy* his conviction that we (as Americans) have now attained that stage of political maturity wherein "each recognizes his substantial side to be the State as such," and in a true Hegelian this must imply the primacy of the State as a higher stage in the realization of the ethical Idea, but that Harris himself held such a view his writings nowhere show. They do reveal that he was all for nationalism, big business,[21] organized religion, and the institutional status quo; but beyond these practical preferences they do not go. For the political theory of the St. Louis Movement, we have to look elsewhere.

4. Denton Snider

HARRIS HIMSELF was inclined to agree with Denton Snider that Brockmeyer was the one man of their circle preeminently qualified by personal experience and speculative study to expound the theory of the State. Unfortunately, Brockmeyer never did get around to writing his long-projected work on the American Constitution. "It remained," so Snider tells us, "like his other works and like himself, and somewhat like his city (St. Louis), unrealized and perhaps unrealizable." [22] In the end it fell to Snider to give the movement its political and social philosophy.

Of the three major works he wrote on the subject, the most important is *The State, specially the American State, Psychologically Treated.* His theme is the State as Will, for to Snider the first fact of the State is that it has power (Will), otherwise it is no State. "It has Will; we may deem it a Will, distinct, working in its sphere, according to its own law . . . With this conception . . . we reach down to its fundamental psychical trait, and thus bring it back to the human Self, which also has Will, and correlates with the same." [23] Psychologically, then, the State and the Self are ultimately one, since the latter, properly conceived, is precisely what the former is. "The man who denies Government," thinks Snider, "denies his Self as a reality, making himself a mere inner shadow, or subjective phantasm which exists for him alone. Government is the process of the Ego as actual, and is for all Egos, not simply for one . . . the fact is that as man develops, so the State develops. We cannot too often repeat that the Government is the very Self of man made real, made a true entity, which otherwise would be unreal, untrue, having no objective validity in the world." [24] Only in the State is man fully man and actually person.

Man is, by nature, a political animal; so Aristotle had premised, and Snider would agree—adding that it follows from this that the State also is a natural institution having its origins in the social instinct (Will) rather than in any social contract or compact. Thus the definition of the State must unfold as the State evolves. The spiritual evolution of man is at the same time the evolution of his political institutions. "The first Institution of man is the Family, in which he is born; the early State will be in more or less immediate unity with the Family, and so may be called the Parental State. The second Institution (secular) of man is Society, and so we shall see a second great group of States whose essential relation is social not domestic. The third Institution (secular) of man is the State, which in the long process of History will turn back upon itself and produce the State of States as distinct from the Society of states." [25]

In world-history this dialectic of institutional evolution begins with the oriental state (Parental), ruled by an absolute monarch whose dignity and authority are in essence familial; passes over into the European state (Social), in which the institution is manifested as a Single-State or as an Empire-State; and culminates in the occidental state (State-producing), wherein "the European conflict between the Single-State and the Empire-State (or central authority) is reconciled and transformed into a process of unity whereby the Single-State produces the Empire-State and the latter (the Federal Union) produces the Single-State." [26] In sum, "the sweep of the State through Orient, Europe and Occident (America) is a vast process of evolution which is in its essence psychical, showing a triple movement which we may call a world-psychosis. This movement has just begun to manifest its third (or American) stage, which seems to complete the circle of the earth." [27]

That Snider's inspiration here is Hegelian is obvious. Yet in a way he has gone far beyond Hegel, for as he himself points out, the idea of the State-producing State is something of which Hegel never dreamed. The Hegelian dialectic sees no further than the particular European Nation-State (Single-State), even though his (Hegel's) conception of a World-Spirit as the presiding Genius of History clearly implies an institutional evolution beyond the Single-State to the State-producing State.

> Now we are to see that the World-Spirit has transcended the philosopher's conception of it; no longer is it something outside or over but within the States, and is actually existent as the universal State creating them yet created through them . . . Hegel's mighty conception of the World-Spirit is to remain, it cannot be cast away; still it too is in the evolutionary process, it is to be transformed and transcended, passing from its European to its American manifestation . . . Now the World-Spirit embodies itself anew in a State-producing State . . . It lays down its law beforehand, which is in essence that the Single-State must will actualized Will, not assail it or destroy it (as the Confederacy had tried to do), and this law is uttered and enforced from the central Institution or from the State of States. In such fashion the capricious European World-Spirit of Hegel has unfolded into the American institutional World-Spirit.[28]

Since the United States, apart from the single-states comprising it, has no permanent territory of its own, this World-Spirit must be thought of as expressing itself in that central institution wherein these United States find their unity—the American Constitution. Thus the major portion of Snider's psychological analysis of the American State is given over to showing how the Federal State unfolds, in its various constitutional divisions, articles, sections, and clauses, into the State-producing State through the exercise of the Free-Will of the American people. This process of unfolding, Snider thinks, must continue "till its principle be made universal, which will happen only when there is a United-States of the world." [29]

It was and is a noble vision, for all that it was conceived in obscurity and destined to oblivion. Fortunately for Snider, he lived long enough to see the admission of the forty-eighth single-state complete the continental union, and died before the failure of the League of Nations cast doubt upon the efficacy of the Genius of World-History. Most probably this last would not have overly disturbed him. He was no stranger to disillusion. His history of the St. Louis Movement anticipates its passing and chronicles its end— or rather its psychological renascence in Snider's System of Psychology. But that is another story altogether.

SUGGESTED READINGS

The best concise account of the development of Hegel's System is that of Herbert Marcuse, *Reason and Revolution*, 2nd ed. (New York, 1954). How Hegel came to America J. H. Muirhead makes plain in his article of this name in the *Philosophical Review*, Vol. 37 (1928), 423-47. For the history of the St. Louis Movement, see Denton J. Snider, *The St. Louis Movement in Philosophy, Literature, Education and Psychology; with chapters of autobiography* (St. Louis, 1920), Henry A. Pochmann, *New England Transcendentalism and St. Louis Hegelianism* (Philadelphia, 1948), and Frances Bolles Harmon, *The Social Philosophy of the St. Louis Hegelians* (New York, 1943). Charles M. Perry, *The St. Louis Movement in Philosophy, some source material* (Norman, 1930), contains much valuable biographical material and excellent bibliographies.

Despite his enormous output (13,475 items in the Collected Papers), there is hardly an article, let alone a book, by William Torrey Harris in print today. His most important works, available in some libraries, are *Hegel's Logic, A Book on the Genesis of the Categories of the Mind, A Critical Exposition* (Chicago, 1890), and *Psychologic Foundations of Education: An Attempt to show the Genesis of the Higher Faculties of the Mind* (New York, 1901). Most of his important articles are to be found in the various issues of *The Journal of Speculative Philosophy* (1867-1892); see especially Vols. I, II, XV, XVII and XIX. Much of this same material, together with other writings not readily available in their original source, has been collected by Marietta Kies and issued in a single volume under the title *Introduction to the Study of Philosophy* (New York, 1890).

A really first-class biography of Harris remains to be written. Kurt Leidecker's *Yankee Teacher, the Life of William Torrey Harris* (New York, 1946), the only major work on the subject, contains much valuable information but suffers from wordiness, poor organization, and the author's determination to find no wrong in his subject. An excellent antidote is Merle Curti's lucid study of Harris as a conservative, "William T. Harris, The Conservator," Ch. IX in *The Social Ideas of American Educators* (New York, 1935). A recent and readable account of Harris as a moral educator is to be found in Part Three of Neil G. McCluskey's, *Public Schools and Moral Education* (New York, 1958).

It is one of the tragedies of American publishing that the works of the most original and philosophically significant of the thinkers of the St. Louis group, Denton Snider, are not available outside of a few midwestern university and public libraries. The reader fortunate enough to have access to these should begin his study with the autobiographies, *A Writer of Books in his Genesis* (St. Louis, 1910), and *The St. Louis*

Movement, etc. A substantially complete bibliography is given in Perry. Of secondary materials, there is nothing important.

REFERENCES

1. *Journal of Speculative Philosophy,* Vol. 1 (1867), Preface.
2. *The Poetry and Prose of Walt Whitman,* edited by Louis Untermeyer (New York: Simon & Schuster, 1949), p. 778 n.
3. It is hardly likely that Whitman had any first-hand knowledge of Hegel. True, he did subtitle his poem "Roaming in Thought," "After Reading Hegel," but, as Herbert Schneider has noted, "there is abundant evidence that he wrote it *before* reading Hegel; in fact, the poem is itself the best evidence." *A History of American Philosophy* (New York: Columbia University Press, 1946), p. 178 n. In truth, Whitman's understanding of the Hegelian formulas derived in most instances from the accounts of disciples who themselves had often only a cloudy idea of the meaning, and no clear idea of the implications, of the teaching they so enthusiastically espoused.
4. In 1916, at the age of seventy-five, he married an ex-pupil, a golden-haired beauty some forty years his junior, and for a brief period he abandoned his room in the St. Louis "Ghetto." However the marriage did not last. There was a quarrel, and Mrs. Snider left St. Louis for California and never returned. Snider eventually returned to the "Ghetto" and there lived out his days.
5. Nearly all of them were published by Snider himself under the imprint of the Sigma Publishing Company (S for Shakespeare, St. Louis, and Snider).
6. Founded in 1867 by Harris, and edited by him throughout most of its twenty-five years of existence, this organ of the St. Louis Philosophical Society was the first periodical in the English language specifically dedicated to Philosophy. As such, it commanded a wide audience among professional philosophers in England and America, and throughout the last third of the Nineteenth Century it was a dominant influence on the course of Anglo-American metaphysics.
7. *Journal of Speculative Philosophy,* Vol. 1 (1867), Preface.
8. David Hume, *A Treatise of Human Nature,* edited by L. A. Selby-Bigge (Oxford: Clarendon Press, 1949), pp. 252-53.
9. *Journal of Speculative Philosophy,* Vol. 1 (1867), p. 5.
10. Ibid.
11. Ibid., Vol. II (1868), p. 2.
12. Ibid., Vol. XVII, p. 297.
13. Ibid., p. 302.
14. Ibid.
15. Ibid., p. 304. See also William Torrey Harris, *Psychologic Foundations of Education* (New York: Appleton, 1901), Chapter VII.
16. Ibid., p. 306.
17. Quoted in Neil G. McCluskey, *Public Schools and Moral Education, The Influence of Horace Mann, William Torrey Harris, and John Dewey* (New York, 1958), p. 165.
18. Ibid., pp. 161-62.

19. Ibid., p. 164.

20. Ibid., p. 167.

21. He favored the Trusts, so much so that he would have heiresses trained in tax law to the end that they might use such knowledge to evade the anti-trust acts.

22. Denton J. Snider, *The St. Louis Movement in Philosophy, Literature, Education, Psychology, with chapters of autobiography* (St. Louis: Sigma Publishing Company, 1920), p. 191.

23. *The State*, etc., p. 6.

24. Ibid., p. 405.

25. Ibid., p. 412.

26. Ibid., p. 413.

27. Ibid.

28. Ibid., pp. 493-94.

29. Ibid., p. 495.

XVI

The Apostle of Evolution

JOHN FISKE

"The universe is not a machine,
but an organism, with an indwelling principle of life. It
was not made, but it has grown." [1]

JOHN FISKE

John Fiske

ON JULY 1ST, 1858, the Linnaean Society of London assembled to hear a joint communication from Charles Darwin and Alfred Russel Wallace, announcing Wallace's independent discovery of the principle of natural selection and Darwin's evidence for the theory of evolution it entailed. Sixteen months later, stimulated to early publication by Wallace's findings, Darwin brought out his monumental *Origin of Species*. Shortly thereafter, Herbert Spencer issued the prospectus of his Synthetic Philosophy, to be completed in ten volumes, and in 1862 volume one, *First Principles,* appeared. The essentials of the theory and the metaphysics of evolution were now before the public. Henceforward, every scientist, philosopher, and theologian with a claim to the truth would be required to take account of them. Not by chance, then, was William Torrey Harris led to devote the lead article of the first issue of *The Journal of Speculative Philosophy* to an analysis of the philosophy of Herbert Spencer; for Harris realized that here was a system which, if not refuted or sublated, must render all its predecessors, including the System of Hegel, obsolete!

By way of preface to his system, Spencer dedicated Part I of *First Principles* to the Unknowable. In *An Autobiography* he tells us why. "I saw," he writes, "that it would be needful to preface the exposition by some chapters setting forth my beliefs on ultimate questions, metaphysical and theological; since, otherwise, I should be charged with propounding a purely materialistic interpretation of things. Hence resulted the first division—'The Unknowable.' " [2] It encompasses all ultimates, scientific or religious. Space, Time, Matter, Motion, Infinity, First Cause and Absolute per se are all alike—beyond any comprehension; for every effort to understand them must end, as Kant has shown in his Antimonies of Pure Reason, in fathomless contradiction. What can be known, then, are the impressions of sensation, the phenomena manifest to consciousness; that these phenomena have a noumenal foundation, that our impressions are caused by something, Spencer does not doubt; but he is equally sure that whatever this something is, it passes understanding. The Ultimate (Reality) is at once unknowable and undeniable. In this truth, he believes, Science and Religion find their reconciliation:

> Common Sense asserts the existence of a reality; Objective Science proves that this reality cannot be what we think it; Subjective Science shows why we cannot think of it as it is, and yet are compelled to think of it as existing; and in this assertion of a Reality utterly inscrutable in nature, Religion finds an assertion essentially coinciding with her own. We are obliged to regard every phenomenon as a manifestation of some Power by which we are acted upon; though Omnipresence is unthinkable, yet, as experience discloses no bounds to the diffusion of phenomena, we are unable to think of limits to the presence of this Power; while the criticisms of Science teach us that this Power is incomprehensible. And this consciousness of an Incomprehensible Power, called Omnipresent from inability to assign its limits, is just that consciousness on which Religion dwells.[3]

The exposition of the Unknowable occupies the first fifth of *First Principles;* the remainder of the book is given over, as are the nine subsequent volumes of the Synthetic Philosophy, to the analysis of the knowable. What is it, then, asks Spencer, that we know? "In what sense do we know it? And in what consists our highest knowledge of it? Having repudiated as impossible the Philosophy which professes to formulate Being as distinguished from Appearance, it becomes needful to say what Philosophy truly is—not simply to specify its limits, but to specify its character within those limits." [4] His answer is that Philosophy is the title for knowledge of the highest generality, i.e., that which fuses the data of physical, biological, and social science into a single system or whole. "As each widest generalization of Science comprehends and consolidates the narrower generalizations of its own division; so," according to Spencer, "the generalizations of Philosophy comprehend and consolidate the widest generalizations of Science. . . . Or to bring the definition to its simplest and clearest form:—Knowledge of the lowest kind is *un-unified* knowledge; Science is *partially-unified* knowledge; Philosophy is *completely-unified* knowledge." [5]

Now if we analyze the ultimate generalizations of Science, i.e., Matter, Motion, Space and Time, we find, says Spencer, "that these are either built up of, or abstracted from, experiences of Force. Matter and Motion, as we know them, are differently conditioned manifestations of Force. Space and Time, as we know them, are disclosed along with these different manifestations of Force as the conditions under which they are presented." [6] Force, then, is the ultimate of ultimates, and the "Persistence of Force" is, he argues, that "widest truth which can be merged in no other, or derived from no other. . . . This being the basis of experience, must be the basis of any scientific organization of experiences. To this an ultimate analysis brings us down; and on this a rational synthesis must build up." [7]

If force persists, then matter must be indestructible and motion continuous, for it is as impossible to think of something becoming nothing as it is to think of nothing becoming something. "The annihilation of Matter is unthinkable for the same reason that the creation of Matter is unthinkable." [8] Rather is it, Spencer believes, that everywhere and eternally there is transformation of force according to the rhythm of least resistance. Everything evolves or dissolves; the imperceptible emerges, the perceptible disappears. "All things are growing or decaying, accumulating matter or wearing away, integrating or disintegrating. All things are varying in their temperatures, contracting or expanding, integrating or disintegrating." [9] "Absolute rest and permanence do not exist. Every object, no less than the aggregate of all objects, undergoes from instant to instant some alteration of state. Gradually or quickly it is receiving motion or losing motion, while some or all of its parts are simultaneously changing their relations to one another. And the question to be answered is—What dynamic principle, true of the metamorphosis as a whole and in its details, expresses these ever-changing relations?

Just this, says Spencer: *"Evolution is an integration of matter and concomitant dissipation of motion; during which the matter passes from an indefinite incoherent homogeneity to a definite coherent heterogeneity; and during which the retained motion undergoes a parallel transformation."* [10]

Such is the law of evolution as Spencer conceives it. It is, he contends, ultimate, and taken in conjunction with the law of dissolution, i.e., the same formula inverted, it constitutes the widest generalization thus far discovered concerning the universe as a whole. Through it, all particular phenomena receive their complete interpretation; by it, phenomena in general are understood. In sum, "the deepest truths we can reach, are simply statements of the widest uniformities in our experience of the relations of Matter, Motion, and Force." [11]

This sounds very much like materialism, and British orthodoxy took it to mean just that. Spencer was denounced for an atheist who would undermine all spiritual values and dissolve the sacred foundations of Christianity. His insistence, several times repeated in his books and in public, that "Matter, Motion, and Force are but symbols of the Unknown Reality," and as such no more materialistic than spiritualistic, went unregarded. Like Darwin and Huxley, he was marked by the English biblicists as an enemy of the True Faith and treated accordingly. To their way of thinking, the enormous popularity of his philosophy in the United States was but one more evidence of American barbarism.

That Spencer should have been well received on this side of the Atlantic might have been expected, for as Hofstadter has pointed out, his philosophy was admirably suited to the American scene. "It was scientific in derivation and comprehensive in scope. It had a reassuring theory of progress based upon biology and physics. . . . It offered a comprehensive world-view, uniting under one generalization everything in nature from protozoa to politics. . . . Moreover it was not a technical creed for professionals. Presented in language that tyros in philosophy could understand, it made Spencer the metaphysician of the homemade intellectual, and the prophet of the cracker-barrel agnostic." [12] The statistics confirm that it was so. In a note appended to Spencer's *Autobiography,* his publishers, the Messrs. Appleton, reported sales of 368,755 copies of the *authorized* editions of Spencer's works from 1860 to 1903. How many of these copies were further read at second-hand, or in pirated editions, it is impossible to say; but the total must have been very large. It was no obscure philosophy that William Torrey Harris thought to prove inadequate.

That his argument should have fallen on deaf ears is an unfortunate tribute to Spencer's and empiricism's hold on the post-bellum American Mind. Unfortunate, because the argument lays bare a series of contradictions in Spencer's system which, had they been recognized at the time, might have altered the subsequent course of American thought.

Consider the Unknowable. Spencer holds that Matter, Motion, Force, Infinity and Ultimate Cause are alike unknowable. How, then, is it possible to distinguish between them? Spencer does not say. He does tell us that the phenomenon is the manifestation of the noumenon; but if so, the noumenon is surely known, for if it is not, how is it that we recognize the phenomenon to be its manifestation? Again, Spencer does not say. Nor can he ever, since if Harris is right the dualistic character of his system debars him from asserting that unity of knowable and unknowable, phenomenon and noumenon, in which alone these contradictions could be resolved. As Harris notes, "Thought is the only crucible capable of dissolving the many into the one." [13] Unfortunately for Spencer, it is a crucible he has cut himself off from using. Having declared the phenomena of mind (thought) to be a symbol of noumenal Force, he is in no position to identify this noumenal unknown as Mind or its analogue Spirit. He must and does hold that the phenomenal (world of nature) and the noumenal (cause of nature's order) are separate, signs of an "Unknown Reality" which he claims underlies both. Yet how or why these should combine so as to constitute this Unknown Reality a comprehensive whole, he nowhere explains. His failure to do so, Harris contends, illustrates the inferiority of the Synthetic Philosophy to its Hegelian competitor. The fatal flaw in Spencer's system is its inability to demonstrate a genuine synthesis.

This fact, which seemed to Harris decisive evidence of the inadequacy of Spencer's *First Principles,* bothered the American Spencerians not at all. It was enough, they thought, to have brought "all known truths concerning the coexistence and succession of phenomena into relation with one another as the corollaries of a single primordial truth," [14] without, as John Fiske put it, "making appeal to data that are ontological or to agencies that are extra-cosmic." [15] That the "Unknown Reality" to which Spencer himself had appealed might be something ontological and extra-cosmic was a possibility that Fiske, in his enthusiasm for the system, did not pause to consider.

II

Fiske's conversion to the Synthetic Philosophy was sudden and unqualified. He was browsing in a Boston bookstore when he chanced upon Spencer's original prospectus. He read it and felt his soul on fire. Then and there he decided that he must have the complete series. "I consider it," he wrote his mother, "my duty to mankind as a Positivist to subscribe; and if I had $2,000,000 I would lay $1,000,000 at Mr. Spencer's feet to help him execute this great work." [16] Instead, he laid out $2.50 for a year's subscription, and sat back to wait for the first quarterly installment of the *First Principles*. He was eighteen, and in three months he would enter Harvard.

Even at this young age, however, he was no stranger to the idea of evolution. He had studied in translation the greatest of the pre-Darwinian works on evolution, Humboldt's *Cosmos,* and at the time of his discovery of Spencer he was working through it in the original German. He was familiar with the pioneering work of the great English geologist, Lyell; he had read Herschel's *Outlines of Astronomy* and Asa Gray's *Structural and Systematic Botany*. He had mastered the Positive Philosophy of Auguste Comte. Some months prior to the great event noted above, he had finished the *Origin of Species*.

At Harvard he early gained a reputation as an advocate of Darwinism, and later was threatened with expulsion for expressing "mischievous opinions" tending, in the opinion of President Felton, "to undermine the faith of his associates." Harvard had not yet forgiven the infidelity of Mr. Emerson; not yet was it prepared to tolerate the heresy of evolution. After all, had not Harvard's own Professor Louis Agassiz, internationally recognized for his contributions to geology (he was the discoverer of the Ice Age) and zoology (he updated Cuvier's classification of animal species), affirmed in his famous *Essay on the Classification of the Animal Kingdom* the special creation of separate species by God! If Agassiz could find no evidence for the evolution of species, who was this undergraduate, Fiske, that he should set himself against such authority! [17]

Fiske graduated from Harvard in 1863, and after a brief and not too successful fling at the law, he abandoned it for his first love —philosophy. Henceforth he would be a propagandist for evolution in all its aspects. His first essays attracted favorable attention here and in England, and Fiske was encouraged to begin a correspondence with his idol, Spencer. Of more immediate importance to his academic future were his articles on university reform. Published in the *Atlantic Monthly* and the *Nation,* they helped to pave the way for the election in 1869 of Charles W. Eliot as President of Harvard.

Eliot was determined that the "thoughts that move mankind" should receive a hearing in Cambridge, and to that end he invited Ralph Waldo Emerson and John Fiske to deliver during the academic year 1869-70 two sets of lectures on recent philosophic thought. It was Eliot's intention that Fiske should expound the Positive Philosophy; what Fiske delivered were lectures on the philosophy of evolution as contrasted with the positive philosophy of Comte. Published later in *The New York World,* they aroused a storm of criticism from conservative Christians. The secular and academic worlds, however, were most favorably impressed. Spencer, to whom Fiske had sent copies of the *World,* protested against being coupled with Comte, but approved the lectures as being "extremely serviceable." Eliot must have agreed, since he promptly reappointed Fiske to deliver a second series of lectures the following year.

Encouraged by this backing, Fiske set himself to rethink the whole question of evolution. That the scientific side of the theory was sound, he never doubted; it was the religious and social side that bothered him. Spencer, in his letter acknowledging receipt of Fiske's lectures, had made clear his conviction that the religious side was incidental and secondary to the main theme of "the interpretation of all concrete phenomena in terms of the redistribution of

Matter and Motion." But Spencer, Fiske thought, could be wrong, and in his second series he addressed himself to the task of supplying the Synthetic Philosophy with a theology. Revised and combined with his 1869 lectures, the lectures of 1871 were published in 1874 under the title *Outlines of Cosmic Philosophy*.

In essence the *Outlines* is an exposition, a very thorough and well-argued exposition, of Spencer's system. Nothing Spencerian is rejected, nothing omitted. However, as Fiske notes in his Preface, while the book "does not, as a whole, lay any claim to the character of an original work, it has nevertheless come to contain so much new matter, both critical and constructive, that it can no longer be regarded as a mere reproduction of Mr. Spencer's thoughts." [18] Fiske was too loyal to say so, but the fact was that Mr. Spencer's thoughts were incomplete. His theory of the evolution of man was inadequately developed, and he had really no theology to speak of. Moreover, he had neglected to take account of his competition.

It was not that Fiske was worried about this last. On the contrary, as he saw it, the only alternatives to Spencer were Agassiz and Hegel, and he took neither seriously. The doctrine of special creations maintained by the former was, he thought, "superlative nonsense," [19] a worthy companion to the "supremely ridiculous" dialectic of the latter. Like the logical empiricists of today, he was sure that what was not common sense was not science; to him, as to them, science was synonymous with empirical verification, and he found none such for the views of Hegel and Agassiz. These he classified as ontology, and with ontology the Cosmic Philosophy, as he defined it, simply had nothing to do.

It had very much to do, however, with the problem of the genesis of man. Just how had the transition from animality to humanity been accomplished? Darwin had suggested "natural selection, aided by inherited habit," and Spencer had echoed Darwin. But this, Fiske thought, hardly sufficed to account for the origin of that moral sense which marked man's separation from his ape-like progenitor. "Natural selection of physical variations might go on for a dozen eternities without any other visible result than new forms of plant and beast in endless and meaningless succession . . . But the moment we consider the minds of man and ape, the gap between the two is immeasurable." [20] Alfred Russel Wallace, recalled Fiske, had pointed out the fact that man's body had hardly changed in a million years, and had concluded from this that the evolution of ape into man was primarily a matter of the development of intelligence. If Wallace was right, and Fiske was sure that he was, here was the clue to the answer. As intelligence evolves in complexity, so, he reasoned, must the period of infancy lengthen. Why this should be, he did not pretend to know; but that it is so, experience confirmed. "The prolongation of infancy accompanying the development of intelligence, and the correlative extension of parental feelings, are facts established by observation wherever observation is possible." [21] Given the uniformity of nature, there is, then, no reason to doubt that it has been ever the same. But if so, the problem of transition is solved.

> For the process here described, when long enough continued, must inevitably differentiate and integrate a herd or troop of gregarious ape-like men into a number of small family communities such as are now found among the lowest savages. The prolonged helplessness of the offspring must keep the parents together for longer and longer periods in successive epochs; and when at last the association is so long kept up that the older children are growing mature while the younger ones still need protection, the family relations begin to become permanent . . . Thus we cross the chasm which divides animality from humanity, gregariousness from sociality, hedonism from morality, the sense of pleasure and pain from the sense of right and wrong.[22]

Thus is born in man that moral sense which is the foundation of all ethics and religion.

From the phenomena of moral sense to the phenomena of religion was but a step, and Fiske found it a natural one to take. As a youth he had accepted as a matter of course the Puritan faith of his family and the Calvinism of his church. Grown to manhood, he continued to search for an adequate faith even as he repudiated the anthropomorphic God of his fathers. In Spencer he had found, so he thought, a philosophy at once scientifically and religiously satisfactory. Imagine, then, the shock he must have felt as he read Spencer's candid admission that Part I (The Unknowable) of *First Principles* was written "simply for the purpose of guarding myself against the charges of atheism and materialism, which I foresaw would most likely be made in its absence." [23] The implicit cynicism he could overlook; the implication of agnosticism he must reject. The doctrine of the Unknowable was plainly theistic, and if the master did not choose to develop it as such, it was the duty of the disciple to do so.

"The question which we have to answer is not," Fiske insists,

> whether there exists a God. . . . Our Cosmic Philosophy is based upon the affirmation of God's existence, and not upon the denial of it, like irreligious Atheism, or upon the ignoring of it, like non-religious Positivism. The question which we have now to answer concerns the existence of a limited personal God, who is possessed of a quasi-human consciousness, from whose quasi-human volitions have originated the laws of nature, and to whose quasi-human contrivance are due the manifold harmonies observed in the universe. Is this most refined and subtilized remnant of primitive anthropomorphism to be retained by our Cosmic Philosophy, or is it to be rejected? [24]

Rejected, answers Fiske, for reasons we shall see very shortly. But first we must be clear in our minds as to who it is that is being rejected.

That it is the God of traditional Christianity is not immediately apparent, for while all Christians would agree that God is personal, none would admit that He is *limited*. On the contrary, He is absolutely unlimited as regards His might, majesty, dominion, and power; absolutely perfect in goodness, wisdom, justice, and love. Indeed, so far is He from being a "limited personal God" that all Christians properly denominate Him—Infinite Personality. So might any Christian argue, but if he did, thinks Fiske, he would be wrong. For the difference the Christian remarks turns out upon examination to be no difference at all, and this because a personal God cannot be conceived as an infinite God!

". . . An anthropomorphic God cannot be conceived as an infinite God. *Personality* and *Infinity* are," to Fiske's way of thinking, "terms expressive of ideas which are mutually incompatible. The pseud-idea 'Infinite Person' is neither more nor less unthinkable than the pseud-idea 'Circular Triangle.' As Spinoza somewhere says, *Determinatio negatio est,*—to define God is to deny Him; and such being the case, what can be more irrational," Fiske wants to know, "than to insist upon thought and volition, phenomena only known to exist within quite narrow limitations, as the very nature and essence of the infinite Deity." [25] The word "person," taken in reference to a particular human being, has a specific meaning understood by all men of common sense; taken in reference to God, it retains that meaning only to the extent that God is conceived as quasi-human. A person who has absolutely nothing in common with human persons simply is not a person in any meaningful sense of the word. And as it is with "person," so is it, Fiske insists, with every word we speak of God. If the word as applied to God does not mean what it means in ordinary usage, then, for all we or any theologian may know, it may mean anything or nothing. Insofar as the Christian idea of a personal God is conceivable, then, it is the idea of a God limited in some manner quasi-human. Is there any admissible evidence to justify the belief that God, so conceived, exists?

Fiske finds none. Science repudiates the idea of a creation out of nothing. It offers no support for the notion of Divine Providence. It is silent on the subject of redemption. The truth of the matter is that the limited personal God of anthropomorphic theism can in no way be harmonized with those demonstrated scientific truths on which the Cosmic Philosophy rests. "Thus from every point of view the doctrine of a quasi-human God appears equally unsatisfactory to the scientific thinker. It rests upon unsupported theories of causation, upon a mistaken conception of law, and upon a teleological hypothesis whose origin renders it suspicious, and whose evidence fails it in the hour of need." [26] It will be said that it does not really matter, that to the man of faith this scientific evidence is irrelevant. Fiske does not think so.

The noble quest in which Science engages is the quest, not of faith or of consolation, but of truth; and, with the scientific philosopher, loyalty to truth is the first principle of religion. The disagreeableness of a well-supported conclusion furnishes no sort of justification for not accepting it, save to those minds which are irreligious as well as unscientific. He who is loyal to Truth will never harbour the misgiving that her paths may lead to Hades: he will fearlessly follow the guidance of Science, never doubting that consolation must come of knowing the truth.[27]

Fortunately, the truth, as Fiske conceives it, is still recognizably Christian. The consolation that comes with its knowledge is the realization that Christianity need only to raise itself from the level of anthropomorphic theism to that of cosmic theism, and all will be well.

"In using the phrase 'Cosmic Theism' . . . to denote the religious phase of the philosophy based on the Doctrine of Evolution, I do not," Fiske tells us, "use it as descriptive of a new form of religion before which Christianity is gradually to disappear. I use it as descriptive of that less-anthropomorphic phase of religious theory into which the present more-anthropomorphic phase is likely to be slowly metamorphosed . . . The result is not the destruction of religion, but the substitution of a relatively adequate for a relatively inadequate set of symbols." [28] To the earliest theists God was, *literally,* Father, Maker, Judge, and Redeemer. As Christianity outgrew its childhood, the literal was transformed into the symbolic. God was still Father, but metaphorically or analogically rather than literally so. Today the metaphorical stands revealed as the mythologic, and Christianity, grown to manhood, must be prepared to substitute new scientific symbols for those mythological forms in which hitherto it has been clothed.

When we have divested deity as far as is possible of all of its anthropomorphic characteristics, and ceased to think of God as someone acting on the universe from outside, what remains, Fiske believes, is an awareness of *"a POWER, to which no limit in time or space is conceivable, of which all phenomena, as presented in consciousness, are manifestations, but which we can know only through these manifestations."* [29] So long as we remember that these manifestations are only symbols of an Inscrutable Reality which is their cause, we cannot fall into the error of identifying this POWER with blind-force. "The use of this, and of the kindred epithet 'brute matter,' implies that matter and force are real existences,—independent 'data objective to' consciousness. To the scientific inquirer," i.e., Fiske himself, "the terms 'matter' and 'force' are mere symbols which stand *tant bien que mal* for certain generalized modes of Divine manifestation: they are no more real existences than the x and y of the algebraist are real existences. The question as to identifying Deity with Force is, therefore, simply ruled out." [30] For

Fiske, Force is POWER symbolized; POWER in and of itself is God.

That this POWER is, we know from its manifestations in mind and matter; *what* it is, is forever Unknowable. We may, he allows, if we choose, call it Spirit; but we must not forget that Spirit, like Force, is only a symbol and never a literal description of God. Whatever we call it will, as Fiske recognizes, involve us in some degree of anthropomorphism: "there is anthropomorphism even in speaking of the unknown Cause as a *Power* manifested in phenomena." [31] Indeed, "the total elimination of anthropomorphism from the idea of God abolishes the idea itself." [32] Yet if we can never entirely rid our reference to God of anthropomorphism, we can recognize it for what it is.

> It is enough to remind the reader that Deity is unknowable just in so far as it is not manifested to consciousness through the phenomenal world,—knowable just in so far as it is thus manifested; unknowable in so far as infinite and absolute,—knowable in the order of its phenomenal manifestations; knowable, in a symbolic way, as the Power which is disclosed in every throb of the mighty rhythmic life of the universe; knowable as the eternal Source of a Moral Law which is implicated with each action of our lives, and in obedience to which lies our only guaranty of the happiness which is incorruptible, and which neither inevitable misfortune nor unmerited obloquy can take away. Thus, though we may not by searching find out God, though we may not compass infinitude or attain to absolute knowledge, we may at least know all that it concerns us to know, as intelligent and responsible beings. They who seek to know more than this, to transcend the conditions under which alone is knowledge possible, are, in Goethe's profound language, as wise as little children who, when they have looked into a mirror, turn it around to see what is behind it.[33]

Perhaps so. But the fact is that Fiske passes over too lightly too many problems of legitimate concern even to those who, like himself, are empirically inclined. He has no adequate account to give of Mind and its relation to Matter and Motion. They are, he insists, parallel manifestations of the Unknowable; neither is translatable into the other, and yet, "owing to the mysterious but unquestionable correlation which exists between the phenomena of Mind and the phenomena of Matter and Motion, it is possible to describe the evolution of the former by the same formula which describes the evolution of the latter." [34] But how and why, he does not say. Presumably, the resolution of the mind-body problem that has occupied the attention of philosophers and scientists since the age of Descartes is one of those things which it does not concern us to know. A similar attitude is evident in his treatment of the relation between God and the universe. That God is, in some sense, the cause of the universe is obvious; but just what the nature of this causality is, again Fiske does not say. Presumably, this too is something it does not concern us to know.

That these negative conclusions should find favour in religious circles was hardly to be expected. Fiske's rejection of traditional (anthropomorphic) theism infuriated conservative Christians and was widely misunderstood by the liberals. His Cosmic Theism was taken for agnosticism thinly disguised, and Spencer's known indifference to religion was now attributed to his American disciple. Naturally, Fiske was disturbed by what he took to be a rank distortion of his views, but for a decade his circumstances left him no time to set the record straight. From 1872 until 1878 his time was fully taken up with his duties as Assistant Librarian at Harvard. Thereafter most of it was given over to his historical work. Finally, in 1884, opportunity arrived in the form of an invitation to deliver one of a scheduled series of addresses on the subject of "Man's Immortality" before the Concord Summer School of Philosophy. So successful was it that Fiske was invited to return the following year, this time to lecture on a subject of his own choosing. He elected to speak on The Idea of God as Effected by Modern Knowledge, and when he had done, it was apparent that his idea of God and Its relation to the universe had undergone considerable development in the decade that had elapsed since the publication of the *Cosmic Philosophy*.

Now he saw clearly, what previously he had hardly noticed, that acceptance of the doctrine of evolution meant the rejection of the classical Newtonian picture of the universe as a machine operating in accordance with fixed laws decreed by the Divine Mechanic who had made it. The universe, he recognizes, is no longer to be conceived on the analogy of a watch fashioned by a cosmic watchmaker. (Archdeacon) "Paley's simile of the watch is no longer applicable to such a world as this. It must be replaced by the simile of the flower. The universe is not a machine, but an organism, with an indwelling principle of life. It was not made, but it has grown." [35]

This cardinal truth is not, of course, original with Fiske. To him, however, belongs the credit of being the first American to sense its truly revolutionary implications as regards our picture of the universe and God. To begin with, "it means," he informs his Concord hearers, "that the universe as a whole is thrilling in every fibre with Life . . ." [36] It means "that nowhere in Nature is inertness or quiescence to be found." [37] It means, in brief, panpsychism.

Panpsychism becomes panentheism in the realization that this "Life" manifest in all Nature is "only a specialized form of the Universal Life," [38] which is that "eternal God indwelling in the universe, in whom we live and move and have our being." [39] For if, as noted earlier, God cannot be conceived as something *outside* the universe (as maintained in anthropomorphic theism), and if, as has been shown, we cannot identify Him or It with the universe phenomenally manifest (since this would be pantheism), then it must be that the one (theistic) alternative remaining is the truth: the universe is (as panen*theism* teaches) *inside* God! Fiske himself had said as much when he remarked at the conclusion of his exposition of the Cosmic Philosophy that, "from first to last it has been implied that, while the universe is the manifestation of Deity, *yet is Deity something more than the universe*." [40] Whether he was really aware of the significance of what he was saying is another question, and one that is not easily answered. In his last theological work, *Through Nature to God* (1899), Fiske allows that "the advance of modern science carries us irresistibly to what some German philosophers call monism," [41] but that these same German philosophers had another name for such a monism, he did not know. His own term, first adopted in *The Idea of God,* was "monotheism," which, as he defined it in use, signified "the universe as an organic whole, animated by the omnipresent spirit of God." [42] More than this he had nothing to say about it. Most likely, he did not realize just how revolutionary a conception his "monotheism" really was.

If so, his failure was no greater than that of his theological generation. Of all his contemporaries, only George Holmes Howison understood what cosmic theism meant, and even he misunderstood Fiske's version of it. As for the rest, they simply ignored it. Some few sought to effect an accommodation of religion with evolution by limiting the province of the latter to the phenomena of growth. With origins, they argued, evolution had nothing to do. Most, however, happy in their faith, refused to argue at all. As they saw it, evolution was simply irrelevant to revelation. And there, for the time being, the matter rested.

SUGGESTED READINGS

The Origin of Species has been recently reprinted in paperback (New York: Mentor Books, 1958), but Spencer's *First Principles* is long out of print. Most libraries, however, will have copies of this latter and the nine other volumes of the Synthetic Philosophy. The centenary of the publication of Darwin's great work has inspired the appearance of a score of books on the subject of evolution. One of the best is Loren Eiseley's *Darwin's Century* (Garden City: Doubleday Anchor, paperback, 1961). The stranger to the history of Darwinism will find this scholarly and eminently readable volume an excellent introduction to the movement and its masters. For the American sequel, consult Richard Hofstadter, *Social Darwinism in American Thought* (Boston: Beacon Press, paperback, 1955). The impact of Darwin and Huxley on English thought is described by William Irvine, *Apes, Angels, and Victorians* (New York: Meridian Books, paperback, 1959).

The student of John Fiske has no recourse but to his local library, since all of Fiske's works, philosophical and historical, are also out of print, as is the standard biography, John Spencer Clark, *The Life and Letters of John Fiske,* 2 Vols. (Boston: Houghton Mifflin, 1917). The only recent study of Fiske's thought is H. Burnell Pannill, *The Religious Faith of John Fiske* (Durham: Duke University Press, 1957). A Ph. D. dissertation reworked, it has few of the vices and most of the virtues of the genre, and not the least of the latter is its provision of a complete bibliography of books and articles by and about its subject.

REFERENCES

1. *The Idea of God* (Boston: Houghton Mifflin, 1887), p. 131. Hereafter cited as Idea.

2. Herbert Spencer, *An Autobiography,* Vol. II (New York: Appleton, 1904), p. 86.

3. Herbert Spencer, *First Principles,* 4th Edition (New York: Appleton, 1896), p. 99.

4. Ibid., p. 127.

5. Ibid., pp. 133-34.

6. Ibid., p. 169.

7. Ibid., p. 192.

8. Ibid., pp. 177-78.

9. Ibid., p. 282.

10. Ibid., p. 396. The italics are Spencer's.

11. Ibid., p. 557.

12. Richard Hofstadter, *Social Darwinism in American Thought* (Boston: Beacon Press, 1955), pp. 31-32.

13. *Journal of Speculative Philosophy,* Vol. I (1867), p. 8.

14. John Fiske, *Outlines of Cosmic Philosophy Based on the Doctrine of Evolution, with Criticisms on the Positive Philosophy,* 2 Vols. (Boston: Houghton Mifflin, 1874), Vol. I, p. x. Hereafter cited as Cosmic Philosophy.

15. Cosmic Philosophy, p. x.

16. John Spencer Clark, *The Life and Letters of John Fiske,* 2 Vols. (Boston: Houghton Mifflin, 1917), Vol. I, p. 139. Hereafter cited as Life.

17. Some years later Fiske published an article in which he undertook to show that Agassiz's rejection of the Darwinian theory was based upon personal bias and insufficient knowledge of the scientific facts. Fiske's points were well taken, but his timing was unintentionally brutal. He did not know at the time that Agassiz was critically ill, and he could not anticipate that his rival would die two months after the publication of the article. As a result, the merits of Fiske's essay were overlooked by a public that saw only that a great American had been kicked while down. For the article in question, see "Agassiz and Darwinism," *Popular Science Monthly,* Vol. III (1873), pp. 692-705.

18. Cosmic Philosophy, I, p. vii.

19. Ibid., II, p. 321.

20. *Through Nature to God* (Boston: Houghton Mifflin, 1899), pp. 81-82. Hereafter cited as Nature.

21. Cosmic Philosophy II, p. 344.

22. Ibid., pp. 344-46.

23. Life, I, p. 368.

24. Cosmic Philosophy II, pp. 377-78.

25. Ibid., pp. 408-9.

26. Ibid., p. 408.

27. Ibid., pp. 382-83.

28. Ibid., p. 505.

29. Ibid., p. 415. Fiske's italics.

30. Ibid., p. 430.

31. Ibid., p. 449. See also Cosmic Philosophy I, p. 183.

32. Idea, p. 135.

33. Cosmic Philosophy II, p. 470.

34. Ibid., p. 162.

35. Idea, p. 131.

36. Ibid., p. 149.

37. Ibid., p. 150.
38. Ibid., p. 149.
39. Ibid., p. 155.
40. Cosmic Philosophy II, p. 424. My italics.
41. Nature, p. 23.
42. Ibid.

XVII

Champion of the Forgotten Man

WILLIAM GRAHAM SUMNER

"Who is, then, the Forgotten Man? He is
the clean, quiet, virtuous, domestic
citizen, who pays his debts and his taxes
and is never heard of out of his little
circle. Yet who is there in the society
of a civilized state who deserves to be
remembered and considered by the legislator and statesman before this man?" [1]

WILLIAM GRAHAM SUMNER

William Graham Sumner

WHILE THE THEOLOGIANS QUIBBLED about the relevance of evolution to the faith, a new social philosophy, nourished by the conversion of the leaders of American science [2] to the Darwinian theory, was finding favor across the land. Social Darwinism, as it was later known, had had its origin in Darwin's and Spencer's conviction that what was true of Nature as a whole could not be false of nature's social part. If they were right, then the factors controlling the life of man in society, their followers thought, must be identical with those governing every evolutionary process. The struggle for existence, culminating in the survival of the fittest, was, then, as true of society as of the jungle. The difference between them was merely a matter of sophistication. The laws that sociology sought, biology had already discovered. What remained was to apply them to the new science of society and educate the people to its truth, and this the social Darwinists now undertook to do.

If only the fittest deserved to survive, then, it was argued, those who lost out in the competitive struggle had no cause for complaint. Exploitation was nature's way, and laissez-faire [3] capitalism was its natural manner of expression. Anything, therefore, that interfered with the free development of economic competition was not only unnatural but immoral, since it must inevitably end in the preservation of the unfit. More than this, it must end by destroying liberty, for liberty, as the social Darwinists conceived it, was simply the freedom to do one's best to win the struggle for existence. To refuse to any man his right to win was, they believed, equivalent to denying the cardinal condition making for social progress. The idea that social progress could be identified with the achievement of social equality, they rejected completely. It was unknown in Nature and never illustrated in History. The fact of the matter, as William Graham Sumner observed, was "that when laws and customs are made with a view to equality they crush out progress." [4] It was, he thought, high time that socialists and reformers faced up to The Challenge of Facts. That competition is a law of nature is a fact.

> If we do not like it, and if we try to amend it, there is only one way in which we can do it. We can take from the better and give to the worse. We can deflect the penalties of those who have done ill and throw them on those who have done better. We can take the rewards from those who have done better and give them to those who have done worse. We shall thus lessen the inequalities. We shall favor the survival of the unfittest, and we shall accomplish this by destroying liberty. Let it be understood that we cannot go outside of this alternative: liberty, inequality, survival of the fittest; not-liberty, equality, survival of the unfittest. The former carries society forward and favors all its best members; the latter carries society downwards and favors all its worst members.[5]

To demonstrate the truth of this conviction was Sumner's one grand aim, and the zeal with which he pursued it through a dozen books and twelve-score articles made him the natural leader of those conservatives who found in social Darwinism their philosophical justification.[6]

Yale's greatest teacher was born at Paterson, New Jersey, on October 30th, 1840. His parents were English immigrants. The father, Thomas Sumner, a machinist by trade, had migrated from Walton-le-Dale in Lancashire in 1836 and here married Sarah Graham, daughter of a fellow Lancashireman. After some years of prospecting for opportunity as far west as Ohio, Thomas Sumner moved his family to Hartford, Connecticut, and settled down to a job in the shops of the Hartford and New Haven Railroad. When William was eight his mother died, and the father, left with three small children to support, soon remarried. For two years, in his teens, William worked in a dry goods store to help the family income. That he was able to scrape up the funds to enter Yale following his graduation from Hartford High School in 1859 was due almost entirely to the rigid economies practiced by his stepmother. Shortly before his graduation from Yale in 1863 he was drafted into the Union Army, but escaped service when a wealthy college friend paid his exemption. Through the good offices of this same friend, William C. Whitney, Sumner was advanced sufficient funds to allow him to undertake graduate studies in Europe. During the autumn of 1863 he pursued French and Hebrew at Geneva, and then left for Göttingen. Here he remained for two years, mastering German, continuing Hebrew, and reading theology. In May of 1866, having virtually decided to seek ordination in the Episcopal Church, he went up to Oxford to study Anglican theology. In the meantime, Yale had, all unknown to Sumner, elected him tutor, and in September he returned to New Haven to take up his duties. However, he was still resolved upon a clerical career, and to that end he had himself ordained deacon in the Protestant Episcopal Church in services at Trinity in New Haven on December 28th, 1867. For a year he combined the jobs of tutor and supply preacher, and then in March of 1869 he left New Haven for New York and the dual post of editor of the new periodical *The Living Church* and assistant to the rector of Calvary Church. Unfortunately, neither position panned out. *The Living Church* proved short-lived, and following a quarrel with his rector, Sumner resolved to seek a new assignment. On July 15th, 1869, he was ordained priest, and shortly thereafter accepted a call to be rector of the Church of the Redeemer at Morristown, New Jersey. In April of the following year he married Jeannie Whittemore Elliott, and thought himself permanently settled. But it was not to be. The social instincts, genial disposition, and out-of-doors tastes that a pastor must have, he conspicuously lacked, and thus when the offer of a professorship came from Yale, he eagerly accepted. As things turned out, it was a lifetime commitment. From time to time Sumner would assume outside responsibilities, but his heart, and most of his energies, would henceforth, be dedicated to Yale. For a while he dabbled in New Haven politics. In 1873 he ran for alderman on the Republican ticket and won election. He was re-elected in 1874. Nominated by the Democrats in 1876 (his public support of Tilden in the national campaign of that year alienated his Republican backers), he was narrowly beaten, and retired from politics for good. Years later he referred to his time in politics and his years as a parson as the two wasted periods of his life. From 1882 until his death in 1910 he served as a member of the Connecticut State Board of Education, but apart from this he took no active role in any other than University affairs.

His influence upon three generations of Yale undergraduates was profound; his effect upon the economic and social thinking of the pre-World War I business community scarcely less so. In this present day of conservative revival, he deserves to be rediscovered, for no American has ever put the case for conservatism more clearly or cogently.

II

Such was Sumner's reputation in his later years that most of his students and not a few of his colleagues would have been astounded to hear that he had been a priest before he became a professor. Years later, reminiscing of those days, he confessed to Albert G. Keller that it was the effort of writing sermons that had made him see just how much his interest lay in topics of social science and political economy. "I thought," he continued, "that these were matters of the most urgent importance, which threatened all the interests, moral, social, and economic, of the nation; and I was young enough to believe that they would all be settled in the next four or five years. It was not possible to preach about them, but I got so near to it that I was detected sometimes. . . ." [7] To compound his difficulties, he now fell, as Fiske had fallen earlier, under the spell of Spencer.

It was at this period (1870) that I read, in an English magazine, the first of those essays of Herbert Spencer which were afterward collected into the volume 'The Study of Sociology.' These essays immediately gave me the lead which I wanted, to bring into shape the crude notions which had been floating in my head for five or six years, especially since the Oxford days. The conception of society, of social forces, and of the science of society there offered was just the one which I had been groping after but had not been able to reduce for myself. It solved the old difficulty about the relation of social science to history, rescued social science from the dominion of the cranks, and offered a definite and magnificent field for work, from which we might hope at last to derive definite results for the solution of social problems.[8]

Later, Sumner was to reject Spencer's easy optimism, but in the first flush of discovery he felt himself in possession of the key to the science of society, and suddenly his concern for theology dropped away. "It was at this juncture (1872) that I was offered the chair of Political and Social Science at Yale.[9] I had always been very fond of teaching and knew that the best work I could ever do in the world would be in that profession; also, that I ought to be in an academical career. I had seen two or three cases of men who, in that career, would have achieved distinguished usefulness, but who were wasted in the parish and the pulpit." [10] Sumner was not about to let it happen to him. There was work to be done, and in September of 1872 he was back in New Haven and ready to do it.

That he had been called to be a pioneer, he well knew. Apart from Spencer, and the Frenchman, Auguste Comte, there was no one who as yet had any clear notion of a *science* of society. Even Fiske, for all his insight, had failed to see in social evolution anything more than the general operation of a cosmic purpose. Spencer had shown that society was a seat of forces measurable by science. To define these forces and to measure them was Sumner's problem. Like Fiske, he would build upon the foundations that Spencer had laid down; but where Fiske had found his inspiration in the first part of Spencer's *First Principles,* Sumner would find his in the second.

He had been, he recalled,

definitely converted to evolution by Professor Marsh's horses some time about 1875 or 1876. I had re-read Spencer's 'Social Statics' and his 'First Principles,' the second part of the latter now absorbing all my attention. I now read all of Darwin, Huxley, Haeckel, and quite a series of the natural scientists. I greatly regretted that I had no education in natural science, especially in biology; but I found that the 'philosophy of history' and the 'principles of philology,' as I had learned them, speedily adjusted themselves to the new conception, and won a new meaning and power from it. As Spencer's 'Principles of Sociology' was now coming out in numbers, I was constantly getting evidence that sociology, if it borrowed the theory of evolution in the first place, would speedily render it back again enriched by new and independent evidence.[11]

His enthusiasm aroused, Sumner now began to lecture on the new sociology to his senior class, using as a textbook Spencer's *The Study of Sociology.* That Spencer was regarded as an atheist by the conservative faction at Yale, he well knew. He also knew that Yale stood before the country as a Christian college. It was, therefore, with no surprise that he received President Noah Porter's letter objecting to his teaching Spencer to impressionable undergraduates. "The freedom and unfairness with which it [*The Study of Sociology*] attacks every Theistic Philosophy of society and of history, and the cool and yet sarcastic effrontery with which he [Spencer] assumes that material elements and laws are the only forces and laws which any scientific man can recognize, seem to me," wrote Porter, "to condemn the book as a textbook for a miscellaneous class in an undergraduate course. I ought," he continued, "to have examined the book sooner, but I feel assured that the use of the book will bring intellectual and moral harm to the students, however you may strive to neutralize or counteract its influence, and that the use of it will inevitably and reasonably work serious havoc to the reputation of the college. Having these opinions, I can do nothing else than express them, and," he concluded, "as I am presumed to authorize the use of every textbook, I must formally object to the use of this." [12]

Sumner's reaction was typical. He went immediately to see the President, and proffered him his resignation. "There was," he later told a reporter for the *New York Times,*

an understanding between us that if the use of the book was prohibited, I should resign my position, as I did not think I could properly fill the chair of Political and Social Science if I was hedged about and restricted in such a manner. With Mr. Spencer's individual opinions upon the matter of religion I have nothing to do, but this work on sociology is the only book of the kind in the English language, and coming from as great a philosopher and student as Mr. Spencer, and embodying, as it does, the results of years of the most exhaustive and discriminating investigation into a particularly complex subject, it naturally commends itself to those engaged in the study of social science. Indeed, it would be difficult to see how English students could study social science at all if the works of so high an authority as Spencer were to be debarred them.[13]

Porter apparently agreed, for the book remained on the schedule, and was used by Sumner during the Spring Term of 1880. Here the matter might have rested, had not some mischief maker given the story to the newspapers. Yale's standing as a seat of Christian learning was now publicly called in question, and the ensuing widespread publicity forced the college authorities to take note of the issue. The conservatives wanted a resolution clearly spelling out the right of the President to forbid the use of unacceptable books. To avoid its passage, which he knew must have disastrous consequences, President Porter now informed the Yale Corporation that Sumner had given assurance that Spencer's book would not be used by him again. Actually, Sumner had done no such thing, and when, some months later, Porter wrote him enclosing a copy of the statement he (Porter) had made to the Corporation, Sumner exploded with indignation. He now determined to resign, and circulated a lengthy letter to all concerned setting forth his reasons for such action in detail. Since very few of the Yale family really wanted Sumner to leave, and as he found no other position to his liking, he stayed on, and gradually the controversy died away. Sumner had, in effect, won his battle, and it was not an unimportant victory. Never again would the theologians presume to censor the professors of social or physical science. Henceforward, Yale would stand for academic freedom.

III

While Sumner's heart was in the study of sociology, his list of publications up to and beyond the turn of the century reveals a mind preoccupied with economics. *Folkways,* his sociological magnum opus, did not appear until 1907, three years before his death. The great mass of data eventually published as *The Science of Society* came out long years after. What he wrote about, and was nationally known as an authority on during his lifetime, was money, banking, taxation, and the tariff. Even in his biographies, particularly those of Hamilton and Morris, his interest centered not on the men themselves but on their economic achievements.

Sumner himself dated his interest in economic problems from the day when, still a Hartford schoolboy, he had chanced upon Harriet Martineau's *Illustrations of Political Economy* in the library of the Young Men's Institute. "I read them," he told Keller,

> all through with the greatest avidity, some of them three or four times. There was very little literature at that time with which these books could connect. My teachers could not help me any, and there were no immediate relations between the topics of these books and any public interests of the time. We supposed then that free trade had sailed out upon the smooth sea, and was to go forward without further difficulty, so that what one learned of the fallacies of pro-tection had only the same interest as what one learns about the fallacies of any old and abandoned error. In college we read and recited Wayland's 'Political Economy,' but I believe that my con-ceptions of capital, labor, money, and trade, were all formed by these books which I read in my boyhood.[14]

What they had taught him in theory, his home life reinforced in fact. The near poverty of his youth, coupled with the example of industry, thrift, and self-denial set him by his father, profoundly influenced him. Thomas Sumner believed in hard work and perfect workmanship, a sound dollar and laissez faire, and he impressed them on his son at every opportunity. William Sumner never forgot the lessons. Fifty years later he would acknowledge that his father's "principles and habits of life were the best possible." From his first book to his last article, he too would stand for hard money and free trade.

Into the intricacies of the currency question as it occupied Amer-ica during the Seventies and Eighties of the last century, we need not go. Suffice it to say that Sumner was vehemently and persistently opposed to the demands of the farmers and wage-earners for more and cheaper money. It was, he thought, no part of the obligation of the government to its citizens to make it easier for debtors to pay their legitimately incurred debts. Free silver, bimetallism, protec-tionism, all the economic panaceas of the age were, if the truth be known, simply devices designed to favor one class, the debtors, at the expense of the rest of society, and in his speeches and articles Sumner made clear his contempt for these schemes in terms specifically calculated to give offense to their advocates. And give offense they did. He was bitterly denounced in the Republican press, and pressure was brought to have him dismissed from Yale; but as his national unpopularity grew, so did Yale's pride in its prince of iconoclasts. Even so, there were many at Yale also in thorough disagreement with Sumner's views, particularly those relating to protectionism.

Then, as now, the belief that the prosperity of the nation required the protection of American industry from foreign competition by the imposition of tariffs high enough to prevent American goods from being undersold at home was gospel to the Republicans and sound economics to the vast majority of the American business community. Free trade they abhorred. It was, they were sure, a policy inevitably tending to encompass the ruin of those firms and industries unable to match the competition of cheap foreign labor and materials. Patriotism, no less than economic common sense, dictated that American workers in such industries be protected in their jobs, that industries vital to the military security of the United States be protected from that corrosive competition which would and could destroy them. Imagine, then, the shock they felt at hearing Sumner scorn their noble sentiments as arrant economic quackery and worse. They retaliated with a spate of vilification that was to last for years, but in all that time scarcely a protectionist voice was raised to refute his simple but decisive argument for free trade.

The point was, as Sumner realized and the protectionists did not, that a tariff was a tax.

If a tariff is not a tax, what is it? In what category does it belong? No protectionist has ever yet told. They seem to think of it as a thing by itself, a Power, a Force, a sort of Mumbo Jumbo whose special function it is to produce national prosperity. They do not appear to have analyzed it, or given themselves an account of it, sufficiently to know what kind of a thing it is or how it acts. Any one who says that it is not a tax must suppose that it costs nothing, that it produces an effect without an expenditure of energy. . . . This is the fundamental fallacy of protection . . . Scientifically stated, it is that *protectionism sins against the conservation of energy.* More simply stated, it is that *the protectionist either never sees or does not tell the other side of the account, the cost, the outlay for the gains which he alleges from protection, and that when these are examined and weighed they are sure vastly to exceed the gains, if the gains were real,* even taking no account of the harm to national growth which is done by restriction and interference.[15]

The fact of the matter is that the gains are illusion; only the cost is real.

The high tariffs that enable American industry to charge higher prices for their product than they could otherwise hope to get on a free market are costs (taxes) levied against the consumer by the government for the sole benefit of the protected. As such, they are, to Sumner's way of thinking, neither more nor less than licenses to steal. To maintain, as the protectionists do, that tariffs are in the national interest is, he insists, patently false. "The truth is that protectionism demoralizes and miseducates a people. It deprives them of individual self-reliance and energy, and teaches them to seek crafty and unjust advantages. It breaks down the skill of great merchants and captains of industry, and develops the skill of lobbyists. It gives faith in monopoly, combinations, jobbery, and restriction, instead of giving faith in energy, free enterprise, public purity, and freedom." [16] It is, in sum, "a social abuse, an economic blunder and a political evil"; [17] persisted in, it will inevitably "lessen wealth, reduce prosperity, diminish average comfort, and lower the standard of living." [18] He was right, but very few believed it then, and even fewer believe it now.

That so many could be so blind about the economics of protectionism, Sumner could forgive; after all, economics is at best an esoteric and imprecise sort of science. What he could not forgive was their failure to see that protectionism was socialism.

The protected interests demand that they be saved from the trouble and annoyance of business competition, and that they be assured profits in their undertakings, by 'the State,' that is, at the expense of their fellow-citizens. If this is not socialism, then there is no such thing. If employers may demand that 'the State' shall guarantee them profits, why may not the employees demand that 'the State' shall guarantee them wages? If we are taxed to provide profits, why should we not be taxed for public workshops, for insurance to laborers, or for any other devices which will give wages and save the laborer from the annoyances of life and the risks and hardships of the struggle for existence? [19]

To Sumner's view, such socialist policies, pursued to their logical end, must lead straight to social chaos. If social progress is synonymous with the survival of the fittest (defined as the victors in the economic struggle for existence), then any device tending to protect the unfit, industry or individual, is a crime against society. That protectionism is precisely such a device was to Sumner a fact self-evident. Protectionism, therefore, is something no capitalist concerned for his future has any business defending.

> The 'we' who are to pay changes all the time, and the turn of the protected employer to pay will surely come before long. The plan of all living on each other is capable of great expansion. It is, as yet, far from being perfected or carried out completely. The protectionists are only educating those who are as yet on the 'paying' side of it, but who will certainly use political power to put themselves also on the 'receiving' side of it. The argument that 'the State' must do something for me because my business does not pay, is a very far-reaching argument. If it is good for pig-iron and woolens, it is good for all the things to which the socialists apply it.[20]

But for capitalism, thinks Sumner, it is fatal.

For those inclined to say "so much the worse for capitalism," Sumner has two questions and a fact. The fact is that "modern civilization is built upon machines and natural agents brought into play through machines, that is, through capital . . . Then come these two questions: (1) can we keep the advantages and comforts of a high civilization, based on capital, while attacking the social institutions by which the creation of capital is secured? (2) are we prepared to give up the comforts of civilization rather than continue to pay the price of them?" [21] "No one who forms his judgments on a study of facts," Sumner believes, "can answer the first question in the affirmative; no one who is familiar with current thought will say that people are prepared to give an affirmative answer to the second." The socialists hold out the promise of a golden future when capitalism will have been swept away, but how this is to be accomplished without the instrumentality of capital they do not say. On the question of where capital is to come from when the capitalist has been abolished they are silent, as well they might be since "their diagnosis of the social disease is founded on sectarian assumptions, not on the scientific study of the structure and functions of the social body. In attacking capital they are simply attacking the foundations of civilization, and every socialistic scheme which has ever been proposed, so far as it has lessened the motives to saving or the security of capital, is anti-social and anti-civilizing." [22]

In sum, "the maxim, or injunction, to which a study of capital leads us is, Get capital." [23] This, according to Sumner, is the first and great social commandment, and the second is like unto it: Use capital to better your position in the struggle for existence. It has been said that this is monstrous doctrine; that Christian charity no less than democratic morality demands that we should help one another to the end that the race itself might socially advance. The truth is that we owe to each other only such help as consists in helping the others to help themselves. As we have no duty to mind other people's business, so they have no right to share ours. "There is a beautiful notion afloat in our literature and in the minds of our people that men are born to certain 'natural rights.' If that were true, there would be something on earth which was got for nothing, and this world would not be the place it is at all. The fact is, that . . . there can be no rights against Nature, except to get out of her whatever we can, which is only the fact of the struggle for existence stated over again." [24] "Nature's forces know no pity. Just so in sociology. The forces know no pity." [25]

IV

The forces are facts, and facts, not motives, purposes, or ideals, are the subject matter of the science of society. Herein, Sumner maintains, lies the fundamental distinction between socialism and sociology. The socialist is free to consider society as he would wish that it were; the unproven panacea is his stock in trade. The sociologist, on the other hand, is duty bound to take society as it is. The socialist can and does irresponsibly refuse the challenge of facts; if necessary he will kill society to cure it. No such option is open to the sociologist. "The sound student of sociology can hold out to mankind, as individuals or as a race, only one hope of better and happier living. That hope," as Sumner sees it, "lies in an enhancement of the industrial virtues (industry, frugality, prudence, and temperance) and of the moral forces which thence arise." [26] Fortunately for society, there are those who daily cultivate these virtues in quiet anonymity. Since they invariably mind their own business, they are forgotten by all but the tax collector. Yet on the backs of these forgotten men, the burden of society rests; for it is they who produce the national wealth which the reformers and politicians so lightly give away. It is they who, in Sumner's opinion, "are the real productive strength of the country," [27] they who "are the very life and substance of a society." [28]

All of us have known the man Sumner describes.

He works, he votes, generally he prays—but he always pays—yes, above all, he pays. He does not want an office; his name never gets into the newspaper except when he gets married or dies. He keeps production going on. He contributes to the strength of parties. He is flattered before election. He is strongly patriotic. He is wanted, whenever, in his little circle, there is work to be done or counsel to be given. He may grumble some to his wife and family, but he does not frequent the grocery or talk politics at the tavern. Consequently, he is forgotten. He is a commonplace man. He gives no trouble. He excites no admiration. He is not in any way a hero (like a popular orator); or a problem (like tramps and outcasts); nor notorious (like criminals); nor an object of sentiment (like the poor and weak); nor a burden (like paupers and loafers); nor an object out of which social capital may be made (like the beneficiaries of church and state charities); nor an object for charitable aid and protection (like animals treated with cruelty); nor the object of a job (like the ignorant and illiterate); nor one over whom sentimental economists and statesmen can parade their fine sentiments (like inefficient workmen and shiftless artisans). Therefore, he is forgotten. All the burdens fall on him, or on her, for it is time to remember that the Forgotten Man is not seldom a woman.[29]

Sumner may have been thinking here of his stepmother; almost certainly he had his father in mind. The Forgotten Man was no mere economic abstraction. America might forget how much it owed to Thomas Sumner and his like, but his son remembered.

Unfortunately, he was just about the only one who did remember. Long years after Sumner's death, Franklin D. Roosevelt would misappropriate his phrase to characterize the one third of a nation then ill-fed, ill-housed, and ill-clothed, but Roosevelt's "forgotten man" only served to focus attention away from the men and women who really were, and still are, forgotten, the two thirds who, in Sumner's bitter words, are "weighed down with the cost and burden of the schemes for making everybody happy." We waste our national substance on artificial schemes of social amelioration, when we should, he thinks, if we had an ounce of national common sense, be concerned for the welfare of those "clean, industrious, independent, self-supporting men and women who have not inherited much to make life luxurious for them, but who are doing what they can to get on in the world without begging from anybody."

Still, the poor and weak, the misfit and the unfit, are always with us. Should we, then, in the name of the survival of the fittest, abandon them to their fate? The question, Sumner holds, cannot be answered by a simple yes or no.

Except the pauper, that is to say, the man who cannot earn his living or pay his way, there is no possible definition of a poor man. Except a man who is incapacitated by vice or by physical infirmity, there is no definition of a weak man. The paupers and the physically incapacitated are an inevitable charge on society. About them no more need be said. But the weak who constantly arouse the pity of humanitarians and philanthropists are the shiftless, the imprudent, the negligent, the impractical, and the inefficient, or they are the idle, the intemperate, the extravagant, and the vicious.[30]

Does society owe anything at all to such as these? Before we answer in the affirmative, says Sumner, we ought to recognize

the thing which is overlooked and the error which is made in all these charitable efforts. The notion is accepted as if it were not open to any question that if you help the inefficient and vicious you may gain something for society or you may not, but that you lose nothing. This is a complete mistake. Whatever capital you divert to the support of a shiftless and good-for-nothing person is so much diverted from some other employment, and that means from somebody else . . . Now this other man who would have got it but for the charitable sentiment which bestowed it on a worthless member of society is the Forgotten Man . . . We do not remember him because he makes no clamor; but I appeal to you whether he is not the man who ought to be remembered first of all, and whether, on any sound social theory, we ought not to protect him against the burdens of the good-for-nothing.[31]

Of his own attitude, Sumner is sure. "It is," he tells us, "totally false that one who has done [his share in the work of society] is bound to bear the care and charge of those who are wretched because they have not done so. The silly popular notion is that the beggars live at the expense of the rich, but the truth is that those who eat and produce not, live at the expense of those who labor and produce." [32] Let those who can, then, work; and those who will not work, let them remember that "this is a world in which the rule is, 'Root, hog, or die.' " [33]

That such views must make unpopular all who subscribed to them, Sumner knew very well. No one, he warned his students, could appreciate and advocate the position of the Forgotten Man without becoming "a cold and hard-hearted skeptic" in all matters affecting social welfare. He expected to be misunderstood, and he was. The humanitarians and liberals interpreted his attacks on the good-for-nothing as an apologetic for the conduct of the business magnates then milking the American economy. The Forgotten Men and Women themselves failed to recognize their champion. Such of the working classes as even knew his name, mostly thought of him as the lackey of management. But all of them were wrong. William Graham Sumner was no tool of the interests. To prove it so, one need only to reflect a moment on the source of the many and continuing attempts to deprive him of his professorship. The conservative alumni of Yale and their friends who year after year sought his removal from the faculty were certainly not members of the working classes.

The truth was that this college professor, who never in his life earned more than $4,000.00 a year, was far too independent in his ways and in his thinking to satisfy the wealthy. Capitalists themselves, they were aware, as most of Sumner's critics were not, that his defense of capitalism was as much and more a defense of the rights of the savings bank depositor and the small investor as it was of the privileges of the leaders of industry. Democrats and socialists might ignore the distinction carefully drawn by Sumner between capitalism (the industrial use of wealth) and plutocracy (the political disabuse of wealth), they might not credit his repudiation of the latter, but the wealthy knew of it, and feared him as a man as much opposed to the abuses of wealth as he was to the excesses of welfare.

Distrusted by the one class whose support he should have had, Sumner was, and has remained, a prophet without especial honor in his own country. Abroad it was a different story. In England, France, and Germany he was early recognized as a great man, and his writings were widely read and highly praised. In America, however, he was a hero only to his own students. As they have passed away, so has the popularity of Sumnerology. Today, even at Yale, Sumner is remembered not for his defense of the Forgotten Man but rather for *Folkways,* the major work of his old age. Of this book, Sumner himself confessed to Keller that he didn't know whether it was "a gold mine or just a big hole in the ground." As it turned out, it was neither.

V

To a public long accustomed to thinking of Sumner as a defender of the economics of free enterprise, *Folkways* was a surprise, and something of a disappointment. To begin with, it was almost entirely lacking in that pith and pungency that his readers had come to expect from the author of *Social Classes* and the *Essays.* It was lengthy, very lengthy, and most of it was ethnographical fact. The material was poorly organized, and the style of writing was not such as to attract any but the most dedicated student. Worst of all, the book had no conclusion. Having exhausted his data, Sumner simply stopped. Withal, the critics recognized the work as an important contribution to the science of society, and it sold slowly but steadily. In fact, it has never stopped selling.

For all its length, the thesis of *Folkways* is quickly stated: the roots of society lie in its folkways. The life of society consists in making folkways and applying them. The science of society is their study. In these three propositions, Sumner contends, the whole of the subject and object of sociology is contained. The rest is merely illustration. The notion, still popular in orthodox religious circles, that the life of society is ordained, sustained, and directed by God to some yet distant end finds no support in sociology. "If," says Sumner, "we put together all that we have learned from anthropology and ethnography about primitive men and primitive society, we perceive that the first task of life is to live. Men begin with acts, not with thoughts . . . Need was the first experience, and it was followed at once by a blundering effort to satisfy it." [34] What we call folkways are simply the individual habits and social customs arising from the efforts to satisfy these needs. Just how this happened, no man can say. "All origins are lost in mystery, and it seems vain to hope that from any origin the veil of mystery will ever be raised." [35] Of one thing only can we be sure, and that, Sumner believes, is that the folkways "are not creations of human purpose and wit. They are," he holds, "like products of natural forces which men unconsciously set in operation, or they are like the instinctive ways of animals, which are developed out of experience, which reach a final form of maximum adaptation to an interest, which are handed down by tradition and admit of no exception or variation, yet change to meet new conditions, still within the same limited methods, and without rational reflection or purpose." [36] The institutions of society, and its laws, are, he goes on to argue, only rationalizations of the mores of society, which in their turn are only the folkways made explicit. The folkways are society's primeval articles of faith and morals; it is they that dictate social practice, create status, and in the process make nonsense of the notion that society is subject to immediate reform. The fact is, Sumner points out, that society is not a system, to be discarded or revised according to plan, but rather an environment constituted by the body of its folkways. "Every one born into it must enter into relations of give and take with it. He is subjected to influences from it, and it is one of the life conditions under which he must work out his career of self-realization. Whatever liberty may be taken to mean, it is," he insists, "certain that liberty never can mean emancipation from the influence of the societal environment, or of the mores into which one was born." [37]

If there was, as some of his critics have contended, an inconsistency between this view and the rugged individualism of his earlier writings, Sumner did not see it, and unfortunately there was almost no time left to him in which to take account of the objections of those who thought they did. In 1907, shortly after the publication of *Folkways,* he suffered the first of a series of strokes. He knew he was soon to die and he faced the prospect with equanimity. He clearly foresaw the troubles ahead and he wanted no part of them. "I have lived," he told Keller, "through the best period of this country's history. The next generations are going to see war and social calamities. I am glad I don't have to live on into them." [38] To the end, however, he went on working. The day after Christmas, 1909, he traveled down to New York to deliver his presidential address on "Religion and the Mores" to the American Sociological Society. Arrived at his hotel, he collapsed. Four months later he was dead.

SUGGESTED READINGS

The best of Sumner is his Essays, the preferred edition being that of A. G. Keller and M. R. Davie, *Essays of William Graham Sumner,* 2 Vols. (New Haven: Yale University Press, 1934). This contains a sketch of Sumner's life and a complete bibliography of his writings. A dozen of these essays have been reprinted in a paperback edition, edited by Stow Persons, under the title *Social Darwinism* (Englewood Cliffs: Prentice-Hall Spectrum Books, 1963). *What Social Classes Owe to Each Other* (New Haven: Yale University Press, 1925) is also available in a paperback edition published by Caxton Printers Inc. of Caldwell, Idaho. *Folkways* (Boston: Ginn and Co., 1940; paperback editions by Dover Books and Mentor Books) is essentially a text and casebook, as is *The Science of Society,* 4 Vols. (New Haven: Yale University Press, 1927). The bulk of this last is by Keller and Davie, and should be read as their work rather than Sumner's. Davie is also responsible for *Sumner Today, Selected Essays of William Graham Sumner with Comments by American Leaders* (New Haven: Yale University Press, 1940). Of Sumner's other writings, the only book for the general reader particularly relevant today is his biographical study of the life and times of Andrew Jackson, *Andrew Jackson as a Public Man* (Boston: Houghton Mifflin, 1882).

The standard, and only, biography of Sumner is that of Harris E. Starr, *William Graham Sumner* (New York: Holt, 1925). Albert G. Keller's delightful volume of *Reminiscences (Mainly Personal) of William Graham Sumner* (New Haven: Yale University Press, 1933) provides an excellent supplement. Oddly enough, considering his importance in the history of American conservatism, there are no full-length critical studies of Sumner's thought.

REFERENCES

1. Albert Keller and Maurice Davie (editors), *Essays of William Graham Sumner,* 2 Vols. (New Haven: Yale University Press, 1934), I, p. 481. Hereafter cited as Essays.

2. Agassiz, the last great holdout against Darwinism, died in 1873. Henceforward, American science would accept evolution as a confirmed fact.

3. According to William Graham Sumner, *laissez faire,* translated into "blunt English," means "Mind your own business." *What Social Classes Owe to Each Other* (New York: Harper, 1903), p. 120. Hereafter cited as Social Classes.

4. Essays, II, p. 314.

5. Ibid., p. 95.

6. Although Richard Hofstadter has called him "the most vigourous and influential social Darwinist in America" (*Social Darwinism in American Thought,* p. 51), the label, strictly speaking, is not quite accurate, since Sumner's evolutionary ideas were, as Herbert Schneider has pointed out (*History of American Philosophy,* p. 427), "specifically those of Spencer."

7. Essays, II, p. 9.

8. Ibid., pp. 9-10.

9. The reasons why a thirty-two-year-old clergyman with small teaching experience should be offered a full professorship in a subject he had never taught or written about are, according to his biographer, as follows: "Earlier at Yale he had made a decided impression as a teacher. . . . He was known, too, as one whose scholarship was broad and thorough. His general training had been the best America and Europe afforded. . . . The objection that he had not had technical traning in the field of political and social science could not be raised then as it would be now, for the training available was meagre. . . . His power to penetrate to fundamental causes and to ultimate significance, and his independence and fearlessness in dealing with what ever he discussed, was equally well known. . . . In addition . . . he had the confidence and admiration of the younger alumni. His activities in connection with the 'Young Yale' movement had brought him into prominence as one who had sound and progressive ideas regarding educational matters. . . . Altogether, therefore, he was regarded as just the kind of man needed on the faculty for the difficult work of reconstruction which was to go on in the years immediately ahead." Harris E. Starr, *William Graham Sumner* (New York: Holt, 1925), pp. 161-63. Hereafter cited as Starr.

10. Essays, II, p. 11.

11. Ibid., p. 10.

12. Starr, pp. 346-47.

13. Ibid., p. 348.

14. Essays, II, p. 5.

15. Ibid., pp. 378-79. Sumner's italics.

16. Ibid., p. 455.

17. Ibid., p. 366.

18. Ibid., p. 406.

19. Ibid., p. 435.

20. Ibid., pp. 435-36.

21. Ibid., I, p. 403.

22. Essays, II, p. 109.

23. Social Classes, p. 78.

24. Ibid., pp. 134-35.

25. Ibid., p. 154.

26. Essays, II, pp. 121-122.

27. Social Classes, p. 149.

28. Essays, I, p. 493.

29. Ibid., pp. 492-93.

30. Ibid., p. 476.

31. Ibid., pp. 476-77.

32. Ibid., p. 478.

33. Ibid., II, p. 127. How Sumner impressed this principle on one of his students is told by William Lyon Phelps: "Professor, don't you believe in any government aid to industries? No! it's root, hog, or die. Yes, but hasn't the hog got a right to root? There are no rights. The world owes nobody a living. You believe, then, Professor, in only one system, the contract-competitive system? That's the only sound economic system. All the others are fallacies. Well, suppose some professor of political economy came along and took your job away from you. Wouldn't you be sore? Any other professor is welcome to try. If he gets my job, it is my fault. My business is to teach the subject so well that no one can take the job away from me." And no one ever did. See William Lyon Phelps, "When Yale was given to Sumnerology," *Literary Digest International Book Review*, Vol. III (1925), p. 662.

34. *Folkways* (Boston: Ginn & Company, 1906), p. 2.

35. Ibid., p. 7.

36. Ibid., p. 4.

37. Ibid., p. 68.

38. Albert Keller, *Reminiscences (Mainly Personal) of William Graham Sumner* (New Haven: Yale University Press, 1933), p. 109.

XVIII

The Case for Sociocracy

LESTER FRANK WARD

"There is one power and only one
that is greater than that which now
chiefly rules society. That power
is society itself. There is one
form of government that is stronger
than autocracy or aristocracy or
democracy, or even plutocracy, and
that is *sociocracy*." [1]

LESTER FRANK WARD

Lester Frank Ward

The whole book is based on the fundamental error that the favors of this world are distributed entirely according to merit. Poverty is only a proof of indolence and vice. Wealth simply shows the industry and virtue of the possessors! . . . Those who have survived simply prove their fitness to survive; and the fact which all biologists perfectly understand, viz.; that fitness to survive is something wholly distinct from real superiority, is, of course ignored by the author because he is not a biologist, as all sociologists should be.[2]

THUS DOES LESTER FRANK WARD dismiss the argument of Sumner's *Social Classes,* an argument, he thinks, nearly every proposition of which involves a fallacy. He was well qualified to judge. Only six months earlier his own monumental *Dynamic Sociology* had appeared. Fourteen years in the writing, fourteen hundred pages in length, it was the first American work of its kind, the first to call in question Spencer's interpretation of the meaning of social evolution. And unlike Sumner's little book, it was the work of a man whose training and profession eminently fitted him to discuss the detail of biological and biosocial evolution.

The tenth and last child of Justus Ward, an itinerant mechanic, and Silence Rolph Ward, a clergyman's daughter, Lester Frank Ward was born at Joliet, Illinois, June 18th, 1841. His childhood was one of hardship. The family was poor, and young Frank, as he was then called, did his share of helping make ends meet. When he was sixteen his father died, and he and his brother Erastus left for Pennsylvania to make their fortune in brother Cyrenus Osborn's wagon factory. The venture failed, and Frank became an unskilled laborer and sometime farm hand. Evenings he studied by candle-light the few precious textbooks he had managed to buy out of his meagre earnings. He was twenty before he scraped together suffi-cient funds to allow him to attend his first real school. The Susque-hanna Collegiate Institute of Towanda, Pennsylvania, for all its grand name, wasn't much. In fact, young Ward found to his surprise that his private studies had put him considerably ahead of his classmates in almost every subject! He stayed but a term, and left to take a job teaching school. By now the Civil War had begun, and in August of 1862 he got married and enlisted as a private. Three times wounded at Chancellorsville, he was invalided home in December, 1863, and shortly thereafter left for Washington with his wife. He hoped to secure a government clerkship, and eventu-ally he succeeded. His salary was minute, and his prospects for advancement were dim, but he had boundless ambition and an un-slakable thirst for knowledge. In 1867 he persuaded Columbian University (now George Washington University) to give evening classes in academic subjects, and two years later he had earned his B.A. In 1871 he qualified as a Bachelor of Laws; the following year he received his Master's degree. His main interest was science, in particular botany and geology, and soon his talents began to attract the notice of his superiors. In 1883 he achieved the rank of Geologist in the U.S. Geological Survey. In this same year was published his first great work in sociology, and in the years that followed, four more books and innumerable articles on a wide variety of sociological and scientific subjects made their appearance. In 1892 he was promoted Paleontologist, a post he held until his resignation in 1906 to accept an invitation from Brown University to become its first full-time professor of sociology. Here he remained until his death on April 18th, 1913.

The American Aristotle, Samuel Chugerman has called him, and the title is well deserved, for Ward too was a master of those who know. During his forty years as a civil serv-ant he did important work in statistics, botany, paleobotany, and geology. Throughout these years he was also writing the pioneering works which were to seal his reputation as a social philosopher and sociologist.

Like Sumner, he was more appreciated abroad than at home. Ludwig Gumplowicz, the famous Austrian sociologist, who crossed intellectual swords with Ward on an occasion memorable to both, thought him "a giant of a scholar." [3] Spencer corresponded with him for twenty years; he was honored by the French, and the Russians burned the first volume of *Dynamic Sociology*. The Americans, not being for the most part a race of readers, were hardly aware of his existence. Neglected in his lifetime by all save a handful of professors and scientists, in death he has been consigned to oblivion.

To see why is at once to understand the narrow conservatism of the contemporary American mind. To begin with, Ward was a nonconformist. His ideas fitted into no established patterns of thought. His sociocracy sounded to American ears too much like socialism; his attacks on the social evils of capitalism struck staunch conservatives as subversive. Nor did he show forth the reassuring character of a Christian believer. In his youth he had been such, but as his mastery of science grew, his faith fell away, as did the Christian claim to uniqueness when viewed in the cold light of the sociology of evolution. In sum, he was, as the title of the periodical he edited during the early seventies proclaimed, an iconoclast, and Americans, even professorial Americans, have never taken kindly to the breed.

His crime in the eyes of the professors was simple yet sufficient: he belonged to no one discipline. To the physical scientists he was too much the sociologist; the sociologists thought him too philosophical; as for the philosophers, misled by the titles of his books, they never thought of him at all. And yet, the world-view of Lester Frank Ward may well be, when all is said, the most important philosophical synthesis yet produced by an American.

II

Ward was a professional scientist, Spencer and his American disciples were not; to this simple fact, every difference between his world view and theirs may be traced. As a scientist, he will have nothing to do with the Unknowable. Spencer intended it as a sop to the religious, let it remain so. The business of science is the elucidation of the real, and what is real, including man, is—matter. "Besides matter itself, only the relations of matter can be conceived to exist." [4] Spencer to the contrary, the ultimate is not force, for force is, "when properly viewed, one of the readiest to take its place as a derivative relation of moving matter." [5] Matter moves. This is the fundamental fact on which every scientific world-view must build. Energy seizes upon matter and expresses itself as motion. To the question, why? no answer is possible. Matter in motion is, says Ward, simply what it appears to be. The task of the scientist is rather to explain the "how."

According to Ward, "all the motions of matter fall under two general classes: those which tend to *unite* and those which tend to *separate* the particles or atoms." [6] This much Spencer had also seen. What Spencer failed to see, however, was that the evolution of the cosmos is brought about by the predominance of the first of these classes, whereas organic evolution is due to the prevalence of the second. The scientist in Ward would not permit him to allow one word, "evolution," to do the work that properly belonged to two. Accordingly, he renames unitary motion "aggregation" and its opposite becomes "segregation." This avoids any possible confusion, but more important it leads to a re-expression of the fundamental law of nature. The authority of Spencer notwithstanding, it is not the law of evolution which is basic, but that of aggregation. "The great law of progress in the universe, therefore, is the law of aggregation, and evolution is due to the resistance which this law meets with from the opposite law of dispersion, out of which conflict not only substances and worlds but organic forms are evolved." [7]

Matter moves, and gradually the material molecules contract into the primary aggregations (inorganic) which constitute the subject matters of astronomy, physics, chemistry, and geology. It develops in complexity, and eventually evolves into those secondary aggregations (organic) which are the topics of biology, anthropology, and psychology. When it becomes protoplasm, life begins. "The great truth that now comes squarely home to us is that *life is a property of matter*. It is simply the result of the movements going on among the molecules composing a mass of protoplasm. It is a phenomenon presented by this most highly complex form of matter, and which is never absent from it." [8] In brief, *"life is the result of the aggregation of matter."* [9]

That such frank materialism was bound to offend the tender-minded, Ward well knew. With these, however, he was not especially concerned. The several hundred pages in the *Dynamic Sociology* and others of his writings devoted to the scientific justification of his conclusion were not so much designed to persuade the average reader as they were to lay a firm foundation for the refutation of Spencer's interpretation of evolution and its social implications. If the case for sociocracy was to be successfully made out against the individualism and *laissez faire* defended by the Englishman and his American hearers, the latter's unscientific oversimplification and misinterpretation of the bio- and phylogenetic facts had to be made clear.

One fact in particular had Spencer misunderstood, which failure, as Ward sees it, invalidates the whole of his sociology. In brief, Spencer had failed to grasp the nature and significance of the human mind in social evolution. "True, his system embraces two volumes on psychology. Nevertheless I make bold to affirm not only that he did not base his sociology upon his psychology, but that his psychology is of a kind such that sociology could not be based upon it." [10] Both, properly conceived, are sciences in the sense that each rests, or should rest, upon a body of uniform laws discoverable by investigation; but of neither, as Spencer develops them, is this true. His psychology, far from attempting a scientific account of mind, concedes it rather to be a something unknown, "the Unknowable as manifested to us within the limits of consciousness in the shape of feeling." More than this, Spencer believes, we cannot say. "Mind still continues to us a something without any kinship to other things; and from the science (psychology) which discovers by introspection the laws of this something, there is no passage by transitional steps to the sciences (sociology included) which discover the laws of these other things." [11] If Spencer is right the sociological function of mind is virtually non-existent. But is Spencer right? Ward does not think so. Not only, he insists, is the human mind a factor in sociology, but its function is of such sort as to justify sociological conclusions precisely the opposite of those proclaimed by Spencer.

Mind is of natural origin. On this Ward and Spencer are agreed. The divergence between their views starts with Ward's assumption "that the phenomena of mind stand in the same relation to the brain and nervous system that all other phenomena stand to the substances that produce them—in a word, that the mind is a property of the organized body." [12] Mind is a state of matter. Once recognize this, Ward argues, and the so-called "mystery of mind" dissolves. For Spencer notwithstanding, the mind is not a mysterious something of whose kinships we must be forever ignorant. On the contrary, its laws are as discoverable as those of matter. In fact, "they are the laws of matter in its most highly developed form." [13] If men have hitherto failed to see this, it is only owing to the fact that for centuries the requirements of their religion have accustomed them to think of mind as something separate from the body. Like Spencer they have presumed the physical (body) and the psychical (mind) to be different in kind, whereas in truth they differ only in degree.

Just how and when mind evolved out of living matter (protoplasm) no man knows; what is certain, however, Ward argues, is that its evolution is a question of feeling. For as feeling grew out of life and life grew out of chemism, so does intellect grow out of feeling. The fact, ignored by most philosophers and all theologians ancient and modern, is that mind has two sides: "the one begins with sensation and ends with sentiment; the other begins with perception and ends with reason. The one constitutes the feelings, the other the intellect," and of the two feeling is the earlier and primary. In its most primitive form it constitutes the phenomenon of irritability manifested by the simplest protoplasmic bodies. It is, in more complex organisms, that sensitivity to pain or pleasure which is the indispensable condition for their survival. As the organic evolves so does its capacity for feeling deepen until in man feeling itself divides into the intensive and the indifferent. Under the former, as Ward defines it, are included all the appetites and passions denoted by the word "desire"; from the latter, consisting of those sensations and intuitions of objects exciting neither pain nor pleasure, the intellect is born. What men untrained in the biology of the mind call reason is, then, simply the end product of the evolution of feeling. "The soul of man has come from the soul of the atom after passing through the great alembic of organic life." [14]

It is no small part of the greatness of Lester Ward that he alone of all his contemporaries and immediate successors saw the revolutionary consequences the scientific establishment of this fact of the primacy of feeling must have for sociology, i.e., philosophy and religion. If it is true, as the evidence indicates, that feeling (desire) rather than intellect (reason) "is the all-pervading, world-animating principle, the universal nisus and pulse of nature, the mainspring of all action, and the life-power of the world," then every previous metaphysic or theology founded upon the assumption of the primacy of intellect must be false. Not intellect but feeling is, then, the dynamic basis of society. A true philosophy of man and society will, therefore, begin with the recognition of feeling as the force that explains them both.

III

The particular form under which feeling manifests itself as a force is *desire,* and the social forces consist in human desires. They are true natural forces and obey all of the Newtonian laws of motion. They are either negative—desire to escape pain—or positive—desire to secure pleasure. In either case they impel the individual to action.[15]

The social forces are natural forces. If so, we are, Ward holds, justified in speaking of a *science* of society since science is "an *explanation* of the phenomena of the universe as presented to the senses," [16] and these, by any standard, must include the phenomena of feeling. So much would Spencer and Sumner concede. What they would not admit, however, is that these social forces are, as Ward goes on to claim, also psychic forces. Rather is it the case as they see it that the social forces are natural forces precisely and only because they are *vital* forces. In other words, the science foundational to sociology, if Spencer and Sumner are to be believed, is not that whose domain is the psychic forces, i.e., psychology, but that (biology) whose subject is the vital forces. The distinction is important because if they are right the scientific explanation of the social forces can only be such as to justify *laissez faire.* If the forces which animate and motivate society are essentially the same as those which activate the rest of nature, then the law of society, no less than the law of the jungle, is manifestly that of the survival of the fittest.

This conclusion, whose implications Sumner had made plain in his *Social Classes,* the reformer in Ward would not allow him to abide any more than the scientist in him would permit him to admit that sociology was not a science. There must be a way around the Spencerian theory of society, and as it turned out there was. The key to the solution of the problem he thought to see in the fact of nature's total indifference to feeling and pleasure. The end of nature is function, i.e., life. Whether or not the organism enjoys or suffers its life is no part of nature's aim. It functions to proliferate life; its end is purely biological. From the standpoint of nature, then, feeling is simply a means to function. From the standpoint of the higher organisms, however, exactly the opposite holds true. Here function is simply a means to feeling. Where the end of nature was simply to preserve and perpetuate life, the end of every higher organism, including man, is the satisfaction of its desires. It seeks not merely to live but to enjoy. "This enjoyment of life, which we may say was not contemplated by Nature . . . and which forms no necessary part of the general scheme of Nature, becomes, once it has been introduced, the sole end of the beings capable of it." [17] To this end mind is born. Through the dynamic agency of desire the vital forces are transmuted into psychic forces. It remains only to identify these last as social forces in order to see that the science properly foundational to sociology is not, as Spencer preached, biology but rather psychology.[18] That sociology as a whole rests primarily upon psychology should, thinks Ward, surprise no one, for after all "this is its natural basis in the hierarchy of the sciences." [19] "Even the social activities of animals are due to their psychic faculty, and this is as true of bees and ants as it is of wolves or buffaloes. Human society, therefore, which is the highest product of evolution, naturally depends upon mind, which is the highest property of matter." [20]

It matters not that psychology rests in its turn upon biology. Once admit that the natural forces inspiring social activity are psychic rather than vital, and the scientific case for *laissez faire* collapses. For the fact is that men are not powerless pawns driven by forces over which they have no control. On the contrary, all that man has accomplished in the course of civilization is owing entirely to his refusal to let nature take its senseless course. "There are philosophers who cry: *laissez faire!* but every step that man has taken in advance, every invention he has made, all art, all applied science, all achievement, all material civilization, has been the result of his persistent refusal to let things alone, and of his determination to conquer the dominion of nature, to emancipate himself from his bondage to nature, and to become master of nature and of nature's powers." [21]

That man can do these things and hope to do still greater is owing entirely to the operation of the psychic forces. Society is the product of mind functioning dynamically to secure the satisfaction of its desires, and directively to insure that these desires are such as conduce to social progress. On this dynamic and directive agency of mind society is built. How, then, can it be that heretofore it has received so little attention from philosophers? For the fact is, as Ward notes, that "no one seems to have seen in the subjective phenomena of mind any great causational factor as the motive power of human activities or as a basis for the scientific treatment of social phenomena; and this is as true of those who are devoting themselves to social science as to those who confine their labors to any department of mental science." [22] The answer, he believes, lies in recognizing the fatal error of the Greeks in divorcing mind from nature.

The theories set on foot by Plato and his followers . . . gave an impetus to the study of the most abstruse of all problems, and caused the discussions to be directed chiefly to the question as to whether anything really exists except the thinking subject. Thus cut loose from its realistic base, philosophy floated for ages in the air and fought the battles of the shades. Brought partly back to earth by Locke, Descartes, and Kant, it continued the struggle with one foot on the ground until physiological psychology at length pricked the metaphysical bubble and it collapsed.[23]

Yet even now the dearth of knowledge concerning the causes of mental phenomena still encourages philosophers to search through "the rubbish of metaphysical speculation" for a truth which is not there. To this day philosophers, psychologists, and sociologists continue to ignore the psychic factors of civilization, although the writings of Bergson, Whitehead, and F. H. Bradley have in our time done much to justify Ward's theory of mind as feeling generating intellect. Had he lived to read their vindications of his ideas, Ward would have been greatly pleased if not overly impressed. For his vision was and is greater than that of his successors. He realized clearly, what no one save John Dewey has seemed to realize at all, that society must evolve as mind evolves and the social forces fall under its control. We are, as he was fond of saying, socially still stone-age savages compared to what it lies within our social power to become.

IV

The individual has reigned long enough. The day has come for society to take its affairs into its own hands and shape its own destinies.[24]

How is this to be done? More specifically, how are the social forces which at present serve the interests of the individual to be made to serve the interests of society? There are, as Ward sees it, two possibilities. The first, and perhaps the best, would be to apply to humans those principles of scientific breeding now used on other animals; the second, and more practical, is education. "Of all the panaceas that have been so freely offered for the perfectionment of the social state there is none, he thinks, that reaches back so far or down so deep or out so broad as that of the increase and diffusion of knowledge among men." [25] The universal distribution of extant knowledge underlies all social reform. Were the basic truths of science to be universally diffused, every evil which today afflicts society must, he is sure, soon vanish. In brief, "education is everything." [26] "Give society education . . . and all things else will be added." [27]

Notice that Ward does not argue that it is education as such that is to bring about this happy result but rather education in *knowledge,* and by "knowledge" he understands no more and no less than that acquaintance with the environment gained through scientific observation and generalization. This alone, he argues, is deserving of dissemination. That culture which commonly passes for knowledge among cultivated men is, he feels, a luxury society can well do without. What matters is that every citizen should have *information* of those great scientific truths on which the future of society depends. "It is obviously less important that a great amount of intelligence (knowledge) shall exist than that the data of intelligence shall be in possession of all alike." [28] That all possess the native capacity to absorb and profit by this information, he does not doubt. Such differences in native intelligence as exist among men are for the most part the result of differences in environment:

> If the same individuals who constitute the intelligent class at any time or place had been surrounded from their birth by exactly the same conditions that have surrounded the lowest stratum of society, they would have inevitably found themselves in that stratum; and if an equal number taken at random of the lowest stratum of society had been surrounded from their birth by exactly the same conditions by which the intelligent class have been surrounded, they would in fact have constituted the intelligent class instead of the particular individuals who happen actually to constitute it. In other words, class distinctions in society are wholly artificial, depend entirely on environing conditions, and are in no sense due to differences in native capacity.[29]

If he is right, then the social task is obviously such as he conceives it: by education to transform the environment so as to bring within the range of all that knowledge which is at present the monopoly of the fortunate few.

To the objection that it is manifestly impossible to educate every man up to even the present level of the intelligentsia, Ward's answer is that this is not what he is proposing. Not the details but the basic principles of science are what the ignorant need to master, and this, he insists, it lies within their power to accomplish. Granted that not every man or woman is capable of appreciating the subtler nuances of the Darwinian theory; still, virtually all are capable of grasping the basic idea of evolution. Could this idea and those of similar scientific generality and importance be made the common property of all, the chasm between the ignorant and the intelligent, which is, to Ward's view, "the worst evil under which society labors," [30] must certainly be narrowed and may in time be reduced to insignificance. The point is that "knowledge is power, and power has ever been wielded for self-aggrandizement, and must ever be so wielded. To prevent inequality of advantages there must be equality of power, i.e., equality of knowledge." [31]

Since government alone has at present sufficient resources and authority to insure that this knowledge reaches those who need it most, it follows that education must be public; since the ignorant cannot be expected to appreciate immediately the boon being conferred upon them, it must be compulsory and universal. Finally, it must be coeducational, for "while the female mind may, and doubtless does, differ from the male in many important and fortunate respects, it is only the emotional part of it. Intellect is one and the same every-where, and the proper nourishment of intellect is truth. Therefore what women require as education is the same that men require, viz., knowledge." [32]

This faith in education as "the great panacea," Ward never lost. From his first book to his last, his hopes for a better society ride with the democratization of knowledge. I say "his hopes" because Ward is no utopian visionary. He is as well aware as Sumner that slow mitigation of the severity of nature's laws is all that can reasonably be expected in the near future. That day is still far distant when men shall recognize the survival of the fittest as a social anachronism. Sociocracy is as yet a dream, even though the law of social evolution marks it for a dream that must come true.

Shall we then dream on and wait? Obviously not. "What must be," grants Ward, "will be, but everything depends upon the manner of its being. The problem of today is how to help on a certain evolution by averting an otherwise equally certain revolution." [33] Its solution, he feels, is possible, provided society can be brought to believe in the gospel of meliorism. As things are now, the mass of men are torn between believing in the pessimism of those who, like Spencer and Sumner, hold that nothing can be done to change the natural course of social evolution, and those who, like the Christians, hold that God has already done it all. They stand passive and society stands still. Obviously, the remedy is action, and for Ward the sufficient motive for action lies in the realization that we can make our world a better place—if we are willing to work at it. "To the developed intellect nature is as clay in the potter's hands. It is neither best nor worst. It is what man makes it, and rational man always seeks to make it better. The true doctrine, then, is meliorism—the perpetual bettering of man's estate." [34] Its end is sociocracy—man's estate brought under scientific control by the collective mind of society itself.

The formula for sociocracy is—society acting for itself. As the individual acts now in his own best interests, so society in the sociocratic state will "imagine itself an individual, with all the interests of an individual, and becoming fully *conscious* of these interests it [will] pursue them with the same indomitable *will* with which the individual pursues his interests . . . In a word, society [will] do under the same circumstances just what an intelligent individual would do. It would further, in all possible ways, its own interests." [35] Since these interests, economically speaking, require a maximum distribution of goods to the greatest number at the lowest price, this means eventual control by society, for society, of every presently private enterprise of concern to the general public. This sounds like socialism, and many, some among them Ward's disciples, have so interpreted it. Ward himself, however, denies the identification. The difference between socialism and sociocracy as he understands it is precisely that between a collectivism artificially imposed and one naturally evolved. Whereas the socialist would abolish all artificial inequalities by legislative fiat, the sociocrat is content to arrive at equality via the gradual process of social evolution. He sees, as the socialist does not, that the end is not to be had without the means, that society can no more be reformed from the top down than a house can be begun with the roof. "It is," writes Ward, "high time for socialists to perceive that, as a rule, they are working at the roof instead of at the foundation of the structure they desire to erect. Not that much of the material which they are now elaborating will not 'come in play' when society is ready to use it, but that their time would be better spent in working out the basal principles which will render social reform possible." [36] In other words, take care of the means (education), and the end (collectivism) will take care of itself.

As a practicing scientist and eminently practical man, Ward knows better than to try to pin down the shape of the future. Just how sociocracy will come to pass, or when, he does not venture to predict. That it will differ from any form of government thus far devised by men, and yet not differ so much as to require a revolution to bring it to being, he feels sure. Most probably it will emerge out of democracy, since democracy as it ought to be would be already sociocracy. Democracy as it is, i.e., government by faction or majority, is, of course, far from sociocratic. A faction or majority acting for itself, or even for society, is a vastly different thing from a society acting for itself. On the other hand, it takes no great awakening of man's social consciousness to effect the transition from the democratic to the sociocratic state. It needs no Walt Whitman celebrating democratic man; a simple broadening of educational opportunity will do. With Socrates, Ward holds that men who know the good are bound to do the good. A people awake to the real interests of society will, he has no doubt, act always to advance those interests. As with Socrates, events may ultimately prove him to have been wrong, but, if so, then Thoreau, Emerson, Lincoln, Whitman, and all those who have shared this dream of a purer democracy are also wrong.

V

Are democracy and free enterprise synonymous—or even compatible? Most Americans of Ward's day, and even our own, have never doubted it. And yet, if the case for sociocracy is sound, they certainly are in error. Free enterprise, as understood by its defenders, implies individualism, which in its turn presupposes a social evolution based directly upon biology. Democracy, on the other hand, understood as government of, by, and for *all* the people, just as plainly implies collectivism, which in its turn presupposes a social evolution directly based upon psychology, i.e., psycho-physiology. As earlier noted, it makes no difference that this psychology itself rests upon biology, for once admit the psychological into social evolution and all is changed. *"In biology the environment transforms the organism, while in sociology man transforms the environment."* [37] The slave of biological evolution has in psychological evolution become the master. The animal mastered by its environment has become man the master of the world in which he lives. The individual bound to his own interests has become the collectivist bound ultimately to the interests of society. From here to sociocracy, if Ward is right, it is only a matter of time.

If Ward is right democracy and free enterprise are inconsistent terms, and he who would hold fast to the one must abandon the other. That Ward is right the conservative attitude towards democracy bears witness. Forced to choose between free enterprise and democracy, conservatives have invariably elected to abandon the latter. For Hamilton, Calhoun, and Sumner, no less than for the partisans of Barry Goldwater, the truth is that our form of government is not a democracy but a republic, and all would endorse the current slogan that calls upon us to keep it that way. For if free enterprise is, as conservatives assume, in principle synonymous with patriotism, then democracy, like every other form of collectivism, must be rejected as un-American.

Whether or not democracy is un-American is a question we cannot here undertake to decide. Ward certainly did not think so. Unlike many Americans today, he was not prepared to concede that any scientific theory of society must be by definition—Marxist. Indeed, for Ward the hallmark of any science, social or physical, is precisely its independence of any and every ideology. That there is bad sociology as well as bad physics, etc., he would admit, but that either is made bad by the ideology of the person advancing it he would roundly deny. The law of gravitation is as true for the sinner as for the saint. Whatever goes up comes down in Russia as well as the United States. Similarly with sociocracy; it will, thinks Ward, stand or fall on its scientific merits alone. Whether it is, as James E. Fleming contends,[38] tainted by its advocacy of ideals identical to those of anarchism, or whether, as Ward himself believes, it is expressive of the democratic ideal of freedom, is ultimately irrelevant. Sociocracy is a scientific hypothesis and requires to be judged as such. If it is false there is no danger that it will permanently prevail. Science has its own ways of burying its errors. However, if it is true, then Ward has proved something that it is surely in the interest of every American to have proved—that a democratic science of society is possible.

SUGGESTED READINGS

The first of Ward's major works is *Dynamic Sociology*, 2 Vols. (New York: Appleton, 1883). Begun in 1869, finished fourteen years later, it offers a complete perspective of his world-philosophy as originally conceived. Virtually ignored by the general public at the time of issue, it is, like all of Ward's books, now long out of print, but your local library may have it, as well as one or more of the following. *The Psychic Factors of Civilization* (Boston: Ginn & Co., 1892) supplements and amends the above by its stress on the social role of mind. In Ward's opinion, it is the best of all his books. The system in brief is rethought and summarized in *Outlines of Sociology* (New York: Macmillan, 1897). *Pure Sociology: A Treatise on the Origin and Nature of Society* (New York: Macmillan, 1903) is rated by Ward's commentators his greatest work. With its sequel, *Applied Sociology: A Treatise on the Conscious Improvement of Society by Society* (Boston: Ginn & Co., 1906), the world-philosophy in its final form is complete. *A Textbook of Sociology*, an abridged version of the *Pure Sociology* redacted by James Q. Dealey and approved by Ward, was for many years in use as a text in various university departments of sociology. Many college libraries will have it. The publishing history of all of the above, as well as of everything Ward ever wrote, is given in *Glimpses of the Cosmos*, 6 Vols. (New York: Putnam's, 1913-1918). This last, assembled by Ward and his biographer, Emily Palmer Cape, was begun in 1909 and finished short months before the author's death in the spring of 1913. It contains all of his more important articles, and gathers up many shorter pieces otherwise unavailable. From his eighteenth year until his death, Ward kept a diary. Unfortunately, most of this unique and extremely valuable material was destroyed by his second wife at the time of his death. However, the diary up to the point of his proposing to his second wife has been preserved and published as *Young Ward's Diary 1860-1870*, edited by Bernhard Stern (New York: Putnam's, 1935).

Of books about Ward, there are only two, and both are intensely partisan. Samuel Chugerman, *Lester F. Ward, The American Aristotle* (Durham: Duke University Press, 1939), offers a vigorously written and admirably detailed summary and interpretation of the genesis and development of Ward's world-philosophy. Complete with bibliography. Emily Palmer Cape, *Lester F. Ward, A Personal Sketch* (New York: Putnam's, 1922), suffers from a bad case of hero worship.

REFERENCES

1. *The Psychic Factors of Civilization*, 2nd Edition (Boston: Ginn, 1906), p. 323. Hereafter cited as Psychic Factors.

2. *Glimpses of the Cosmos,* 6 Vols. (New York: Putnam's, 1913), III, pp. 303-4. Hereafter cited as Glimpses.

3. The story of their encounter is given by Gumplowicz in his article, "An Austrian Appreciation of Lester F. Ward," *The American Journal of Sociology,* Vol. 10 (1904-05), pp. 643-53.

4. *Dynamic Sociology,* 2 Vols. (New York: Appleton, 1883), I, p. 222. Hereafter cited as DS.

5. DS, I, p. 228.

6. Ibid., p. 232.

7. Ibid., p. 249.

8. Glimpses, V, p. 320.

9. Ibid., p. 318.

10. "Herbert Spencer's Sociology," in Glimpses, VI, p. 172.

11. *The Principles of Psychology,* 2 Vols. (New York: Appleton, 1886), I, p. 140. See also Glimpses, V, p. 83.

12. "Status of the Mind Problem," in Glimpses, V, p. 86.

13. Ibid., p. 95.

14. Psychic Factors, p. 56.

15. *Outlines of Sociology* (New York: Macmillan, 1921), p. 166. Hereafter cited as Outlines.

16. DS, I, p. 45. Ward's italics.

17. Outlines, p. 98.

18. It is important that the reader not confuse Ward's notion of psychology with that rather vague and ill-defined discipline which common sense mistakes for the science of mind. "Psychology" for Ward is rather the physics of the mind, "and its phenomena are as uniform and its laws as exact as are those of the physics of the inorganic world. If this were not so it would not be a science, and there would be no use in attempting to treat it at all." Psychic Factors, p. 34. See also pp. 123, 139.

19. Psychic Factors, p. 2. Ward, following Comte, conceives the hierarchical principle as from the most ample in scope to the most complex in detail. Thus astronomy, the most ample in scope, is followed in ascending order by physics, chemistry, biology, psychology, and sociology, the last named being, to Ward's view, the most complex in detail.

20. Psychic Factors, pp. 2-3.

21. *Pure Sociology,* 2nd Edition (New York: Macmillan, 1916), p. 512.

22. Psychic Factors, p. 4.

23. Ibid., p. 218.

24. Ibid., p. 323.

25. Glimpses, III, p. 148.

26. Ibid.

27. "Solution of the Great Social Problem," unpublished manuscript, quoted in Samuel Chugerman, *Lester F. Ward, The American Aristotle* (Durham: Duke University Press, 1939), p. 465.

28. DS, II, p. 596.

29. *Applied Sociology* (Boston: Ginn, 1906), pp. 100-1. In an article written about the same time (1906) he puts the case even more vehemently: ". . . so far as the native capacity, the potential quality, the 'promise and potency,' of a higher life are concerned, these swarming, spawning millions, the bottom layer of society, the proletariat, the working classes,

the 'hewers of wood and drawers of water,' nay, even the denizens of the slums—that all these are by nature the peers of the boasted aristocracy of brains that now dominates society and looks down upon them, and the equals in all but privilege of the most enlightened teachers of eugenics." "Social Darwinism," *The American Journal of Sociology,* Vol. 12 (1907), p. 710.

30. DS, II, p. 602.

31. Ibid.

32. Ibid., p. 619. Very early in his scientific career, Ward had become convinced of the biological superiority of women. His gynaecocentric theory of life, first stated in *Dynamic Sociology* and reiterated in all of his later books, helped to make the cause of women's suffrage scientifically respectable, and made Ward the idol of those few women who were emancipated enough to appreciate the far-reaching implications of his theory.

33. Glimpses, IV, p. 315.

34. Outlines, p. 26.

35. Psychic Factors, pp. 324, 327.

36. DS, II, p. 597.

37. *Pure Sociology,* p. 254.

38. "The Role of Government in a Free Society: The Conception of Lester Frank Ward," *Social Forces,* Vol. 24 (1946), pp. 257-66.

XIX

The Pragmatic Creed

CHAUNCEY WRIGHT

CHARLES SANDERS PEIRCE

WILLIAM JAMES

"By their fruits ye shall know
them." [1]

1. Chauncey Wright

I BELIEVE THAT the meaning of a word is its use, that the true is what comes true, and I acknowledge as truth only that which works. Belief itself I hold to be that on which the believer is prepared to act, and I maintain that the total value of any act is the consequences it involves. I respect the right to believe of every man who has the will to believe in God, even as I deny the right of any man to impose his personal beliefs on others. For this also I believe, that everything worthy of belief has its origin in the common experience of mankind, and that apart from this experience there is nothing real or true at all.

Such is the creed of pragmatism (from the Greek *pragma,* action) and it is nothing new. As sophism it flourished in Athens four centuries before the birth of Christ. The middle ages knew it as nominalism. British empiricism and French positivism are its European forebears, but nowhere has it proved as popular or as enduring as in these United States. Its articles of faith are already to be found in the writings of Franklin, and to a lesser and somewhat different degree in Edwards. Thoreau has been counted a pragmatist by many, as has Abraham Lincoln. The view is implicit in Fiske, and rather more explicit in Sumner. Long before the pragmatic method was a commonplace of American thinking, Lester Ward was using it to promote sociocracy. As a specific and distinct philosophy, however, pragmatism is usually and properly held to have originated with a group of young Boston and Cambridge intellectuals who during the sixties and seventies of the last century were accustomed to meet informally to try out their ideas on one another. "The Metaphysical Club" had a distinguished roster. Charles Sanders Peirce and William James were regulars, as was young Oliver Wendell Holmes. John Fiske attended frequently, and Francis Ellingwood Abbott was sometimes present. Oddly enough, considering the fame that each of these was later to attain, the member Peirce himself rated their strongest intelligence was none of the above, but rather a man whom posterity has all but forgotten—Chauncey Wright.

"Our boxing-master" Peirce called him, and the name was not unfitting, for Wright was the sort who gave no quarter in debate, and his cool intelligence and skill in dialectic were such as would win for him after his death the nobler title, an American Socrates. This is not to imply that his life was at all dramatic. In truth it was about as undramatic as a life could be. From his early youth on he shrank from anything out of the ordinary. He was, by his own admission, "indisposed to active exercise, to any kind of excitement or change." [2] To put it bluntly, he was lazy.

Fresh out of Harvard in 1852 he obtained a position as computer in the Nautical Almanac office of the U.S. Naval Observatory at Cambridge. The great attraction of the job was that it paid well enough for him to live for a year on what he made for three months' work, and for eighteen years he did precisely that until in 1870 the receipt of a small legacy made it possible for him to give up work entirely. Apparently his wants were simple. He lived in rooms. He never married. He seems to have had no family obligations. His greatest delight was the conversation of friends like himself scientifically inclined. In 1870, and again in 1874, he lectured at Harvard; in 1872 he visited England and met Darwin. For the rest there were his studies—and the writings. It was not that he was prolific. He wrote no books, and the number of his articles, added to his letters and reviews, make up but one moderately sized volume. Nor was he an avid reader. On the contrary, he was, according to the testimony of his good friend and sometime neighbor, E. W. Gurney, "utterly averse to reading." [3] What little he did read, however, stuck with him.

During his college days he had been exposed to the works of the Scots philosopher, Sir William Hamilton. From Hamilton he got his knowledge of the history of philosophy, as well as his conviction of the impossibility of attaining to any knowledge of the reality behind appearances. Later, in the writings of Hamilton's great English critic, John Stuart Mill, he made the acquaintance of that principle of utility [4] which was to become the touchstone of his own social philosophy. Darwin he studied carefully. With the theory of evolution he had no quarrel. The basic facts were, he was convinced, beyond dispute. What was clearly not beyond dispute though were the metaphysical and theological conclusions drawn from these facts by Darwin and his disciples. Wright rejected them all. They had, he felt, no place in science, for science, as he understands it, is entirely—observation and experiment. Its realm is fact; with fancy however disguised it has absolutely nothing to do. As far as metaphysics and theology are concerned it is and must be absolutely neutral. Believing thus, he could not help but hold the speculative generalizations of Herbert Spencer in contempt. The vast sweep of the Synthetic Philosophy which his friend John Fiske found so appealing moved Wright not at all. "Mr. Spencer's writings," he thinks, "evince an extensive knowledge of facts political and scientific, but extensive rather than profound, and all at second hand." [5] Spencer's famed law of evolution he dismisses as a perfect example of "that kind of orderliness which the human mind spontaneously supplies in the absence of facts sufficiently numerous and precise to justify sound scientific conclusions." [6] For himself, Wright prefers Aristotle and that view which, banishing cosmology from the realm of scientific inquiry, reduces "natural phenomena in their cosmical relations to an infinite variety of manifestations (without a discoverable tendency on the whole) of causes and laws which are simple and constant in their ultimate elements." [7]

That everything natural admits of explanation in terms of physical causation, Wright firmly believes. On this postulate, he feels, all science must rest. "The very hope of experimental philosophy, its expectation of constructing the sciences into a true philosophy of nature, is based on the induction, or, if you please, the a priori presumption, that physical causation is universal; that the constitution of nature is written in its actual manifestations, and needs only to be deciphered by experimental and inductive research; that it is not a latent invisible writing, to be brought out by the magic of mental anticipation or metaphysical meditation." [8] What science seeks is natural explanations. Its proper objects "are all of them processes and the results of processes . . . the immutable elements in the orders of all changes, the permanent relations of coexistences and sequences, which are hidden in the confusions of complex phenomena. Thought itself is a process and the mind a complex series of processes, the immutable elements of which must be discovered . . . by the aid of physiological researches and by indirect observation." [9] In brief, there are no phenomena, physical or psychical, intrinsically capricious and arbitrary. Causation may be hidden, but it is never absent.

Yet even as we claim this, we must, Wright holds, concede the incapacity of our finite minds to probe into the ultimate causes of events. Our knowledge extends no further than the conditioned. What the Unconditioned, i.e., that Reality existing independent of our perceptions, is we do not and cannot know. Like the weather, the universe as it discloses itself to scientific observation is of such causal complexity as to render every cosmic speculation suspect. Consider, for instance, the law of evolution. Can we, asks Wright, assert with any scientific confidence that it applies to phenomena not connected, either directly or remotely, with the life of the individual organism? He thinks not. "Of what we may call cosmical weather, in the interstellar spaces, little is known. Of the general cosmical effects of the opposing actions of heat and gravitation, the great dispersive and concentrative principles of the universe, we can at present only form vague conjectures." [10] No evolutionary pattern is discernible. Cyclic process there certainly is, but for its explanation simple thermodynamics suffices. "The living forces of all moving bodies, *minus* the potentials of their forces of gravitation, *plus* the mechanical values of their heat, *equal* to a constant quantity,— is the precise formula to which our cosmical speculations should conform." [11] The wise man will then take note of the cosmic weather, but never will he, like Spencer and, to a lesser extent, like Darwin, deceive himself into believing it teleological. Rather will he, trusting always and only to experiment and observation, proportion his belief to the empirical evidence and count nothing true but what a reasonable induction from the facts says must be so.

Where no facts exist, as in the speculative realms of faith and morals, wisdom demands that we suspend judgment. God may exist. We cannot prove it, but neither can the atheist disprove it. Where all is purely speculative, character and common sense alike enjoin a discreet silence and an open mind. "I may," notes Wright in a letter to Francis Ellingwood Abbott,

> appear to you to evade the speculative questions. I do not think that I do; for though I may not consistently hold on all occasions the even balance of judgment and the open mind which I think as proper in such matters . . . it is at any rate my design to do so. Whichever way we yield assent, we feel ourselves carried, not by evidence, but by the prejudices of feeling. We fall into one or another form of superstitious belief. Suspension of judgment appears to me to be demanded, therefore, not merely by the evidence, but as a discipline of character—*that faith and moral effort may not waste themselves on idle dreams but work among the realities of life.*[12]

Are we justified in taking this last to imply that there is a *practical* meaning of faith and moral effort? Wright does not deny it, and the tenor of his subsequent remarks to Abbott, and to others of his correspondents, is such as to indicate that he does find religion, conceived as devotion to human ideals, something of practical value. Faith and moral effort serve a useful function when they are directed to the betterment of mankind. Religion as the revelation of "all that is noble and beautiful and delightful in the possibilities of human nature" [13] is something we should all be the poorer for rejecting. To dignify so amorphous an attitude with the title of religious pragmatism would not perhaps be appropriate. What we have here is rather the germ of that doctrine which thirty years later will emerge full grown as William James' *Will to Believe.*

As in his view of religion, so also in his philosophy of science and society, what Wright has to offer is not a system but a suggestion. The worth of scientific theories is, he indicates, simply "their utility in enlarging our concrete knowledge of nature." [14] Similarly, social customs are to be valued or disvalued as they do or do not promote the greatest happiness of the greatest number. For theory and custom alike the proper measure of utility is human experience. Do scientific abstractions afford consequences capable of sensuous verification?—then they are meaningful. Are social customs beneficial on the whole?—then they are good. These maxims, learned from Mill, served Wright to the end of his short life. Whether he would have worked out their implications had he been spared to live as long as Peirce and James is difficult to say. As things turned out, it would not have been necessary for him to have done so, since a thinker greater than he was shortly to make good the defect.

2. Charles Sanders Peirce

CHARLES SANDERS PEIRCE, second son of the eminent Harvard mathematician Benjamin Peirce, was unusually well equipped for his task. A child prodigy, thoroughly grounded in mathematics by his father, he had gone on to specialize in physics and chemistry at Harvard. He was, as he noted many years later, "saturated, through and through, with the spirit of the physical sciences." [15] They would be his life's work. Following graduation in 1859 he joined the United States Coast and Geodetic Survey as a researcher in astronomy and geodetics. In 1863, on temporary leave from his job, he earned the first Sc.B. ever granted by Harvard. His book, *Photometric Researches* (1878), secured his scientific reputation, even as his pioneering work in symbolic logic and sign theory has earned him a permanent place in the history of philosophy of science.

Withal, Peirce's is no narrowly empirical mind. Throughout his life, as in his writings, he has time and concern for the poetic as well as the precise. In his conviction of the need for philosophy to take account of the human as well as the scientific situation in its cosmic setting, he goes far beyond Wright. He clearly sees, as Wright did not, that utilitarianism—"that improved substitute for the Gospel" [16]—presupposes the admission of some purpose to the world; that this, in turn, implies a cosmic philosophy. Like Fiske, he founds his system on the fact of evolution. "The only possible way of accounting for the laws of nature and for uniformity in general is," he is convinced, "to suppose them the results of evolution." [17] Unlike Wright, he recognizes Love (Eros) as "the great revolutionary agency of the universe." [18] Without Love, no growth; such, as Peirce interprets it, is the gospel of St. John, and the philosophy he draws from it "is that this is the way mind develops; and as for the cosmos, only so far as it yet is mind, and so has life, is it capable of further evolution. Love, recognizing germs of loveliness in the hateful, gradually warms it into life, and makes it lovely. This is the sort of evolution which every careful student of my essay 'The Law of Mind' must see that *synechism* calls for." [19]

By "synechism" Peirce understands cosmic continuity, which last he associates with the universal operation of mind. "The one intelligible theory of the universe," as he sees it, "is that of objective idealism, that matter is effete mind, inveterate habits becoming physical laws." [20] In the beginning—infinitely remote—

there was a chaos of unpersonalized feeling, which being without connection or regularity would properly be without existence. This feeling, sporting here and there in pure arbitrariness, would have started the germ of a generalizing tendency. Its other sportings would be evanescent, but this would have a growing virtue. Thus, the tendency to habit would be started; and from this, with the other principles of evolution, all the regularities of the universe would be evolved. At any time, however, an element of pure chance survives and will remain until the world becomes an absolutely perfect, rational, and symmetrical system, in which mind is at last crystallized in the infinitely distant future.[21]

When this happens, mind will have emerged as God; until it happens, we confront a universe characterized by a creativity which is God in the making.[22]

What is the relevance of this world-view to pragmatism? Apparently, very little. As Peirce understands it, "Pragmatism is, in itself, no doctrine of metaphysics, no attempt to determine any truth of things. It is merely a method of ascertaining the meanings of hard words and abstract concepts." [23] That hard words such as synechism and tychism [24] might owe their meaning to the truth of the abstract conception of reality above proposed is a possibility he does not consider. He does admit that pragmaticism [25] involves as an essential *consequence* acceptance of a realistic, as opposed to a nominalistic, theory of universals; that is to say, he holds that a thing in general (for example, manhood) is as real as the particular thing (the individual man) of which it (manhood) is predicated. But that it *presupposes* that metaphysic of which this theory of universals is a part, he nowhere attempts to show. Synechism, like every other concept, is justified pragmatically—or not at all.

That this is so, Peirce had first undertaken to demonstrate in a "little paper" written for presentation to the Metaphysical Club. "This paper was received with such unlooked-for kindness, that [he] was encouraged, some half-dozen years later to insert it, somewhat expanded, in the *Popular Science Monthly* for November 1877 and January 1878." As the dates imply, this "paper" is actually two essays, "The Fixation of Belief" and "How to Make our Ideas Clear." Their argument is presupposed throughout his later work.

The root idea is that thinking itself is essentially a process of fixing belief. Never, Peirce contends, would thought arise were it not that our minds are stimulated by doubts demanding resolution. "The irritation of doubt is the only immediate motive for the struggle to attain belief." [26] The doubt resolved and belief established, mind rests and "mental action on the subject comes to an end." [27] A habit of thought has been formed, and whether or not it is a good one only the consequences of our acting on it will make clear.

> If there be a unity among our sensations which has no reference to how we shall act on a given occasion, as when we listen to a piece of music, why we do not call that thinking. To develop its meaning, we have, therefore, simply to determine what habits it involves . . . What the habit is depends on *when* and *how* it causes us to act. As for the *when,* every stimulus to action is derived from perception; as for the *how,* every purpose of action is to produce some sensible result. Thus, we come down to what is tangible and conceivably practical, as the root of every real distinction of thought, no matter how subtle it may be; and there is no distinction of meaning so fine as to consist in anything but a possible difference of practice.[28]

Synechism, then, means the continuity we actually experience plus our success in acting upon the assumption that such continuity really exists, and apart from this it means nothing. In other words, our idea of synechism, or of anything, "*is* our idea of its sensible effects; and if we fancy that we have any other we deceive ourselves." [29] Where no sensible effects can be observed to follow, there, we may be sure, is nothing meaningful. "It appears, then, that the rule for attaining the third grade [30] of clearness of apprehension is as follows: Consider what effects, that might conceivably have practical bearings, we conceive the object of our conception to have. Then, our conception of these effects is the whole of our conception of the object." [31]

The phrasing is clumsy and deliberately so, for Peirce wishes to emphasize that his pragmatism has to do only with the consequences of conceptions. His concern is always with the *intellectual purport* of ideas; with their emotive or feeling aspect he will have nothing to do, and this for the obvious reason that feelings and emotions as such do not directly entail consequences or issue in habits of action. The advantage of such a restriction, and it is a great one, is that it enables the pragmatist to dispense with most of philosophy past.

> It will serve to show that almost every proposition of ontological metaphysics is either meaningless gibberish—one word being defined by other words, and they by still others, without any real conception ever being reached—or else is downright absurd; so that all such rubbish being swept away, what will remain of philosophy will be a series of problems capable of investigation by the observational methods of the true sciences—the truth about which can be reached without those interminable misunderstandings and disputes which have made the highest of the positive sciences (i.e., Philosophy) a mere amusement for idle intellects, a sort of chess—idle pleasure its purpose, and reading out of a book its method." [32]

Were Peirce, like Wright, an avowed nominalist of pronounced anti-speculative tendencies, such sentiments would be natural, but as we have seen, he is not, and this being the case, we may well wonder whether in his eagerness to consign metaphysics to the philosophical garbage-pail he has not gone further than his own position allows. Has he emptied out the baby with the bath-water? It certainly seems so, for despite his insistence that pragmatism, being only a method, has no bearing on metaphysics as such, the pure philosophy that is left to pragmatic contemplation can hardly include the sort of realism he endorses. No scholastic realist could or would think of conceding the problem of universals resolvable by observation. On the contrary, if observation is the sine qua non of meaning, then Peirce is a nominalist in spite of himself! The fact of the matter is that the empiricism implied by his pragmatic method is irreconcilable, not only with his realism, but with the fragment of a metaphysic sketched out above, as well as with that theory of categories [33] he elsewhere develops. The illusion of compatibility fostered by the claim of pragmatism to be merely a method dissolves away the moment we recognize the impossibility of separating our notion of the known from the way of our knowing it. For method must and does dictate content and impose limitations. And if the method be that of pragmatism, then the real must be such as to admit of observation, since an unobserved or unobservable consequence would be a contradiction in terms. If seeing is believing, and what is seen is real, then the unreal and the unseen are synonymous. If the ontological metaphysics of Aristotle, Duns Scotus, Kant, and Hegel is meaningless, then the realistic metaphysics of Peirce, owing something to each of these, is like all of them—rubbish; if, that is, philosophy really is what Peirce declares it to be, i.e., either science or balderdash.[34]

Philosophy is, then, science, or rather, the logic of science. Had Peirce said no more than this, he would today be honored as the founder of modern logical empiricism. But he went further, and by declaring for realism and against nominalism he cut himself off from the empiricist tradition, for its advocates are nominalists to a man. Had he restricted himself to arguing the realistic character of scientific propositions, his today would be the honors accorded to Whitehead. But he went further, and by denying metaphysics he diminished his standing as a cosmologist. So I believe, and it is only fair to add that many of his interpreters would disagree. Since Peirce himself has nothing definite to say on the subject, it is unlikely that the question of interpretation will be settled soon or ever.

A similar vagueness of expression characterizes Peirce's philosophy of religion, and impels the same unsatisfactory conclusion. Having rejected ontological metaphysics, he is, naturally, in no position to theologize, and he does not try. Into "the fallacious logical disputations" of the theologians he does not propose to enter. "Can you induce the philosophic world to agree upon any assignable creed, or in condemning any specified item in the current creeds of Christendom?" [35] He thinks not, although he himself confesses to believing in the reality of God. Reality, not existence, for "whatever there may be of *argument* in all this is as nothing, the merest nothing, in comparison to its force as an appeal to one's own instinct, which is to argument what substance is to shadow, what bed-rock is to the built foundations of a cathedral." [36] Instinct, he insists, demonstrates that God is continuously creator eternal even as reason denies the possibility of any further definition of his nature. "Let a man drink in such thoughts as come to him in contemplating the physico-psychical universe without any special purpose of his own; especially the universe of mind which coincides with the universe of matter. The idea of there being a God over it all of course will be often suggested; and the more he considers it, the more he will be enwrapt with Love of this idea. He will ask himself whether or not there really is a God. If he allows instinct to speak, and searches his own heart, he will at length find that he cannot help believing it." [37] This argument, which Peirce elsewhere names the Neglected Argument, is, he insists, no less persuasive for not being subject to formal proof. "I cannot," he declares,

tell how every man will think . . . But I can tell how a man must think if he is a pragmatist. . . . If a pragmatist is asked what he means by the word "God," he can only say that just as long acquaintance with a man of great character may deeply influence one's whole manner of conduct, so that a glance at his portrait may make a difference, just as almost living with Dr. Johnson enabled poor Boswell to write an immortal book and a really sublime book, just as long study of the works of Aristotle may make him an acquaintance, so if contemplation and study of the physico-psychical universe can imbue a man with principles of conduct analogous to the influence of a great man's works or conversation, then that analogue of a mind—for it is impossible to say that *any* human attribute is *literally* applicable—is what he means by "God." [38]

What a man's instinct tells him he must believe, that he has every right to believe, and if his belief adds meaning and purpose to his life, why that is all the justification pragmatism requires. That such a doctrine is liable to misinterpretation, not to say caricature, Peirce knew from his own experience of his critics. Since he was clear in his own mind as to what he meant, however, their barbs and jibes did not greatly disturb him. Besides, he was no longer alone in advocating pragmatism. By the turn of the century, F. C. S. Schiller, Giovanni Papini, John Dewey, and William James were all actively engaged in promoting the pragmatic cause. Even as pragmatism flourished, however, the fortunes of its founder were on the wane. Having severed his connection with the Geodetic Survey in 1891, he had hoped to make his living by his writing, but although he turned out great amounts of work, it was not of the sort to interest publishers, and finally he was reduced to doing reviews and dictionary articles to make ends meet. By 1902 he was close to absolute poverty and failing in health, and had it not been for the generosity of James, he and his wife must have ended their days in the poorhouse. As it was, the last dozen years of Peirce's life were lived in debt and destitution. In 1912 he contracted cancer; two years later he passed away, unnoticed in death as he had been unrecognized by all but William James in life.

3. William James

THEY HAD KNOWN OF EACH OTHER SINCE 1861. James, a callow and none too physically robust nineteen, was newly enrolled in chemistry at Harvard's Lawrence Scientific School. Peirce was twenty-two, a year ahead of James at Lawrence, and already known on campus as a man of the world. He was, James wrote his sister, "a very 'smart' fellow with a great deal of character," albeit "pretty independent and violent." [39] Soon these two, in company with Chauncey Wright and Wendell Holmes, would be meeting regularly to thrash out the eternal problems. In 1866 Henry James, Sr. moved his family from Boston to Cambridge, and Peirce now became the intimate of them all. William James, who thought his father "the wisest of men," could not help but be impressed by the growing attachment between Peirce and Henry Senior. Whom the latter admired, he must admire too, and his difficulty in understanding just what it was that his brilliant friend was driving at in his early lectures and articles only served to sharpen his suspicion that he was in the presence of genius. It was a suspicion destined never to be dispelled. To the end of his life he would promote the cause and philosophy of this strange man whom Harvard and the rest of academic America were content to ignore.

It may have been that James misunderstood Peirce. Ralph Barton Perry, whose monumental study of James still stands as the last word on the subject, is inclined to think that he did. Certainly there is in their respective pragmatisms a difference of outlook distinctly discernible. Where Peirce is satisfied "to analyze sundry

concepts with exactitude," James wants to know the why and wherefore of their working. That neglect of formal logic which so bothers
Peirce worries James not at all. Consequently, his version of
pragmatism is simpler, more direct, more concerned with everyday
applications. The gulf that seems to make of Peirce's metaphysics
and method two separate doctrines is scarcely visible in James's
work. The pragmatic principle clearly grasped, felicitously stated,
and strikingly illustrated, here leads naturally to radical empiricism
and issues, as it obviously must, in a panpsychic metaphysic. It
is as if the cimmerian darkness had lifted to disclose the commonplace. No wonder, then, that James should win the popularity
Peirce never had. If, in truth, he did misunderstand him, his error
was such as any man trying to make common sense of pragmatism
might commit.

The common sense of it was there from the beginning, and the
beginning can be dated: August 26th, 1898; the place, Berkeley,
California; the occasion, James's address to the Philosophical Union
of the University of California. His subject was "Philosophical
Conceptions and Practical Results," and having disposed of the
amenities and acknowledged his indebtedness to Peirce, he pro-
ceeded immediately to remark his reinterpretation of the pragmatic
principle. It should, he thought,

> be expressed more broadly then Mr. Peirce expresses it. The ultimate
> test for us of what a truth means is indeed the conduct it dictates
> or inspires. But it inspires that conduct because it first foretells some
> particular turn to our experience which shall call for just that con-
> duct from us. . . . The ffective meaning of any philosophical propo-
> sition can always be brought down to some particular consequence,
> in our future practical experience, whether active or passive; the
> point lying rather in the fact that the experience must be particular,
> than in the fact that it must be active.[40]

Thus, as between any two philosophical propositions supposedly
contradictory of each other, "if, by supposing the truth of the one,
you can foresee no conceivable practical consequences to anybody
at any time or place, which is different from what you would foresee if you supposed the truth of the other, why then the difference
between the two propositions is no difference—it is only a specious

and verbal difference, unworthy of further consideration." [41] In sum, "there can be no difference which doesn't make a difference—no difference in abstract truth which does not express itself in a difference of concrete fact, and of conduct consequent upon the fact, imposed on somebody, somehow, somewhere, and somewhen." [42]

To see that this is so, we need only to reflect how meaningless the question of whether all things are produced by matter or by God would be if "the world were finished and no more of it to come." [43] Such a question, "reasonable enough in a consciousness that is prospective, as ours now is, and whose world is partly yet to come, would be," James insists, "absolutely senseless and irrational in a purely retrospective consciousness summing up a world already past." [44] "Thus if no future detail of experience or conduct is to be deduced from our hypothesis, the debate between materialism and theism becomes quite idle and insignificant. Matter and God in that event mean exactly the same thing—the power, namely, neither more nor less, that can make just this mixed, imperfect, yet completed world—and the wise man is he who in such a case would turn his back on such a supererogatory discussion." [45]

Every proposition of significance, then, must be such as makes a difference, and making a difference always involves reference to some particular fact or situation present or future. Take again the question, materialism or theism. If the world has a future, it is certainly, James thinks, a matter of some practical concern as to which of these alternatives is true. It surely makes a difference whether there is or is not a God guiding the course of the world. Our actions, not to say our morale, must differ as we live with or without the hope that such a divine being exists. On the other hand, we must never forget that the truth of theism, or of anything else, is as much and no more than its "cash-value." We have always to ask ourselves what difference it would make in our lives whether theism were true or false; we have always to remember that its meaning for us is simply the sum of those "voices and visions, responses to prayer, changes of heart, deliverances from fear, inflowings of help, assurances of support" [46] which we really experience. "That the God of systematic theology should exist or not exist is a matter of small practical moment. At most it means that you may continue uttering certain abstract words and that you must stop using others. But if the God of these particular experiences be false, it is an awful thing for you, if you are one of those whose lives are stayed on such experiences. The theistic controversy, trivial enough if we take it merely academically and theologically, is of tremendous significance if we test it by its results for actual life." [47] Perhaps so—if, that is, the voices and visions, etc., are really evidences of God, and not, as some would claim, delusions or worse. Here at Berkeley James leaves the issue in abeyance, since it is, after all, no part of his present task to decide between the alternatives, but only to demonstrate that pragmatic method and give voice to that sound English spirit of common sense which, as opposed to "the circuitous and ponderous artificialities of Kant" and his metaphysical successors, "is intellectually, as well as practically and morally, on the saner, sounder, and truer path." [48]

His purpose accomplished, James returned to Cambridge. Whatever thoughts he may have at this time entertained with regard to the further development of the pragmatic thesis never took written shape, for shortly thereafter he suffered a recurrence of the ill-health which had plagued him since childhood, and for over a year he did no work at all. After that there were his Gifford Lectures on the varieties of religious experience to prepare, and thus it was not until 1903, his Giffords delivered and in print, that he was free to turn his mind again to pragmatism. For some time now he had been minded to expand his views into a book, and the assignment to teach the undergraduate course in the philosophy of nature gave him the excuse he needed to put his thoughts in order. The result was Syllabus for Philosophy 3; on it all his later works would build. From this syllabus he drew in 1906 the plan for those Lowell Lectures which in May of 1907 were published under the title *Pragmatism, A New Name for Some Old Ways of Thought.*

Basically, the book is pretty much the mixture as before, with this one difference; that whereas in the 1898 lecture James had restricted himself to an identification of the *meaning* of an idea with the method of its verification, now he boldly equates the verifiable with the *true. "True ideas are those that we can assimilate, validate, corroborate and verify. False ideas are those that we can not. That,"* he now feels, "is the practical difference it makes to us to have true ideas: that, therefore, is the meaning of truth, for it is all that truth is known-as." [49] Rationalism and Idealism to the contrary, the truth is not, as James understands it, something absolute, before which we must bow in all humility; it is not something eternal, forever above and beyond our limited ability to comprehend it in its entirety. Rather is it that the truth is made; the true is what works. "Its verity *is* in fact an event, a process: the process namely of its verifying itself, its veri-*fication*. Its validity is the process of its valid-*ation*." [50]

Obviously, much, if not everything, depends here on what James takes "verification" and "validation" to mean. If these are, as his statement appears to imply, merely synonyms for sense experience, then pragmatism, for all its pretense of philosophical open-mindedness, must be classed with those narrow empiricisms which find all metaphysics meaningless and ethics and religion emotive nonsense. Does pragmatism belong in such company? James seems to be conceding as much, when he remarks, apropos of the harmony of pragmatism with the empirical tradition, that "it agrees with nominalism, for instance, in always appealing to particulars; with utilitarianism in emphasizing practical aspects; with positivism in its disdain for verbal solutions, useless questions and metaphysical abstractions." [51] With all of these it stands a pole apart from rationalism. Such difference as may exist, then, between pragmatism and these other empiricisms is at most one of attitude. Considered as theories of truth, pragmatism, nominalism, utilitarianism, and positivism are one and the same point of view.

The significance of this identification cannot be overstressed, since it is precisely the neglect of it that allows James to claim, as he does throughout his books and letters, that pragmatism is only a method, and as such neutral as regards the truth or falsity of any particular school of thought, including that radical empiricism [52] which he himself professes. And yet if it is true, as empiricism claims, that the meaning and truth of any idea is the method of its verification; if, further, every form of verification other than that of pragmatic sense experience is ruled out, then it is certainly true that all non-empirically oriented philosophies are nonsense. We have found it to be so with Peirce; it is even more clearly so with James, since unlike his mentor he has no doctrine of realism to obscure the fact of his nominalism. Thus when James tells us that pragmatism "has no dogmas, and no doctrines save its method," [53] he is overlooking his presupposition of the greatest dogma and doctrine of them all, i.e., nothing sensed, nothing true. To repeat, then, such difference as exists between pragmatism and its fellow empiricisms is simply one of attitude. Whereas they candidly proclaim the falsity of every proposition and idea inherently unverifiable, it reserves the right to hope that such ideas and propositions may be true.

The right to hope—this, in a word, is meliorism, and on James's finding it is that which marks off pragmatism from, and constitutes it clearly superior to, all other varieties of empiricism. "It is," he believes, "clear that pragmatism must incline towards meliorism," [54] and this because there is nothing in empiricism which prevents our faith in the possibility of our bettering ourselves and the world in which we live.

> 'If we do *our* best, *and* the other powers do *their* best, the world will be perfected'—this proposition expresses no actual fact, but only the complexion of a fact thought of as eventually possible. As it stands, *no* conclusion can be positively deduced from it. *A conclusion would require another premise of fact, which only we can supply. The original proposition* per se *has no pragmatic value whatsoever, apart from its power to challenge our will to produce the premise of fact required.* Then indeed the perfected world emerges as a logical conclusion.[55]

"We can *create* the conclusion, then. We can and we may, as it were, jump with both feet off the ground into or towards a world of which we trust the other parts to meet our jump—and *only so* can the *making* of a perfected world of the pluralistic pattern ever take place. Only through our precursive trust in it can it come into being." [56] With this statement of the meliorist faith, the last he ever wrote, James's version of the pragmatic creed is complete.

Is it such as any reasonable man might make his personal rule of life? This is a question only you can answer, since logic has no province where meliorism is concerned. Subtract the meliorism, however, and the case is altered, for now we have to do simply with the question of the adequacy of empiricism as such considered as a theory of truth and as a view of reality. On the side of empiricism there is common sense, as well as that instinct which bids us believe that what we experience is real. Against it is the fact that science proper begins only where common sense leaves off, and the instinct, equally strong, to believe ourselves part of and participant in a greater whole. Since James virtually ignores the fact, and seems of two minds as regards the instinct, he can hardly be said to have effectively disposed of the case against empiricism. On the other hand, his refutation of rationalism, and its prime American exponent, Josiah Royce, must certainly invalidate the greater part of that case—if refutation it really is. Royce, of course, denies it; with what justification we have now to consider.

SUGGESTED READINGS

Edward H. Madden, *The Philosophical Writings of Chauncey Wright, Representative Selections* (New York: Liberal Arts Press, paperback, n.d.), provides a good cross-section of Wright's work. For those who dislike bits and snippets, the whole, available in some libraries, is contained in Chauncey Wright, *Philosophical Discussions* (New York: Holt, 1877). For an appraisal of the man and his work as viewed by a contemporary, see John Fiske, "Chauncey Wright," in *Darwinism and Other Essays* (Boston: Houghton Mifflin, 1879), pp. 79-110. Wright's letters, slightly edited so as to put their author in his most favorable light, have been published by his good friend James Bradley Thayer. However, it is most unlikely that any but the very largest libraries will have a copy of the *Letters of Chauncey Wright, with some account of his life* (Cambridge, 1878). On the other hand, most will have copies of the following journals which contain such other limited materials on Wright as are available: Josephy L. Blau, "Chauncey Wright: Radical Empiricist," *New England Quarterly,* Vol. 19 (1946), pp. 495-517, is a rather pedantically written survey of the basic positions of Wright's philosophy, with special emphasis on the ethical aspects of his thought. Much better as regards readability are two articles by Philip P. Wiener, "Peirce's Metaphysical Club and the Genesis of Pragmatism," *Journal of the History of Ideas,* Vol. 7 (1946), pp. 218-33; and "Chauncey Wright's Defense of Darwin and the Neutrality of Science," *Journal of the History of Ideas,* Vol. 6 (1945), pp. 19-45. This last is prefaced by a daguerreotype of Wright.

The standard edition of Peirce is Hartshorne, Weiss, and Burks, *Collected Papers,* 8 Vols. (Cambridge: Harvard University Press, 1958). Virtually all the references in articles and books about Peirce are to this edition. For the serious student of Peirce it is indispensable. Philip P. Wiener (ed.), *Values in a Universe of Chance: Selected Writings of Charles S. Peirce* (Garden City: Doubleday Anchor Books, paperback, 1958), offers a balanced selection complete with brief introductions to each by the editor. Also available in paperback is Justus Buchler, *Philosophical Writings of Peirce* (New York: Dover Books, paperback, 1955). Of the several books about Peirce, the two best for my money are James Kern Feibleman, *An Introduction to Peirce's Philosophy, interpreted as a system* (New York: Harper, 1946), and Manley Thompson, *The Pragmatic Philosophy of C. S. Peirce* (Chicago: University of Chicago Press, 1953). Justus Buchler, *Charles Peirce's Empiricism* (New York: Harcourt, Brace and Co., 1939), is somewhat dated but still well worth your reading time. Unless you possess some familiarity with the major themes of contemporary logic and epistemology you had best avoid W. B. Gallie, *Peirce and Pragmatism* (London: Penguin Books, Pelican paperback, 1952).

Virtually every library of any size will have all or most of the works of William James in one or more editions. *Pragmatism and Other Essays* (New York: Meridian Books, paperback, 1955) affords a good introduction to his thought, as does Alburey Castell (ed.), *Essays in Pragmatism* (New York: Hafner, paperback, 1952). The best of the books about James is still Ralph Barton Perry, *The Thought and Character of William James*, 2 Vols. (Boston: Little, Brown and Co., 1935). Contains a chronology and complete bibliography of James's works. Also available in a one-volume abridged edition. George Santayana, *Character and Opinion in the United States* (Garden City: Doubleday Anchor Books, paperback, 1960), contains a wickedly perceptive study of the man and his influence. For those wishing an analysis of more recent vintage, there is Lloyd R. Morris, *William James; the message of a modern mind* (New York: Scribner, 1950).

A comprehensive bibliography of articles, monographs, reviews, and books on pragmatism and other related varieties of empiricism is given in Herbert Schneider, *A History of American Philosophy* (New York: Columbia University Press, 1946), pp. 572-87.

REFERENCES

1. Matthew 7:20. Quoted by Charles Sanders Peirce as illustrative of the basic thesis of pragmatism. See *Collected Papers of Charles Sanders Peirce* (Cambridge: Harvard University Press, 1958), 5.465 (the numbers refer to volume (5) and paragraph (465); hereafter cited as Collected Papers).

2. Edward H. Madden (editor), *The Philosophical Writings of Chauncey Wright* (New York: Liberal Arts Press, 1958), p. viii. Hereafter cited as Wright.

3. Wright, p. 130.

4. "The creed which accepts as the foundation of morals 'utility' or the

'greatest happiness principle' holds that actions are right in proportion as they tend to promote happiness, wrong as they tend to produce the reverse of happiness. By happiness is intended pleasure, and the absence of pain; by unhappiness, pain, and the privation of pleasure." John Stuart Mill, *Utilitarianism* (New York: Liberal Arts Press, 1949), p. 7.

5. Wright, p. 13.

6. Ibid., p. 21.

7. Ibid., p. 113.

8. Ibid., p. 37.

9. Ibid., pp. 21-22.

10. Ibid., pp. 115-16.

11. *Philosophical Discussions* (New York: Holt, 1877), p. 19. Wright's italics.

12. Wright, p. 44.

13. Ibid., p. 54.

14. *Philosophical Discussions,* p. 56.

15. Collected Papers, 1.3.

16. Ibid., 6.297.

17. Ibid., 6.13.

18. Ibid., 1.287.

19. Ibid., 6.289.

20. Ibid., 6.25.

21. Ibid., 6.33.

22. No part of Peirce's metaphysics has given rise to a greater diversity of opinion among his critics than this notion of God. Actually, Peirce never defines what he means by God with any precision. At times he speaks of God in a manner reminiscent of Whitehead; sometimes his references appear to imply a conception not far removed from the traditional deity of Christian orthodoxy; mostly he tends to think of God as a being of whom nothing exact or even meaningful can be said. Thus, "we cannot so much as frame any notion of what the phrase 'the performance of God's mind' *means*. Not the faintest! The question is gabble." Collected Papers, 6.508. See also 6.494-507; 6.509-21.

23. Ibid., 5.464.

24. In Peircian language, tychism, from the Greek *tyche,* chance, fortune, luck. Although Peirce's philosophy has been called Tychism, he himself denies that the label is properly descriptive of the system as a whole. "For although tychism does enter into it, it only enters as subsidiary to that which is really, as I regard it, the characteristic of my doctrine, namely, that I chiefly insist upon continuity. . . . Accordingly, I like to call my theory Synechism, because it rests on the study of continuity." Collected Papers, 6.202.

25. "Pragmaticism" rather than "Pragmatism" because Pierce wishes to mark off his usage of the term to indicate a theory of meaning differing from that of William James, F. C. S. Schiller, and others who, in Peirce's opinion, tend to employ it as a name for a type of philosophy. Essentially, there is only the smallest of differences in the connotation of the two terms; often they are used interchangeably. See Collected Papers, 5.414f.

26. Collected Papers, 5.375.

27. Ibid., 5.376.

28. Ibid., 5.400.

29. Ibid., 5.401.

30. The first two grades are those of (1) clearness and (2) distinctness as distinguished by Descartes and his logical predecessors. For Peirce's criticism of their adequacy, see Collected Papers, 5.388-93.

31. Collected Papers, 5.402.

32. Ibid., 5.423.

33. There are three basic characters of the universe. Peirce calls them First, Second, and Third. "First is the conception of being or existing independent of anything else. Second is the conception of being relative to, the conception of reaction with, something else. Third is the conception of mediation, whereby a first and second are brought into relation. . . . The origin of things, considered not as leading to anything, but in itself, contains the idea of First, the end of things that of Second, the process mediating between them that of Third. . . . In psychology Feeling is First, Sense of reaction Second, General conception Third, or mediation. In biology, the idea of arbitrary sporting is First, heredity is Second, the process whereby the accidental characters become fixed is Third. Chance is First, Law is Second, the tendency to take habits is Third. Mind is First, Matter is Second, Evolution is Third." Collected Papers, 5.32.

34. Peirce to William James in Ralph Barton Perry, *The Thought and Character of William James* (Boston: Little, Brown, 1935), II, p. 438. Hereafter cited as Perry.

35. Collected Papers, 6.446.

36. Ibid., 6.503.

37. Ibid., 6.501.

38. Ibid., 6.501-2.

39. Perry, I, p. 211.

40. *Collected Essays and Reviews* (New York: Longmans, Green, 1920), p. 412. Hereafter cited as CER.

41. CER, p. 413.

42. Ibid.

43. Ibid., p. 414.

44. Ibid., p. 415.

45. Ibid., p. 417.

46. Ibid., p. 428.

47. Ibid., p. 429.

48. Ibid., p. 436.

49. *Pragmatism, A New Name for Some Old Ways of Thinking* (New York: Longmans, Green, 1921), p. 201. Hereafter cited as Pragmatism.

50. Pragmatism, p. 201. James's italics.

51. Ibid., pp. 53-54.

52. According to James, "Radical empiricism consists first of a postulate, next of a statement of fact, and finally of a generalized conclusion.

"The postulate is that the only things that shall be debatable among philosophers shall be things definable in terms drawn from experience. . . .

"The statement of fact is that the relations between things, conjunctive as well as disjunctive, are just as much matters of direct particular experience, neither more so nor less so, than the things themselves.

"The generalized conclusion is that therefore the parts of experience hold together from next to next by relations that are themselves parts of experience. The directly apprehended universe needs, in short, no extraneous trans-empirical connective support, but possesses in its own right a concatenated or continuous structure." *The Meaning of Truth* (New York: Longmans, Green, 1911), pp. xii-xiii. In this work and also in *Pragmatism* James remarks in several places the lack of any logical connection between pragmatism and radical empiricism. Occasionally, however, he appears to contradict himself on this point. See *Pragmatism*, pp. 161f, 258-59.

53. Pragmatism, p. 54.

54. Ibid., p. 286.

55. *Some Problems of Philosphy* (New York: Longmans, Green, 1916), p. 230. James's italics.

56. Ibid. James's italics.

XX

Biographer of the Absolute

JOSIAH ROYCE

"Individual Consciousness is but
a shadow; what is permanent is
the world." [1]

JOSIAH ROYCE

Josiah Royce

IN THE HISTORY OF WESTERN THOUGHT it is more often true than not that what one philosopher takes another to hold, the other philosopher does not really hold at all. Thus one thinker will fasten upon the central idea of the other and, having maltreated it in ways never intended by its original proponent, will end by finding the other's view inadequate or false. Inevitably, this calls forth a reply from the author of the rejected idea, which reply, far from setting the record straight, usually results in a compounding of the mutual misunderstanding. So it has ever been; so is it with the most famous rivalry in American philosophy, that of William James and Josiah Royce.

The heart of the matter is Royce's contention that a Many which is not at once a One, and this not merely as an abstract unity but as a concrete Whole inclusive of its parts, is nothing intelligible, and hence nothing real.

One is [then] the Absolute, because in *mere* multiplicity there would be no finality of insight. *Many* is the Absolute, because in the interrelationships of contrasted expressions of a single Will lies the only opportunity for the embodiment of wholeness of life, and for the possession of Self-consciousness by the Absolute . . . *Individuals* are all the various expressions of the Absolute, in so far as they are Many; just because, where the One is individual, every aspect and element of its self-expression is unique. *Free,* in its own degree, is every individual will amongst all the wills that the world-life expresses, because every such will, as unique, is in some respect underivable from all the others. *Temporal,* is the world order, because, so far as we can know, time is the universal form of the expression of Will. *Eternal* is this same world order, because past, present, and future time equally belong to the Real, and their Being implies, by definition, that they are present, in their wholeness, to the final insight. And Time, surveyed in its wholeness, is Eternity.[2]

Such is Royce's central idea, and that James, unintentionally or otherwise, misconceives it his strictures on the subject make plain.

Given his philosophical temperament, it is not surprising that he should, for James was never the man to rest easy in monism of any sort. The fact is, as he repeatedly insists, that the universe we live in is through and through pluralistic. One it may be, but if so our experience does not confirm it. Pragmatically speaking, it adds nothing to Reality to call it One. Granted that such a *confessio fidei* has its emotional value for those stout souls dedicated to "One Life, One Truth, one Love, one Principle, One Good, one God . . . But if we try to realize *intellectually* what we can possibly *mean* by such a glut of oneness we are," James feels, "thrown right back upon our pragmatistic determinations again."[3]

It means either the mere name One, the universe of discourse; or it means the sum total of all the ascertainable particular conjunctions and concatenations; or, finally, it means some one vehicle of conjunction treated as all-inclusive, like one origin, one purpose, or one knower. In point of fact it always means one *knower* to those who (like Royce) take it intellectually today. The one knower involves, they think, the other forms of conjunction. His world must have all its parts co-implicated in the one logical-aesthetical-teleological unit-picture which is his eternal dream.[4]

In sum, for James the One is either an empty word or a reality which by implication reduces the Many to the status of an illusion. Most probably, he thinks, it is the former, since the latter alternative is so patently contrary to fact as hardly to deserve the courtesy of a refutation. That the One might be, as Royce claims, an infinite Self or Life or Person conscious of and sustaining the manifold reality which in It lives and moves and has its being is a possibility James does not consider, probably because it never occurred to him, any more than it did to any other of Royce's critics, that the

One here at issue was not, as he seems to have thought, the One of pantheism but rather the One of *panentheism*. This is not to say that James' failure to distinguish the One of pantheism from that of panentheism invalidates his criticism of the Roycian monism. It may be that monism panentheistically conceived is no more valid or viable a philosophy than that pantheistic monism so lightly dismissed by James. Even so, fairness to Royce requires that judgment be suspended until he too has had his hour in court.

II

His parents were English. Brought to this country as children, raised in rural New York, in 1849, like hundreds of other families drawn by the chance for fortune and a new life, they joined a wagon-train for California and the gold-fields. There, in the mining camp town of Grass Valley, high in the Sierras, their fourth child and only son was born on November 20th, 1855. His first schooling was from his mother. Later, the family having moved to San Francisco, he attended schools there and across the bay in Oakland. In 1871 he entered the newly-opened University of California at Berkeley. He was a brilliant student, so much so that a group of local businessmen, impressed by his senior thesis, offered to pay his way for a year of study abroad. At the Universities of Leipzig and Göttingen he read Schelling and Schopenhauer, heard Lotze lecture, and acquired his conviction of the truth of Absolute Idealism. Back in America in 1876, he enrolled as a graduate student at Johns Hopkins. First the Ph.D. and then a job teaching philosophy in some eastern university, such was his aim, and two years later the first half of it was fulfilled. The second unfortunately not materializing, he returned to California and for the next four years eked out a living instructing University of California freshmen in the rudiments of rhetoric, mathematics, and logic. Nights, holidays, and vacations he read and wrote, building a scholarly reputation against the day when he would be invited east. Finally in 1882 the invitation came. Would he care to take over the classes of a Harvard philosopher going on leave? The job was strictly temporary; there was, he was told, no guarantee of reappointment. He decided to take the gamble, and such was the impression that he made that at the expiration of his year, wires were pulled to keep him at Harvard. In 1885, following the publication of his first book, he was promoted to assistant professor. The die was cast, a Harvard professor he would be for the remainder of his life. In 1892, after the appearance of his second book, he attained the rank of full professor. He was a prolific author and a famous teacher; his Gifford Lectures, delivered at the University of Aberdeen during 1899 and 1900, would establish his reputation in England and in America as a leading exponent of Idealism.

When and where the question prompting that Idealism first occurred to him, Royce does not say. Presumably it was in Germany, at Göttingen or Leipzig, possibly during one of Lotze's unforgettable lectures, that it first popped into his mind. Certain it is that he brought the question home with him, for one finds it raised in his doctoral dissertation and answered in his first book. How is error possible? Or, in other words, what is an error? That, Royce believes, is the question on which, as we shall find, everything depends; for its answer is at once the key to Truth and our introduction to the Absolute.

That there is such a thing as error, Royce thinks not even the skeptic can deny. For suppose that he says that there is no difference between truth and error. If we are not to conclude that he is talking nonsense, it must be that his statement "there is no difference between truth and error" is itself either true or false. And if so, then our skeptic is confounded out of his own mouth. Either he is caught up in a self-contradiction, for surely it is self-contradictory to affirm the truth of a denial of the distinguishability of truth, or he refutes himself, since if it is false to say that there is no difference between truth and error, then that difference must exist. " 'No absolute truth exists'—can you," asks Royce, "say that if you want to? At least you must add, 'No absolute truth exists *save this truth itself, that no absolute truth exists.*' Otherwise your statement has no sense. But if you admit this truth, then there is in fact an absolute distinction between truth and error." [5] That this "absolute distinction" is not simply one of logic but of reality as well, the skeptic himself bears witness; "for does he not after all argue for relativity against 'absolutists,' holding that he is really right and they really wrong?" Royce finds that he does.

Truth and error having been found to be distinct, the question reappears: What is an error? Common sense tells us that it is the failure of a judgment to agree with its object. If I judge the person across the street to be my friend James, and then on coming closer find that it is not James at all but a stranger, to the view of common sense I have erred. What common sense overlooks, however, is the fact that to have made the error at all I must antecedently have had in mind *both* my judgment and its object, and this because I could not possibly know my error as such unless I already knew that there was a truth to which my error failed to measure up. That is to say, my error, properly understood, is not that I have failed to conform my judgment to its object; rather is it that my judgment and its object taken together have failed to agree with that higher thought which includes them both. What, then, is error? "An error," Royce replies, "is an incomplete thought, that to a higher thought, which includes it and its intended object, is known as having failed in the purpose that it more or less clearly had, and that is fully realized in this higher thought. And without such higher inclusive thought, an assertion has no external object, and is no error." [6]

Error is possible therefore only because there exists an Ultimate Knower to whose true thought our false thoughts and their objects are present as fragments of Its truth. Taken in isolation, no judgment is true or false, and this because "alone, as a separate fact, a judgment has no intelligible object beyond itself." [7] What makes it true or false is its inclusion together with its object in the unity of an infinite thought. That this thought must be infinite in comprehension, the endlessness of possible error makes evident. For however great the error, that truth which includes it must, Royce points out, be greater still.

There is no chance of escape. For all reality is reality because true judgments can be made about it. And all reality, for the same reason, can be the object of false judgments. Therefore, since the false and the true judgments are all true or false as present to the infinite thought, along with their objects, no reality can escape. You and I and all of us, all good, all evil, all truth, all falsehood, all things actual and possible, exist as they exist, and are known for what they are, in and to the absolute thought; and are therefore all judged as to their real character at this everlasting throne of judgment.[8]

Such, Royce maintains, is the inevitable conclusion to which we are impelled by our recognition of the meaning and possibility of error. *"Either there is no such thing as error, which statement is a flat self-contradiction, or else there is an infinite unity of conscious thought to which is present all possible truth."* [9]

He may be right, although William James is not alone among those of Royce's contemporaries and successors who are not convinced, and indeed when we examine the argument more closely it does show forth a certain weakness. Granted that error, *known as such,* presupposes the existence of an encompassing truth, it does not follow that this truth, or its possessor, must be infinite. The most inclusive thought thus far attained by human mind is Einstein's unified field theory. It may be false. Most probably it is shot through with errors. Eventually some scientist will come along and point them out. But for all that his thought will encompass a truth as yet undreamed of, it will still be the thought of a man, and as such— finite. If infinite error exists, so must infinite truth. But does infinite error *actually* exist? What Royce says is that there is no limit to the possibility of error. From this, given his premise, it would seem to follow only that infinite truth is a possibility; but possibility, even multiplied to infinity, no more adds up to actuality than an infinity of zeroes adds up to one!

That this conclusion would be justified if the possibility at issue was a mere abstraction, Royce concedes. The point is, as he sees it, that it is not. To say of anything that it is possible is, he insists, to say that the future may see its realization. An unrealizable possibility is simply not a possibility at all. Not that is possible which is barely possible; only that is possible which might actually come to pass. Thus if infinite error is possible it is really possible, and if so, infinite truth really exists, since an infinite truth which was a real, but unrealized, possibility would be, to Royce's way of thinking, a contradiction in terms, since an infinite possibility, known as such, presupposes, demands, and requires the existence of a Knower adequate to such knowledge, which Knower can only be that "infinite unity of conscious thought previously posited." Similarly with finitude. To know that you are finite is, Royce argues, precisely to know yourself as subject to illusion, and hence to know yourself and your thought as included in that wider truth encompassing every illusion. Deny that wider truth and illusion vanishes. Deny the infinite and the finite loses all meaning. Deny actuality and possibility itself is no more.

III

In the autumn of 1889, at the urging of a friend, Royce undertook to prepare a series of lectures on the history of modern philosophy from Spinoza to the rise of evolution. To this end it was necessary that he restudy his predecessors in the Idealist tradition. Evidently, they reminded him of that aspect of the Absolute which he had hitherto ignored, for in the lectures as published [10] the transition from that noetic monism outlined above to a genuinely ontological monism is already accomplished. Where earlier he had thought it sufficient to identify the Absolute with Infinite Thought, he now defines it as Infinite Being. Knowing now is Being manifest as Self,

> the problem-solver, the complete thinker, the one who knows what we mean even when we are most confused and ignorant, the one who includes us, who has the world present to himself in unity, before whom all past and future truth, all distant and dark truth is clear in one eternal moment, to whom far and forgot is near, who thinks of the whole of nature, and in whom are all things, the Logos, the world-possessor . . .[11]

What had brought him to this new expression of the Absolute, he does not tell us, presumably because he sees no basic difference between this and his earlier view. He does remark his awareness of the need to "enrich" the notion of the One, but that this enrichment is anything more than a development of the implications of the position established in *The Religious Aspect of Philosophy*, he is at pains to deny.

> Our whole idealistic analysis . . . from the beginning . . . has been to the effect that facts must be facts for somebody, and can't be

facts for nobody, and that bare possibilities are really impossible. Hence whoever believes, whether truly or falsely, about objects beyond the moment of his belief, is an organic part of a reflective and conscious larger self that has those objects immediately present to itself, and has them in organic relation with the erring or truthful momentary self that believes.[12]

The Absolute is organic Self. How is it, then, that science has failed to see this? Because, answers Royce, it is none of its business to do or to have done so. With the private elements of our experience science is not concerned; no more is its province the private life of the Absolute. Its business is with the permanent, the public, and the universal. Its world is what can be described. Even psychology and psychiatry, for all their profession of interest in the self, treat only of that self which can be objectively specified. Their task, like that of every science, stops short of that appreciation which is the essence of the life of self as such. "Appreciation," this, if Royce is right, is the word and the world which will lead us beyond the limitations of science to the recognition of Reality as absolute, infinite, organic Self.

The difficulty, as Royce himself points out, is that the merely appreciable as such is, in our temporal world, notoriously fleeting. The least fact of nature exemplifies a permanence no emotion, however noble it may be, can ever claim. Were eternity not a real possibility, the transience of all earthly values must lead the philosopher, as it has led so many poets, to despair. Appreciation, then, insofar as it is of eternal significance, "must not be the appreciations of *merely* temporal and transient beings, but of some being that himself does not live in moments, as we mortals on earth do, but that appreciates in eternity, or that shares in such an eternal appreciation." [13] Thus a "World of Appreciation," if such there be,

would be a world such as the organic Self in his wholeness might have present to him at a glance, or such as the community of conceived spiritual mind-readers might share. It would be a world whose Universals were of the type that Hegel defined. It might be free from the type of necessity that our order of nature possesses. It might be a world altogether inspired by appreciative ideals; and yet it would be a world of objective truth, for each individual in it, each conscious moment of it, would find the others as outer and yet not foreign facts.[14]

Does such a world actually exist? The fact that we communicate with each other, thinks Royce, bears witness that it must.

> If I cannot really communicate with my neighbor, and think of meanings that are like his, there is no truth in any of our descriptions. Without the multitude of genuinely interrelated experiences, no true similarities, no describable universality of experience; without the facts of appreciation, no laws of description; without the cloud of witnesses, no abstract and epitome of the common truth to which they can bear witness. Destroy the organic and appreciable unity of the world of appreciative beings, and the describable objects all vanish . . . The world of science, then, *presupposes the world of spiritual oneness;* the unity of the Self is through and through His Own, and is in so far appreciative.[15]

As error implies its encompassing truth, so, he believes, does the World of Description imply that World of Appreciation which is the Absolute appreciative of all values. In short, the true world, "the deeper reality," is "the system of the thoughts of the Logos." [16] What men call true, the world of nature and the universe of stars in empty space, is simply "show," the appearance of a reality indescribable by the methods of science. "If we could grasp the whole truth at a glance, as the Logos does, we should see what now is dark to us, namely, why and how the world of appreciation, when viewed under the conditions of our finite experience, has thus to seem a world of matter in motion. As it is, however, we already know that the world of matter in motion is simply an external aspect of the true and appreciable world." [17] That is to say, we know already that there is nothing dead in nature, for if the descriptive is but the external aspect of the appreciative, then it must be that even inorganic nature has its own inner and appreciable aspect. Nor is this all. "We have, indeed," Royce insists,

> a perfect right thus to say that the world of the stars is, like the brains of our friends, the well-founded show in space and time of an appreciative consciousness, and that the unity of the laws of physical nature is the outer aspect of some deep spiritual unity of

will and plan in the world. We have a right to interpret this unity, in hypothetical forms, as well as we are able. Only we must not say that this will and plan are in any physical sense the causes of our show-world. On the contrary, all physical causation is itself part of the show, in so far as the show is describable.[18]

The Absolute does not create the world. He contains it.

IV

Theologically speaking, Royce's Address to the Philosophical Union of the University of California,[19] together with its sequel the Supplementary Essay in reply to his critics, is the most significant of his many works. True, the argument as formulated five years later in his two volumes *The World and the Individual* is much more elaborately worked out, but for all of that it is neither as precise nor as directly to the point as that of the Essay and Address, and this for the simple reason that in these articles Royce is not primarily concerned with general problems raised and resolved by himself but with specific issues and objections posed by others. His answers to them are presupposed throughout his later writings. On their theological validity his case depends and rests.

To the conception of God as already stated, the Address itself has little to add. Now, as before, God is regarded as possessing to the full all logically possible knowledge, which knowledge, as Royce continues to teach, implies a Being "conceived as essentially world-possessing." The conception remains panentheistic. There is an Absolute Experience, endless in its variety, "related to our experience as an organic whole to its own fragments." [20] To prove it the argument from error is reiterated, as is the notion that "every *if* implies an *is.*" In sum, "God is [still] known as Thought fulfilled; as Experience absolutely organized, so as to have one ideal unity of meaning; as Truth transparent to itself; as Life in absolute accordance with idea; as Selfhood eternally obtained. And all this the Absolute is in concrete unity, not in mere variety." [21]

The Absolute exists. This, Royce's first critic, Professor Sidney Mezes, is not disposed to deny. But is the Absolute—God? That he doubts. For consider what it is that Royce has proved. He has shown, Mezes believes, that the contents of the Absolute consist "of the outer world of science, of your present feelings, thoughts, puzzles, and aspirations, and, in addition, of the answers to your present puzzles and the satisfaction of your present aspirations." [22] What he has not shown is that the Ultimate Being which encompasses all these is a spiritual being, i.e., a being of that worth and dignity commonly ascribed to God. He has argued that the Absolute is eternally complete, and he has claimed that as such it is moral since in it all error and immorality are overcome by truth and goodness. But are completeness and goodness compatible? Mezes does not think so. Goodness implies progress and the chance to grow in worth.

> The very life of morality is toil, struggle, *achievement;* we must *overcome* difficulties; the stream of morality must rise higher than its source. Take progress away, and you destroy morality. This, after all, is very obvious, nor would I be understood to say that Professor Royce denies this. On the contrary, he is at considerable pains to assert and illustrate it . . . But I venture to suggest that Goodness *requires* progress, and of the whole. That there is progress in *bits* of the Inclusive Self, Professor Royce does maintain; but if the Inclusive Self is to be moral, he must be in his *totality* progressive. The *whole* of him must advance without limitation towards some goal.[23]

No goal, no God; that, if Mezes is right, is the sum and substance of the matter. Granted the Absolute exists, it does not follow that It is He whom men call God, for God is Good, and Goodness is quite destitute of consistency with Completeness.

That Royce has failed to establish the Absolute as God, Professor George Holmes Howison agrees. But neither, he thinks, has Mezes, for both are guilty of the same mistake; both fail to take account of the difference in kind between Creator and creature. It makes no difference whether or not the Absolute is conceived as growing in goodness through time. Whether growing or complete, the Absolute is Reality. Neither conception provides adequately for a *public* of thinkers, a *manifold* of selves.

> If the Infinite Self *includes* us all, and all our experiences,—sensations and sins, as well as the rest,—in the unity of one life, and

includes us and them *directly;* if there is but one and the same final Self for us each and all; then, with a literalness indeed appalling, He is we, and we are He; nay, He is I, and I am He. And I think it will appear later, from the nature of the argument by which the Absolute Reality as Absolute Experience is reached, that the exact and direct way of stating the case is baldly: *I am He.* Now if we read the conception in the first way, what becomes of our ethical independence?—what, of our *personal* reality, our righteous *i.e.* reasonable responsibility—responsibility to which we *ought* to be held? Is not He the sole real *agent?* Are we anything but the steadfast and changeless modes of his eternal thinking and perceiving? Or, if we read the conception in the second way, what becomes of *Him?* Then, surely, He is but another name for *me;* or, for any one of *you,* if you will. And how can there be talk of a Moral Order, since there is but a single mind in the case?—we cannot legitimately call that mind a *person.*[24]

Whatever logic may say, our moral sense, Howison insists, must rebel against an Idealism which reduces the finite individual to naught. Instinct, not to mention common sense, simply will not allow that all we are is what the Absolute is. "It is impossible for the religious reason to accept this, no matter what the apparently philosophical reason may say in its behalf. In that fealty which is the true 'substance of things hoped for,' the religious reason firmly avers there must be some flaw in such philosophising, and in the name of *all* reason, protests against the claim that this conception of God is 'the inevitable outcome of a reflective philosophy.' " [25]

Royce saw no flaw, perhaps because there was none. Nonetheless, he was disturbed by Howison's implication that his conception of the Absolute was like that of a night in which all cows are black. There was, he thought, room enough in his conception for ethical individuality. The problem was—to prove it. A year later opportunity, in the form of an invitation from the Philosophical Union to put on record his replies to his critics, knocked, and he responded with a supplementary essay on The Absolute and the Individual.

It begins, as ought every inquiry into the problem of the Many and the One, with the most fundamental of all philosophical questions: What is Real? Common sense tells us that it is the world outside our eyes, the world we cannot wish or think away. Something there is that is independent of each and all of us. To this conviction our consciousness bears witness; on it Realism is founded. Is Realism true? Common sense does not doubt it, and neither, when all is said and done, do most philosophers including, Royce believes, Professor Howison. Idealism, of course, must and does deny that *anything* is independent of that Absolute which is for it the Real. To some extent, therefore, it must and does contradict the common sense of consciousness. Obviously, then, if Realism is true, Idealism must be false; since it is not, Realism must be, as Royce thinks it is, refutable.

Take, for instance, this book: you see black on white, plus a certain shape; you feel a smooth hardness; perhaps you smell a faint papery odor. If asked to explain how it is that you have come to have these sensations, you would cite the object (book) in front of you as their cause. Might it be that you are dreaming, that the book is not really there? But no, you check your sensations again; they compel the conclusion—here is an independent object. Does it vanish when you turn your attention from it? You think not. You put down the book and leave the room; you return and here it is just as and where you left it. The independence is a fact. For all that you may sympathize with Royce, your experience has confirmed and justified the Realist point of view. Or has it?

Consider the situation further: you have assumed a cause, the book (call it x), of your sensations, the effect (call it p). In other words, you have assumed the existence of a relation of cause and effect (call it R). Now, asks Royce,

What do you *mean* by this relation R? I care not how you know that such a relation is necessary, or must exist. This your knowledge may be a human convention or a primal 'intuition.' That here concerns us not. What I ask is, how you express to your mind the *nature* of this relation R, whatever it is, and wherever it may exist or be known to exist. Do you or do you not mean, by this relation R, a relation which you at once conceive as capable of being presented to you in some possible experience? You say: 'the relation is real.' You mean something by the assertion, and something said to be well known to you. For the relation R is by hypothesis especially clear to you. You are so sure of it that you use it to prove the presence of that otherwise unknowable and transcendent x; and you define x as that which stands in the relation R to any fact *p* of our experience. Is not, then, this relation R clear to you just because, however it is supposed to be realized, a possible experience could present to you the known situation that the relation expresses? . . . Now, if this be true, how can *p,* which is a fact of experience, be viewed as standing in a certain relation R (which also is, by hypothesis, a fact of a *possible* experience) to something, *x,* whose very nature is that it is no fact of any possible experience, being a reality that is utterly transcendent? [26]

The answer is, Royce argues, that it cannot, for surely it would be absurd to say that "contents of experience (the sensations) stand in a known and clear relation (of cause and effect), that itself is, as such, an object of possible experience, to something (the book) that is to be expressly defined as no object of any possible experience whatever." [27] Obviously, then, if the relation R between the book *x* and your sensations *p* of it is, as such, an object of a possible experience, then the terms of that relation, i.e., the book and the sensations (*x* and *p*), must be so too!

Nor, Royce adds, is this conclusion to be escaped by positing the relation R as being itself something transcendent.

One asks you, again: What evidence can you give for this transcendent and unexperienced existence, beyond consciousness, of R,— say, of causation, or of some other form of explanatory relation? Afresh you must answer, if you still cling to the present line of argument: 'Because the facts of experience demand, for their explanation, the existence of some such transcendent relation to transcendent realities.' But this new demand for explanation introduces a new relation, R', between the facts of experience, *p,*[28] and the first relation R, which was to be that relation to *x* whereby they were explained. All our questions as to R now recur as to R', the new mediator that is to bring us to the assumption of R.[29]

The infinite regress has begun. For, concludes Royce, if you hold the new mediator R' transcendent, then you are obliged to introduce still another relation R" in order to explain R', and after that another, R''', to explain R", and so on to infinity. In sum:

If, by saying that *an experience, p, needs an explanation in the existence of some fact x, which stands to p in the relation* R, one refers to a relation R identical with an already known and experienced relation, one inevitably implies the assertion: 'If the fact *p* were properly known, it would be experienced as in the relation R to *x';* and hereupon *x,* as well as *p,* must be viewed as the object or content of a possible experience. Thus *x* ceases to be anything that we have so far regarded as a transcendent (independent) object. But if one regards the relation R itself as a transcendent relation, a new mediating relation, R', is needed to make valid any argument for the transcendent reality of the first relation R; and an infinite regress becomes necessary.[30]

The unknown, known as such, is not, in fact, unknown. This having been established, the first stage of the refutation of Realism is complete.

The second starts with the claim of the realist to have evaded the onus of stage one by accepting its conclusion. Granted that *x* is not a something unknown or independent, but is rather a "possible experience," it does not follow from this that *x* is not transcendent. On the contrary, if this as yet unexperienced "possible experience" is, as Royce himself maintains, a real possibility, then it must be transcendent since "transcendent" *means* that which is real but unexperienced. Is Realism hereby re-established? As against that half—or subjective idealism which contents itself with the claim to have reduced all objects to states of private experience, the answer, Royce concedes, is—yes. As against Absolute Idealism, however, the realist, as Royce portrays him, has no case. Indeed, his Realism, properly understood, turns right around into Idealism!

The realist asserts that when one says: 'A given experience is possible, but not here presented,' one inevitably holds that there is fact, both beyond the range of the fragmentary experience that is here and now present, and beyond the range of the bare assertion of the possibility itself. The realist is right. On the other hand, the half-idealist of our first statement of the case is right in maintaining that as soon as you define the beyond, and tell what you mean by it, you cannot make its nature incongruous with the conception 'content of experience,' present or possible. The solution of the antimony lies in asserting that *the beyond is itself content of an actual experience,* the experience to which the beyond is presented being in such intimate relation to the experience which asserts the possibility, that both must be viewed as aspects of one whole, fragments of one organization. The realist, in so far as he is opposed to the half-idealist, is merely a thoroughgoing idealist who does not know his own mind. He rejects bare possibilities, in favour of something beyond them which is their ground. He is right. Only, this beyond is the Concrete Whole of an Absolute Experience, wherein the thoughts of all the possibilities of experience get their right interpretation, their just confirmation, or their refutation,—in a word, their fulfillment.[31]

It is important that you be clear in your mind as to just what Royce is claiming in this passage, the more so since most philosophers themselves habitually misconstrue this Absolute Idealism. Notice that he is not denying that there is transcendence. This book, he would say, is really there—outside your eyes and hands. The finite individuals about whom Professor Howison is so concerned are really there. The point is that they, yourself, the book, and every other object of possible experience all fall *within* the purview of the Absolute. "I agree," says Royce, "that Individuality is a fact. I agree that it is an ethical fact. I agree that the fact of other individuality than mine is to me, *in my private capacity,* something transcendent. . . .

But just as past and present, from an idealistic point of view, are fragments of the eternal Now,—of the Absolute Experience,—so the fact of the relative finite isolation of individuals is a real fact in so far as the Absolute Experience finds it to be such.[32]

Transcendent—yes, independent—no. Grant this distinction, and the second stage of the refutation is accomplished.

The third and last follows, on Royce's finding, from our recognition of the true implication of the one argument remaining to the realist. This is the argument from sameness, and according to Royce it runs thus:

The sameness of the objects of experience, in so far as these objects can be thought of at various times, can be referred to by various subjects, can be objects for many points of view, demands that at least the relations whereby this same reference is secured, if not the facts themselves to which reference is made, should transcend the stream of experience itself, and should be really external to it. Into the stream of experience, as into the flux of Heraclitus, nobody descends twice at the same point. If, however, the sameness of reference is still possible, whereby many experiences bear upon, many thoughts portray, the same content of fact, existent beyond them all, then the relations of reference, if not the facts referred to, must be real beyond all experience.[33]

And so they must, if "all experience" is taken to mean the sum of finite experience. If, however, it means what it says, then the argument is unintelligible, since a relation of reference known to no one could not, by definition, exist as a relation. "To suppose *such* a relation objectively realized without a transcendent objective unity of consciousness in which it is realized, is to suppose a question answered without an answer being given, a wish fulfilled without any concrete fact of fulfillment. In brief, an objective relation of meaning or reference, existing apart from any unity of consciousness, is precisely like an unfelt pain or an undesired object of desire." [34]

To be real a relation of reference must be such for somebody, and in the last analysis that somebody, thinks Royce, must be the Absolute. "For if not, the concept of Reality has no meaning, philosophy has served us no whit, and we are yet in our sins." [35] In other words, "all this Realism, when duly considered, becomes either Absolute Idealism or nothing." [36] To have recognized this, Royce believes, is already to have accounted for the essence of Howison's objection, since if Realism as such is untenable, so must be any objection based upon it, and that Howison, for all his protestations to the contrary, is, as regards his theory of individuality, a realist, Royce is convinced. The existence of the Absolute, then, is not to be refuted by any emotional appeal to the religious reason or moral sense of independent finite individuals, for none such exist. What does exist is the manifold of finite selves within the Infinite Self. What does exist is individuals encompassed by The Individual.

The Absolute is an Individual, and so presumably are you, and so am I. What, then, is it that makes us each the individuals we are? What is it that individuates? How is it that we who live and move and have our being in the Absolute Individual are not, as Howison claims, swallowed up in Him; or, if we are truly individual, how is it that He is not reducible to us? As the refutation of Realism has constituted the negative argument for Absolute Idealism, so do the answers to these questions comprise the positive argument.

Ask common sense what an individual is, and the answer is that it is just this unique composition of matter presented to the senses as this particular body occupying this localized region of space. Ask common sense how it knows that this body is unique, and the answer is: "it is a fact." But is it? Certainly, mere experience cannot assure us that the object present to our senses is *unique,* for what experience really presents is simply a something particularized in space and time. Perhaps, then, it is our thought of the object that supplies the element of uniqueness? "But, now," asks Royce, "how could one define an idea so as to forbid any multiple exemplification? To define is to specify, but not to individualize. Define a man of such shape, size, colour, eyes, hair, 'finger-prints,' feeling, knowledge, and fortune. You have only defined a type. That this type has but one exemplification, you must leave to experience to prove." [37] But if thought must appeal to experience, and experience is incapable of grasping the unique, what is it that individuates? Divine and human love, answers Royce:

> Man individuates the objects of his knowledge because he is an ethical being. God individuates the objects of his own world and knows them as individuals for no other reason. This will be my own thesis. In short, to use familiar but still not unphilosophical terms, I propose briefly to show that the Principle of Individuation, in us as in reality, is identical with the principle that has sometimes been called Will, and sometimes Love. Our human love is a good name for what first individuates for us our universe of known objects. We have good reason for saying that it is the Divine Love which individuates the real world wherein the Divine Omniscience is fulfilled.[38]

Exactly what this "good reason" is, unfortunately his exposition never does make fully clear. The Divine Omniscience must, he is sure, involve other attributes than Omniscience alone. "As a fact, the conception of an experience wherein an absolute system of ideas gets a fulfillment, and wherein all truth forms the content of a single whole moment, demands, for its own completion, the presence of a factor whereby the Individual Whole of the Absolute Moment gets a more positive definition than we have yet given it." [39] This factor is will, and as it pervades our whole being, so also, he feels, must it pervade that of the Absolute. In brief, "The unity of the Absolute consciousness involves immediate data, fulfillment of ideas in these data, consciousness of the adequacy of this fulfillment, and Will, whereby not merely this adequacy is secured in general, but also the adequacy is concretely secured in one whole and single content of the total experience." [40] But if Will, then Love, otherwise Will has no motive. Having thus established, to his own satisfaction if not that of his critics, that the Absolute is Divine Love, it only remains to show how Love functions to individuate and "the circle of the argument is complete."

Unfortunately, at this point in his account Royce is at his vaguest. Human love, he maintains, tends to individuate both lover and loved, the more so as the loved becomes the lover's exclusive interest and passion. Thus, for instance, does the mother's all-enfolding love for her infant individuate them both, as does your love of God tend to individuate you as a moral self and He as a Person. As for those who neither love nor are loved enough to put on individuality of their own, they, he seems to suggest, become such only as they partake of the Divine Love, for ultimately it is the Absolute (God) alone who is and guarantees the individual.

But if so, is not Howison right when he says that all Royce's position amounts to in the end is *I am He?* Royce will not concede it. We are, it is true, what God is; still, were we not ourselves, God would be less than He is. "For so the individual can say: Without just my unique experience in its wholeness, and in its meaning as a totality of life progressively fulfilling an individual ideal, God's life would be incomplete; or, in other words, God would not be God." [41] My experience is at once identically a part of God's experience, that, he holds, we can and should admit. "On the other hand, I insist that this individual experience . . . is . . . when metaphysically viewed, a *unique* experience, and consequently a unique constituent of the Divine life, nowhere else capable of being represented in God's universe, and therefore metaphysically necessary to the fulfillment of God's own life." [42] The difficulty is, now as before, wherein to locate the source of this uniqueness. When all is said and done, Royce's answer is—God's moral will: ". . . the finite individuals are as real as the moral order requires or permits them to be." [43] We end, then, by going round in circles. I am an individual because God wills it; since God wills it, it must be that he needs me to complete his life; hence I am unique. Is it really so? Howison will not admit it, but then he has no other defence to offer against Royce's refutation of his (Howison's) moral realism than to deny that his view of individuals is, in fact, realistic. Mezes is reluctant to accept it, but for the present he has nothing to offer by way of rebuttal. Nor, as it turned out, has anybody else then or since.

V

By the end of the Nineties Royce was riding high. His books had established his position as the leader of American idealism. At Harvard he was set for life. All that he lacked was European recognition, and that came in 1898 in the form of an invitation from the University of Aberdeen to deliver the Gifford Lectures. These lectures, somewhat revised and enlarged, appeared a year later as Volume I of *The World and the Individual*.

His thesis, as before, is that the Individual Being which is the World is that Absolute in which all individual beings live, move, and are real. What is new is the way in which he comes to this conclusion. There are, he now tells us, four historical conceptions of Being, four answers, that is, to the fundamental question: What does it mean to be? The first of these, the answer of Realism, i.e., "the view which, recognizing independent beings as real, lays explicit stress upon their independence as the very essence of their reality," [44] he finds inadequate for the same reasons as advanced in the essay on "The Absolute and the Individual." [45] The second, that of Mysticism, i.e., the view which takes Being to be One alone, is, he thinks, almost as unsatisfactory, for in denying any reality to the finite or the many it ends by denying any content to the Absolute itself.

Our result, in case of the mystic, is accordingly very simple. To the realist we formerly said: Your ideas are Independent Beings as surely as their objects are such. Hence your world is rent in twain, and you cannot put it together again. To the mystic we now say: Your Absolute is defined merely as the goal of the finite search. That it is such a goal, this alone, according to your own hypothesis, distinguishes it from mere nothing, for to save the unity of Being, you have deprived it of all other characters than this. Therefore, since your Absolute is only a goal, an attainment, and is naught else, its sole meaning is due to your process of search . . .[46]

Like Realism's independent Being, it is an abstraction which upon analysis is seen to dissolve into a Nothing. As Realism has pointed to its opposite—Mysticism—so the defect of the latter suggests that the answer to the question of Being lies somewhere between the two.

This middle ground, as Royce surveys it, is the terrain of the third historical conception of Being, Critical Rationalism, i.e., the view which holds that to be real means to be valid. This idea of the real as that to which my idea, if valid, corresponds has had many distinguished adherents, among them Augustine, Aquinas, and Kant. Royce himself finds no wrong in it—as far as it goes. The difficulty is that it does not go far enough.

Ask me how I discover, in a concrete case, the validity of my idea, how I make it out for certain that a given experience is possible; and then I have to answer, 'By actual experience alone.' When I say then, 'A given idea is certainly valid,' I primarily mean merely, 'A given idea is fulfilled in actual present experience.' But if you ask me what I regard as the range of possible experience, and of the truth of ideas, then I can only say that the range of valid possible experience is viewed by me as infinitely more extended than my actual human experience. . . . Now what our Third Conception so far fails to explain to us is precisely the difference between the reality that is to be attributed to the valid truths that we do not get concretely verified in our own experience, and the reality observed by us when we do verify ideas.

In brief, *What is a valid or a determinately possible experience at the moment when it is supposed to be only possible?* What is a valid truth at the moment when nobody verifies its validity? [47]

Since Critical Rationalism affords no answers to these most important questions, it too must give way to that Idealism which, as we have seen, resolves these and all other questions by its hypothesis of an Absolute whose infinite compass guarantees the reality of possibility and insures that the Valid is at once the True. Hereby, we have reached the fourth (Idealist) Conception of Being.

Being, as our Third Conception declared, is what gives true ideas their truth; or in other words, to be real is to be the object of a true idea. We are ready, now that we have defined both object and truth, to assert, as our Fourth and final Conception of Being, this, that *What is, or what is real, is as such the complete embodiment, in individual form and in final fulfillment, of the internal meaning of finite ideas.*[48]

Thus, as regards the answer to the question: What does it mean *to be?* the Fourth, or Roycian, Conception of Being replies: "To be means simply to express, to embody the complete internal meaning of a certain absolute system of ideas," [49] in sum, to be the Absolute.

VI

To be, we have said, means *to fulfil a purpose,* in fact, to fulfil in final, individual expression, the *only* purpose, namely, the Absolute purpose.[50]

Granted that this is so, it remains to remark the nature of this purpose as it bears first upon the moral life, and ultimately upon religion. ". . . We assert that this world which we have been characterizing is a Moral Order. In what sense, and for what reason, do we assert this?" [51] It is, Royce holds, a moral order in the sense that it represents the fulfillment of God's will that good should prevail in eternity. What in time is evil because incomplete is, in eternity, transformed into good by virtue of being taken up into the life of God and thereby made complete. "The moral order of your idealistic world means, then, not that no moral ill can be done, but that, in the temporal order, *every evil deed must somewhere and at some time be atoned for, by some other than the agent, if not by the agent himself,* and that this atonement, this overcoming of the evil deed, will in the end make possible that which in the eternal order is directly manifest, namely, the perfection of the whole." [52] The Whole is good. As Royce has defined it, it could not be otherwise. This, if he is right, is reason enough to characterize the world as a moral order.

Given such a world, man's moral duty is plain. He ought ever to strive to imitate God. As He serves the cause of His community, so ought we to serve the cause of ours. By this, Royce does not mean merely that we should all do good works. Good works are, of course, important; but even more important to Royce's way of thinking is the spirit from which they are done. What is vital is that we should be *loyal* to whatever cause we espouse, for in a world such as that described above, loyalty is the virtue of virtues. Loyalty first to the community, loyalty finally to God in whom all causes find their meaning. Be loyal to loyalty: this, for Royce, is the first and great commandment. Observe it, and all else shall be added unto you.

Could all men be brought to not only believe in the Eternal, but to give their loyalty to God as such, the religious ideal would be a reality, for religion, as Royce defines it, is, in its highest form, *"the interpretation both of the external and of the spirit of loyalty through emotion, and through a fitting activity of the imagination."* [53] Is such a view Christian? Royce believes that it is—if by Christian you mean, as he does, one who consciously serves that "Beloved Community" which is the mystical body of Christ spiritually understood. However, if by Christian you mean one who simply and uncritically pledges allegiance to the doctrines and dogmas of some one of the various institutions of Christianity, then perhaps not. But if Christianity merely means assent to creeds outworn, who then is a Christian? Certainly not the Church Fathers; in their time hardly a dogma had yet been established. Certainly not St. Paul. Nowhere in his epistles does he concern himself with the question of the historicity of Jesus; nor has he anything concrete to say about the doctrine of the Two Natures or the dogma of the Trinity. Do these defects debar us from calling him a Christian? Or rather do they not point up the fact that the heart of Christianity is to be sought elsewhere than in the person of the individual founder. "Now you are the body of Christ and individually members of it," says St. Paul. Just so. And what does this signify? As Royce reads it, simply this: that men shall in community love one another, and in community, through Christ, be saved. Not Jesus then, but our membership in the Beloved Community constitutes the condition of our salvation. "We are saved in and through the community." [54]

> If Christianity, in the future, triumphs, that will be because some active and beloved community comes gradually more and more to take control of human affairs, not because religion has fled to the recesses of any wilderness of the Godhead.[55]

For that way is no man saved.

You may disagree. If so, let it be on the basis of the adequacy of that panentheism out of which this conclusion grows. Is the Roycian version of panentheism adequate *as panentheism?* [56] This depends on how well you judge him to have met the twin criteria against which every species of panentheism must be measured; (a) the cogency of its demonstration of the existence of an Encompassing One, God, or Absolute; (b) the satisfactoriness of its explanation of how the Many in the One yet remain a Many. If William James is right, Royce has failed to meet the first of these criteria; if Howison is correct, he has failed the second. Subsequent American philosophical opinion, siding with neither specifically, has, for the most part, tended to acquiesce in the verdict passed on Royce by his junior colleague, George Santayana:

> There was a voluminous confusion in his thought; some clear principles and ultimate possibilities turned up in it, now presenting one face and now another, like chips carried down a swollen stream; but the most powerful currents were below the surface, and the whole movement was hard to trace.[57]

SUGGESTED READINGS

The original statement of the argument from error is given in the eleventh chapter of *The Religious Aspect of Philosophy* (New York: Harper Torchbooks, paperback, 1958). Follow it, if possible, with the Macmillan edition of *The Conception of God* (New York, 1898). This last, consisting of an address by Royce to the Philosophical Union of the University of California, criticisms of same by Professors Mezes, LeConte, and Howison, and a long supplementary essay (missing from the California edition) in which Royce replies to his critics, is the only one of Royce's books to explore both the pros and the cons of Absolute Idealism, and if you can come by a copy of it (it is out of print and rather rare) read it from start to finish. Idealism as manifested in the works of Royce's great European predecessors is traced out, criticized, and updated in *The Spirit of Modern Philosophy* (New York: George Braziller, 1955). It has been remaindered by the publisher, but your bookseller may still have it in stock. The most thorough statement of the case for and content of Roycian Idealism is *The World and the Individual*, 2 Vols. (New York: Dover Books, paperback, 1959). This, Royce's Gifford Lectures, is generally acknowledged to be his magnum opus, and fortunately it is readily available. Idealism as it applies to ethics and religion is the continuing theme of the later works, *The Philosophy of Loyalty* (New York: Macmillan, 1911), *The Sources of Religious Insight* (New York: Scribner 1912), and *The Problem of Christianity*, 2 Vols. (New York: Macmillan, 1913). The second of these is now available in paperback; the first and last are, unfortunately, long out of print, but most university and some public libraries will have copies. Of the six volumes of essays published during and after Royce's lifetime, none is at present in print, although Liberal Arts Press has announced a paperback edition of the important *Lectures on Modern Idealism* (New Haven: Yale University Press, 1923). Some of this material, however, may be found in the two volumes of selections edited by Stuart Gerry Brown, *The Social Philosophy of Josiah Royce* (Syracuse: Syracuse University Press, 1952). Both are in print.

There are three books about Royce's philosophy, all of them in print. John E. Smith, *Royce's Social Infinite: the community of interpretation* (New York: Liberal Arts Press, 1950), is a careful study of Absolute Idealism as it issues in the idea of the Beloved Community. James Harry Cotton, *Royce on the Human Self* (Cambridge: Harvard University Press, 1954), critically evaluates the Roycian conception of the relation of finite to infinite self. Gabriel Marcel, *Royce's Metaphysics* (Chicago: Henry Regnery, 1956), is a translation of an early work by the famous French Catholic existentialist. Oddly enough, considering Royce's high place in the history of American philosophy, there is no biography.

REFERENCES

1. The concluding sentence of Royce's doctoral dissertation, "Of the Interdependence of the Principles of Knowledge . . . Elements of Episte-

mology," handwritten manuscript (microfilm); original in the Johns Hopkins University Library.

2. *The World and the Individual,* Second Series (New York: Dover Books, 1959), pp. 336-37. Hereafter cited as WI II.

3. *Pragmatism,* p. 150.

4. Ibid., pp. 150-51.

5. *The Religious Aspect of Philosophy* (Boston: Houghton Mifflin, 1885), pp. 375-76. Royce's italics.

6. Ibid., p. 425.

7. Ibid., p. 393.

8. Ibid., p. 433.

9. Ibid., p. 424. Royce's italics.

10. *The Spirit of Modern Philosophy* (New York: George Braziller, 1955).

11. Ibid., p. 374.

12. Ibid., pp. 377-78.

13. Ibid., p. 393.

14. Ibid., p. 397.

15. Ibid., p. 410. Royce's italics.

16. Ibid., p. 415.

17. Ibid., pp. 416-17.

18. Ibid., pp. 421-22.

19. Delivered at Berkeley, August 30th, 1895; published later with the Supplementary Essay and criticisms and comments by Professors Sidney Mezes, Joseph LeConte, and George Holmes Howison, under the title *The Conception of God* (New York: Macmillan, 1898). Hereafter cited as CG.

20. CG, p. 44.

21. Ibid., pp. 45-46.

22. Ibid., p. 58.

23. Ibid., p. 63. Mezes' italics.

24. Ibid., pp. 98-99. Howison's italics.

25. Ibid., p. 123.

26. Ibid., pp. 157-58.

27. Ibid., p. 158.

28. Royce's phrasing is "a, b, c, etc.," which represents the instances of the type, *p.*

29. CG, p. 159.

30. Ibid., p. 151.

31. Ibid., p. 168.

32. Ibid., p. 170.

33. Ibid., pp. 174-75.

34. Ibid., p. 179.

35. Ibid., p. 181.

36. Ibid.

37. Ibid., p. 248.

38. Ibid., p. 259.

39. Ibid., p. 186.

40. Ibid., pp. 212-13.

41. Ibid., p. 293.

42. Ibid.

43. Ibid., p. 337.

44. *The World and the Individual, First Series* (New York: Dover Books, 1959), p. 62.

45. Ibid., p. 143.

46. Ibid., p. 194.

47. Ibid., pp. 259-60. Royce's italics.

48. Ibid., p. 339. Royce's italics.

49. Ibid., p. 36.

50. WI II, p. 335.

51. Ibid., p. 337.

52. Ibid., p. 368. Royce's italics.

53. *The Philosophy of Loyalty* (New York: Macmillan, 1908), p. 377. Royce's italics.

54. *The Problem of Christianity*, Vol. II (New York: Macmillan, 1913), p. 390.

55. Ibid., Vol. I, p. 400.

56. Whether or not panentheism *as such* is adequate is a question whose answer would carry us far beyond the concerns of our present subject. I personally believe that it is. For my reasons, see my "Prolegomena to a Modern Philosophical Theism," *Tulane Studies in Philosophy*, Vol. 5 (1956), pp. 87-93, and articles on the panentheistic philosophies of Iqbal (*Review of Metaphysics*, Vol. 9, pp. 681-99); Hegel (*Philosophy*, Vol. 31, pp. 36-54), and (*Tulane Studies in Philosophy*, Vol. 9, pp. 134-64); Karl Heim (*Concordia Theological Monthly*, Vol. 30, pp. 824-37); and Whitehead (*Modern Schoolman*, Vol. 11, pp. 56-74).

57. *Character and Opinion in the United States* (Garden City: Doubleday Anchor Books, 1960), p. 79.

XXI

The Poet of Animal Faith

GEORGE SANTAYANA

"The life of reason as I conceive
it is a mere romance, and the life
of nature a mere fable. . . ." [1]

GEORGE SANTAYANA

George Santayana

APPROPRIATELY ENOUGH, the judgment that Santayana had passed on Royce, Harvard and the American philosophic world passed on Santayana himself. For between their thought there was but this one difference, that what in the one was swollen was, in the other, deceptively clear.

Boston hardly knew what to make of Santayana. He wasn't quite one of them, but on the other hand, he was hardly a foreigner, even granting the fact of Spanish parents and Madrid as a birth-place. After all, his mother had been the widow of a Sturgis, and she saw to it that George and her Sturgis children were reared as proper Bostonians.[2] So he went to Boston Latin and afterwards to Harvard; traveled abroad, mingled with all the best people and, for all his European panache, was, as his onetime student, Baker Brownell, has reported, "no mysterious stranger among [Harvard] students or staff."[3] And yet, no one sensed as well as Santayana himself that he belonged not where he lived.

"This sense of belonging elsewhere, or rather of not belonging where I lived, was," he tells us,

nothing anomalous or unpleasant to me but, as it were, hereditary. My father had done his life-work in a remote colony; my mother had had no home as a child, her first husband had been of one nationality and her second husband of another, and she had always been a stranger, like me, wherever she was. This is rather consonant with my philosophy and may have helped to form it. It is not a thing

I regret. So that my intentional detachability from America is balanced by an equal detachability from every other place.[4]

In 1912 he received a legacy large enough to allow him to live where and do as he would. Intentionally detaching himself from his professorship, he now left America for good. He had forty years still to live, and he would spend all of them in Europe. There the majority of his books were written, and there in 1952, in Rome, he died. Since he had never bothered to become an American citizen, no one could honestly call him even an expatriate. Yet all this notwithstanding, his critics and admirers alike have claimed him as an American philosopher, and he himself has said that it is as an American writer that he must be counted, if he is counted at all.

On the face of it, there are two—and only two—aspects of his philosophy that would seem to justify such a conclusion. Like most Americans he has a healthy respect for common sense.

I think that common sense, in a rough dogged way, is technically sounder than the special schools of philosophy, each of which squints and overlooks half the facts and half the difficulties in its eagerness to find in some detail the key to the whole. I am animated by distrust of all high guesses, and by sympathy with the old prejudices and workaday opinions of mankind: they are ill expressed, but they are well grounded.[5]

Of all these "workaday opinions" none is sounder, he thinks, than that which simply accepts the physical world as it finds it, and sees in common matter the content of everything real.

I do not profess to know what matter is in itself, and feel no confidence in the divination of those *esprits forts* who, leading a life of vice, thought the universe must be composed of nothing but dice and billiard-balls. I wait for the men of science to tell me what matter is, in so far as they can discover it, and am not at all surprised or troubled at the abstractness and vagueness of their ultimate conceptions: how should our notions of things so remote from the scale and scope of our senses be anything but schematic? But whatever matter may be, I call it matter boldly, as I call my acquaintances Smith and Jones without knowing their secrets: Whatever it may be, it must present the aspects and undergo the motions of the gross objects that fill the world.[6]

Materialism and common sense—these two are the foundation of that introduction to a system of philosophy which is Santayana's *Scepticism and Animal Faith*.

Strictly speaking, what is set forth in its pages is not a *system* at all—at least in the ordinary meaning of the term. It is no part of Santayana's intention to describe a world-view or make of this multiverse a universe. Modesty, no less than common sense, must forbid any such grandiosity.

I do not pretend to place myself at the heart of the universe nor at its origin, nor to draw its periphery. I would lay siege to the truth only as animal exploration and fancy may do so, first from one quarter and then from another, expecting the reality to be not simpler than my experience of it, but far more extensive and complex. I stand in philosophy exactly where I stand in daily life; I should not be honest otherwise. I accept the same miscellaneous witnesses, bow to the same obvious facts, make conjectures no less instinctively, and admit the same encircling ignorance.

My system, accordingly, is *no system of the universe*. The Realms of Being of which I speak are not parts of a cosmos, nor one great cosmos together: they are only kinds or categories of things which I find conspicuously different and worth distinguishing, at least in my own thoughts.[7]

Of these several kinds of things, the most elemental is—Substance, meaning by this term nothing metaphysical but rather the various stuffs of the world, met in action. Substance is, then, the self-existent, the material object independent of anyone's awareness of it, whatever is—out there.

What is independent of knowledge is substance, in that it has a place, movement, origin, and destiny of its own, no matter what I may think or fail to think about it. This self-existence is what the name object jeopardises, and what the name substance indicates and asserts. . . .

Substances are called things when found cut up into fragments which move together and are recognizable individually; and things are called substances when their diffuse and qualitative existence is thought of rather than their spatial limits. Flour is a substance and a loaf of bread is a thing; but there is nothing metaphysical about flour, nor is there any difference of physical status between a thing and the substance of it.[8]

I hold in hand this loaf of bread, and perhaps I bite it; what knowledge is involved here? Common sense would have it that I know what I now experience—this object as a loaf of bread. Reflection tells me that what I really know are those qualities, brownness, hardness, roundness, etc., which the loaf exhibits to my five senses. Scepticism suggests that the qualities which my senses discover perhaps do not exist at all, since the *existence* of a loaf of bread is not included in the congeries of qualities constituting the datum immediately present. And scepticism, according to Santayana, is right, for the beginning of wisdom is the recognition that nothing given exists.

That is to say, nothing given exists—merely because it is given. "The obvious is only the apparent," [9] and that this is so is evidenced by the fact that we never think to insist: this loaf that appears, exists. "This fact, the existence of the intuition (of the loaf), would not be asserted until the appearance ceased to be actual, and was viewed from the outside, as something that presumably had occurred, or would occur, or was occurring elsewhere. In such an external view there might be truth or error; not so in each appearance taken in itself, because in itself and as a whole each is a pure appearance and bears witness to nothing further." [10]

Hence an important conclusion which at first seems paradoxical but which reflection will support; namely, that the notion that the datum (the loaf perceived) exists is unmeaning, and if insisted upon is false. That which exists is the fact that the datum is given at that particular moment and crisis in the universe; the intuition, not the datum, is the fact which occurs; and this fact, if known at all, must be asserted at some other moment by an adventurous belief which may be true or false. That which is certain and given, on the contrary, is something of which existence cannot be predicated, and which, until it is used as a description of something else, cannot be either false or true.[11]

If there is any existence at all, presence to consciousness is neither necessary nor sufficient to render it an existence.[12]

Notice that Santayana is not saying that nothing exists, only that nothing *given* exists. Obviously, the facts and events of nature exist, but the fact and event independent of my awareness of it is not at all the same thing as the fact or event imaged in my intuition.

The animal mind treats its data as facts, or as signs of facts, but the animal mind is full of the rashest presumptions, positing time, change, a particular station in the midst of events yielding a particular perspective of those events, and the flux of all nature precipitating that experience at that place. None of these posited objects is a datum in which a sceptic could rest. Indeed, existence or fact, in the sense which I give to these words, cannot be a datum at all, because existence involves external relations and actual (not merely specious) flux: whereas, however complex a datum may be, with no matter what perspectives opening within it, it must be embraced in a single stroke of apperception, and nothing outside it can belong to it at all. The datum is a pure image; it is essentially illusory and unsubstantial, however thunderous its sound or keen its edge, or however normal and significant its presence may be.[13]

"If we refuse to bow to the yoke of animal faith, we can find in pure intuition no evidence of any existence whatsoever." [14]

What we do find is something which for all its immateriality is at once infinitely richer and more precious; what we intuit is— essence. No word in Santayana's vocabulary has given his critics more trouble; no term of his system is harder to define. As he himself describes it, the realm of essence

is not peopled by choice forms or magic powers. It is simply the unwritten catalogue, prosaic and infinite, of all the characters possessed by such things as happen to exist, together with the characters which all different things would possess if they existed. It is the sum of mentionable objects, of terms about which, or in which, something might be said.[15]

In short, essences are whatever comes to mind in fancy or through sense. Ideas are essences, and so are symbols; qualities are essences, and dreams also. In fact, "the realm of essence . . . is absolutely infinite, and contains images of all the events that any existing world could enact, or that all possible worlds could enact together." [16] Since essences do not exist (they are the given, remember, and nothing *given* exists), they suffer no infection of temporality nor are they localizable in space; each is at once eternally everywhere and nowhere. Finally, each is real.

This is hard doctrine, and Santayana does not make it any easier to understand by denying to this realm of essence all metaphysical status. Essences are real, but they are not, like Plato's Forms, the only truly real in which all things participate.

> My doctrine lends no countenance to the human presumption that whatsoever man notices or names or loves ought to be more deeply seated in reality or more permanent than what he ignores or despises. The good is a great magnet over discourse and imagination, and therefore rightly rules the Platonic world, which is that of moral philosophy only; but this good is itself defined and chosen by the humble animal nature of man, demanding to eat and live and love. In the realm of essence this human good has no pre-eminence, and being an essence it has no power. . . . No essence, except temporarily and by accident, is the goal of any natural process, much less its motive power.[17]

On the other hand,

> If there were no purely ideal characters present to intuition yet not existentially a part either of the mind or of the environment, nothing ulterior could ever be imagined, much less truly conceived. Every supposed instance of knowledge would be either a bit of sentience without an object, or an existing entity unrelated to any mind. But an essence given in intuition, being non-existent in itself and by no means the object at that moment intended by the animal in his alertness or pursuit, may become a description of that object. . . . What is given becomes in this manner a sign for what is sought, and a conventional description of it; and the object originally posited by faith and intent in the act of living may be ultimately more and more accurately revealed to belief and to thought. . . . Thus intuition of essences first enables the mind to say something about anything, to think of what is not given, and to be a mind at all.[18]

So it is that the realm of essence intuited enriches the realm of existence known by animal faith and makes possible the discovery of the timeless and supernatural realm of spirit.

Like all of Santayana's realms of being, Spirit is best defined negatively. Thus it is not to be confused with any life force ingredient in substance, nor is it to be identified with any Idealist Absolute growing to consciousness in history, and certainly it is not of the nature of a ghost—holy or otherwise. "Spirit can never be observed as an essence is observed, nor encountered as a thing is encountered. It must be enacted; and the essence of it (for of course it has an essence) can be described only circumstantially, and suggested pregnantly." [19] To Santayana's understanding, it is

> the light of discrimination that marks in that pure Being (substance) differences of essence, of time, of place, of value; a living light ready to fall upon things, as they are spread out in their weight and motion and variety, ready to be lighted up. Spirit is a fountain of clearness, decidedly windblown and spasmodic, and possessing at each moment the natural and historical actuality of an event, not the imputed or specious actuality of a datum. Spirit, in a word, is no phenomenon, not sharing the aesthetic sort of reality proper to essences when given, nor that other sort proper to dynamic and material things; its peculiar sort of reality is to be intelligence in act. Spirit, or the intuitions in which it is realized, accordingly forms a new realm of being, silently implicated in the apparition of essences and in the felt pressure of nature, but requiring the existence of nature to create it, and to call up those essences before it. By spirit essences are transposed into appearances and things into objects of belief. . . .[20]

However misty you may find this definition to be, and plainly it is far from clear, on one point it is clear enough: Spirit, so defined, is a quality of human activity in its natural setting. Its ground is this arbitrary existing world. It might be wondered just how this could be, if spirit truly is, as has been described above, a timeless and supernatural realm. The resolution of the paradox is the realization that the timeless and supernatural signify here only the nonexistent in the sense previously remarked, and not some heavenly world beyond the world of nature. In the language of Santayana, it is nothing other than that "wakefulness of attention," that "light of intuition" which, "when it thoroughly dominates experience, transmutes it into pure flame, and renders it religious or poetical. . . ." [21] In sum, as the realm of essence is the realm of matter transmuted by intuition, so the realm of spirit is the realm of essence transmuted by active mind. Each realm but reveals another facet of that Reality which is all that Nature is, has been, or yet might be. Each marks out still another dimension of that Being which is for Santayana the ultimate principle of unity.

For Santayana, then, the real is this common-sense world of things and selves with whom we live. There is no going behind nature to any other reality, nor is there anything real above it. This universe which science analyzes and poets spiritualize is all that there is. Matter alone exists. How do we know this? According to Santayana, by animal faith alone, for neither experience nor reason can ever disclose to us the existent as it is in itself. We are the prisoners of our senses, and the discrimination of our sensations yields only essence. Essences, however, are real. My idea of the loaf of bread is no less real for lacking physical existence in my mind. The aspirations and enthusiasms of the minds of men may and often do enrich the world for all that they cannot be reduced to mundane materiality. Thus spirit, rising out of substance, touches nature with beauty and reveals man as something more than matter.

Since this system is, on Santayana's own submission, no system of the universe, we should hardly expect to find implied in it any ethical or religious absolutes, and in fact we do not. The moral absolutist, Santayana believes, proclaims nothing but his own intellectual provinciality. "They [the absolutists] may be beautifully virtuous, but they do not understand the world nor their place in it." "Morality is relative." [22]

Ethics, if it is to be a science and not a piece of arbitrary legislation, cannot pronounce it sinful in a serpent to be a serpent; it cannot even accuse a barbarian of loving a wrong life, except in so far as the barbarian is supposed capable of accusing himself of barbarism. If he is a perfect barbarian he will be inwardly, and therefore morally, justified. The notion of a barbarian will then be accepted by him as that of a true man, and will form the basis of whatever rational judgments or policy he attains. It may still seem dreadful to him to be a serpent, as to be a barbarian might seem dreadful to a man inbued with liberal interests. But the degree to which moral science, or the dialectic of will, can condemn any type of life depends on the amount of disruptive contradiction which, at any reflective moment, that life brings under the unity of apperception. The discordant impulses therein confronted will challenge and condemn one another; and the court of reason in which their quarrel is ventilated will have authority to pronounce between them.[23]

This vision of the ethical life as the life of reason he never recants, although in a writing of much later date he pulls back from making reason the sole criterion of the moral life: "Reason alone can be rational, but it does not follow that reason alone is good. The criterion of worth remains always the voice of nature, truly consulted, in the person that speaks." [24]

Not only morality but religion too has its expression in this "voice of nature." To those who would identify the life of nature as divine, Santayana has no objection. We are, he holds, free to view God as we will, and to choose that faith most satisfying to our hearts and our imaginations.

Does not modern philosophy teach that our idea of the so-called real world is also a work of imagination? A religion—for there are other religions than the Christian—simply offers a system of faith different from the vulgar one, or extending beyond it. The question is which imaginative system you will trust. My matured conclusion has been that no system is to be trusted, nor even that of science in any literal or pictorial sense; but all systems may be used and, up to a certain point, trusted as symbols. Science expresses in human terms our dynamic relation to surrounding reality. Philosophies and religions, where they do not misrepresent these same dynamic relations and do not contradict science, express destiny in moral dimensions, in obviously mythical and poetical images: but how else should these moral truths be expressed at all in a traditional or popular fashion? Religions are the great fairy-tales of conscience.[25]

Literally false, they are as true as your imagination cares to make them, and who is to say that the works of the human imagination are worthless? Not Santayana. "What should mind be, if it were not a poetic cry? Mind does not come to repeat the world but to celebrate it." [26] What does it matter that God exists nowhere but in my fancy? Whatever helps my spiritual growth is truth for me; whatever serves to bring about the harmony with nature that my self requires is to me of genuine worth. "That is all my message: that morality and religion are expressions of human nature; that human nature is a biological growth; and finally that spirit, fascinated and tortured, is involved in the process, and asks to be saved." [27]

One seems to hear in all of this an echo—not so faint—of William James. The true is what works; the true is what becomes true —in religion no less than in our daily lives. Is this pragmatic note what Santayana has in mind in telling us that he must be counted an American writer? Possibly. The subtlety of his thought permits no more definite conclusion. Is he right in his assessment of himself as an American? It would, in my opinion, be wrong to deny him the name. All the native elements—pragmatism, materialism, common-sense—are there. If a man's country is where his spirit rises and his influence lies, we must, I think, count Santayana one of us.

SUGGESTED READINGS

Every one of the thirty books that Santayana wrote is of a literary quality to delight the serious reader, and for such as are interested primarily in the man and his style, any one of them will do to begin with. Those seeking the essentials of his thought, however, should read first *Scepticism and Animal Faith* (New York: Dover, paperback, 1955), and then, leisure and inclination permitting, take up the four volumes of its sequel, *The Realms of Being* (New York: Scribner, 1942). *Character and Opinion in the United States* (New York: Doubleday Anchor, paperback, 1960) is Santayana's often caustic reflections on the mind and mores of America, with special attention to the philosophies of his Harvard colleagues, Royce and James. His best known essays are collected in *Winds of Doctrine and Platonism and the Spiritual Life* (New York: Harper, paperback, 1957). *The Last Puritan* (New York: Scribner, paperback, 1960), Santayana's only novel, very long and very philosophical, was a best seller of 1936. A best buy is Irwin Edman's selections from all the works, *The Philosophy of Santayana* (New York: Scribner, 1953).

Not to be confused with this last is P. A. Schilpp, *The Philosophy of George Santayana* (Evanston: Northwestern University Press, 1940). It offers articles covering every phase of Santayana's philosophy, together with the philosopher's reply to his critics, "Apologia Pro Mente Sua," and his autobiography, "A General Confession." Included is a complete bibliography of Santayana's writings up to October, 1940. Of more recent vintage is Richard Butler's excellent study of *The Mind of Santayana* (Chicago: Regnery, 1955). It too provides a good bibliography.

REFERENCES

1. *Scepticism and Animal Faith* (New York: Dover Books, 1955), p. 101. Hereafter cited as SAF.

2. As Santayana tells it, "Her first husband, an American merchant established in Manila, had been the ninth child of Nathaniel Russell Sturgis, of Boston (1779-1856). In Boston, accordingly, her three Sturgis children had numerous relations and a little property, and there she had promised their father to bring them up in case of his death. When this occurred, in 1857, she therefore established herself in Boston. . . ." "A General Confession," in P. A. Schilpp, *The Philosophy of George Santayana* (Evanston: Northwestern University Press, 1940), p. 5. Hereafter cited as Schilpp. In 1862 Mrs. Sturgis while on a visit to Spain married Santayana's father. "He had been an old friend of hers and of her first husband's, and was well aware of her settled plan to educate her children in America. . . . The matter eventually ended in a separation. . . . My mother returned with her Sturgis children to live in the United States and my father and I remained in Spain. Soon, however, this compromise proved unsatisfactory. The education and prospects which my father . . . could offer me in Spain were far from brilliant; and in 1872 he decided to take me to Boston. . . . I was then in my ninth year, having been born on December 16, 1863, and I did not know one word of English." Ibid.

3. Schilpp, p. 35.

4. Ibid., p. 602.

5. SAF, p. v.

6. Ibid., pp. vii-viii.

7. Ibid., pp. v-vi.

8. Ibid., p. 203.

9. Ibid., p. 43.

10. Ibid., pp. 44-45.

11. Ibid., p. 45.

12. Ibid.

13. Ibid., p. 34.

14. Ibid., p. 50.

15. Ibid., p. 77.

16. Ibid., p. 125.

17. Ibid., pp. 78-79.

18. Ibid., pp. 80-82.

19. Ibid., pp. 274-75.

20. Ibid., pp. 273-74.

21. Ibid., pp. 284, 288.

22. Schilpp, p. 562.

23. *The Life of Reason,* Vol. V *Reason in Science* (New York: Scribner, 1906), p. 234.

24. Schilpp, p. 563.
25. Ibid., p. 8.
26. Ibid., p. 29.
27. Ibid., p. 23.

XXII

The Great Dissenter

OLIVER WENDELL HOLMES, JR.

"I say—and I say no longer with
any doubt—that a man may live
greatly in the law as well as
elsewhere; that there as elsewhere
his thought may find its unity in
an infinite perspective; that there
as well as elsewhere he may wreak
himself upon life, may drink the
bitter cup of heroism, may wear his
heart out after the unattainable." [1]

OLIVER WENDELL HOLMES, JR.

XXII

The Great Disaster

Oliver Wendell Holmes

The judicial power of the United States shall be vested in one Supreme Court, and in such inferior courts as the Congress may from time to time ordain and establish. . . . In all cases affecting ambassadors, other public ministers and consuls, and those in which a State shall be party, the Supreme Court shall have original jurisdiction. In all the other cases before mentioned, the Supreme Court shall have appellate jurisdiction, both as to law and fact, with such exceptions, and under such regulations, as the Congress shall make.[2]

IN THAT SYSTEM of checks and balances which is the government of the United States, the Supreme Court, from the time of Chief Justice Marshall on, has reserved to itself the right to review State and Federal laws and to declare null and void any act of Congress or of the several state legislatures which in its opinion contravenes the Constitution. Is it justified in its assumption of such a role? Throughout most of its history the majority on the Court have maintained the affirmative. To their view the Court is, and should be, in effect the guardian of public welfare and morality. Believing this, they have used, and still employ, the power of judicial review in the interest of what they consider the common good. It is no small power they invoke. Indeed, one need only reflect for a moment upon the consequences to date of the Court's 1954 decision outlawing racial segregation in the public schools to see just how powerful an instrument of social policy judicial review can be in the hands of a majority determined to use it for such ends. The public reaction to the decision of the Court in this case is, of course, nothing novel. From the beginning there has existed a school of thought whose conviction, loudly maintained, it is that it is no part of the proper function of the Supreme Court to save the people from themselves. That a majority of nine old men should have the power to nullify the legislative will and set aside the social custom of generations is to the partisans of judicial limitation a scandal. Unfortunately for them, the fact of the matter is that judicial review is firmly established as part of the American system, and it is extremely unlikely that Congress will in the near or distant future take it upon itself to alter the system, for all that the Constitution permits it to do so. If change is to come, then, it will have to come from within; it will have to reflect a change in the disposition of the Court itself. Is such a change to be expected? The answer is that it has been in the making ever since December 8th, 1902, on which day Oliver Wendell Holmes, Jr., newly appointed Associate Justice, walked for the first time into the old Supreme Court Building and took his seat on the Court.

His new "brothers" had not long to wait for an expression of his views on the question of judicial tolerance of legislative acts. Less than a month later, in his opinion for the majority upholding a provision of the California constitution allegedly in violation of the Fourteenth Amendment, he declared the position he was to maintain with but few exceptions throughout his term on the Court.

It is true, no doubt, that neither a state legislature nor a state constitution can interfere arbitrarily with private business or transactions, and that the mere fact that an enactment purports to be for the protection of public safety, health or morals, is not conclusive upon the courts . . . But general propositions do not carry us far. While the courts must exercise a judgment of their own, it by no means is true that every law is void which may seem to the judges who pass upon it excessive, unsuited to its ostensible end, or based upon conceptions of morality with which they disagree. Considerable latitude must be allowed for differences of view, as well as for possible peculiar conditions which this court can know but imperfectly, if at all. Otherwise a constitution, instead of embodying only relatively fundamental rules of right, as generally understood by all English-speaking communities, would become the partisan of a particular set of ethical or economical opinions, which by no means are held *semper ubique et ab omnibus.*[3]

Live and let live, such, in essence, was Holmes' advice to his colleagues, and in the hundreds of cases that he and they would hear over the next thirty years, he would find occasion to repeat that advice time and again.

II

I, Oliver Wendell Holmes, Jr., was born March 8, 1841, in Boston . . . All my three names designate families from which I am descended.[4]

The note of quiet pride here struck was justified. Few Bostonians could boast a more illustrious pedigree. Among his colonial forbears were Quincys and Bradstreets. A long line of Olivers and Wendells was, as he noted, commemorated in the *Memorials of the Dead in Boston.* His grandfather Holmes was a much-loved clergyman; his grandfather Jackson sat on the Massachusetts Supreme Court. His father, the perennially popular Autocrat of the Breakfast Table, was at once a distinguished poet and professor of medicine at Harvard. With such a tradition behind him, his upbringing was foreordained. He attended E. S. Dixwell's Private Latin School (years later he would marry the headmaster's daughter) and in 1857 entered Harvard. When the Civil War broke out he enlisted as a private, but remained in the vicinity of Boston long enough to graduate with his class.

Soon thereafter, newly commissioned, Lieutenant Holmes rode south to battle with his regiment, the Twentieth Massachusetts. They saw hard fighting. At Balls Bluff Holmes was seriously wounded; at Antietam he was wounded again. Returned to active duty in November of 1862, he fought through the Fredericksburg campaign until wounded for a third time at Maryes Hill. In 1864 he was mustered out, a lieutenant-colonel. The harsh realities of life which the war had brought home to him would remain with him all his life. In later years it gave him pain to talk about those days; to the end he had no taste for the literature spawned by the war. But he had learned at first hand what later he would read in Darwin: man is a predatory animal; life is battle; "force, mitigated so far as may be by good manners, is the *ultima ratio.*" [5] Withal, he is no pessimist. For all that war is horrible and dull, there is, he thinks, something of imperishable value in it.

> It is only when time has passed that you see that its message was divine. I hope it may be long before we are called again to sit at that master's feet. But some teacher of the kind we all need. In this snug, over-safe corner of the world we need it, that we may realize that our comfortable routine is no eternal necessity of things, but merely a little space of calm in the midst of the tempestuous untamed streaming of the world, and in order that we may be ready for danger. We need it in this time of individualist negations, with its literature of French and American humor, revolting at discipline, loving fleshpots, and denying that anything is worthy of reverence,— in order that we may remember all that buffoons forget. We need it everywhere and at all times. For high and dangerous action teaches us to believe as right beyond dispute things for which our doubting minds are slow to find words of proof. Out of heroism grows faith in the worth of heroism.[6]

The words of a realist, these, but not, be it quickly added, those of a cynic. Life is battle, yes, but battle, as Holmes understands it, is that which alone gives to life its zest and glory.

> That the joy of life is living, is to put out all one's powers as far as they will go; that the measure of power is obstacles overcome; to ride boldly at what is in front of you, be it fence or enemy; to pray, not for comfort, but for combat; to keep the soldier's faith against the doubts of civil life, more besetting and harder to overcome than all the misgivings of the battle-field, and to remember that duty is not to be proved in the evil day, but then to be obeyed unquestioning; to love glory more than the temptations of wallowing ease, but to know that one's final judge and only rival is oneself—with all our failures in act and thought, these things we learned from noble enemies in Virginia or Georgia or on the Mississippi, thirty years ago; these things we believe to be true.[7]

Himself a hero, he would and did keep the soldier's faith. At ninety he would put into words what at twenty-three he had not the words to say: "Death plucks my ears and says, Live—I am coming." [8]

Returned from the war, in September of 1864 he entered Harvard Law School; in 1867, following graduation and a European tour, he was admitted to the Massachusetts bar. His aim was to become not a trial lawyer but a scholar, and in this he was eminently successful. Three years of grinding study had their reward in an invitation to lecture on constitutional law at Harvard. In the same year (1870) he was offered, and accepted, the editorship of the *American Law Journal*. This, in turn, lead to an invitation to edit the twelfth edition of Kent's *Commentaries on American Law*. Published in 1873, it firmly established his reputation as a legal scholar. Somehow he found time for the amenities. The year before he had married Fanny Dixwell. There were long philosophical discussions with Chauncey Wright (whom he admired) and with William James (whose point of view he temporarily shared).[9] There were periodic visits to England and the Continent. There was Boston society.

His permanent mistress, proudly adknowledged, was, however, the common law. From her he was never long absent. His editorships required him to read widely; his character and abilities encouraged him to think deep. Like his contemporaries, Ward and Sumner, he was concerned about the theory of evolution, particularly as it bore upon the question of the origins and development of the common law. If the Social Darwinists were right in their application of the theory to society, and Holmes was early convinced that they were, then law, no less than all other social institutions, must arise out of and vary with the feelings and demands of society. In brief, "Law, being a practical thing, must found itself on actual forces." [10] Having arrived at this conclusion, Holmes, with characteristic thoroughness, now set himself the task of working out its implications. A number of articles on the subject, which he published during the late 70's, having captured the attention of the trustees of the Lowell Institute, he was in 1880 asked by them to develop his ideas in a series of Lowell Lectures. The result was *The Common Law*.

"The object of this book," according to its author, "is to present a general view of the Common Law. To accomplish the task, other tools are needed besides logic. It is something to show that the consistency of a system requires a particular result, but it is not all. The life of the law has not been logic: it has been experience." [11] As its origins have their roots in the desire of primitive man to revenge himself on those who have done him injury, so its development, Holmes argues, is inevitably conditioned by the prevalent human situation. "The felt necessities of the time, the prevalent moral and political theories, intuitions of public policy, avowed or unconscious, even the prejudices which judges share with their fellow-men, have had a good deal more to do than the syllogism in determining the rules by which men should be governed." [12] The fact is, as every evolutionist knows, that men ultimately live not by logic but by force. "The truth is, that the law is always approaching, and never reaching, consistency. It is forever adopting new principles from life at one end, and it always retains old ones from history at the other, which have not yet been absorbed or sloughed off. It will become entirely consistent only when it ceases to grow." [13] Since this is a contingency not to be anticipated, it behooves those entrusted with the keeping of the law to recognize its relativity, and not allow themselves to be misled by the false vision of a natural law or moral absolute that never was and is not now.

Holmes did not expect his relativistic view of the common law (heresy to the tradition-bound Boston bar) to arouse much local enthusiasm, and in truth it did not. His peers (the Harvard Law faculty) felt its appeal to the custom of the community rather too radical; his fellow lawyers simply ignored it. As before in American intellectual history, the author was more honored abroad than at home. Such good notices as the published version of the lectures received were all from English sources. Holmes, however, was satisfied. He had said what he thought needed to be said, and he was fortunate that there were a few men of influence present who recognized the importance of his words. One of these, Charles W. Eliot, President of Harvard, remembered them fifteen months later when an alumnus came to him with an offer to endow a new professorship of law. He offered the chair to Holmes, who accepted, enjoyed the delights of teaching for three months, and then, much to Eliot's disgust, resigned to take another chair he had always coveted, that of justice of the Massachusetts Supreme Court.

The next twenty years (from 1882 to 1902) were, for Holmes,

the best years of his life. At last he was doing exactly what he had always wanted to do. He had congenial colleagues, sufficient income, and a prestige sufficient to finally lay to rest the inferiority complex the presence of his famous father had always induced in him. In 1899 on the death of Chief Justice Field, Holmes succeeded to the office. Chief Justice in Massachusetts! It was the pinnacle of his ambition, and he was well content to have attained it, the more so as he had but three years before handed down a dissenting opinion in *Vegelahn v. Guntner and Others* which, as he thought at the time, forever shut him off from judicial promotion.

Vegelahn owned a store. Guntner and the Others picketed it— peacefully. Still, Vegelahn felt his business suffering and appealed to the Court for an injunction to halt the picketing, which relief the majority of the Court voted to grant. Holmes dissented. At no time, he noted, had the pickets threatened or used force; no property had been damaged; no individual had been shamed.

> I can [he wrote] remember when many people thought that, apart from violence or breach of contract, strikes were wicked, as organized refusals to work. I suppose that intelligent economists and legislators have given up that notion today. I feel pretty confident that they equally will abandon the idea that an organized refusal by workmen of social intercourse with a man who shall enter their antagonist's employ is wrong, if it is dissociated from any threat of violence, and is made for the sole object of prevailing if possible in a contest with their employer about the rate of wages. The fact, that the immediate object of the act by which the benefit to themselves is to be gained is to injure their antagonist, does not necessarily make it unlawful, any more than when a great house lowers the price of goods for the purpose, and with the effect of driving a smaller antagonist from the business.[14]

The point was, as Holmes saw and the majority did not, that peaceful picketing was as much a part of the competitive struggle as any contest between concerns of the same type competing for the same end. If free competition was lawful as between commercial houses, then it is no less lawful when it is between employer and employee. In both instances what is involved is, as the majority conceded and precedent allowed, the battle for life. Why, then, should the majority rule otherwise? Because they, like most middle and upper class Americans of the late Nineteenth Century, feared and hated organized labor. The memory of the violence engendered by labor's attempts to organize the steel, oil, and meatpacking industries was still green in their minds. All they saw was that violence imperiled that property right which the founding fathers had declared it to be the prime function of government to uphold and protect. Conditioned to thinking thus, they could not understand how a man of Holmes' background and beliefs could possibly side with those they sincerely took to be opposed to the American Way. That Holmes' opinion was based not on any particular partiality for the side of labor but rather on the conviction, derived from Darwin and supported by the common law, that all have equal rights of participation in the free struggle for life was a fact they could and did not credit. Some of Holmes' friends cut him dead. Henceforth, all true-blue conservatives would rate him an "unsound" man.

Theodore Roosevelt, however, thought otherwise. Newly promoted to the Presidency by the bullet that had killed McKinley, he was determined to curb the spreading power of big business, and to this end he needed a Supreme Court composed of men whose class and business connections did not inhibit their concern for the rights of labor, small business, and consumers. In Holmes he saw just such a man.[15] His dissent in *Vegelahn v. Gunter* qualified him, in Roosevelt's eyes, as a liberal. His distinguished war record and "soldier's faith" stamped him as the sort of patriot the President himself most admired. Thus, when in the summer of 1902 Justice Gray was forced by illness to resign his seat on the Court, Roosevelt nominated Holmes for his place.

Should he accept? Holmes was not sure. He was sixty years old. In Washington he would be the lowliest junior, where here in Massachusetts he was Chief. There was his wife to think of. Would she, a recluse from society since her illness, be able and willing to adjust to the social demands of the new position? Secretly dreading the prospect, Mrs. Holmes reassured her husband that she would. Apprehensive, but unable to resist the challenge of the job, Holmes decided to accept. It was, he told his friends and colleagues at the testimonial dinner tendered him just before his departure for Washington, "a good deal of a wrench to leave old friends."

But gentlemen, it is a great adventure, and that thought brings with it a mighty joy. To have one's chance to do one's share in shaping the laws of the whole country spreads over one the hush that one used to feel when awaiting the beginning of a battle.

We will not falter. . . . We will reach the earthworks if we live, and if we fail we will leave our spirit in those who follow, and they will not turn back. All is ready. *Bugler, blow the charge.*[16]

III

To find the thread of consistency in a body of writing consisting of four score and more major opinions delivered over a period of thirty years is no easy matter. Indeed, if some of Holmes' commentators are to be believed, it is impossible. Even among those who claim to have discovered the common denominator there is little unanimity of view. Holmes has been hailed as a liberal; held up as an examplar of humanitarianism; decried as a formalist; and damned for a reactionary. Actually, he was all of these at various times, and none of them at others.

Take, for example, the Northern Securities case. Northern Securities was a holding company formed by J. P. Morgan and James J. Hill for the purpose of bringing under single control the hitherto competitive Great Northern and Northern Pacific railroads. To President Roosevelt this was simply the latest in a long series of devices aiming to create monopoly in restraint of trade, and at his urging the Government sued to dissolve the company, alleging violation of the Sherman Anti-Trust Act. In December of 1903 the case reached the Supreme Court, which, after due deliberation, voted five to four in favor of the Government. The nation, solidly behind Roosevelt's trust-busting policies, rejoiced. Roosevelt, however, for all that he had won a famous victory, was annoyed, very annoyed. His own appointee, the supposed liberal, pro-labor Justice Holmes, had voted with the conservative minority, had, in his very first dissent, come down on the side of the Trusts.

The conservatives, foreseeing a pro-business majority in the making, were jubilant. Like Roosevelt, however, they were doomed to disappointment, and for the same reason: They had grossly misjudged their man. Finding him on their side, they automatically assumed that his reasons for being there were the same as their own. It no more occurred to them than it had to the President that Holmes' support of their position was independent of his personal preferences. And yet it was so. True, Holmes did have his share of prejudices. He voted Republican and paid due honor to most of Boston's sacred cows. Where he differed from the majority of his brothers on the bench was in his refusal to allow these private sentiments to obtrude into his public opinions. Being only human, he sometimes failed to live up to this ideal. Still, he did succeed often enough to make nonsense of the arguments of those who think to find in him a doctrinaire of the right—or of the left.

This is not to say that there is nothing doctrinaire about Holmes; rather is it that his doctrine is of a different sort, biological rather than political. Its ruling principle is Spencerian. Free competition, free struggle for life, is, he believes, the policy on which our law is founded. If Northern Securities is legal, it is, Holmes argues, because the Government has failed to prove any attempt on the part of the company to stifle competition or combine in restraint of trade, and combination, however vast its scope, is, of itself, no necessary evil. If Guntner and Others are justified in their picketing, it is because they too are entitled to their chance to win the battle for life. And as in these cases, so also in the rest, the common denominator, the thread of consistency, is—judicial tolerance of legislative acts, justified by social Darwinism.

"For those who will cling to a lingering belief that Holmes was a humanitarian liberal in his impulses, the 'Alabama peonage' case should be required reading." So says Max Lerner,[17] and surely he is right. No case more clearly illustrates Holmes' continuing concern with principles rather than individuals than does *Bailey v. Alabama.* Lonzo Bailey was a Negro farmhand who in 1907 had signed a contract with his employer agreeing to work for a year at a salary of $12.00 per month. In return for his signature he received an advance on wages of $15.00, which sum was to be deducted from his pay in equal monthly installments. Bailey worked for a month plus a few days and then quit—without refunding the advance. Evidently this was a fairly common occurrence in rural Alabama, for the State had on its books a statute making contract-jumping an offense punishable by a fine; failure to refund an advance was evidence of "prima facie intent to defraud." Bailey was tried, convicted, and fined thirty dollars and costs. Since he had no money to pay, the court substituted sentence of 136 days at hard labor. His lawyers appealed, charging involuntary servitude in violation of the 13th Amendment. When the case reached it, the Supreme Court sustained the appeal and reversed the conviction. Holmes dissented. It did not matter, he thought, that the law in question was directed mainly against the Negro; it did not matter that it was, as Justice Hughes remarked in his opinion for the majority, "a convenient instrument for coercion particularly effective against the poor and ignorant, its most likely victims." The sole question at issue was whether or not there had been a violation of the 13th Amendment. For himself Holmes found none. Involuntary servitude as a punishment for a crime was, as he pointed out, expressly exempted from the ban of the Amendment. In any case, the State of Alabama had a right to exact a punishment to fit the crime. Legally, he was on fairly solid ground. If the case was, as he insisted, "to be considered and decided in the same way as if it arose in Idaho or New York," obviously Bailey was guilty. The fact that the defendant's skin was black in a State where justice wore a white face was irrelevant. What mattered was the principle. Breach of contract without excuse was wrong conduct and the State was right to judge it so. Humanitarians might shudder, but then they could not be expected to appreciate the inexorability of the law.

To those prone to judging cases with their hearts but not their heads, Holmes' dissent in *Hammer v. Dagenhart* seems clearly inconsistent with the view above ascribed to him, for of all his opinions this is the one which has drawn most praise from liberals and humanitarians. And yet it too, coldly viewed, showed evidences of social Darwinism at work. The ultimate issue raised by the case was the constitutionality of the Keating-Owen Act. Passed by Congress in 1916, it prohibited the shipment in interstate or foreign commerce of any product of a cotton mill situated in the United States, in which within thirty days before the removal of the product children under fourteen have been employed, or children between fourteen and sixteen have been employed more than eight hours in a day, or more than six days in any week, or between seven in the evening and six in the morning. Dagenhart, whose two teen-age sons were millhands, sought an injunction to prevent

Hammer, the local United States Attorney, from enforcing the Act. The Federal District Court in granting the injunction held the Act to be in violation of states-rights as guaranteed by the 10th Amendment, and on appeal the Supreme Court by a vote of five to four sustained the ruling of the lower court. Holmes dissented.

> The notion that prohibition is any less prohibition when applied to things now thought evil I do not understand. But if there is any matter upon which civilized countries have agreed . . . it is the evil of premature and excessive child labor. I should have thought that if we were to introduce our own moral conceptions *where in my opinion they do not belong,* this was preeminently a case for upholding the exercise of all its powers by the United States.
>
> But I had thought that the propriety of the exercise of a power admitted to exist in some cases was for the consideration of Congress alone and that this Court always had disavowed the right to intrude its judgment upon questions of policy or morals. It is not for this Court to pronounce when prohibition is necessary to regulation if it ever may be necessary—to say that it is permissible as against strong drink but not as against the product of ruined lives.
>
> The Act does not meddle with anything belonging to the States. They may regulate their internal affairs and their domestic commerce as they like. But when they seek to send their products across the state line they are no longer within their rights . . . Under the Constitution such commerce belongs not to the States but to Congress to regulate. It may carry out its views of public policy whatever indirect effect they may have upon the activities of the States.[18]

Just so, but the point to notice is that Holmes justifies his opinion solely by appeal to constitutional principle and legislative right. His explicit disavowal of the right of the Court to "intrude its judgment upon questions of policy or morals" leaves no doubt that his presence here on the side of the angels is due more to his belief in the legal soundness of their case than to his conviction of the righteousness of their cause. As earlier in his dissent in *Lochner v. New York* on behalf of the right of the State to enforce legislation relating to the health of its workers, and later in his defence in *Gitlow v. People of New York* of the right of free speech, so here his primary concern is with the *law* of the matter; with its *heart* he has no business.

From this point of view, Justice Brandeis, his comrade at the bar from 1916 on, strove mightily to wean him—with evident success, to judge by the disgruntlement of Chief Justice Taft. "I am," Taft wrote to Henry Stimson, "very fond of the old gentleman [Holmes], but he is so completely under the control of Brother Brandeis that it gives to Brandeis two votes instead of one. He has more interest in, and gives more attention to his dissents than he does to the opinions he writes for the Court, which are very short and not very helpful." [19] Perhaps it was the fact that "his dissents" were so often from the opinions of Taft himself and the conservative majority he aspired to lead that made the Chief Justice so irritated, even so, there was a core of truth in his complaint. Holmes himself bears witness in his correspondence to the pressure Brandeis put upon him to "speak out in dissent." Apart from this, there is little evidence to back up Taft's charge. Holmes and Brandeis were, it is true, most often to be found on the same side of the case before the Court, but given their respective temperaments and judicial attitudes this is not to be wondered at. Nor was Holmes ever the mental dodderer that Taft by implication makes him out to be. Physically, he came in time to share the feebleness common to all men going on ninety; intellectually, however, his powers remained undimmed to the end. His last dissent, delivered at the age of eighty-nine, lacks nothing of the vigor and cogency of his first.

Ostensibly, the problem at issue in *Baldwin v. Missouri* was one of double taxation. Actually, the problem was the same one that Holmes had raised in his very first opinion for the Court, and again in *Lochner v. New York,* the problem, that is, of judicial tolerance of legislative acts. Carrie Pool Baldwin, "a resident of Illinois, dying there, willed all her property to her son (Thomas A. Baldwin), also a resident of that State. The will was probated in Illinois and an inheritance tax was there laid upon all her intangible personalty, wherever situate. At the time of her death she owned credits for cash deposited in banks located in Missouri, and coupon bonds of the United States and promissory notes, all physically within that State (Missouri). Some of the notes had been executed by citizens of Missouri, and some were secured on lands there." [20] In consequence, Missouri also levied an inheritance tax on the property. Thomas Baldwin refused to pay and was upheld by the State circuit court. The State appealed, and judgment was reversed by the Missouri Supreme Court. Baldwin, charging violation of that section of the Fourteenth Amendment which forbids any State to "deprive any person of life, liberty, or property without due process of law," now appealed to the United States Supreme Court. Without passing specifically on the question of the constitutionality of double taxation, the Court ruled that due process had indeed been denied, and it ordered the Missouri Supreme Court's judgment reversed. Holmes dissented, Brandeis concurring.

Both were deeply concerned about the Court's interpretation of the due process clause. That it was legal, Holmes conceded. A long train of decisions handed down by conservative majorities over a period of fifty years and more had firmly established the right of the Court to decide what did or did not constitute due process of law. The problem was to persuade the majority that such a right should be invoked rarely, and even then never in such a way as to lay the Court open to the suspicion of imposing its economic and social theories on the people. "I have not yet," writes Holmes in his dissent,

adequately expressed the more than anxiety that I feel at the ever increasing scope given to the Fourteenth Amendment in cutting down what I believe to be the constitutional rights of the States. As the decisions now stand, I see hardly any limit but the sky to the invalidating of those rights if they happen to strike a majority of this Court as for any reason undesirable. I cannot believe that the Amendment was intended to give us *carte blanche* to embody our economic or moral beliefs in its prohibitions. Yet I can think of no narrower reason that seems to me to justify the present and the earlier decisions to which I have referred. Of course the words 'due process of law' if taken in their literal meaning have no application to this case; and while it is too late to deny that they have been given a much more extended and artificial signification, still we ought to remember the great caution shown by the Constitution in limiting the power of the States, and should be slow to construe the clause in the Fourteenth Amendment as committing to the Court, with no guide but the Court's own discretion, the validity of whatever laws the States may pass . . . Very probably it might be good policy to restrict taxation to a single place, and perhaps the technical conception of domicil may be the best determinant. But it seems to me that if that result is to be reached it should be reached through understanding among the States, by uniform legislation or otherwise, not by evoking a constitutional prohibition from the void of 'due process of law' when logic, tradition and authority have united to declare the right of the State to lay the now prohibited tax.[21]

Let the judiciary be tolerant of legislative acts. As it was in the beginning, so is this at the end the essence of Holmes' philosophy of law. On January 12th, 1932, having achieved his ambition of beating Justice Taney's record for age and length of service, he retired from the Court. He was ninety-one years old, and, as he confessed in a letter to Pollock, "tired most of the time." He had outlived duty; he was prepared to say goodbye.

IV

For three years he lived quietly in the house on I Street, and then on March 6th, 1935, just as quietly he passed away. It was the obituaries that brought him back to public mind. They were very long, very fulsome; all agreed that a link with the glorious past had been broken. The post mortems began. What was the sum of his accomplishment? In 1935 it appeared rather small. The conservative majority continued to see its duty as the protection of the people and the States from the consequences of their collective folly. Not until the late 30's, when death and Franklin Roosevelt had had their way, did the disposition of the Court show any tendency to change. Since then it has become more liberal. Whether it has become more Holmesian is still an open question.

SUGGESTED READINGS

For the general reader, *The Mind and Faith of Justice Holmes* (New York: Modern Library, 1943) should suffice. Herein are all of the important speeches, essays, and judicial opinions together with a sampling of Holmes' extensive correspondence, the whole edited with Introduction and commentary by Max Lerner. The comprehensive bibliography lists the various collections of Holmes' writings, and surveys the literature up to 1942. Those interested in the man and his private opinions should supplement the above with the new Harvard edition of the *Holmes-Pollock Letters* edited by Mark DeWolfe Howe (Cambridge: Belknap Press, 1961).

There are three biographies. Silas Bent, *Justice Oliver Wendell Holmes* (New York: Vanguard Press, 1932), is poorly organized and, on some points, incorrect. Catherine Drinker Bowen, *Yankee from Olympus, Justice Holmes and His Family* (Boston: Little, Brown, 1944), is very readable but light on philosophy. Far superior to either from the standpoint of scholarly thoroughness are the two volumes thus far completed of a projected four-volume study by Mark DeWolfe Howe, *Oliver Wendell Holmes: The Shaping Years 1841-1870* (Cambridge: Belknap-Harvard University Press, 1957) and *Justice Oliver Wendell Holmes: The Proving Years 1870-1882* (Cambridge: Belknap-Harvard University Press, 1963). For Holmes the jurist and legal philosopher, see Felix Frankfurter, *Mr. Justice Holmes and the Supreme Court*, 2nd edition (Cambridge: Belknap Press, 1961), and Samuel J. Konefsky, *The Legacy of Holmes and Brandeis, A Study in the Influence of Ideas* (New York: Collier Books, paperback, 1961).

REFERENCES

1. Max Lerner (editor), *The Mind and Faith of Justice Holmes, his speeches, essays, letters, and judicial opinions* (New York: Modern Library, 1943), p. 31. Hereafter cited as Mind and Faith.

2. The Constitution of the United States, Article III, Sections 1 and 2.

3. *Otis v. Parker*, 187 U.S. 606 (1903). In legal notation the name refers to the principals in the case; the first figure indicates volume number, followed by volume identification, followed by the second figure, which is the number of the page from which the quotation is taken. The year in which the decision was handed down is given in parentheses. Thus 187 U.S. 606 (1903) signifies: United States Reports, cases adjudged in the Supreme Court, volume 187, page 606, given in the year 1903. All subsequent citations of cases will be made in this form.

4. Mind and Faith, p. 6.

5. Mark DeWolfe Howe (editor), *Holmes-Pollock Letters*, 2 Vols. (Cambridge: Harvard University Press, 1941), II, p. 36. Hereafter cited as H-P. The entire passage bears repeating for the clear light that it throws upon Holmes' basic outlook on life. "I am not an admiral or a general. I loathe war—which I described when at home with a wound in our Civil War as an organized bore—to the scandal of the young women of the day who thought that Captain Holmes was wanting in patriotism. But I do think that man at present is a predatory animal. I think that the sacredness of human life is a purely municipal ideal of no validity outside the jurisdiction. I believe that force, mitigated so far as may be by good manners, is the *ultima ratio,* and between two groups that want to make inconsistent kinds of world I see no remedy except force."

6. Mind and Faith, p. 23.

7. Ibid., pp. 23-24.

8. Ibid., p. 451.

9. Later they would grow apart as their interests diverged. Pragmatism is prospective, the law retrospective, and Holmes was dedicated to the law.

Much later he would dismiss pragmatism as "an amusing humbug." H-P I, pp. 139, 167.

10. *The Common Law* (Boston: Little, Brown, 1881), p. 213.

11. Ibid., p. 1.

12. Ibid.

13. Ibid., p. 36.

14. 167 Massachusetts 92, 104 (1896).

15. "Judge Holmes' whole mental attitude . . . is," Roosevelt wrote to Senator Lodge, "such that I should naturally expect him to be in favor of those principles in which I so earnestly believe." *Selections from the Correspondence of Theodore Roosevelt and Henry Cabot Lodge 1884-1918* (New York: Scribner, 1925), I, pp. 517-18. In this expectation Roosevelt was sorely disappointed. He never forgave what he took to be Holmes' betrayal of his principles in the Northern Securities case. Holmes' side of the story appeared years later in one of his letters to Pollock. Apropos of his recent reading of *Theodore Roosevelt and His Time* he adds: "Of course I pretty well made up my package about him a good while ago, and I don't think I was too much disturbed by what you admit to and what was formulated by a Senator in his day, thus: 'What the boys like about Roosevelt is that he doesn't care a damn for the law.' It broke up our incipient friendship, however, as he looked upon my dissent to the Northern Securities case as a political departure (or, I suspect, more truly, couldn't forgive anyone who stood in his way). We talked freely later but it never was the same after that, and if he had not been restrained by his friends, I am told he would have made a fool of himself and would have excluded me from the White House—as in his case about the law, so in mine about that, I never cared a damn whether I went there or not." H-P II, pp. 63-64.

16. Quoted in Catherine Drinker Bowen, *Yankee from Olympus* (Boston: Little, Brown, 1944), p. 348.

17. Mind and Faith, pp. 336-37.

18. 219 U.S. 280, 281. My italics.

19. Samuel J. Konefsky, *The Legacy of Holmes and Brandeis* (New York: Collier Books, 1961), p. 93.

20. 281 U.S. 586.

21. 281 U.S. 596, 597.

XXIII

Learning As Living

JOHN DEWEY

"Learning? certainly, but living
primarily, and learning through
and in relation to this living." [1]

JOHN DEWEY

John Dewey

How SHALL WE EDUCATE the rising generation? The question is not unimportant. The future, perhaps the very survival of our society, depends upon the answer and on the action that we as Americans take to enforce that answer. Nor is it a question easily evaded. The tremendous achievements of Soviet science in recent years have laid upon us all the burden of responsibility for the adequacy of our educational ideals. Some there are who having thought the matter through have come to the conclusion that nothing less than a revolution in methods and theory is needed. Nothing less, they tell us, will suffice—if we are to meet successfully the Russian challenge. For such as these, our present educational practice is an open invitation to national disaster. If they are right, our duty is plain: we ought to join the revolution. That they are right, however, hundreds of thousands of public school teachers and administrators trained in the techniques and principles of progressive education would deny. Having themselves worked to accomplish one educational revolution, they are not about to join another. Better, as they see it, that we allow our present practice time to prove its worth, for that in time it must do so they are certain. How, then, shall we train our children? How else, answers the progressive, save along the lines long since described by John Dewey in his epoch-making little book, *The School and Society*.

Let them, he argues, learn by doing, by practice, yes, by play, for in these instinctive, impulsive attitudes and activities of the child all education worthy of the name is rooted. Let them pursue *their* interests, not at haphazard but under guidance, for only thus is effort generated and intellectual growth sustained. Lastly, let them learn those things that fit them for life in society, for "the primary business of school is to train children in co-operative and mutually helpful living; to foster in them the consciousness of mutual interdependence; and to help them practically in making the adjustments that will carry this spirit into overt deeds." [2] Such is Dewey's teaching; such was his practice from 1896 to 1904 in the experimental school he organized and directed at the University of Chicago. On the results of this practice, his educational philosophy is founded; from this educational philosophy derives, in turn, that progressivism which in our time has come to dominate the thinking of those who run our public schools.

Not that progressivism as such was original with John Dewey. He himself acknowledges his indebtedness to the educational theories of Friedrich Froebel, and to the previous practice of them by Colonel Francis W. Parker. In truth, the educational problems progressivism was devised to solve are as old as the common schools themselves. Horace Mann had recognized that the methods appropriate to the teaching of an elite few must change as that few expanded into a many diverse in social background and intellectual ability. His successors had to cope with a classical curriculum ill-suited to the needs of children destined to serve society in factories and on farms. Industry, rapidly developing in the decades following the Civil War, wanted manually as well as mentally trained workers. By the Eighties, the vocational training movement, sparked by Calvin Woodward, had arisen to fill its needs. Nor were the schools of the time permitted to forget their social responsibilities. Lester Ward was but one of a distinguished host of reformers who, sickened by the excesses and corruption of the Gilded Age, thought to find in the schools an instrument for social betterment. Meanwhile, in the world outside the classrooms, the winds of politics were blowing populist and progressive. Inevitably, those schools within the sphere of influence of these movements came to reflect something of their democratic ideal. Thus progressivism in politics bred progressivism in education and paved the way for that Deweyism which was and is its pedagogical and philosophical adjunct.

As for Dewey's own politics, these, like his educational ideals, reflect the influence of his New England background. On both sides his family histories traced back five American generations. His mother's family were gentry, landowners, lawyers, and a congressman. The Deweys were mostly farmers, some were in trade. Archibald Dewey, John's father, had a grocery business in Burlington, Vermont. Here, on October 20th, 1859, John Dewey was born.

His upbringing was nothing extraordinary. He attended the local schools, mastered the standard curriculum, did his recitations and was bored. As his daughter has remarked,[3] his passion for educational reform had its inception in the stupidities and inadequacies of the educational practice he himself had been subjected to. At fifteen, finished with high school, he entered the University of Vermont. It was in those days a small and not particularly distinguished institution. However, it did have two great advantages: it was located just down the street from the Dewey house, and it was cheap. Dewey was a good student, and in his senior year, in consequence of his first exposure to philosophy, a dedicated one. Not yet however was he prepared to take the plunge into philosophy as a life work, and so for two years following his graduation in 1879 he taught a little of everything at the High School in South Oil City, Pennsylvania. In 1882, his mind finally made up, he left for Baltimore to enter upon graduate study at the Johns Hopkins University. It was, as he noted many years later,

something of a risk; the work offered there was almost the only indication that there were likely to be any self-supporting jobs in the field of philosophy for others than clergymen. Aside from the effect of my study with Professor Torrey, another influence moved me to undertake the risk. During the years after graduation I had kept up philosophical readings and I had even written a few articles which I sent to Dr. W. T. Harris, the well-known Hegelian, and the editor of the *Journal of Speculative Philosophy,* the only philosophic journal in the country at that time, as he and his group formed almost the only group of laymen devoted to philosophy for non-theological reasons. In sending an article I asked Dr. Harris for advice as to the possibility of my successfully prosecuting philosophic studies. His reply was so encouraging that it was a distinct factor in deciding me to try philosophy as a professional career.[4]

At Hopkins he soon came under the influence of Professor George Sylvester Morris. Morris introduced him to the works of Hegel, and his readings in the English Hegelians confirmed a philosophical allegiance that was to endure for a dozen years and leave a permanent deposit in Dewey's thinking. "The form, the schematism, of his [Hegel's] system," he wrote in 1930, "now seems to me artificial to the last degree. But in the content of his ideas there is often an extraordinary depth; in many of his analyses, taken out of their mechanical dialectical setting, an extraordinary acuteness. Were it possible for me to be a devotee of any system, I should still believe that there is greater richness and variety of insight in Hegel than in any other single systematic philosopher." [5]

Out of Hopkins in 1884, his Ph.D. in hand, Dewey, through the good offices of Morris, obtained an instructorship in the Department of Philosophy at the University of Michigan. Here, except for an interlude of a year of teaching at Minnesota, he would remain until his call to Chicago. It was a time for making his philosophical reputation, and young Dewey soon gave evidence of a mind to be reckoned with. His *Psychology,* reflecting the influence of William James, and a growing preoccupation with intelligence as an instrument of individual and social progress, came out in 1887. Eventually this instrumentalism would drive him to a complete break with the Idealist tradition he yet adhered to, albeit with a steadily diminishing fervor. As if to prove that he could produce a work of precise scholarship, in 1888 he published his critical exposition of *Leibniz's New Essays Concerning the Human Understanding,* a study that, for all the passage of the years, still ranks as the best book on the subject. *Outlines of a Critical Theory of Ethics* (1891), together with its sequel, *The Study of Ethics* (1894), further emphasized his drift away from Hegel. Intelligence, as he now envisages it, is "mediation of native impulses with respect to the consequences of their operations." [6] The transition from absolutism to experimentalism was nearly complete.

All the while his interest in and concern with the learning process had been growing as his family grew. He was determined that his children should not suffer the intellectual boredom of his own school days, and gradually this determination translated itself into the conviction of the philosophic primacy of education. Four decades after, remarking this progression of his thought, he recalled

but one critic who has suggested that my thinking has been too much permeated by interest in education. Although a book called *Democracy and Education* was for many years that in which my philosophy, such as it is, was most fully expounded, I do not know that philosophic critics, as distinct from teachers, have ever had recourse to it. I have wondered whether such facts signified that philosophers in general, although they are themselves usually teachers, have not taken education with sufficient seriousness for it to occur to them that any rational person could actually think it possible that philosophizing should focus about education as the supreme human interest in which, moreover, other problems, cosmological, moral, logical, come to a head.[7]

Dewey, at all events, thought it possible enough to allow the prospect of combining pedagogy and psychology with philosophy to lure him from his pleasant situation at Michigan (he was then a full professor, with tenure) to Chicago. In 1894 he was appointed Chairman of these combined departments. Henceforth philosophy for him would be, in the broadest sense of the term, philosophy of education.

II

The most penetrating definition of philosophy which can be given is, then, that it is the theory of education in its most general phases.

The reconstruction of philosophy, of education, and of social ideals and methods thus go hand in hand.[8]

According to Hegel, the task of philosophy is to discover what is, and this it can do because what is is reason—the bond uniting all persons, things, and institutions into one continuous whole. For Dewey also the business of philosophy is with what is—continuous; only now, this continuity is defined as experience, while philosophy now is taken to be a form of thinking aiming at the resolution of the manifold difficulties that experience presents. Herein, Dewey contends, philosophy differs from science and coincides with education, for whereas science restricts itself to the enumeration and collation of the facts, philosophy, like education, is always concerned with their consequences.

At this point, the intimate connection between philosophy and education appears. In fact, education offers a vantage ground from which to penetrate to the human, as distinct from the technical, significance of philosophic discussions. . . . If a theory makes no difference in educational endeavor, it must be artificial. The educational point of view enables one to envisage the philosophic problems where they arise and thrive, where they are at home, and where acceptance or rejection makes a difference in practice.[9]

That this is often forgotten is, Dewey argues, owing to the fact that philosophers, in their efforts to carve out a special intellectual province for themselves, traditionally have had recourse to a technical vocabulary whose net effect has been to perpetuate the illusion that philosophy has to do with a truth beyond nature and without application to social life. Thus have arisen the various dualisms which from the time of the Greeks on have afflicted philosophy and its cousin theology. Misled by their own language, philosophers have sought to sunder man from nature, mind from body, knowing from doing, and means from ends. Having created for themselves a dualistic world, they have wasted their substance on a perennial attempt to resolve a series of antinomies that never have and do not now exist. For the truth is that the real world, as it discloses itself to our experience and to science, is a unified realm of ends in view, whose worth and nature it is philosophy's business to uncover and exploit. In Dewey's words,

philosophy is at once an explicit formulation of the various interests of life and a propounding of points of view and methods through which a better balance of interests may be effected. Since education is the process through which the needed transformation may be accomplished and not remain a mere hypothesis as to what is desirable, we reach a justification of the statement that philosophy is the theory of education as a deliberately conducted practice.[10]

As if to illustrate his own maxim of learning by living, Dewey had worked this conclusion out in practice long before he got around to setting it down on paper. *Democracy and Education,* the book from which the views just expressed are taken, was not written until 1915; the epistemological and cosmological justification of the revolt against dualism here implied would not be composed until 1925. The argument of both these later works, however, represents the conclusions drawn from the practice followed at the Laboratory School in the years just before and after the turn of the century. What, in general, that practice was we have already noted. What we have now to note is the educational credo of which it was the first and finest expression.

In 1897, scarcely a year after the founding of his school, Dewey was invited by the editor of *The School Journal* to summarize the educational philosophy behind his experiment. The result was *My Pedagogic Creed,* a statement which has since become a part of the professional bible of every progressive educationist. "I believe," writes Dewey, "that

the only true education comes through the stimulation of the child's powers by the demands of the social situations in which he finds himself. . . . The child's own instincts and powers furnish the material and give the starting-point for all education. Save as the efforts of the educator connect with some activity which the child is carrying on of his own initiative independent of the educator, education becomes reduced to a pressure from without. It may, indeed, give certain external results, but cannot truly be called education. . . .
—the school is primarily a social institution. Education being a social process, the school is simply that form of community life in which all those agencies are concentrated that will be most effective in bringing the child to share in the inherited resources of the race.
—education, therefore, is a process of living and not a preparation for future living. . . .
—the teacher's place and work in the school is to be interpreted from this same basis. The teacher is not in the school to impose certain ideas or to form certain habits in the child, but is there as a member of the community to select the influences which shall affect the child and to assist him in properly responding to these influences.
—the discipline of the school should proceed from the life of the school as a whole and not directly from the teacher.
—the teacher's business is simply to determine, on the basis of larger

experience and riper wisdom, how the discipline of life shall come
to the child. . . .

—the true center of correlation on the school subjects is not science,
nor literature, nor history, nor geography, but the child's own social
activities. . . .

—there is, therefore, no succession of studies in the ideal school
curriculum. If education is life, all life has, from the outset, a scientific aspect, an aspect of art and culture, and an aspect of communication. It cannot, therefore, be true that the proper studies for
one grade are mere reading and writing, and that at a later grade,
reading, or literature, or science, may be introduced. The progress
is not in the succession of studies, but in the development of new
attitudes towards, and new interests in, experience.

—education must be conceived as a continuing reconstruction of experience; that the process and the goal of education are one and
the same thing.[11]

The autocratic ideal of learning by listening must give way to the
democratic ideal of learning by doing, for not until this reconstruction of ideals has been accomplished will American education be,
as Dewey thinks it ought to be, truly representative of those principles for which we as a people stand. Not until we have taken hold
"of the organic, positive principle involved in democracy, and put
that in entire possession of the spirit and work of the school," [12]
will we have insured that democracy has a future in America.

A democratic society presupposes democracy in education. This
proposition, first defended by Dewey in 1903 in his article "Democracy and Education," and later developed at length in the book
of the same title, is foundational to his philosophy of education.
From it the motivation to reconstruction of education *and* philosophy is derived. That a democratic society is, morally and sociolog-
ically, the ideal, Dewey simply assumes. "Modern life," he tells
us, "means democracy, democracy means freeing intelligence for
independent effectiveness—the emancipation of mind as an individual organ to do its own work." [13] The statement is vague enough,
but Dewey's subsequent utterances on the subject of democracy and
intelligence make it plain that for him the instrumentality of intelligence is the root from which all else grows. Because it alone
permits intelligence to operate with perfect freedom, democracy is

the political and social ideal. Because progressivism is democracy in action in the schools, it is the educational ideal. The task before us, as Dewey conceives it, is, then, to see that this ideal becomes a reality.

Reconstruction begins with the teacher. *"All other reforms are conditioned upon reform in the quality and character of those who engage in the teaching profession."* [14] That we must bend every effort to obtain teachers of the highest character and quality is obvious; that such teachers once obtained must be given a voice in the direction of school affairs is not so obvious, but, thinks Dewey, it is equally essential.

Until the public school system is organized in such a way that every teacher has some regular and representative way in which he or she can register judgment upon matters of educational importance, with the assurance that this judgment will somehow affect the school system, the assertion that the present system is not, from the internal standpoint, democratic seems to be justified. Either we come here upon some fixed and inherent limitation of the democratic principle, or else we find in this fact an obvious discrepancy between the conduct of the school and the conduct of social life—a discrepancy so great as to demand immediate and persistent effort at reform.[15]

So long as control of the school is vested in a board untrained as educators, or in the school superintendent, the interests of democracy will not be served. For no matter how wise, expert, or benevolent they or he may be, the result is still—autocracy. "I know," he writes,

it will be said that this state of things, while an evil, is a necessary one; that without it confusion and chaos would reign; that such regulations are the inevitable accompaniments of any graded system. It is said that the average teacher is incompetent to take any part in laying out the course of study or in initiating methods of instruction or discipline. Is not this type of argument which has been used from time immemorial, and in every department of life, against the advance of democracy? What does democracy mean save that the individual is to have a share in determining the conditions and the aims of his own work; and that, upon the whole, through the free and mutual harmonizing of different individuals, the work of the world is better done than when planned, arranged, and directed by a few, no matter how wise or of how good intent that few? How can we justify our belief in the democratic principle elsewhere, and then go back entirely upon it when we come to education? [16]

Dewey's answer is, of course, that we cannot. If democracy is to flourish in society, its lessons must already have been learned by practice in the schools. Ultimately, this means the extension of the democratic ideal to every phase of school life. The abolition of autocracy in administration is but the first in a series of needed reforms which, for Dewey, includes the abandonment of all curricula based upon the assumption of an aristocracy of studies or of students.

This assumption, the bequest of Greek education to the educators of the modern world, has, Dewey insists, no place in a society which, unlike that of the Greeks, brooks no sharp division of classes into laboring or leisure, master and slave. "Democracy cannot flourish where the chief influences in selecting subject matter of instruction are utilitarian ends narrowly conceived for the masses, and, for the higher education of the few, the traditions of a specialized cultivated class." [17] To assume that these traditions, as preserved in the so-called "liberal arts," have an intrinsic value in and of themselves apart from their function as "organs of initiation into social values" [18] is to assume a truth that never was. The Greeks to the contrary, "we cannot establish a hierarchy of values among studies. It is futile to attempt to arrange them in an order, beginning with one having least worth and going on to that of maximum value." [19] Does this mean that all are equal in value? Dewey neither affirms nor denies it. He does imply by his emphasis on consequences that no one type of subject matter, such as science, is intrinsically and invariably superior to others as regards their mutual potential for the enrichment of life.

All information and systematized scientific subject matter have been worked out under the conditions of social life and have been transmitted by social means. But this does not prove that all is of equal value for the purposes of forming the disposition and supplying the equipment of members of present society. The scheme of a curriculum must take account of the adaptation of studies to the needs of the existing community life; it must select with the intention of improving the life we live in common so that the future shall be better than the past. Moreover, the curriculum must be planned with reference to placing essentials first, and refinements second. The things which are socially most fundamental, that is, which have to do with the experiences in which the widest groups share, are the essentials. The things which represent the needs of specialized groups and technical pursuits are secondary. There is truth in the saying that education must first be human and only after that professional. But those who utter the saying frequently have in mind in the term human only a highly specialized class: the class of learned men who preserve the classic traditions of the past. They forget that material is humanized in the degree in which it connects with the common interests of men as men.[20]

Classics no less than cooking finds its value in the measure of its contribution to individual and social welfare. Mathematics as much as manual training proves its worth by its use.

Which is to say, as Dewey does, that there is no distinction, intrinsic and absolute, between culture and utility. Each may be, and virtually always is, ingredient in the other. Significant knowledge and practical achievement go hand in hand. "If the living, experiencing being is an intimate participant in the activities of the world to which it belongs, then knowledge is a mode of participation, valuable in the degree in which it is effective. It cannot be the idle view of an unconcerned spectator." [21] For nowhere, in or out of nature, is such a spectator to be found.

III

Experience and Nature is John Dewey's most important book, important because in it, as nowhere else in his writings, he is concerned to explicate and justify the philosophical ground on which his general theory of education rests. Regrettably, it is, as regards style and clarity of content, also one of his worst. Justice Holmes, no mean judge of literary quality, thought it "incredibly ill-written." Withal, he wrote to Pollock,

it seemed to me after several rereadings to have a feeling of intimacy with the inside of the cosmos that I found unequaled. So methought God would have spoken had He been inarticulate but keenly desirous to tell you how it was.[22]

Only Holmes would have found Dewey's addiction to the use of polysyllabic words evidence of inarticulateness. For most others of his critics what troubles is not his inarticulateness but his ambiguity. The difficulty is to understand what Dewey means when he refers to "experience," "nature," and "man."

In part the diffuse character of these central concepts is owing to Dewey's taking them as concepts in process. Every idea, these included, is, to him, "largely the obverse side of action; a perception of what might be, but is not, the promise of things hoped for, the symbol of things not seen." [23] "Standardizations, formulae, generalizations, principles, universals, have their place, but the place is that of being instrumental to better approximation to what is unique and unrepeatable." [24] With Heraclitus he agrees that change is all. Anticipating Whitehead, he proclaims every existence an event.

This fact is nothing at which to repine and nothing to gloat over. It is something to be noted and used. . . . The important thing is measure, relation, ratio, knowledge of the comparative tempos of change. In mathematics some variables are constants in some problems; so it is in nature and life. The rate of change of some things is so slow, or is so rhythmic, that these changes have all the advantages of stability in dealing with more transitory and irregular happenings—if we know enough.[25]

Unfortunately, the history of philosophy from the Greeks on is replete with thinkers who have not known enough to distinguish the constancy of change from changeless Being as such. Having begun by exalting Being over Becoming, they ended by divorcing Reality from Nature, thus raising the host of pseudo-problems that to this day continue to plague philosophy. For this sort of thinking the cure is simple and, once taken, complete. We must face up to the fact that Reality is not Being but Becoming. The laws of nature are themselves not invariant, for all that they may seem so from the standpoint of our cosmic epoch. Similarly, what we call matter or substance is nothing permanent. "The name designates a character in operation, not an entity." [26]

'This,' whatever *this* may be, always implies a system of meanings focussed at a point of stress, uncertainty, and need of regulation. It sums up history, and at the same time opens a new page; it is record and promise in one; a fulfillment and an opportunity. It is a fruition of what has happened and a transitive agency of what is to happen. It is a comment written by natural events on their own direction and tendency, and a surmise of whither they are leading.[27]

It is, in sum, a process taking time, an act of experiencing, the present as big with the past and pregnant for the future. As known, it is a meaning, and, as such, object. Insofar as it is significant, it is an end in view.

"It goes without saying," says Dewey, "that man begins as a part of physical and animal nature." [28] First life, then consciousness, finally mind; such is the order of human development.

The distinction between physical, psycho-physical, and mental is thus one of levels of increasing complexity and intimacy of inter-action among natural events. The idea that matter, life and mind represent separate kinds of Being is a doctrine that springs, as so many philosophic errors have sprung, from a substantiation of eventual functions. The fallacy converts consequences of interaction of events into causes of the occurrence of these consequences—a reduplication which is significant as to the *importance* of the functions, but which hopelessly confuses understanding of them. 'Matter,' or the physical, is a character of events when they occur at a certain level of interaction. It is not itself an event or existence; the notion that while 'mind' denotes essence, 'matter' denotes existence is superstition. It is more than a bare essence; for it is a property of a particular field of interacting events.[29]

What we call mind is, then, only consciousness raised to the level of reflection upon that series of episodes, i.e., the immediate aware-ness of colours, tastes, sounds, and smells, etc., which is conscious-ness itself. "There must be a story, some whole, an integrated series of episodes. This connected whole is mind, as it extends beyond a particular process of consciousness and conditions it." [30] What gives meaning to events, uses events, takes notice of and acts upon the consequences of events, that is mind. In other words, mind, or soul, is what the conscious body does. The solution of the age-old problem of the relation of mind and body lies in the recognition that these aspects of the organism never have been separate entities requiring to be related. "To see the organism *in* nature, the nervous system in the organism, the brain in the nervous system, the cortex in the brain is the answer to the problems that haunt philosophy." [31]

The fact is that man is continuous with nature. "The thing essential to bear in mind is that living as an empirical affair is not something which goes on below the skin-surface of an organism: it is always an inclusive affair involving connection, interaction of what is within the organic body and what lies outside in space and time, and with higher organisms far outside." [32] The idea, native to every species of dualism, of man as a something apart from nature, an eternal essence, finds no foundation in modern psychophysiology or, for that matter, in any science, physical or biological. Rather are his aims natural, his ends empirical ends in view. Man's task naturalistically conceived is not to escape nature but to appreciate it and to use it.

When man finds he is not a little god in his active powers and accomplishments . . . when he perceives clearly and adequately that he is within nature, a part of its interactions, he sees that the line to be drawn is not between action and thought, or action and appreciation, but between blind, slavish, meaningless action and action that is free, significant, directed and responsible.[33]

Ethically, this implies his recognition that "morals mean custom, folkways, established collective habits." [34] It marks his understanding of the good as goods in process of achievement. Religiously, it signifies his repudiation of the supernatural, together with its corollary emancipation of the religious from religion. In short, it means that truth of any sort is nothing fixed or finished. Whatever truths may be are always truths *if,* truths validated by consequences, truths in use. To criticize their usefulness is the function of science; the office of philosophy is the criticism of these criticisms. "There may be those to whom it is treason to think of philosophy as the critical method of developing methods of criticism. But this conception of philosophy also waits to be tried, and," if Dewey is right, "the trial which all approve or condemn lies in the eventual issue. The import of such knowledge as we have acquired and such experience as has been quickened by thought is," he concludes, "to evoke and justify the trial." [35]

With this conception of philosophy, and with the scientific outlook it presumes, few contemporary critics are disposed to quarrel. Even those most vigorously opposed to Dewey's application of democracy to education tend to approve his idea of the universe as a social process atomized by events, although, in truth, it is not so much Dewey's formulation of this cosmological idea as it is that of his great contemporary, Alfred North Whitehead, which today finds general acceptance. Be that as it may, the question remains as to whether or not acceptance of the Dewey-Whitehead version of Reality commits one to acceptance of democracy as the social and educational ideal. Dewey himself nowhere specifically claims a connection. Democracy has no part in *Experience and Nature*. On the other hand, there is his statement, earlier cited, to the effect that cosmological and other philosophical problems ought to come to a head as problems of education; and in the works of his later years, particularly in *Experience and Education,* he does appear to be saying that what one holds concerning education is all of a piece with what one believes about the nature of the Real. Beyond these very general and tenuous suggestions, however, he does not go; nor could he even if he wished, since, by his own admission, what he has to offer is not a system but a method.

IV

Of all the men and women who have contributed to the making of the American mind, none can boast an influence more immediate and pervasive than that exercised by John Dewey. The disciples he attracted during twenty-six years at Columbia today control the operations and curricula of the majority of our public school systems. Others of them dominate the faculties and administrations of virtually all the normal schools and university departments of education. Not a few State Boards of Education are in their hands. The most famous of the Deweyites, Professor William Heard Kilpatrick of Teachers College, Columbia, in the course of a career spanning five decades, himself preached progressivism to 35,000 teacher trainees. Every year thousands more trained in the methods and philosophy of Dewey take their places in American education. Add to these the large numbers who continue to purchase and study the many volumes of Dewey's writings still in print, and it is easy to see that Kilpatrick speaks but the simple truth when he says that "no one in a position to judge would deny that he [Dewey] is the foremost leader in educational philosophy that America has produced." [36]

Certainly Dewey's educational enemies would not deny it, for it is in just this blanket dominance of our educational institutions by his ideas and disciples that they find the danger to lie. Indeed, Mortimer Adler has gone so far as to imply that Dewey is more dangerous to America than was Hitler,[37] and if Adler's scholastic assumptions are justified he may be right. Even those most disposed to admire the goodness of Dewey's intentions have remarked their disastrous consequences. For the fact is, as these see it, that progressivism has failed. Having begun by confusing traditional subject matters with traditional ways of teaching them, it has ended by providing a corps of teachers as learned in methods as they are ignorant of the contents of the subjects they supposedly teach. For all its emphasis on life-adjustment and the interests of the child, it has raised up a succession of generations of neurotics, each class more troubled in spirit than that which preceded it. It has not produced in sufficient quantity or quality the scientists and technicians our society so sorely needs. It has produced a citizenry trained to believe that what counts is to be well heeled and well liked.

It is a harsh indictment, and were Dewey alive to read it, he might well wonder what went wrong with his educational revolution. Many things, of course, but two transcending all others in importance—the inadequacy of his conception of democracy, the apostasy of his disciples. Like most philosophers before him, Dewey has been unfortunate in his followers. Thus it was not Dewey but Kilpatrick who de-emphasized the role of the curriculum. Not

Dewey but Burton Fowler it was who proclaimed "the obvious hypothesis that the child rather than what he studies should be the centre of all educational effort." [38] "We don't teach subjects, we teach children." To such puerile slogans Dewey himself never subscribed. Nor should he be blamed for the failure of most State and local school boards to raise teacher salaries, qualifications, and prestige to those high levels at which alone progressive education, as Dewey conceives it, can work. On the other hand, he is responsible for the oversimplification that vitiates his argument for democracy in education. "How," he has asked us in a passage earlier quoted, "can we justify our belief in the democratic principle elsewhere, and then go back entirely upon it when it comes to education?" So put, the question plainly admits of none other than a negative answer. Actually, however, the matter is not nearly as simple as Dewey would have us believe. For the issue is not whether the schools ought to be *entirely* democratic or autocratic. The evils consequent upon our adherence to one extreme do not transpose into goods as we swing to the other. The dictatorial schoolmaster is as much and no more a caricature of the good teacher than is the playmate schoolmarm. The assumption that the democratic principle can or should apply the same way in school as out is patently absurd. Granted that the legislative chamber and the classroom are both institutions essential to the health of any democracy, it does not follow that the rules of procedure appropriate to the one are right for the other. Our society is no less democratic for its denial of the vote to children.

Were this particular oversimplification all that is wrong with Dewey's conception of democracy, the issue might well be allowed to drop. Unfortunately it is not. There is a graver deficiency in his view, that is, his failure to perceive that education for life-adjustment must end by producing a race of group-adjusted men, herd-men incapable of that independent thinking so essential to the proper functioning of a truly democratic society. Dewey forgets, or perhaps it is simply that he chooses not to remember, that children require to be taught the *nature* as well as the *practice* of the good life. He ignores their need to learn that freedom is something over and above the liberty to live as prosperously as possible. His ultimate failure, and in justice it ought to be noted that it is the failure of most Americans, lies in his not realizing that while learning is living, it is also and always more than this; it is living to some knowable purpose and end—beyond the end in view. What this end is, it is, according to Whitehead, the major business of philosophy to discover. That philosophy is competent to its task, Whitehead is convinced. With what justification we have now to see.

SUGGESTED READINGS

Dewey himself regarded *Democracy and Education* (New York: Macmillan, 1916; Macmillan paperback edition, 1961) as the most comprehensive of his several books on the philosophy of education, and *Experience and Nature* (Chicago: Open Court, 1925; Dover paperback edition, 1958) as his best specifically philosophic work. Fortunately, both are readily available, and it makes little difference which of them you read for a starter. Those who prefer samplers should begin with Sidney Ratner's volume of Dewey selections, *Intelligence in the Modern World* (New York: Modern Library Giant, 1939). The material here included traverses the whole range of Dewey's life and thought, telescoping into 800 pages writings that in their uncut versions total considerably more than 50,000 pages. The Introduction adds 200 pages more, and it is well worth your attention. For summaries and criticism of these and others of Dewey's works, see P. A. Schilpp (editor), *The Philosophy of John Dewey* (Evanston: Northwestern University, 1939). This last also provides a biography of Dewey edited by his daughter, Jane M. Dewey, as well as a virtually complete bibliography of the writings up to October, 1939.

Most libraries will have copies of one or more of the following studies, all by students of Dewey, all highly favorable to his point of view: Sidney Hook, *John Dewey, An Intellectual Portrait* (New York: John Day, 1939); Jerome Nathanson, *John Dewey* (New York: Scribner, 1951); George Geiger, *John Dewey in Perspective* (New York: Oxford, 1958). Among the myriad of books and articles concerning Dewey and progressive education, Lawrence A. Cremin, *The Transformation of the School* (New York: Knopf, 1961), stands out like a fire in the fog.

REFERENCES

1. *The School and Society* (Chicago: Phoenix Books, n.d.), p. 36. Hereafter cited as SS.

2. SS, p. 117.

3. Jane M. Dewey, "Biography of John Dewey," in Paul Arthur Schilpp (editor), *The Philosophy of John Dewey* (Evanston: Northwestern University Press, 1939), p. 9. Hereafter cited as Schilpp-Dewey.

4. "From Absolutism to Experimentalism," in George P. Adams and William Pepperell Montague (editors), *Contemporary American Philosophy* (New York: Macmillan, 1930), II, p. 16. Hereafter cited as CAP.

5. Ibid., p. 21.

6. Schilpp-Dewey, p. 22.

7. CAP II, pp. 22-23.

8. John Dewey, *Democracy and Education* (New York: Macmillan, 1916), p. 386. Hereafter cited as DE.

9. DE, p. 383.

10. Ibid., p. 387.

11. "My Pedagogic Creed," *The Journal of the National Education Association,* Vol. XVIII (1929), pp. 291-93. Hereafter cited as NEAJ.

12. "Democracy in Education," in NEAJ 18:290.

13. NEAJ 18:287.

14. Ibid., p. 288. Dewey's italics.

15. Ibid., p. 287.

16. Ibid., p. 288.

17. DE, p. 226.

18. Ibid., p. 414.

19. Ibid., p. 281.

20. Ibid., p. 225.

21. Ibid., p. 393.

22. Holmes-Pollock Letters II, p. 287.

23. *Experience and Nature* (Chicago: Open Court Publishing Company, 1925), p. 350. Hereafter cited as EN.

24. EN, p. 117.

25. Ibid., p. 71.

26. Ibid., p. 73.

27. Ibid., p. 352.

28. Ibid., p. 370.

29. Ibid., p. 261-62.

30. Ibid., p. 307.

31. Ibid., p. 295.

32. Ibid., p. 282.

33. Ibid., p. 435.

34. *Human Nature and Conduct* (New York: Modern Library, 1930), p. 75.

35. EN, p. 437.

36. "Dewey's Influence on Education," in Schilpp-Dewey, p. 471.

37. *Time,* March 17th, 1952, p. 77.

38. "President's Message," in *Progressive Education,* Vol. 7 (1930), p. 159.

XXIV

Adventurer in Ideas

ALFRED NORTH WHITEHEAD

"It is the business of the future
to be dangerous; and it is among
the merits of science that it
equips the future for its duties." [1]

ALFRED NORTH WHITEHEAD

Alfred North Whitehead

EXPERIENCE IS ALL. In this assumption the philosophies of Whitehead and Dewey coincide. On it their respective world-views build. As Dewey himself has pointed out, for both "the background and point of departure seems to be the same." [2] For both, "the truth is that the brain is continuous with the body, and the body is continuous with the rest of the natural world." [3] Here, however, the resemblance ends as of course it must if Whitehead is justified in his belief that there is some cosmic end or purpose transcending and informing each particular end in view. The problem is to show, by examination of the implications of experience and nature, that Reality is such as to require our recognition of this cosmic purpose.

If Dewey is right, any such attempt must end in failure since our human experience is not such as to permit the conclusion that we are parts of one organic whole. This Whitehead categorically denies. The principle of relativity is, he thinks, warrant enough for holding that "there are no brute, self-contained matters of fact, capable of being understood apart from interpretation as an element in a system." [4] To describe this system is, to his view, the business of philosophy. Its proper objective is the elaboration of a categorical scheme, internally coherent and externally consistent with the witness of experience. "Also, it must be one of the motives of a complete cosmology, to construct a system of ideas which bring the aesthetic, moral, and religious interests into relation with those concepts of the world which have their origin in natural science." [5] Only as this is accomplished, Whitehead believes, does philosophy free itself from the taint of ineffectiveness. "It attains its chief importance by fusing the two, namely, religion and science, into one rational scheme of thought . . . Philosophy finds religion and modifies it; and conversely religion is among the data of experience which philosophy must weave into its own scheme." [6] Its task is to explain, not to explain away. Its obligation is to all of the evidence, not merely that specific selection of it which certain men of science and of common sense declare important. "Philosophy may not neglect the multifariousness of the world—the fairies dance, and Christ is nailed to the cross." [7]

Whitehead comes by this concern for things religious naturally. His father was a rural vicar, there were other clergy in the family; Canterbury Cathedral with its splendor and its memories was, he recalled a lifetime later, but sixteen miles removed from Ramsgate, Isle of Thanet, Kent, his birthplace and his boyhood home. Reverend Whitehead was a familiar of the Archbishop; it was foreordained that his son's education would be strictly classical. At fifteen young Whitehead went down to Sherborne in Dorsetshire; at twenty he went up to Trinity College, Cambridge. Here he remained, "first as 'scholar' and then as 'fellow,'" for thirty years. His subject was mathematics, and his contributions to it were to be not inconsiderable.

For seven of these years he worked away at his *Treatise on Universal Algebra* (1898). On its merits he was in 1903 elected a fellow of the Royal Society. Ten years more were spent on the development of the original theories published as *The Axioms of Projective Geometry* (1906) and *The Axioms of Descriptive Geometry* (1907). Finally, in 1910, appeared Volume One of the monumental *Principia Mathematica*. Composed in collaboration with his sometime pupil, afterwards colleague, at Cambridge, Bertrand Russell, it is his most famous work, and justly so, for on its demonstrations of the logical foundations of mathematics much of the modern science of symbolic logic depends. One other of Whitehead's mathematical writings requires mention. This is *An Introduction to Mathematics* (1911), in which he undertakes to demonstrate the mathematical foundations of all science. Written in the ten months' interval between his permanent removal from Cambridge and his assumption of new academic duties at University College, London, it has proved to be the most popular of his pre-philosophical books.

It was during the tragic years of World War I that Whitehead, stimulated by his appointment as Dean of the Faculty of Sciences at the Imperial College of Science and Technology, Kensington, began to develop an interest in philosophy itself. From the first, he saw as clearly as ever Dewey did that everything begins and ends with an appeal to experience. "Has science," he asks us in an essay composed in 1916, "to wait for the termination of the metaphysical debate till it can determine its own subject matter?"

> I suggest that science has a much more homely starting ground. Its task is the discovery of the relations which exist within that flux of perceptions, sensations, and emotions which forms our experience of life. The panorama yielded by sight, sound, taste, smell, touch, and by more inchoate sensible feelings, is the sole field of activity. . . . The most obvious aspect of this field of actual experience is its disorderly character. It is for each person a continuum, fragmentary, and with elements not clearly differentiated. . . . To grasp this fundamental truth is the first step in wisdom, when constructing a philosophy of science. This fact is concealed by the influence of language, moulded by science, which foists on us exact concepts as though they represented the immediate deliverances of experience. The result is, that we imagine that we have immediate experience of a world of perfectly defined objects implicated in perfectly defined events which, as known to us by the direct deliverance of our senses, happen at exact instants of time, in a space formed by exact points, without parts and without magnitude: the neat, trim, tidy, exact world which is the goal of scientific thought.
>
> My contention is, that this world is a world of ideas, and that its internal relations are relations between abstract concepts, and that the elucidation of the precise connection between this world and the feelings of actual experience is the fundamental question of scientific philosophy.[8]

The extension of experience to include the primitive emotions, its continuity, the distrust of language, the denial of clarity and distinctness as the criteria of truth, the rejection of absolute space and time and its corollary belief in the possibility of locating objects exactly, the insistence upon a thorough-going doctrine of internal relations, all of these ideas, here merely hinted at, are, as later developed, foundational to the system, as is the contention that philosophy is concerned not so much with the facts as with the justification of the forms to which the facts give rise. As Whitehead puts it in his remarks preliminary to the setting forth of the categorical scheme of *Process and Reality:*

> The explanatory purpose of philosophy is often misunderstood. Its business is to explain the emergence of the more abstract things from the more concrete things. It is a complete mistake to ask how concrete particular fact can be built up out of universals. The answer is, 'In no way.' The true philosophic question is, How can concrete fact exhibit entities abstract from itself and yet participated in by its own nature?
>
> In other words, philosophy is explanatory of abstraction, and not of concreteness.[9]

Experience is all. The only problem is, How shall we describe it?

II

In 1924 Whitehead was sixty-three years old. His career, now drawing to its close, had been brilliant. His reputation as a mathematician was secure. Three books of philosophy, *An Enquiry Concerning the Principles of Natural Knowledge* (1919), *The Concept of Nature* (1920), and *The Principle of Relativity* (1922), had made his name familiar to academicians on both sides of the Atlantic. Now, at an age when most professors are happily contemplating the joys of retirement, he received an invitation to join the faculty of Harvard as Professor of Philosophy. What led him to accept he does not tell us, but accept he did. Shortly thereafter, in company with his wife, he took ship for America, and in the fall of 1924 entered upon a new life. The February following he gave in Boston a series of Lowell Lectures, later published, with additions, under the title *Science and the Modern World.*

"The key to the book," he tells us in its Preface, "is the sense of the overwhelming importance of a prevalent philosophy." [10] So it is, but that is not the point Whitehead here seeks to make. The point is that a philosophy may so dominate the mentality of its epoch as to lead men to ignore or even to deny completely the efficacy of those modes of life and thought it disavows. Its importance may be such as to promote a universal conviction of the triviality or error of everything alien to it. Thus the medieval mind, accepting Scholasticism, sees nothing of permanent value in secular science. Conversely, the modern, ruled by the assumptions of scientific materialism, finds no intrinsic worth in reason or emotion. That these must finally pass away, as have all prevalent philosophies dedicated to the foreshortening of man's vision of the nature of things, Whitehead is certain. Inevitably the quality of narrowmindedness calls forth that "Nemesis which waits upon those who deliberately avoid avenues of knowledge. Oliver Cromwell's cry echoes down the ages, 'My brethren, by the bowels of Christ I beseech you, bethink you that you may be mistaken.'" [11]

Are they mistaken, then, who throughout the past three hundred years of Western civilization have presupposed the ultimate truth of things to be "brute matter"? It is Whitehead's thesis that they are, insofar, at least, as they assume materialism suited to the scientific situation of our time. What they forget in their reliance on sense-experience and common sense is the fact that "the new situation in the thought of today arises from the fact that scientific theory is outrunning common sense." [12] Thus any philosophy which takes seriously the law of evolution must and does imply the falsity of materialism, since

the aboriginal stuff, or material, from which a materialistic philosophy starts is incapable of evolution. This material is in itself the ultimate substance. Evolution, on the materialistic theory, is reduced to the role of being another word for the description of the changes of the external relations between portions of matter. There is nothing to evolve, because one set of external relations is as good as any other set of external relations. There can merely be change, purposeless and unprogressive. [13]

When we pass from a consideration of the sort of view permitted by evolution to that presupposed by the theory of relativity, the unsuitability of materialism is even more marked. For the materialist it is self-evident that any piece or particle of matter occupies a certain point in space at a definite instant of time. "In fact, as soon

as you have settled, however you do settle, what you mean by
a definite place in space-time, you can adequately state the relation
of a particular material body to space-time by saying that it is just
there, in that place; and, so far as simple location is concerned,
there is nothing more to be said on the subject." [14] On the other
hand, if the requirements of the modern relativistic world-view are,
as Whitehead maintains, such as to compel the denial of simple
location as the primary way in which things are involved in space-
time, and this because "in a certain sense, everything is everywhere
at all times," [15] then matter, as a property of simple location, is, like
it, a mere abstraction. What is wrong, therefore, with materialism
is that it commits what Whitehead calls the Fallacy of Misplaced
Concreteness, the fallacy, that is, of mistaking the abstract for the
concrete, the mistake, in this instance, being to confuse matter with
ultimate matter of fact.

To discover what this ultimate matter of fact is, we need only to
attend to the present situation in science itself. For there, Whitehead points out, we find science

> taking on a new aspect which is neither purely physical, nor purely
> biological. It is becoming the study of organisms. Biology is the
> study of the larger organisms; whereas physics is the study of the
> smaller organisms. . . . The organisms of biology include as in-
> gredients the smaller organisms of physics; but there is at present
> no evidence that the smaller of the physical organisms can be
> analyzed into component organisms. It may be so. But anyhow we
> are faced with the question as to whether there are not primary
> organisms which are incapable of further analysis. It seems very
> unlikely that there should be any infinite regress in nature. Accord-
> ingly, a theory of science which discards materialism must answer
> the question as to the character of these primary entities. There
> can only be one answer on this basis. We must start with the event
> as the ultimate unit of natural occurrence. [16]

"The event is the unit of things real." [17] Focus on the unit, and
event means organism; think of it as process, and it becomes a
synonym for actual occasion. Throughout *Science and the Modern
World* these three terms, event, organism, and occasion, are used
interchangeably. The definition of any one of them is, in this book,

approximately the definition of them all. What, then, is an event? Primordially, it is an adventure of energy, the grasping into unity of some particular pattern of spatio-temporal activity such as the life history of an electron or a cell. Subjectively, it is the ingathering of the specific events antecedent to it, events which, as gathered in, make it to be what it is. From the standpoint of evolution, it is organic process, the perpetual emergence of organic occasions out of their predecessors and into their successors. Relativistically regarded, it is "one among a multiplicity of occasions without which it could not be itself." [18] Which is to say that nowhere in the universe does there exist an occasion, organism, or event sufficient unto itself. "The concept of an organism includes, therefore, the concept of the interaction of organisms." [19] "Actuality is through and through togetherness." [20] Literally, all things, molecules and men, galaxies and God, are members one of another.

The reference to God requires further explanation, the more so as the concept here maintained is alien to the notion of God entertained by Christian orthodoxy. It is, however, in Whitehead's opinion, a concept no less justified for all that it sounds strange to churchmen. As these demand a God to account for the origin of things and the presence of purpose exhibited by them, so does the philosophy of organism necessitate a principle of limitation to explain why and how actual occasions, conceived as emergent limitations imposed upon possibility, come to manifest just the values and relationships that they do. As Whitehead puts it,

the fact that there is a process of actual occasions, and the fact that the occasions are the emergence of values which require such limitation, both require that the course of events should have developed amid an antecedent limitation composed of conditions, particularisation, and standards of value.

Thus as a further element in the metaphysical situation, there is required a principle of limitation. Some particular *how* is necessary, and some particularisation in the *what* of matter of fact is necessary. The only alternative to this admission, is to deny the reality of actual occasions. Their apparent irrational limitation must be taken as a proof of illusion and we must look for reality behind the scene. If we reject this alternative behind the scene, we must provide a ground for limitation which stands among the attributes of the substantial activity. This attribute provides the limitation for which no reason can be given: for all reason flows from it. God is the ultimate limitation, and His existence is the ultimate irrationality. For no reason can be given for just that limitation which it stands in His nature to impose. God is not concrete, but He is the ground for concrete actuality.[21]

He is, in brief, the Principle of Concretion.

As such, He is that "underlying eternal energy in whose nature there stands . . . first, the envisagement of eternal objects; secondly, the envisagement of possibilities of value in respect to the synthesis of eternal objects; and lastly, the envisagement of the actual matter of fact which must enter into the total situation which is achievable by the addition of the future." [22] In less technical language, this is to say that God has eternally in mind the idea of whatever might, has, or will come to pass. Eternally He entertains all possibilities and guides to actualization all those which serve His purposes. Because there is a future, there are possibilities as yet unrealized in the universe, thoughts thus far unthought by any one, values still unrecognized, ideals and ideas to date undiscovered. Since all of these eternal objects must subsist somewhere and somehow, otherwise there would be something coming out of nothing, and this, as Whitehead points out in *Process and Reality,* is an impossibility, and since, as St. Augustine and St. Thomas Aquinas long ago discovered, the only event in which such a subsistence is eternally possible is God; in Him it is that all eternal objects have their location. So too it is that these define the nature of the limitation above remarked as being ingredient to the actual occasions composing this universe. God, therefore, as the locus of eternal objects is, as He must be, the Principle of Limitation and Concretion.

Beyond this characterization of the function of deity, Whitehead does not go in *Science and the Modern World.* His chapter on Religion and Science has much to say about our collective need to recognize the evolution of religion as the great adventure of the spirit, but it has nothing whatever to add to the conception of God just stated. That Whitehead himself was dissatisfied with this conception, his complete recasting of it in *Process and Reality* makes plain. Indeed, save as seen from the enlarged view of the nature and function of God as given in this later work, the position as expressed in *Science and the Modern World* makes little sense.

III

Few there are today, in philosophy or out, who would deny that *Process and Reality* belongs on any list of the great books of the first half of the Twentieth Century. Certainly there is nothing in recent philosophical literature at all comparable to it in analytic depth or breadth of synthesis. Like the Logic of Hegel and the Summas of St. Thomas it stands alone, above and beyond every other book of its age. Competitors, at present, it has none; although in all fairness to those who deny that the business of philosophy is system-building, it should be noted that it has critics aplenty. In essence it constitutes an expansion and development of the ideas first suggested in *Science and the Modern World;* in fact it is much more than this. Not only is its terminology new; the ideas the words denote are different.

The ultimate matter of fact is now called Creativity, the One uniting the many actual entities (events). Each actual entity is conceived as arising out of its past through the process of appropriating that past to itself; each perishes into objective immortality as it is appropriated by events future. According to Whitehead,

> 'Actual entities'—also termed 'actual occasions'—are the final real things of which the world is made up. There is no going behind actual entities to find anything more real. They differ among themselves: God is an actual entity, and so is the most trivial puff of existence in far-off empty space. But, though there are gradations of importance, and diversities of function, yet in the principles which actuality exemplifies all are on the same level. The final facts are, all alike, actual entities; and these actual entities are drops of experience, complex and interdependent.[23]

Actual entities prehend each other, that is to say, they feel each other and through so doing are together. As together they comprise a nexus (singular of nexūs). Collectively, these three, actual entities, prehensions, and nexūs, are the ultimate facts of immediate actual experience. The problem is to show how and why, out of these concrete components of reality, the relatively abstract objects of our human experience arise and endure.

Recalling what he had previously remarked concerning the organic character of the real, Whitehead begins his approach to the solution with a reminder:

> The philosophy of organism is a cell-theory of actuality. Each ultimate unit of fact is a cell-complex, not analysable into components with equivalent completeness of actuality.[24]

The cell, he continues, can be considered genetically (as in process of formation or concrescence) and morphologically (as a concrete whole). Both ways are considered in *Process and Reality*. The former, as here taken, constitutes a theory of feelings, the latter culminates in a theory of coordinate division. On the cogency of these two theories, and on the efficacy of the tie (God) which binds them together, the philosophy of organism rests.

According to Whitehead, we must begin with feelings, for these, collectively, are what an actual entity really is. What, then, is a feeling? Essentially, answers Whitehead, a transition effecting a concrescence, i.e., a positive prehension. "Its complex constitution is analysable into five factors which express what that transition consists of, and effects. The factors are: i) the 'subject' which feels, (ii) the 'initial data' which are to be felt, (iii) the 'elimination' in virtue of negative prehensions, (iv) the 'objective datum' which is felt, (v) the 'subjective form' which is *how* that subject feels that objective datum."[25] Translated into ordinary English, this is to say that a feeling is at once the feeler and the felt, for, and this is the crux of the matter, "the feelings are inseparable from the end at which they aim; and this end is the feeler."[26]

> The feelings are what they are in order that their subject (the actual entity) may be what it is. Then transcendently, since the subject is what it is in virtue of its feelings, it is only by means of its feelings that the subject objectively conditions the creativity transcendent beyond itself. In our own relatively high grade of human existence, this doctrine of feelings and their subject is illustrated by our notion

of moral responsibility. The subject is responsible for being what it is in virtue of its feelings.[27]

Just as you, as a person, are that character which is at every moment of your life in the process of making, so, at the submicroscopic level of the actual entity, it (the actual entity) is the feelings that it entertains.

In putting forth this view, Whitehead is, of course, aware of just how far removed it is from our everyday idea of the subject (person) as someone existing apart from and prior to those objects in which it thinks to find the source of its feelings. Nonetheless, it is, he insists, a view which must be mastered. "It is," he tells us, "fundamental to the metaphysical doctrine of the philosophy of organism, that the notion of an actual entity as the unchanging subject of change is completely abandoned." [28] As in modern physics we have come to realize the utter inadequacy of all descriptions of the universe framed in terms of Newtonian space-time and Euclidean geometry, so in modern biology we must come to recognize the inherent falsity of all descriptions couched in subject-predicate terms. For the truth is that there is no subject *having* experiences; rather is it that the subject *is* its experience; it *is* what it *becomes,* and antecedently to this experiencing and this becoming it is literally nothing at all.

Thus, in compliance with the category of subjective unity, the first of the nine categoreal obligations which, in Whitehead's schema of the universe, define and describe the conditions to which every entity, God included, must conform, every actual entity is to be conceived as literally self-realizing.

Self-realization is the ultimate fact of facts. An actuality is self-realizing, and whatever is self-realizing is an actuality. An actual entity is at once the subject of self-realization, and the superject which is self-realized.

As superject it is the subject complete, the actual entity as having achieved that "one complex fully determinate feeling" which is its "satisfaction." It is the actual occasion as available for feeling by those events posterior to it. What it has felt it bequeathes to those who feel it. In sum, the process of reality is eternally and everywhere an infinity of local processes of feeling becoming feelers, and as such passing into objective immortality as feelers felt.

Into the details of this feeling process it is not, for our present purpose, necessary to go. Nor need we consider in depth that theory of coordinate division descriptive of the various relationships of entities in extensive connection. Suffice it to recognize that there is a variety of types of feeling, simple and complex, which vary with the nature, complexity, and relations of the actual entities and eternal objects involved. However, before we leave the theory of feelings, it is necessary to remark that one feature of the system which insures the continuity of process at the same time as it gives process its direction. This is the "subjective aim" illustrated by the subject (occasion) controlling its own process of becoming. It is, in Whitehead's phrase, "this subject itself determining its own self- creation as one creature"; [29] that subject feeling a proposition with the subjective form of purpose to realize it in that process of self-creation." [30] That a subject, itself incomplete, should be able to determine the direction of its completion would be a miracle were it not for the fact that the "proposition" here presented for its feeling derives initially from God, who in this aspect of his triune nature functions as the "lure for feeling, the eternal urge of desire . . . establishing the initial phase of each subjective aim." [31] What this means as regards Whitehead's conception of the relation of God to the world we have now to consider.

There are those who, by reason of commitment to gods more conventional or to no god at all, believe that it is possible to make sense of *Process and Reality* without having recourse to its doctrine of God. They are wrong. This system stands or falls as a whole, and this whole, conceived as the all-inclusive cosmic event, the infinitely actual entity prehending and prehended by all finite actual entities, *is* God. "He is," says Whitehead, "the beginning and the end," [32] primordial, also consequent. From Him issues all order, purpose, and form; unto Him whatever is realized returns, is perfected and reused. "What is done in the world is transformed into a reality in heaven, and the reality in heaven passes back into the world." [33] As here employed, "heaven" and "world" are, of course, metaphors. Even so, they express a notion of passage which Whitehead intends us to take in all literalness.

God is the beginning, but not in the sense ordinarily understood. "He is not the beginning in the sense of being in the past of all members." [34] The Father Almighty, Maker of Heaven and Earth, worshipped by orthodox Jews and Christians is not the God of *Process and Reality*. For this latter deity "is not before all creation, but *with* all creation"; [35] not outside the universe, but ingredient in it. In Whitehead's words, "He is the presupposed actuality of conceptual operation, in unison of becoming with every other creative act." [36] As such, His function is virtually identical with that previously remarked in *Science and the Modern World*. Here, as there, God is envisaged as the primordial manifestation of the principle that makes for order and value. But whereas in the earlier book the relation of God to the physical universe was not further defined, in the later, Whitehead has expanded his conception of God to include the experience of the universe as well as its ordering. As before, He is felt, but now He also feels. What He has set in train, He sums up. Thus, analogously to all actual entities, the nature of God is triune. Triune, however, in a rather different way, for whereas all finite actual entities have the character "given" for them by the past,

in the case of the primordial actual entity, which is God, there is no past. . . . There is still, however, the same threefold character: (i) the 'primordial nature' of God is the concrescence of an unity of conceptual feelings, including among their data all eternal objects. The concrescence is directed by the subjective aim, that the subjective forms of the feelings shall be such as to constitute the eternal objects into relevant lures of feeling severally appropriate for all realizable basic conditions. (ii) The 'consequent nature' of God is the physical prehension by God of the actualities of the evolving universe. This primordial nature directs such perspectives of objectification that each novel actuality in the temporal world contributes such elements as it can to a realization in God free from inhibitions of intensity by reason of discordance. (iii) The 'superjective' nature of God is the character of the pragmatic value of his specific satisfaction qualifying the transcendent creativity in the various temporal instances.[37]

More simply, God is (as primordial) the ground of value; (as consequent) the ingathering of actuality; (as superjective) the valuation and re-expression of the actuality ingathered. "For the perfected actuality passes back into the temporal world, and qualifies this world so that each temporal actuality includes it as an immediate fact of relevant experience. For the kingdom of heaven is with us to-day." [38]

The "today" is important, since it calls our attention back to a most important fact, i.e., to the fact that this conception, like that of the orthodox Christian trinity, is of a three-in-One, which One is omnipresent. No more than the Church Fathers is Whitehead willing to be bound by that defect of language which implies a temporal succession of natures: Father, Son, *and* Holy Ghost; primordial, consequent, *and* superjective. As the persons of the trinity are eternally co-*operative* at every temporal moment, so are the natures of Whitehead's God momentarily and eternally interwoven. Realizing this, many scholars, particularly those denominationally affiliated, have sought to modernize their faith by assimilating to it the Whiteheadian conception of God. For the most part, however, they have been unsuccessful because the two conceptions of the trinity, for all their superficial resemblance, are fundamentally quite different.

Like God the Father, God as primordial holds in Himself all possibilities for creation; but whereas the former, by an act of will, actualizes these possibilities by creating for them a home in some sense external to Himself, the latter, by persuasion (the lure for feeling), insinuates the possibilities into that creative flux which He Himself instances. Like God the Son, God as consequent saves the world; but whereas the former is God as man present in the world, the latter is the world become divine as present in God. Like God the Holy Ghost, God as superjective floods the world with love; but whereas the former is God as spirit present in the hearts of those who trust in Him, the latter is purpose operative in every entity from cell to cosmos. The difference, in brief, is between that view which speaks of God *and* the world, and that which prefers to think of the world *in* God. As earlier, in the metaphysics of Fiske and Royce, so here, the conception of God maintained by Whitehead is not theistic but *panentheistic!* As previously, in the cosmologies of Peirce and James, so here, the idea is one of God in the making, God evolving as that universe which is His body evolves.

Whether or not this idea is one that a Christian might in good conscience adopt as his own is something for the Christian himself to decide. It is, at all events, an idea to nourish those hearts who long, not for a monarch infinite in majesty and in indifference to the cares of men, but for Him, whom Whitehead describes: "the great companion—the fellow-sufferer who understands." [39]

IV

In putting out these results, four strong impressions dominate my mind: First, that the movement of historical, and philosophical, criticism of detached questions, which on the whole has dominated the last two centuries, has done its work, and requires to be supplemented by a more sustained effort of constructive thought. Secondly, that the true method of philosophical construction is to frame a scheme of ideas, the best that one can, and unflinchingly to explore the interpretation of experience in terms of that scheme. Thirdly, that all constructive thought, on the various special topics of scientific interest, is dominated by some such scheme, unacknowledged, but no less influential in guiding the imagination. The importance of philosophy lies in its sustained effort to make such schemes explicit, and thereby capable of criticism and improvement.[40]

Thirty-five years have elapsed since Whitehead's attempt to set philosophy to this "sustained effort," and the philosophic scene is today more crowded than ever with empiricist, existentialist, and positivist partisans of the "detached question." Where philosophy has not become anti-philosophical, it has become ancillary to science. "Constructive thought," for many today, has no other meaning than the activity of the theoreticians of the exact sciences. Should we, then, accept as fact that Whitehead was wrong? To answer either way is to state the nature of the philosophic enterprise.

The issue is fundamental. If Whitehead's conclusions are rejected, philosophy resolves itself into an adjunct of physical science or psychology. Empiricism and existentialism, the philosophic fashions of our time, can, in themselves, aspire to no higher goals. Alternatively, to assert, as Whitehead does, the autonomy of philosophy is to envisage the task of the philosopher as the framing of the universe in some scheme of ideas whereby all experience, personal or scientific, finds its interpretation and explanation. Between philosophy as adjunctive and philosophy as autonomous there would seem to be no settled middle ground. The direction of one's view as to the nature of the philosophical enterprise has been irrevocably determined when one or the other of these alternatives has been chosen.

Failing to see this, Whitehead's critics have spent the decades before and after his death reproaching his lack of concern for those specific problems they happen to find important. Thus John Dewey chides him for his indifference to ends in view, while Stephen Ely finds the unavailability of his God for religion sufficient grounds for abandoning it altogether. His usage of language, particularly his employment of "value" and "mind" is discovered by W. M. Urban to be inconsistent with ordinary usage, hence wrong. In similar vein, Nathaniel Lawrence taxes him with failure to provide a theory of the self descriptive of man as he ordinarily is. By their lights each of these scholars is right, for it is true that Whitehead has little to say on these matters of mundane importance. He wastes no time debating adjunctivist philosophers. He has no patience for that sort of scholarship which contents itself with savoring the subtler thoughts of great men gone. This way, he thinks, lies decadence and the death of civilization. A society survives and prospers by looking forward, not back.

A race preserves its vigour so long as it harbours a real contrast between what has been and what may be; and so long as it is nerved by the vigour to adventure beyond the safeties of the past. Without adventure civilization is in full decay.[41]

Nothing stands still.

The foundation of all understanding of sociological theory—that is to say, of all understanding of human life—is that no static maintenance of perfection is possible. This axiom is rooted in the nature of things. Advance or Decadence are the only choices offered to mankind.[42]

When man has ceased to adventure, he has already begun to die.

To preserve this sense of adventure is the obligation nature lays upon us all. To exemplify it in his speculations is the philosopher's particular responsibility. Which is to say that we must not expect philosophy to provide us with any final answers, for if reality is process there are none such. Any philosophy may be, as perhaps that of Whitehead is, sufficient unto its day. But there is always tomorrow, and in its turn every philosophy will suffer deposition if for no other reason than that it must inevitably fail to account for the totality of future fact. As men of reason we owe it to ourselves to preserve an open mind.

The duty of tolerance is our finite homage to the abundance of inexhaustible novelty which is awaiting the future, and to the complexity of accomplished fact which exceeds our stretch of insight.[43]

SUGGESTED READINGS

Process and Reality (New York: Harper Torchbooks, paperback, 1961) is just possibly the greatest work of philosophy so far produced in our century. It is certainly the most difficult, and very definitely not a book to be attempted by the reader new to Whitehead. Where then to begin? Since Whitehead's philosophy evolves from work to work, a chronological reading is much to be preferred. Begin, then, with *Science and the Modern World* (New York: Mentor Books, paperback). This book, in order of writing the fifth of Whitehead's philosophical works, is, from the standpoint of his final synthesis, of the nature of an introduction to the system, the earlier works being devoted to the presentation of a point of view much modified in the system proper. If after it you still feel unprepared for the intricacies of *Process and Reality,* read next *Adventures of Ideas* (New York: Mentor Books, paperback, 1955). For the beginner, this is perhaps the best, if not the easiest, introduction to the philosophy of organism in all its aspects. As for Whitehead's four shorter books of lectures, these may be read in any order—after you have mastered the above. *Religion in the Making* (New York: Meridian Books, paperback) presupposes some understanding of the ideas earlier expounded in *Science and the Modern World. Symbolism, Its Meaning and Effect* (New York: Capricorn Books, paperback) will mean more to you if you have read *Process and Reality,* as will *The Function of Reason* (Boston: Beacon Press, paperback, 1958) and *Modes of Thought* (New York: Capricorn Books, paperback). For those who prefer everything wrapped in one package, there is *Alfred North Whitehead: An Anthology* (New York: Macmillian, paperback, 1961), edited with introduction and commentary by F. S. C. Northup and M. W. Gross.

As yet no biography exists. Whitehead himself has contributed a sketch of his life to P. A. Schlipp, *The Philosophy of Alfred North Whitehead* (New York: Tudor, 1951). This anthology of articles explanatory and critical of Whitehead's philosophy is still the best thing of its kind in print. The same sketch, together with other personalia, is reprinted as Part I of Whitehead's *Essays in Science and Philosophy* (New York: Philosophical Library, 1948). Of books and articles about Whitehead there is no end. The most recent bibliography, listing continental European, English, and American titles is that by Jacques Ruytinz, "Alfred North Whitehead: une bibliographie," *Revue Internationale de Philosophie,* 56-57 (1961), pp. 267-77. The best of the commentaries are Nathaniel Lawrence, *Whitehead's Philosophical Development* (Berkeley: University of California Press, 1956), and William Christian, *An Interpretation of Whitehead's Metaphysics* (New Haven: Yale, 1959). The former covers the works up to *Process and Reality;* the latter, in my opinion the best book on Whitehead so far, offers an extremely thorough analysis of Whitehead's magnum opus and its sequels.

REFERENCES

1. *Science and the Modern World* (New York: Macmillan, 1950), pp. 298-99. Hereafter cited as SMW.

2. "The Philosophy of Whitehead," in P. A. Schilpp, *The Philosophy of Alfred North Whitehead* (New York: Tudor, 1951), p. 645.

3. Alfred North Whitehead, *Adventures of Ideas* (New York: Macmillan, 1933), p. 290. Hereafter cited as AI.

4. Alfred North Whitehead, *Process and Reality* (New York: Social Science Book Store, 1941), p. 21. Hereafter cited as PR.

5. PR, p. vi.

6. Ibid., p. 23.

7. Ibid., p. 513.

8. *The Organization of Thought, Educational and Scientific* (London: Williams and Norgate, 1917), pp. 109-10.

9. PR, p. 30.

10. SMW, pp. xi-xii.

11. Ibid., p. 24.

12. Ibid., p. 166.

13. Ibid., p. 157.

14. Ibid., p. 72.

15. Ibid., p. 133.

16. Ibid., pp. 150-51.

17. Ibid., p. 219.

18. Ibid., p. 253.

19. Ibid., p. 151.

20. Ibid., p. 251.

21. Ibid., pp. 256-57.

22. Ibid., p. 154.

23. PR, pp. 27-28.
24. Ibid., p. 334.
25. Ibid., pp. 337-38.
26. Ibid., p. 339.
27. Ibid.
28. Ibid., p. 43.
29. Ibid., p. 108.
30. Ibid., p. 37.
31. Ibid., p. 522.
32. Ibid., p. 523.
33. Ibid., p. 532.
34. Ibid., p. 523.
35. Ibid., p. 521.
36. Ibid., p. 523.
37. Ibid., pp. 134-35.
38. Ibid., p. 532.
39. Ibid.
40. Ibid., p. x.
41. AI, p. 360.
42. Ibid., pp. 353-54.
43. Ibid., p. 65.

Postscript

IF THE BEST of the recent commentators on the American scene are to be believed, we the people are today, spiritually and intellectually, in a bad way. There is in us, thinks Thomas Griffith, an inherent hostility to the first rate. We are, says Daniel Boorstin, the most illusioned people on earth. Is it so? From Benjamin Franklin to Mark Twain to now, the most perceptive critics of American society have never doubted it, and I, for one, can find no cogent argument, no *living* exemplar, to say them wrong. All of the men whose thoughts these pages have rehearsed are dead. No one of comparable caliber in any of the major fields of intellectual or sociopolitical or religious endeavour is, at present, on the scene. Or if he or she is, they are, as yet, unknown to lasting fame. It is so: we are hostile to excellence; we do tend to see ourselves as what we advertise ourselves to be, rather than as what we are. How we got this way does not now greatly matter. What does concern us all is how to get from where we are to what we ought to be. My recipe is simple; it is, in truth, the only one I have to offer. If you have read these pages and been spurred to read beyond them, you already have the half of it. As for the rest, it consists entirely of one vitally important and neglected maxim: keep an open mind.

Keep an open mind. In these United States today this is not an easy thing to do. We have only to attend to the news media to realize how frighteningly large a percentage of reputable Americans are moved by their prejudice and emotions to deny that debate which is the life force of a truly republican society. In my own state, at this moment, the Constitution is in process of being subverted in the name of States Rights and White Supremacy. Elsewhere, legislatures similarly minded are now and have been meeting to endorse proposals which, if successful, can only serve to destroy the structure of national government as we have known it. "If proposals of this magnitude had been made in the early days of the Republic, the great debate," Chief Justice Warren believes, "would be resounding in every legislative hall and in every place where lawyers, scholars and statesmen gather." It is not resounding now. Whether or not it does so in the days to come is up to us; for when all has been said, the American Mind is nothing but what we profess and practice.

New Orleans
June, 1963.

INDEX